Under the General Editorship of

Joseph W. Towle
Washington University, St. Louis
Houghton Mifflin Adviser in Management

Personnel Management and Organization Development: Fields in Transition

Edited by

Wendell L. French
University of Washington

Don Hellriegel
University of Colorado

HOUGHTON MIFFLIN COMPANY · BOSTON
New York · Atlanta · Geneva, Ill. · Dallas · Palo Alto

Printed in the U.S.A.

Library of Congress Catalog Card Number: 73–144320

ISBN: 0–395–12035–7

General Editor's Introduction

In his popular text, *The Personnel Management Process* (Second Edition, 1970), Professor French stated that today's questioning extends to many of the assumptions underlying traditional personnel practices. He himself asked provocatively, "How can work become more meaningful in the lives of people?" Here, he continues, with Professor Hellriegel, his search for an answer.

Throughout industry and business, from the machine shop to the conference room, we find evidence of the search for greater satisfactions and opportunities of self-realization for workers in all occupations and at all levels. Many of the newer approaches to the utilization of human resources have yielded, simultaneously, greater satisfactions and opportunities for employees and increased productivity and profitability for firms — often to the amazement of observers.

This readings book constitutes a silent forum. Its diverse and numerous participants — upward of fifty — are able to investigate thoroughly the wide array of newer, as well as older, approaches. As a supplement to standard textbooks by single authors, this volume can provide an important, contemporary "extra dimension." Its skillfully selected readings and succinctly written introductions should help it to become an enthusiastically accepted offering for courses in personnel management, human relations, and organization development.

To convoke this forum, *Personnel Management and Organization Development: Fields in Transition,* Professor French collaborated with Professor Hellriegel, of the University of Colorado. The practical organizational experience of Professors French and Hellriegel, and their research and teaching expertise, join to equip them, outstandingly, for the task of selecting participants from all sides — the behavioralists and the traditionalists, the theoreticians and the practitioners. Professor French has served as Chairman of the Department of Management in the Graduate School of Business Administration at the University of Washington. He has lectured and consulted widely — in the British Isles, in Southern Europe and the Middle East. Closer to home, he has acted as consultant to corporations ranging in size from twenty to one hundred thousand employees. From 1954 through 1958, he acted as Director of Personnel Relations for the Mallinckrodt Chemical Works. Professor Hellriegel, formerly Assistant to the Dean at Southern Illinois University, now serves as Associate Professor, School of Business, University of Colorado.

The Houghton Mifflin Company is pleased indeed to make available — to administrators, executives, educators, and students — this lively forum on contemporary personnel management thought.

Joseph W. Towle
Washington University, St. Louis

Preface

If the organizations of the future are to be more viable and less crisis-ridden than those of today, the reason will be, we believe, that their managers — the students of today — paid attention to the concepts discussed in the following and similar selections. Some of these concepts are simple; some are complex; taken as a whole, they describe what will make for the effective management of human resources in organizations.

Many of these concepts have emerged from disciplines which are, in themselves, interdisciplinary — from systems theory, organization theory, and social psychology (or, more accurately, organizational psychology). We see the behavioral sciences as providing, in large part, the springboard for innovation in human resource administration.

Traditional thought and practice — pertaining to "people" management — provides the other large part. We do not reject the traditional; rather, we build and extend upon it. For instance, authors of the selections ask, sometimes explicitly and sometimes implicitly, questions about the interaction between (1) manpower management and outside forces, (2) group type and leadership style, (3) job design and motivation, and (4) organizational adaptability and leadership behavior. They ask how these interactions can be managed effectively. They ask how we can create an environment which at once optimizes the attaiment of personal goals and organizational objectives — ones congruent with a humanistic, vigorous, and creative society. In asking, and sometimes answering, such questions, the authors increase the range of options open to the practicing and the potential manager.

In designing the book, we had in mind both undergraduate and graduate students. We divided the thirty-six selections under seven parts, each with an introduction. In turn, we divided several of the parts into sections, again with introductions. Overall, our organization adds, we believe, an "extra dimension" to its subject: it will alert students to the nature and vitality of the changes going on within personnel management and organization development — truly, fields in transition.

Our debt is great, of course, to the authors of the selections. It is great also to the various journals and publishers which, with generosity, granted us permission to reprint.

Wendell L. French
University of Washington

Don Hellriegel
University of Colorado

Contents

PART FOUR

PART FIVE

PART SIX

PART SEVEN

PART SEVEN

Organizational Development 353

PART ONE

Systems Concepts and a Behavioral Science Approach

Systems theory — deriving in large part from such disciplines as biology, physics, and cybernetics, as well as from sociology — includes concepts which give a broad perspective on the effective management and development of human resources within organizations. Some of these concepts: inputs, interdependency, feedback, closedness vs. openness, entropy, boundaries.

Theory and research in the behavioral sciences, both drawing upon, and drawn upon by, systems theory, provide an even broader perspective. Indeed, application of the behavioral sciences acounts for most of the advances in personnel management and organization development — fields in transition.

Kast and Rosenzweig (Selection 1), in the tradition of Pareto,[1] Bertalanffy,[2] and others, present a "systems way" of thinking about and analyzing organizations. They are not concerned with a particular method or content area in management; rather, they stress the desirability of considering, and ways in which we can consider organizations and their components as subsystems of larger systems. The systems approach calls attention to the need for coordination and integration of activities and tasks for the attainment of virtually all types of organizational, group, and individual goals. We think it is useful to consider all the selections within this frame of reference — both in terms of how they relate to organizational subsystems and of how they interrelate.

Argyris (Selection 2) emphasizes the use and application of the behavioral sciences in helping to solve human problems within organizations. He is concerned with the "living system," which, of course, is the domain of our concern. In the question and answer format of this selection, the reader will be exposed to a wide range of thoughts which will be explored in later selections. Argyris presents an introduction to the questions of where we were, where we are, and where we seem to be headed vis-a-vis the "living system."

[1] Lawrence J. Henderson, *Pareto's General Sociology,* Harvard University Press, 1935.

[2] Ludwig von Bertalanffy, "The Theory of Open Systems in Physics and Biology," *Science,* January 13, 1950.

1

System Concepts: Pervasiveness and Potential

Fremont E. Kast
University of Washington

James E. Rosenzweig
University of Washington

Introduction

Modern society is becoming increasingly complex as accelerating technology forces change on many fronts. While we have been adapting to scientific and technological progress reasonably well, there is some doubt about ability to adjust psychologically, sociologically, and economically. The inevitable stresses and strains that seem to be concomitant with progress have had an impact both individually and organizationally.

A key element in this complex is management; the institution charged with converting disorganized resources of men, material, and money into useful and effective enterprise. Management's task in a complex environment is not easy. A manager is a combination artist–technician but he relies on scientific endeavor in both the physical and social sciences to provide background information.

Scientists seek to understand complex phenomena by proposing theories and conducting research which may confirm, disprove, or alter them. A key concept is that of trying to understand complexity as it exists in the real world, rather than trying to simplify it for purposes of expediency.

Artists and technicians have been accused, at times, of attempting to oversimplify the real world in order to apply certain operating principles. However, in the long run the manager (artist–technician) may find it fruitful to spend more time trying to understand the complexity. One useful approach may be that of utilizing the systems concept.

It provides a framework for visualizing internal and external environmental factors as an integrated whole. It allows recognition of the proper place and function of subsystems. The systems within which businessmen

Taken and adapted from *Management International Review,* Vol. 7, No. 4–5, 1967, pp. 87–96. Used by permission.

must operate are necessarily complex. However, management via systems concepts fosters a way of thinking which, on the one hand, helps to dissolve some of the complexity and, on the other hand, helps the manager recognize the nature of the complex problems and thereby operate within the perceived environment. Business systems are a part of larger systems — possibly industry-wide, or including several, maybe many, companies and/or industries, or even society as a whole. Further, business systems are in a constant state of change — they are created, operated, revised, and often eliminated.

What does the concept of systems offer to students of management and/or to practising executives? Is it a panacea for business problems which will replace scientific management, human relations, management by objective, operations research, and many other approaches to, or techniques of, management? Perhaps a word of caution is applicable initially. Anyone looking for "cookbook" techniques will be disappointed. There are no "ten easy steps" to success in management. Such approaches, while seemingly applicable and easy to grasp, usually are shortsighted and superficial. Fundamental ideas, such as systems concepts, are more difficult to comprehend, and yet they present a greater opportunity for a large-scale payoff.

In this article we will show how systems concepts pervade scientific endeavor and how similar approaches can be useful frames of reference for managers. Several models of subsystems are presented to indicate the various ways of analyzing and synthesizing organizations. The models include (1) flow concepts, (2) key subsystems, (3) human-social systems — both individuals and groups, and (4) subsystem overlays. A discussion of the use of systems concepts in current, familiar settings gives additional evidence of their pervasiveness. Their potential usefulness for managers is postulated also.

Systems Concepts in Science and Management

A system is "an organized or complex whole; an assemblage or combination of things or parts forming a complex or unitary whole."[1] The term system covers an extremely broad spectrum of concepts. For example, we have mountain systems, river systems, and the solar system as part of our physical surroundings. The body itself is a complex organism including the skeletal system, the circulatory system, and the nervous system. We come into daily contact with such phenomena as transportation systems, communication systems (telephone, telegraph, etc.), and economic systems.

A science is described as a systematic body of knowledge; a complete array of essential principles or facts, arranged in a rational dependence or connection; a complex of ideas, principles, laws, forming a coherent whole. Scientists endeavor to develop, organize, and classify material into connected disciplines. Within a particular discipline there is often a macro-micro-macro sequence of emphasis. Initial attempts in a particular field seem to be directed toward some comprehensive, grand scheme. In physics, for example, Sir Isaac Newton set forth what he called the "system of the world." It dealt with the movement of celestial bodies and was truly universal in outlook.

The micro outlook concentrates on the individual parts that go to make up the total system. The hydrogen atom, consisting of one proton with one electron revolving around it, represents a basic physical system. Certainly, much attention has been focused on the micro aspects of physics in recent years.

The macro-micro-macro cycle is completed when attention is again focused on the relationship of parts to one another and their integration into systems. Eddington describes this process as follows:

> From the point of view of the philosophy of science the conception associated with entropy must I think be ranked as the great contribution of the 19th century to scientific thought. It marked a reaction from the view that everything to which science need pay attention is discovered by microscopic dissection of objects. It provided an alternative standpoint in which the centre of interest is shifted from the entities reached by the customary analysis (atoms, electric potentials, etc.) to qualities possessed by the system as a whole, which cannot be split up and located — a little here and a little bit there. . . .
>
> We often think that when we have completed our study of *one* we know all about *two,* because "two" is "one and one." We forget that we still have to make a study of "and." Secondary physics is the study of "and" — that is to say, of organization.[2]

The problem of AND is a legitimate one for scientists. However, it is also legitimate for scientists to concentrate on individual parts in pushing back the frontiers of knowledge, leaving to others the task of integrating the results. For managers, however, the problem of AND is central. The essence of management is coordination. The functions of planning, organizing, and controlling are undertaken to foster systematic integration of various resources toward objective accomplishment. Systems concepts provide the framework or a "way of thinking" which emphasizes the integrative nature of management.

Management theory has undergone somewhat the same transition as physics (and other physical and social science disciplines). Early attempts to develop organization charts as administrative models are examples of a macro approach. The principles developed concentrated on the whole and how work might best be divided in order to accomplish enterprise objectives. Some have said that this approach emphasized "organizations without people." Emphasis on the human element, on the other hand, has been described as "people without organizations."[3] In this case emphasis has been on understanding the individual, his motivation, and what must be considered in order that he will be a contributing member of the organization. This approach seems to emphasize the parts rather than the whole.

Consideration of organizations as social systems is an attempt to integrate the macro and micro approaches by recognizing that the individual is part of a group and that there are many subgroups in any large-scale organization. Social systems concepts recognize the complexity of the organizational environment and stress understanding rather than development of principles.

Emphasis on decision making is another way of viewing organizations and management. Some would suggest that decision making *is* management; i.e., that decision making is the essence of the managerial task. It is via decisions that the coordinating functions of planning, organizing, and controlling actually are carried out. Some would suggest also that organizations can be identified by pinpointing decision centers and the flow of information necessary for decision making. Such an approach to studying organizations gets at what really happens in day-to-day operations. This may or may not be reflected in more traditional organization charts which depict the job-task hierarchy. Emphasis on information-decision systems is also an attempt to understand the AND. Studying problems of choice or the decision maker *per se* would be an example of emphasizing parts, whereas studying the decision process and the linking mechanism between decision makers is an attempt to focus on relationships within complex systems.

Systems of Systems of Systems

Various models of subsystems have been proposed as ways of analyzing whole systems. Each is appropriate, depending on the purpose at hand.

Flow Concepts

One general approach to systems design involves identification of material, energy, and information flow. These three elements are part of every system and subsystem. Consideration of them plus the use of flow concepts facilitates thinking about systems of systems. The material aspects of any system include the facilities involved and the raw material, if any, which flows through the process. A system must be designed to ensure the acquisition of raw material and/or components necessary for processing into finished products. Whenever the operation in question involves the flow and processing of material, appropriate systems can be identified. For operations such as insurance companies or other commercial institutions, there may be no material flow *per se*. Rather, the material in these systems is represented by the facilities and equipment involved. Regardless of whether there is any material flow, all business operations, whether processing a product or service, contain elements of energy and information flow.

Some source of energy is present in any operating system. It may be electricity obtained from available sources or generated by the firm's own power plant. The process may require natural gas, petroleum, coal, or other fuel for production purposes. A business usually requires electrical energy for operating facilitating systems, if not for the main processing operation itself. Another obvious source of energy is people. Both physical and mental energy are required to operate business or government systems. People represent a renewable source of energy, at least for the short run. And as an energy source, people are quite variable as individuals. However, in total, the group represents a reasonably stable source of energy for the system. An organization maintains a flow of worker energy throughout its life — on a day-to-day basis and from the standpoint of a long-range cycle which includes recruiting, hiring, orientation stages, and employment until retirement. Thus, all energy can be considered as a flow process both in and of itself and as part of other systems.

Another basic element in any system is information. It facilitates inter-relationships among subsystems and provides the linkage necessary to develop systems of systems. Information flow may be developed to flow along with the routing of material to be processed; production control, for example. The accounting system requires a flow of information toward the development of income statements and balance sheets for tax purposes or stockholder reports or both. While many data processing systems are developed on the basis of periodic batch processing, more and more systems are being developed which call for flow concepts approximating real-time activity; that is, the activity to be considered is recorded as it happens and action is taken almost simultaneously. For many systems where manufacturing and material flow are not present — service, commercial, and many governmental organizations — the flow of information is the critical element. Information must flow through key decision points where action is taken with regard to a service to be performed by the organization in question. In such cases, the system can be defined primarily on the basis of the flow of information to appropriate decision points. Subsystems can be identified on this basis, and they in turn can be inter-related to define the total system.

Key Subsystems

There are certain key subsystems and/or functions essential in every business organization which make up the total information-decision system, and which operate in a dynamic environmental system subject to rapid change. The subsystems include:

1. A sensor subsystem designed to measure changes within the system and to provide an interface with the environment.
2. An information processing subsystem such as an accounting, or data processing system.

3. A decision-making subsystem which receives information and emits planning messages.
4. A processing subsystem which utilizes information, energy, and materials to accomplish certain tasks.
5. A control component which ensures that processing is in accordance with planning. Typically this provides feedback control.
6. A memory or information storage subsystem which may take the form of records, manuals, procedures, computer programs or human experience.

The goal setting function will establish the long-range objectives of the organization, and the performance will be measured in terms of factors such as sales, profits, employment, or cost reduction — relative to the total environmental system. As described, these key subsystems seem vague and impersonal. Each statement outlines a function, one which will be performed in some fashion regardless of the size and/or type of organization. Often, technical and mechanical elements are involved — automated equipment, computers, paper-work forms — which are coupled with human effort to close the loop. The specific approach for a subsystem can be tailor-made even though standard "hardware" items are utilized. Customizing can be accomplished via the "software" (sometimes referred to as "brainware") elements of the system. It is particularly important that attention be devoted to the people aspects of key subsystems.

Human–Social Systems

Notions of flow concepts mixed with the six subsystems mentioned above indicate the complexity of organizations. Many of the systems involved are combination man-machine systems. Of particular concern is the human element involved — the social system. Organizations are comprised of people — individually and in groups. In addition, organizations operate within a framework provided by communities and society at large.

Systems concepts seem pertinent and useful in studying the human element. Scott presents this view as follows:

> The distinctive qualities of modern organization theory are its conceptual-analytical base, its reliance upon empirical research data, and, above all, its synthesizing, integrating nature. These qualities are framed in a philosophy which accepts the premise that the only meaningful way to study organization is as a system.
>
> System analysis has its own peculiar point of view. Modern organization theory accepts system analysis as a starting point. It asks a range of inter-related questions which are not seriously considered by the classical and neo-classical theories of organization. Key among these questions are:
>
> 1. What are the strategic parts of the system?
> 2. What is the nature of their mutual interdependency?

3. What are the main processes in the system which link the parts and facilitate their adjustment to each other?
4. What are the goals sought by the system?[4]

It is evident that each individual is a strategic part of a total system. The individual is to the organization theorist what the atom is to the physicist—a basic unit of analysis. Psychologists have used systems concepts in describing and analyzing individuals and their behavior. For example, Dr. James G. Miller, Director of Mental Health Institute of the University of Michigan, conceives of man as a system that processes matter, energy, and information much as a computer does. He draws a set of parallels between the processing or metabolism of matter-energy (food) and the processing of information, "information metabolism."[5]

A key aspect of this concept is that of man as an information processing system. Input is picked up from the environment and used or stored as seen fit by the individual. Man, like other systems, receives inputs from his changing environments and delivers outputs to it. His self-adjusting, internal adaptive mechanisms are what engineers hope to duplicate in their automatic control systems, such as a steel rolling mill run by computers. Psychiatrists are interested in what can go wrong with man's adaptive mechanisms. "Information overload" is one problem that is receiving increasing attention in our fast paced, intensely communicative urban culture.[6]

As an individual interacts with other individuals in groups, additional aspects of systems concepts come into play. The term biosphere was coined to convey the conception of holistic entity which includes both individual and the environment "not as interacting parts, not as constituents which have independent existence, but as aspects of a single reality which can be separated only by abstraction."[7]

The concept as set forth included psychological and sociological processes as well as somatic processes. The psychological domain consists of the symbolic functions of the organisms, that is, perceiving, thinking, remembering, imagining, and the like; the social domain consists of man's interreactions with society. Basic divisions in the biosphere are the organism and the environment. The whole of life consists of the interactions between these two poles. Neither organism processes nor environmental events alone reflect reality but rather, biospheric occurrences, which are bio-pole in character, are the reality with which biological and social scientists must deal.

> Instead of studying the "organism" and "environment" and their interaction, we propose to study life as a unitary whole and endeavor to describe the organization and dynamics of the biosphere.[8]

Angyal prefers systems analysis over relationship analysis for the following reasons:

1. A system may include as many members as are necessary to explain a given phenomenon whereas a relationship involves only two members. The reduction of a complex structure to pairs of related members tends to destroy its natural coherence in unity and oversimplify the kinds of connections that exist.
2. The components of a system are connected with one another by virtue of their respective positions in the system whereas members of a relationship are connected by virtue of possessing some common property, such as color or form. In a power system, such as an organization, the position of each person in the system is far more important than any specific relationship that a person may possess with other members of the system.
3. The members of a system need have no direct connection with one another but the two members of a relationship must be directly connected.

One dimension of social systems involves the continuum of rigidity versus plasticity. In a rigid system events are highly standardized and uniform, whereas in a more plastic system variable approaches are evident. A rigid system is likely to be compartmentalized to the extent that local happenings have little or no effect on neighboring subsystems. In a plastic system on the other hand, local events are likely to inter-react with neighboring subsystems and hence may touch off reactions throughout the system.

A system contains parts which are either fully differentiated or still embedded in the whole and undifferentiated state. Differentiation of parts out of the whole occurs when a complex operation requires a division of labor among the parts of the system. In a highly differentiated whole, parts are more individualized and possess greater relative autonomy. Such a situation tends to produce disunity and disintegration in the system and will eventually destroy it if allowed to go unchecked. Therefore, there has to be some counterbalancing effect such as integration. The expansion of systems comes about by successive stages of differentiation and integration, and the tendency of any system is to be conservative with respect to differentiation and to permit it only when it is absolutely essential. A part of a whole has to have two characteristics: it must be relatively complete in itself and it has to occupy a position in a system which does not require the mediation of intermediary systems for its maintenance. In other words, it has to be relatively autonomous and independent without becoming isolated from the system.

Subsystem Overlays

Individuals interact with other individuals in both small and large groups to comprise the social system that is an organization. Both formal and informal organizations are involved. The organization chart depicts a system of interdependent roles in a job-task hierarchy. This basic job-task hierarchy is modified by a number of other systems which have been called overlays by Pfiffner and Sherwood.[9]

These subsystems or overlays include:

1. The sociometric network
2. The decision network
3. The communication-feedback grid
4. The network of functional relationships
5. The power center network
6. The network of individual personalities
7. The network of personal and industrial values

Each of these is a system with interactions within its own framework. In addition each of these subsystems interacts with some or all of the other systems. The complexity involved is evident. Thus managers would be well advised not to succumb to the temptation to adopt oversimplified views of organizations or "ten-steps to managerial success" which are guaranteed in any situation. The administrator is better advised to attempt to understand the complexity and why straightforward, simple-minded approaches do not seem to work out in the real world.

Implementation of Systems Concepts

Many of the most recent developments in the environment of businessmen and managers have involved systems concepts. For example, automation suggests a self-contained system with inputs, outputs, and a mechanism of control. Sophisticated mechanization or completely automated systems such as oil refineries are commonplace today. Systems concepts are also apparent in the automation of information flow. Here again there is an entire spectrum of sophistication leading from simple, straightforward data-reduction problems to the elaborate, real-time data processing systems.

Physical distribution systems have received increasing attention on the part of manufacturers and shippers. The concepts of logistics, or materials management, have been used to emphasize the flow of materials through distribution channels. The term rhochrematics[10] has been coined to connote the flow process from raw material sources to final consumer. In essence, these ideas embrace systems concepts because emphasis is placed on the total system of material flow rather than on functions, departments, or institutions which may be involved in the processing.

In recent years increasing attention has been focused upon massive engineering projects. In particular, military and space programs are becoming increasingly complex, thus indicating the need for integrating various elements of the total system. Manufacturing the product itself (a vehicle or other hardware) is quite complex, often involving problems of producibility with requirements of extremely high reliability. This is difficult to ensure for individual components or subsystems. In addition, each subsystem also must be reliable in its interrelationship with all other subsystems. Successful integration of subcomponents, and hence successful performance of a particular product, also must be integrated with other elements of the total system. For example, the functioning of the Nike-Zeus antimissile missile must be coordinated with the early warning system, ground facilities, and operating personnel. All elements must function as an operating, integrated whole.

These examples emphasize the mechanistic and structural aspects of the systems concept. Yet, we cannot forget that organizations are social systems; we are dealing with man-made systems. In discussing the impact of the systems concept it should not be assumed that people basically resist systems. Much of man's conscious activities since the dawn of history has been geared to creating system out of chaos. Man does not resist systematization of his behavioral patterns *per se*. Rather, the normal human being seeks satisfactory systems of interpersonal relationship which guide his activities. Without systematization, behavior would be random, nongoal-oriented, and unpredictable. Certainly, our complex, modern, industrial society demands more systematized human behavior than older, less-structured societies. A common characteristic in a rapidly advancing society is to make systems of interpersonal relationship more formal. While many of these systems have been implicit in the past, they are becoming more explicit. This remains one of the basic precepts of our systems model; systematic interpersonal relationships are necessary for accomplishing group objectives and an effective organizational system should be designed to meet this need.

It seems clear that systems concepts are extremely pervasive — psychologically and sociologically, as well as technologically and structurally. The question remains, however, "What is the potential usefulness of such an approach?" It is apparent that the functions of management can be carried out without explicit reference to systems concepts. On the other hand, it seems equally clear that reference to systems concepts would make a manager more effective. The job-task hierarchy as a macro model of the organization can be used as a point of departure. Basic notions such as dividing the work appropriately and integrating efforts toward enterprise objectives can be carried out within the framework of systems concepts. McDonough defines an organization as a collection of problems to be solved.[11] In this context it would be useful to identify kinds of problems involved in terms of some breakdown such as non-programmed vs. programmed decisions (or routine-adaptive-innovative). It may be entirely appropriate for different approaches to be used in problem solving or decision making depending on the kinds of problems identified.

A well-defined bureaucratic system may well be the best approach for programmed decision making within an organization. In such a case the hierarchy would take precedent and relationship would be superior oriented.

The system of policies and procedures would provide a framework for integrated decision making. On the other hand, for non-routine, ill-structured problem solving situations a bureaucratic system would be less appropriate. Some way should be found to facilitate heuristic decision making so that the organization can be adaptive and innovative. Thus the system should be as flexible as possible and allow such systems to be generated, expanded, and disbanded as the situation dictates.

The specific organizational approach to implement systems concepts might take any one of several forms. Committees, either standing or ad hoc, have long been an approach for recognizing the need for subsystems not readily available in the job-task pyramid. The task force approach is another way of dealing with non-routine items in an efficient and effective manner. In such cases the necessary subsystem is developed specifically to accomplish a task and disbanded once the job has been completed. The program management concept is another example of implementing systems concepts. In this case resources — men, materials, and machines — are assembled to concentrate on achieving the objectives of a particular program. The program may be short-lived or it may last several decades. In any case its temporal nature is recognized. It is a subsystem which must be interrelated with others in some organizational or enterprise environment. These various specific approaches to implementing systems concepts in real organizations are primarily ways of maintaining a flexible social system which function effectively in the face of both routine and non-routine problems.

Summary

General systems theory is concerned with developing a systematic, theoretical framework for describing general relationships of the empirical world. While a spectrum, or hierarchy of systems can be established over a considerable range, the systems concept is also a point of view and a desirable goal, rather than a particular method or content area. Progress can be made as research proceeds in various specialized areas but within a total system context.

The business organization is a man-made system which has a dynamic interplay with its environment — customers, competitors, labor organizations, suppliers, government and many other agencies. In addition, it is a system of interrelated parts working in conjunction with each other in order to accomplish a number of goals, both those of the organization and those of individual participants. The concept of the organization in a state of dynamic equilibrium can be used by practising managers in order to integrate the various on-going activities into a meaningful total system. Regardless of specific adjustments or organizational arrangements, there are certain subsystems or essential functions which make up a total information-decision system. However, the exact form utilized by a particular organization may depend upon the task orientation.

Managers are needed to convert disorganized resources of men, material, and money into a useful, effective enterprise. Essentially, management is the process whereby these unrelated resources are integrated into a total system for objective accomplishment. The systems concept provides no cookbook technique, guaranteed to provide managerial success. The basic functions are still planning, organization, control, and communication. Each of these activities can be carried out with or without overt emphasis on systems concepts. Our contention is that the activities themselves can be better accomplished in light of systems concepts. Furthermore, there can be a definite change in emphasis for the entire managerial process if the functions are performed in light of the system as a whole and not as separate entities.

The business organization as a system can be considered as a subsystem of a larger environmental system. Even industry or inter-industry systems can be recognized as sub-elements of the economic system, and the economic system can be regarded as a part of society in general. One of the major changes within business organizations of the future may be the breakdown of traditional functional specialization geared to optimizing performance of particular departments. There may be growing use of organizational structures designed around projects and information-decision systems. The systems concept calls for integration, into a total organizational system, of activities related to particular projects or programs. This approach currently is being implemented in some of the advanced-technology industries where creativity is at a premium.

Increasingly, managers will need a meaningful frame of reference for coordinating activities in large-scale, complex organizations. Systems theory offers such a concept — one that is operational, yet viable.

Notes

1. For a more complete discussion see: R. A. Johnson, F. E. Kast, *The Theory and Management of Systems* (New York: McGraw-Hill Book Co., 1963), pp. 4–6, 91, 92.

2. Sir Arthur Eddington, *The Nature of the Physical World* (Ann Arbor: The University of Michigan Press, 1958), pp. 103–104.

3. Warren G. Bennis, "Leadership Theory and Administrative Behavior: The Problem of Authority," *Administrative Science Quarterly*, December 1959, p. 263 ff.

4. William G. Scott, *Human Relations in Management* (Homewood: Richard D. Irwin, Inc., 1962), p. 138.

5. "Does a Human, Pressured, Really 'Blow a Fuse'?," *National Observer*, January 4, 1965, p. 1 ff.

6. *Ibid.*, p. 12.

7. A. Angyal, *Foundations for a Science of Personality* (New York: Commonwealth Fund, 1941), p. 100.

8. *Ibid,* pp. 100–101.

9. John N. Pfiffner and Frank P. Sherwood, *Administrative Organization* (Englewood Cliffs: Prentice-Hall, Inc., 1960), p. 207.

10. Rhochrematics comes from two Greek roots; rhoe, which means a flow (as a river or stream), and chrema, which stands for products, materials, or things (including information). The abstract ending -ics has been added, as for any of the sciences.

11. Adrian McDonough, *Information Economics and Management Systems* (New York: McGraw-Hill Book Company, 1963).

2

Behavioral Scientist at Large . . . . a Candid Conversation with Chris Argyris

HAROLD M. F. RUSH
The Conference Board

Business consultants of one kind and another can be found in every industrialized country today. Their job, in a word, is to diagnose a company's ills. While some come prepared to prescribe their favorite nostrums, others, more and more these days, attempt to apply new doctrine, and often it is drawn from the most scholarly fields of investigation.

Ever since World War II, industry has been exposed increasingly to the work of one group of specialists in particular. They generally call themselves behavioral scientists, but the conglomerate includes psychologists, sociologists, anthropologists, and sometimes economists and political scientists as well.

Some businessmen have already become enthusiasts for the so-called behavioral approach. Others have refused even to get acquainted with these new philosophies. But most have apparently adopted a wait-and-see attitude.

To get a close-up view of one of the more prominent proponents of behavioral science in industry, and report his candid appraisal of its present status, The Conference Board last month talked with Professor Chris Argyris in his office at Yale University.

We asked Dr. Argyris: In recent years, there has been an increased awareness of the behavioral sciences in management circles. There has also been a lot of criticism of the "behavioral" approach to management. What, in your opinion, is this new element we are talking about?

Argyris answered:

> In the past, people like Urwick and Mooney wrote books to help executives understand the most rational and effective way of designing an organization. And their contributions were important because an organization needs some sense of design if it's ever going to be effective.

Taken and adapted from *The Conference Board Record,* Vol. 4, May 1967, pp. 23–28. Used by permission.

Then came the behavioral sciences. Now, one of the characteristics of the behavioral sciences is indicated by its title; namely, behavior. So we said: Let's see what is actually going on. Let's observe behavior by opening up an organization and looking inside it.

When we looked, we saw at least two things. One, there was a lot of behavior going on that wasn't supposed to be going on, according to plan; and two, some of this behavior facilitated the organization's effectiveness, and some inhibited it.

We thought it a good idea for executives to take a look at this and eventually feed it back in the way they designed organizations. So that what the behavioral scientist does is take a look at what I like to call the "living system," the way people actually behave towards one another, the way they actually deal with one another.

In the study of behavior is it possible to contribute information that will be really useful to the executive or is it just theory? One of the most common criticisms of behavioral scientists is that they oversimplify everything.

I view the traditional formal structures as the ones that are oversimplified. We begin with these formal structures, but we have to ask ourselves another question: Do people actually behave according to these formal structures? If they don't, why not?

So we must try to add another dimension; we must take a new look at the total living system. Here I think we — and I refer to myself too — have miscommunicated. But there's been some considerable misperception on other people's part too. We aren't advocating throwing out the formal structures. Yet those formal structures are only one-dimensional views of the organization.

The Living System

Granted, the organization chart doesn't tell the whole story. You say you feel it is important to take a *new* look at organizations. Is the work that you do something truly new?

Well, yes, I think it's new on the total organizational scene.

Recently I wrote a report for the Secretary of State on the State Department, and that took a look at the living system. What I found, I believe people knew about for years. But I believe that the way I organized and conceptualized it may be somewhat new. This could have been done years ago by a consulting firm, if, in addition to having the traditional managerial point of view, it also had a behavioral point of view and took a look at the "living system."

Let me pursue this expression of yours, "living system." Exactly what do you mean?

I mean, when you open up the roof, so to speak, and look into a company, you map out the way people actually deal with one another, the way they interact, the way they communicate their norms — whether towards conformity or individuality, towards trust or mistrust.

If the norms were towards conformity, would you call this a living system?

Yes, that's part of the living system, except it's one that may be becoming sick. That's one other thing that we behavioral scientists are interested in. For example, we want to know what the difference is between a healthy system and a sick system, and how we can measure and identify a system that is sick and one that is healthy? These kinds of questions, I think, can only come when the "formal" approach is integrated with the "behavioral" approach.

What are your criteria in diagnosing a sick system or a healthy system?

Broadly speaking, I would say some of the most important criteria we use are: To what extent is the system aware of the problems that plague it? To what extent is it able to solve these problems in such a way that they remain solved? And to what extent is it able to accomplish the first two criteria without deteriorating the level of effectiveness of the problem solving process.

Another way of observing system effectiveness is by determining the amount of energy being used inefficiently or ineffectively in a system. "Ineffectively," in this context refers to the amount of energy employees are using to fight the objectives, the strategies, the plans of the organization.

Behavioral scientists have documented that a lot of energy is used fighting the system, ranging from rate setting, goldbricking, apathy, and indifference at the lower levels, to mistrust, politicking and conformity at the upper levels. Our view is that management may want to minimize some of these, so we can cut the cost inherent in this kind of situation.

There are two kinds of cost. One is the sheer financial cost. But more important is the long-range cost of an organization becoming sticky and rigid. I should add here that the main causes of organizational rigidity include such factors as mistrust, lack of openness, and lack of leveling among the people in the organization.

Isn't it possible that a company can be a sick organization, by your standards, and still be profitable?

I think I'd like to answer that question in two different ways. First of all, we need a lot more long-range, longitudinal research to be able to measure how a company becomes healthy and more effective. But in the absence of this research, there is another possible answer to your question.

From some behavioral science research, we can conclude that using the traditional ways we have in dealing with people, especially at the upper levels, there is a built-in tendency for ineffectiveness. This built-in tendency costs money. The cost is built into all accounting systems throughout the entire country. Therefore, no one competes with someone who is more effective. In reality, all accounting systems carry the cost of this human ineffectiveness.

It follows that if you can begin to decrease this ineffectiveness, you should show some difference in the financial payoff; and some of the smaller companies that have experimented with this have begun to show this difference.

I have one other comment on this. It is possible for a firm to make money in the short run and be inefficient. But the question is, what's the firm's long-range legacy in terms of rigidity and flexibility?

I think it can be predicted that the environment is going to become more hostile to a firm, either from greater competition or greater government control. The firm will then have to be, on the one hand, more innovative and quicker. On the other hand, the firm must also be able to get data from the environment to feed back to such organizations as governmental agencies. Well, how do you become more innovative? How do you do it quickly? And how do you generate the data necessary for survival and growth? It cannot be done without openness and trust within this system.

Do you actually observe any real change in management *practice* as a result of behavioral research?

Definitely. I do see examples of how behavioral science research has changed management practices in large and small corporations.

The changes, however, are spotty. There are no major changes overnight, but that's how it should be. Principles should be tested constantly. There's no denying that some companies are dead-set against even exploring the use of behavioral principles.

Why do you think these companies have resisted the behavioral sciences?

One reason is that behavioral science has questioned the fundamental concepts of traditional management practice, and the people involved are threatened by anything that goes against their life-long assumptions; therefore they resist.

Tough-minded Management

In all honesty, wouldn't you admit that that view is perhaps all too "pat;" I mean isn't it too easy to counter with "they're threatened?" It would seem that some pretty successful executives haven't embraced the behavioral sciences.

Many executives believe that human relations means something like "being nice to people." When we observe these men in action, we find that these so-called "tough-minded executives" are the most conservative and relatively inffective in dealing with people. They're uncomfortable in firing people; they're uncomfortable in leveling with them; they'd rather hold all sorts of meetings first to make a decision before coming to a board meeting which ostensibly is for making decisions.

The men who have been most critical of the behavioral sciences are, in my experience, the ones who haven't faced reality. So they are more threatened when the behavioral scientist says, "Let's face the reality." And part of this reality may be focusing on hostility, threats, and conformity — but focusing on it quite openly.

Might their resistance also be founded on the belief that the behavioral sciences aren't really sciences?

No, I don't agree with that. At least I don't agree, if you must apply the usual criteria of scientific method that apply to the physical sciences. I think you'll find that our use of scientific method is rather crude because our field is young. But I have no doubt that as we continue, we're going to become more and more systematic. And when you study human beings, they react differently than leaves, atoms and molecules. We may, indeed, invent some new methods of conducting research.

It has been said that much behavioral science research isn't really valid because of what is called the "Hawthorne effect" — that is, the behavioral patterns of the people being studied aren't necessarily indicative, because the subjects are more submissive as a result of the attention being paid to them. Is this true?

Some of the original interviews from the Hawthorne studies have, for some reason, not been looked at. A conference at Dartmouth in about 1928, as I recall, suggests that one of the men who observed in a bank wiring room asked the girls, "Why do you produce with no breaks in time?" And it wasn't because of the Hawthorne effect, namely, that they were being researched. They were simply so fed up with their supervisor, they were delighted to be outside his control. So the issue of the Hawthorne effect, I think, has to be reexplored.

Out of the Nowhere

I'm sure you're aware that a lot of the resistance to the behavioral approach to managing has come from outside the business community. In fact, some of the most outspoken critics are respected management theorists. At a recent NICB conference a professor from another leading business school referred to behavioral science as a method of "pouring from the empty into the void." Another widely published management authority referred to the use of the behavioral sciences in industry as a fad, and he compared it to a phase of human relations management that emphasized paternalism. Any comment?

I think the traditional management theorists have been caught flat-footed. You know, it may be embarrassing to the forty or so professors of personnel administration and traditional management who were brought to a center by the Ford Foundation to be retrained, or as it was called, "retreaded" because their field was threatened — on its way out.

Then you would reject the allegation of a fad?

The best research being done in universities is not only useful to practical people who are managers, but it's also adding to basic knowledge and theory. So far, in the history of man, nothing that has added to basic knowledge has become a fad.

But what about the criticism that has come from within the psychological disciplines that too much of the research is entirely too empirical and too insignificant? I think one psychologist referred to it as "itsy-bitsy, teeny bits of research."

There is a lot of so-called "behavioral research" that really isn't adding to knowledge, and a lot of it isn't very meaningful. Researchers are aware of the problem, and many would be delighted to see some of it go.

Would you please be more specific?

I'm referring to research that doesn't focus on critical issues. Often, that kind of research attracts people who aren't willing to take risks to turn out research that deals with significant questions.

We've had thousands of studies that have taken a look at attitudes, but they have never really been correlated and effectively tied up with performance and motivation.

One leading researcher told me that he wasn't really concerned whether business picked up what he had researched and documented. He's only interested in the knowledge itself, and he wanted to go on doing his research. Would you say this is a prevalent attitude, or is this man an exception?

I have to admit that that's probably a prevalent attitude among a good number of researchers, and one that is supported by the norms of the university. But I also think many behavioral scientists are deeply concerned over whether our knowledge is used and for two reasons. We're concerned, as human beings, about these problems. Also, if we communicate to our subjects that we do not really care for them, I doubt if we will be able to get the data we need to conduct valid research.

The Computer Cometh

A large amount of the writings that reflect your research and the work of some of your colleagues deals with the concept of self-actualization. In your opinion, will the rise of the computer take away individual responsibility and involvement (in decision making, for example) or do you foresee the computer as an aid to self-actualization?

At the lower level, I think the jobs that are left will engender greater increments of self-actualization because they will provide greater challenge and responsibility. The very routine jobs will eventually go, and that's a problem our society has to face. But the new jobs being created require much more brains and capability.

Let's look at automation outside the computer. What about the man who's had a great deal of training — maybe he's served an apprenticeship and worked at his craft for a long, long time. Now, he can push a button and his work will be done for him. Where's the satisfaction? Where's the opportunity for self-actualization?

Well, there won't be any for him, if that's what we're going to limit him to. But he may, indeed, be the person who will be trained as a computer programmer. He may also be trained as a planner for product design, or he may be used in quality control issues. But I agree, this is a difficult problem.

Dull Jobs for the Frightened

Regarding self-actualization, what happens to the employee whose job is just plain dull? How is this man motivated?

In my own research, I have found people who are emotionally frightened by responsible work; these people often value the dull, routine job.

Suppose that's all he can do?

Then I would say fine, if he chooses to do so.

Yet you talk a lot about integrating his needs with the organization's, or getting him to identify with the organization's goals. How does he get involved and committed if his work is dull and prosaic?

My research shows that people who are interested in dull, routine work and are given this work, are highly committed to the organization. What creates commitment is the fit between the man's needs and the company's needs.

He can conceivably be highly committed to the organization's goals, but he hasn't any way himself of contributing very much to them, except through the mundane, prosaic task that he does. Then what does he do?

Then I think he's in a situation that many people are in now; namely he adapts by psychologically withdrawing and not really being very committed to the work. In effect he learns to believe, "It's managtment's responsibility to keep this organization working."

Then where does he get his kicks?

I wish I could say, "He gets his kicks outside," but my research suggests that he does not.

It suggests that he does *not?*

He does not. That is if, by kicks, we mean real opportunities for self-actualization. There is no data to show that workers seek genuine self-actualization outside the plant, if they don't seek it inside the plant. There are studies to show that what they seek outside is as apathetic, non-involved and non-committed as it is inside.

What about the man who through a series of economic circumstances, or geography or cultural circumstances, finds himself with a third-grade education and, in his late fifties, he's doing a job he's done all of his life, and he hates it. Is there any hope for getting commitment from this man?

I wonder. I think what can be done is at least to help him face up to it.

The point I'm trying to ask management to consider is that workers are capable of facing reality, and that instead of trying to develop programs that tell them their work is meaningful when it isn't, they should stop those programs.

If I were a manager, I'd say, "How can I design my system so that I minimize the dull, boring, routine work? After I start on that, how can I take these people who are in a dull, boring routine job, and help them face up to it, so at least they don't fight me by fighting the system?"

But, none of us will say that *all* work will eventually be fulfilling. That's not true.

Happiness Isn't Everything

But isn't much of your work aimed at creating an organizational atmosphere in which people can achieve higher morale levels — become happier workers, in other words?

I think a careful reading of research will reveal we have *never* said that we're interested in the happiness of people. For example, I have said that the lower you go down the structure, the more you will find that a person feels controlled, dependent and submissive. There are many happy workers who are dependent, submissive and apathetic, and who have enormous trouble when they must react to a stress in the system — mainly an enormous competitive stress. One can have plenty of happy workers who aren't going to be very productive, but they aren't going to create problems either.

What the theory suggested and the data confirmed is that this kind of organization gets in trouble when it really has to move fast and be innovative.

The behavioral approach to managing usually connotes some form of participative atmosphere. Some critics have referred to this kind of situation as "management by consensus." Others have attacked this approach as unethical, claiming it's just a more sophisticated way of manipulating people. Would you care to comment on this?

If, by "manipulate," you mean to create or alter an environment so that a person gives his best and actualizes himself, then I'll have to go along with it.

I think we both know that's not what the critics mean by "manipulate."

If you define "manipulate" as a means of getting people to do what you want them to do, then that is impossible under the conditions that we behavioral scientists are advocating.

Will you elaborate on that for me?

Manipulation is impossible because we are suggesting that both the manager and his subordinates be open . . . that they take risks and trust one another. And above all, they *both* have an opportunity to make an informed choice. When this situation exists, the subordinate has a right to ask, "What are you doing? Are you trying to manipulate me?" Manipulation of the environment works; manipulation of people will eventually boomerang.

I think behavioral science *will* become a fad and die on the vine if someone tries to take the matter of participation only half way. One manager who practiced manipulation said it perfectly. "I love behavioral science," he said. "It means participation. In my company, we have centrally-controlled participation." This is certainly not the point of view of respectable behavioral scientists.

Participating Presidents

Do you see any real trend toward participative methods in problem solving and decision making, particularly at the top of the organization?

Yes. And I want to emphasize that one of the main reasons is the computer. It can turn out enormous amounts of information for the top executive committee to deal with.

Now, if the president tried to handle this amount of information alone, he would find it impossible to do. He needs his team. So there is participation in the exploration and discussion of the decision — real, genuine participation because the president can't make this a game; it has to be for real. And it seems to me what then happens is, if he has a group that he can really trust, he participates fully and concurs fully in the decision and can then be held individually accountable for it.

Would you agree with the statement that an organization is pretty much the "width and breadth" of the chief executive?

No, I'd have to modify that somewhat. The computer revolution has brought about an enormous change in the meaning of responsibility on the part of top management.

The president can't any longer be expected to have all the data in his own head. He, in effect, needs to have a viable decision-making network around him.

I am not suggesting that the president may not be individually responsible. I'm saying that a good way for the president to be individually responsible for decision made is to generate an exploration of problems in his group, where all the data are on the table, so that he can have confidence in the decision for which he accepts individual responsibility.

Creative Non-innovation

Human behavior is an area of responsibility that is usually relegated to the personnel specialist, yet I don't read much in your books about the work of personnel men and, throughout this interview, whenever you talk about organizations you seem to talk in terms of line management. Is this by design?

I must admit it's by design. Whenever I am called in to work with a company, it is usually at the invitation of the line executives. Rarely will I accept an invitation from a personnel officer.

Why not?

In my experience, many line executives feel that their personnel men aren't up-to-date in the field of the behavioral sciences.

There's another reason. Personnel administrators are known for being most innovative in what I call the non-innovative aspects of personnel administration: namely, wage and salary administration of a type that has been used in the past. Or maybe he's oriented to fight the union, rather than to serving as an organizational change agent or organizational diagnostician. In other words, the line executive sees him as a keeper of records; what the accountant is for finance, the personnel man is for human problems.

Aren't you being a little hard on the professional personnel man?

I don't think so. Regarding the behavioral sciences and the whole field of organizational development, I keep hearing line officers say, "I don't want this function to be with training; I don't want it to be assigned to personnel." The reason for this may be the history of the personnel function and its willingness to embrace fads.

I gather that you feel the personnel man will need some kind of new training for the future, since you are optimistic about the expanded use of the concept of organization development. Am I correct?

Yes. As the behavioral sciences develop what I feel will be an enormous impact in the future, the personnel administrator will need to function as an organizational consultant. As the routine aspects of personnel administration are fed into the computer, and as such things as wage and salary are re-examined, the personnel function should grow to meet the new demands and requirements of the organization. The office of the personnel administrator will be composed of men capable of diagnosing and facilitating change within the organization.

This sound as if a whole new education is required for many personnel men. Is this the case?

Perhaps, but it doesn't necessarily mean getting a doctorate. In fact, there are already some outstanding men who are doing research and functioning as successful practitioners of organization development who don't have a Ph.D. In some cases a Ph.D. might even be a hindrance. There are some core skills that can be developed through a relatively small amount of additional, formal education.

What is needed more than academic study is a re-orientation on the part of personnel men — a basic re-orientation and re-evaluation of themselves and their important roles as agents of change.

PART TWO

Ecology of Human Resources Administration

Broad perspective on the effective management and development of human resources enables us to look beyond the boundaries of a given organization — at the external forces which affect its administration. Section A takes such a look — at the organization's "causal texture," at labor force patterns, computer systems, urban crises.

The social disorders of our day suggest the profound influence of goals and values on personnel management and organization development; and suggest the extreme urgency of consideration, and reconsideration, as in Section B, of our traditional and emerging goals and values.

A. ENVIRONMENTAL INFLUENCES

Emery and Trist (Selection 3) conceptualize the different types of environments with which an organization or its subsystem may have to cope. They describe four possible types of environments for an organization and the kinds of strategies which may be appropriate to each environment. Their analysis questions the validity of attempting to apply, in a mechanistic way, universal principles, practices, or decision rules. Rather, they suggest the utility of a diagnostic approach — starting with an analysis of the external environment.

Whereas Emery and Trist emphasize the types of economic environment confronting different organizations, Myers (Selection 4) presents an overview of the technical, social, and political forces with which managers will need to cope in the decade ahead. The four areas of management decisions anticipated by Myers have one common theme — the major challenge to management is the better utilization of people. Many of the selections to follow present value orientations, strategies, and practices which might be useful in coping with such problems.

3

The Causal Texture of Organizational Environments

F. E. Emery
Tavistock Institute on Human Relations

E. L. Trist
University of Pennsylvania

Identification of the Problem

A main problem in the study of organizational change is that the environmental contexts in which organizations exist are themselves changing, at an increasing rate, and toward increasing complexity. This point, in itself, scarcely needs labouring. Nevertheless, the characteristics of organizational environments demand consideration for their own sake, if there is to be an advancement of understanding in the behavioural sciences of a great deal that is taking place under the impact of technological change, especially at the present time. This paper is offered as a brief attempt to open up some of the problems, and stems from a belief that progress will be quicker if a certain extension can be made to current thinking about systems.

In a general way it may be said that to think in terms of systems seems the most appropriate conceptual response so far available when the phenomena under study — at any level and in any domain — display the character of being organized, and when understanding the nature of the interdependencies constitutes the research task. In the behavioural sciences, the first steps in building a systems theory were taken in connection with the analysis of internal processes in organisms, or organizations, when the parts had to be related to the whole. Examples include the organismic biology of Jennings, Cannon, and Henderson; early Gestalt theory and its later derivatives such as balance theory; and the classical theories of social structure. Many of these problems could be represented in closed-system models. The next steps were taken when wholes had to be related to their environments. This led to open-system models.

Taken and adapted from *Human Relations,* Vol. 18, No. 1, Feb. 1965, pp. 21–32. Used by permission.

A great deal of the thinking here has been influenced by cybernetics and information theory, though this has been used as much to extend the scope of closed-system as to improve the sophistication of open-system formulations. It was von Bertalanffy (1950) who, in terms of the general transport equation which he introduced, first fully disclosed the importance of openness or closedness to the environment as a means of distinguishing living organisms from inanimate objects. In contradistinction to physical objects, any living entity survives by importing into itself certain types of material from its environment, transforming these in accordance with its own system characteristics, and exporting other types back into the environment. By this process the organism obtains the additional energy that renders it "negentropic"; it becomes capable of attaining stability in a time-independent steady state — a necessary condition of adaptability to environmental variance.

Such steady states are very different affairs from the equilibrium states described in classical physics, which have far too often been taken as models for representing biological and social transactions. Equilibrium states follow the second law of thermodynamics, so that no work can be done when equilibrium is reached, whereas the openness to the environment of a steady state maintains the capacity of the organism for work, without which adaptability, and hence survival, would be impossible.

Many corollaries follow as regards the properties of open systems, such as equifinality, growth through internal elaboration, self-regulation, constancy of direction with change of position, etc. — and by no means all of these have yet been worked out. But though von Bertalanffy's formulation enables exchange processes between the organism, or organization, and elements in its environment to be dealt with in a new perspective, it does not deal at all with those processes in the environment itself which are among the determining conditions of the exchanges. To analyse these an additional concept is needed — *the causal texture of the environment* — if we may re-introduce, at a social level of analysis, a term suggested by Tolman and Brunswik (1935) and drawn from S. C. Pepper (1934).

With this addition, we may now state the following general proposition: that a comprehensive understanding of organizational behaviour requires some knowledge of each member of the following set, where L indicates some potentiality lawful connection, and the suffix 1 refers to the organization and the suffix 2 to the environment:

$$L_{1\,1},\ L_{1\,2}$$
$$L_{2\,1},\ L_{2\,2}$$

$L_{1\,1}$ here refers to processes within the organization — the area of internal interdependencies; $L_{1\,2}$ and $L_{2\,1}$ to exchanges between the organization and its environment — the area of transactional interdependencies from either direction; and L_{22} to processes through which parts of the environment become related to each other — i.e. its causal texture — the area of interdependencies that belong within the environment itself.

In considering environmental interdependencies, the first point to which we wish to draw attention is that the laws connecting parts of the environment to each other are often incommensurate with those connecting parts of the organization to each other, or even with those which govern the exchanges. It is not possible, for example, always to reduce organization-environment relations to the form of "being included in"; boundaries are also "break" points. As Barker and Wright (1949), following Lewin (1936), have pointed out in their analysis of this problem as it affects psychological ecology, we may lawfully connect the actions of a javelin thrower in sighting and throwing his weapon; but we cannot describe in the same concepts the course of the javelin as this is affected by variables lawfully linked by meteorological and other systems.

The Development of Environmental Connectedness (Case I)

A case history, taken from the industrial field, may serve to illustrate what is meant by the environment becoming organized at the social level. It will show how a greater degree of system-connectedness, of crucial relevance to the organization, may develop in the environment, which is yet not directly a function either of the organization's own characteristics or of its immediate relations. Both of these, of course, once again become crucial when the response of the organization to what has been happening is considered.

The company concerned was the foremost in its particular market in the food-canning industry in the U.K. and belonged to a large parent group. Its main product — a canned vegetable — had some 65 per cent of this market, a situation which had been relatively stable since before the war. Believing it would continue to hold this position, the company persuaded the group board to invest several million pounds sterling in erecting a new, automated factory, which, however, based its economies on an inbuilt rigidity — it was set up exclusively for the long runs expected from the traditional market.

The character of the environment, however, began to change while the factory was being built. A number of small canning firms appeared, not dealing with this product nor indeed with others in the company's range, but with imported fruits. These firms arose because the last of the post-war controls had been removed from steel strip and tin, and cheaper cans could now be obtained in any numbers — while at the same time a larger market was developing in imported fruits. This trade being seasonal, the firms were anxious to find a way of using their machinery and retaining their labour in winter. They became able to do so through a curious side-effect of the development of quick-frozen foods, when the company's staple was produced by others in this form. The quick-freezing process demanded great constancy at the growing end. It was not possible to control this beyond a certain point, so that quite large crops unsuitable for quick freezing but suitable for canning became available — originally from another country (the United States) where a large market for quick-frozen foods had been established. These surplus crops had been sold at a very low price for animal feed. They were now imported by the small canners — at a better but still comparatively low price, and additional cheap supplies soon began to be procurable from underdeveloped countries.

Before the introduction of the quick-freezing form, the company's own canned product — whose raw material had been specially grown at additional cost — had been the premier brand, superior to other varieties and charged at a higher price. But its position in the product spectrum now changed. With the increasing affluence of the society, more people were able to afford the quick-frozen form. Moreover, there was competition from a great many other vegetable products which could substitute for the staple, and people preferred this greater variety. The advantage of being the premier line among canned forms diminished, and demand increased both for the not-so-expensive varieties among them and for the quick-frozen forms. At the same time, major changes were taking place in retailing; supermarkets were developing, and more and more large grocery chains were coming into existence. These establishments wanted to sell certain types of goods under their own house names, and began to place bulk orders with the small canners for their own varieties of the company's staple that fell within this class. As the small canners provided an extremely cheap article (having no marketing expenses and a cheaper raw material), they could undercut the manufacturers' branded product, and within three years they captured over 50 per cent of the market. Previously, retailers' varieties had accounted for less than 1 per cent.

The new automatic factory could not be adapted to the new situation until alternative products with a big sales volume could be developed, and the scale of research and development, based on the type of market analysis required to identify these, was beyond the scope of the existing resources of the company either in people or in funds.

The changed texture of the environment was not recognized by an able but traditional management until it was too late. They failed entirely to appreciate that a number of outside events were becoming connected with each other in a way that was leading up to irreversible general change. Their first reaction was to make an herculean effort to defend the traditional product, then the board split on whether or not to make entry into the cheaper unbranded market in a supplier role. Group H.Q. now felt they had no option but to step in, and many upheavals and changes in management took place until a "redefinition of mission" was agreed, and slowly and painfully the company re-emerged with a very much altered product mix and something of a new identity.

Four Types of Causal Texture

It was this experience, and a number of others not dissimilar, by no means all of them industrial (and including studies of change problems in hospitals, in prisons, and in educational and political organizations), that gradually led us to feel a need for re-directing conceptual attention to the causal texture of the environment, considered as a quasi-independent domain. We have now isolated four "ideal types" of causal texture, approximations to which may be thought of as existing simultaneously in the "real world" of most organizations — though, of course, their weighting will vary enormously from case to case.

The first three of these types have already, and indeeed repeatedly, been described — in a large variety of terms and with the emphasis on an equally bewildering variety of special aspects — in the literature of a number of disciplines, ranging from biology to economics and including military theory as well as psychology and sociology. The fourth type, however, is new, at least to us, and is the one that for some time we have been endeavoring to identify. About the first three, therefore, we can be brief, but the fourth is scarcely understandable without reference to them. Together, the four types may be said to form a series in which the degree of causal texturing is increased, in a new and significant way, as each step is taken. We leave as an open question the need for further steps.

Step One

The simplest type of environmental texture is that in which goals and noxiants ("goods" and "bads") are relatively unchanging in themselves and randomly distributed. This may be called the *placid, randomized environment.* It corresponds to Simon's idea of a surface over which an organism can locomote: most of this is bare, but at isolated, widely scattered points there are little heaps of food (1957, p. 137). It also corresponds to Ashby's limiting case of no connection between the environmental parts (1960, S15/4); and to Schutzenberger's random field (1954, p. 100). The economist's classical market also corresponds to this type.

A critical property of organizational response under random conditions has been stated by Schutzenberger: that there is no distinction between tactics and strategy, "the optimal strategy is just the simple tactic of attempting to do one's best on a purely local basis" (1954, p. 101). The best tactic, moreover, can be learnt only by trial and error and only for a particular class of local environmental variances (Ashby, 1960, p. 197). While organizations under these conditions can exist adaptively as single and indeed quite small units, this becomes progressively more difficult under the other types.

Step Two

More complicated, but still a placid environment, is that which can be characterized in terms of clustering: goals and noxiants are not randomly distributed but hang together in certain ways. This may be called the placid, clustered environment, and is the case with which Tolman and Brunswik were concerned; it corresponds to Ashby's "serial system" and to the economist's "imperfect competition." The clustering enables some parts to take on roles as signs of other parts or become means-objects with respect to approaching or avoiding. Survival, however, becomes precarious if an organization attempts to deal tactically with each environmental variance as it occurs.

The new feature of organizational response to this kind of environment is the emergence of strategy as distinct from tactics. Survival becomes critically linked with what an organization knows of its environment. To pursue a goal under its nose may lead it into parts of the field fraught with danger, while avoidance of an immediately difficult issue may lead it away from potentially rewarding areas. In the clustered environment the relevant objective is that of "optimal location," some positions being discernible as potentially richer than others.

To reach these requires concentration of resources, subordination to the main plan, and the development of a "distinctive competence," to use Selznick's (1957) term, in reaching the strategic objective. Organizations under these conditions, therefore, tend to grow in size and also to become hierarchical, with a tendency towards centralized control and coordination.

Step Three

The next level of causal texturing we have called the disturbed-reactive environment. It may be compared with Ashby's ultra-stable system or the economist's oligopolic market. It is a type 2 environment in which there is more than one organization of the same kind; indeed, the existence of a number of similar organizations now become the dominant characteristic of the environmental field. Each organization does not simply have to take account of the others when they meet at random, but has also to consider that what it knows can also be known by the others. The part of the environment to which it wishes to move itself in the long run is also the part to which the others seek to move. Knowing this, each will wish to improve its own chances by hindering the others, and each will know that the others must not only wish to do likewise, but also know that each knows this. The presence of similar others creates an imbrication, to use a term of Chein's (1943), of some of the causal strands in the environment.

If strategy is a matter of selecting the "strategic objective" — where one wishes to be at a future time — and tactics a matter of selecting an immediate action from one's available repertoire, then there appears in type 3 environments to be an intermediate level of organizational response — that of the operation — to use the term adopted by German and Soviet military theorists, who formally distinguish tactics, operations, and strategy. One has now not only to make sequential choices, but to choose actions that will draw off the other organizations. The new element is that of deciding which of someone else's possible tactics one wishes to take place, while ensuring that others of them do not. An operation consists of a campaign involving a planned series of tactical initiatives, calculated reactions by others, and counteractions. The flexibility required encourages a certain decentralization and also puts a premium on quality and speed of decision at various peripheral points (Heyworth, 1955).

It now becomes necessary to define the organizational objective in terms not so much of location as of capacity or power to move more or less at will, i.e. to be able to make and meet competitive challenge. This gives particular relevance to strategies of absorption and parasitism. It can also give rise to situations in which stability can be obtained only by a certain coming-to-terms between competitors, whether enterprises, interest groups, or governments. One has to know when not to fight to the death.

Step Four

Yet more complex are the environments we have called turbulent fields. In these, dynamic processes, which create significant variances for the component organizations, arise from the field itself. Like type 3 and unlike the static types 1 and 2, they are dynamic. Unlike type 3, the dynamic properties arise not simply from the interaction of the component organizations, but also from the field itself. The "ground" is in motion.

Three trends contribute to the emergence of these dynamic field forces:

(i) The growth to meet type 3 conditions of organizations, and linked sets of organizations, so large that their actions are both persistent and strong enough to induce autochthonous processes in the environment. An analogous effect would be that of a company of soldiers marching in step over a bridge.
(ii) The deepening interdependence between the economic and the other facts of the society. This means that economic organizations are increasingly enmeshed in legislation and public regulation.
(iii) The increasing reliance on research and development to achieve the capacity to meet competitive challenge. This leads to a situation in which a change gradient is continuously present in the environmental field.

For organizations, these trends mean a gross increase in their area of *relevant uncertainty*. The consequences which flow from their actions lead off in ways that become increasingly unpredictable: they do not necessarily fall off with distance, but may at any point be amplified beyond all expectation; similarly, lines of action that are strongly pursued may find themselves attenuated by emergent field forces.

References

Ashby, W. Ross. *Designs for a Brain*. London: Chapman & Hall, 1960.

Barker, R. G., and H. F. Wright. "Psychological ecology and the problem of psychosocial development." *Child Development*, 20 (1949), 131–43.

Bertalanffy, L. von. "The theory of open systems in physics and biology." *Science*, 111 (1950), 23–9.

Chein, I. "Personality and typology." *J. soc. Psychol.*, 18 (1943), 89–101.

Churchman, C. W., and R. I. Ackoff. *Methods of Inquiry*. St. Louis: Educational Publishers, 1950.

Churchman, C. W., and F. E. Emery. "On various approaches to the study of organizations." Proceedings of the International Conference on Operational Research and the Social Sciences, Cambridge, England, 14–18 September 1964. To be published in book form as *Operational Research and the Social Sciences*. London: Tavistok Publications, 1965.

Heyworth, Lord. *The Organization of Unilever*. London: Unilever Limited, 1955.

Lewin, K. *Principles of Topological Psychology*. New York: McGraw-Hill, 1936.

Lewin, K. *Field Theory in Social Science*. New York: Harper, 1951.

Likert, R. *New Patterns of Management*. New York, Toronto, London: McGraw-Hill, 1961.

McGregor, D. *The Human Side of Enterprise*. New York, Toronto, London: McGraw-Hill, 1960.

Pepper, S. C. The conceptual framework of Tolman's purposive behaviorism. *Psychol. Rev.* 41 (1934), 108–33.

Schutzenberger, M. P. "A tentative classification of goal-seeking behaviours." *J. ment. Sci.* 100 (1954), 97–102.

Selznick, P. *Leadership in Administration*. Evanston, Ill.: Row Peterson, 1957.

Simon, H. A. *Models of Man*. New York: Wiley, 1957.

Tolman, E. C. and E. Brunswik. "The organism and the causal texture of the environment." *Psychol. Rev.* 42 (1935), 43–77.

4

Management Decisions for the Next Decade

CHARLES A. MYERS
Massachusetts Institute of Technology

Introduction

Recently, considerable attention has been focused on the Year 2000 and beyond. Herman Kahn, who wrote first about thermonuclear war, has now turned the attention of his Hudson Institute to a series of statements about the turn of the century. Kahn is bolder than most prophets. He lists as one of the characteristics of our society: "Business firms are no longer the major source of innovation."[1] Another prophet is Daniel Bell, a sociologist at Columbia University, who heads an American Academy of Arts and Sciences group that is also attempting to assess our society at the Year 2000. He has coined the phrase "post-industrial society" to describe the United States at that time. Bell defines the post-industrial society "as one in which the organization of theoretical knowledge becomes paramount for innovation in the society, and in which intellectual institutions become central in the social structure."[2]

The American Management Association, through its American Foundation for Management Research, held a conference early this year, publishing papers and discussion under the title, *Management 2000*.[3] The speakers at the conference, on the whole, did not predict as sharp a break with the present as Kahn and Bell visualize. These forecasts about the turn of the millennium (only 32 years away) have initiated considerable thought within the business community.

The intent here is to stimulate further thought about the future by suggesting developments likely to occur in the next decade which will be of paramount significance to management. The effort is more limited, both in scope and in time horizon, than the current predictions about the Year 2000 and beyond. The areas considered are further limited to developments with implications for management decisions. No projections are made concerning international crises or political elections, for example, not because they

Taken and adapted from *Industrial Management Review*, Vol. 10, No. 1, Fall 1968, pp. 31–39.

are without significance for management, but because the uncertainty associated with these events discounts their importance for current management decisions. By selecting a time horizon of the next decade instead of the next century, projections can be made with greater certainty. Furthermore, the validity of forecasts about the Year 2000 by Kahn and Bell is in part dependent on the response of corporate executives to the developments of the next decade discussed here.

Four areas of sufficient importance to warrant in depth consideration are:

1. Changes in the composition of our labor force which accentuate some of the problems managers have already had in dealing with better educated and differently motivated employees, and the shortage of competent managers accentuated by these labor force changes;
2. Rapidly increasing use of computer systems and management science techniques;
3. Further crises in our cities, particularly in the urban ghettos where the persistent problems of black disaffection and hard-core unemployment will not go away during the next decade, or even the decade after that; and
4. Expanding involvement of the multi-national corporation, not only in Western Europe but also in developing countries.

The implications for management decisions of these all-important areas are discussed in the sections which follow.

Changes in the Labor Force Affecting Management

Recent labor force projections by the Bureau of Labor Statistics of the United States Department of Labor, extending to 1975, provide a basis for analyzing emerging population and manpower patterns.[4] According to those projections, the population picture in 1975 will possess the following characteristics:

1. There will be an absolute *decrease* in the age group, 35–54. The number of males 35–44 years of age, the prime age group from which most top managers will be recruited, will be 7.3 per cent lower than the 1965 figure. Unless increased efforts are made to develop more managers, a smaller group of men will be dealing with the tougher problems of the next decade. The significance for management development efforts and for those managerial philosophies and organizational climates which best develop managers on the job is obvious.
2. There will be a 30 per cent increase in the number of people in the age group, 15–24. Although many will be students, a substantial portion will be in the labor force. Their expectations in an affluent society will diverge from their elders' much as the values of today's youth do. To recruit and

motivate young people who have a myriad of options (further graduate study, overseas and domestic service, etc.), management must adjust to these expectations. The increase in this age group provides challenges from other vantages. The market which has emerged to satisfy young people's desires — for sports cars, clothing, rock music — is likely to grow at a rate exceeding the one-third numerical expansion of this young group.

3. An expansion of nearly 40 per cent will take place in the age group, 25–34. This group will be comprised of today's teenagers and young adults, whose behavior and values have led to much head-shaking by their elders. Although the 25's to 34's may sober up a bit with the usual family responsibilities, managers will certainly have to accommodate themselves to the behavior of this new generation. Tomorrow's young people may not be called hippies, but they are likely to continue questioning society's values and rebelling against society's constraints. Managers will have to tolerate considerable diversity in those they hire in the next decade. The challenge of providing opportunities which will interest these future managers must be met if they are to contribute enthusiastically to organizational objectives. Job enlargement, less detailed control of job responsibilities, and business involvement in social problems will be necessary, if indeed anything will attract capable people in this age group to industry from other alternatives now available.

4. The age group 55 and over will increase 17 percent by 1975. In part this reflects increasing longevity, and will necessitate re-examination of rigid compulsory retirement policies and/or more efforts to prepare employees (including executives) for retirement. Perhaps people in this age group should look forward to two occupations, one before compulsory retirement and one after, one full-time and one part-time. Adequate provision must be made for the reduced income of retirement years. Someone has pointed out that while many organizations retire their chief executive at 65, this is about the age when United States Senators and Representatives become chairmen of important Congressional committees.

5. Nearly four-fifths of the young adults (23–34) in the 1975 labor force will be high-school graduates; one-fifth will be college graduates or beyond. This heavy influx of educated people is both an asset and a challenge to management. Employees will be better educated but will also have greater expectations for their careers. This is the upper end of the educational ladder. At the lower end will be a minority "underclass," the 7 per cent with less than eight grades of schooling, whose educational handicap in the working world will be especially severe.

6. The upper and lower ends of the occupational ladder in 1975 will reflect earlier educational backgrounds. The number of professional and technical employees at the top will grow twice as fast (by 45 per cent) from 1965 to 1975. As a further indication of the impact of advancing higher education on our occupational structure, there were only 3.8 million professional and

technical employees in 1947 and 8.9 million in 1965. By 1975, if current projections are accurate, there will be 12.9 million. (It is worth noting that earlier projections have frequently fallen short of their marks.) At the bottom of the occupational ladder, excluding farm workers, are the people classified as "laborers." Their share in the labor force will shrink from 5 per cent in 1965 to 4 per cent in 1975. There will be proportionally fewer jobs for those with brawn but not much education.

To sum up this brief review of the 1975 labor force projections, proportionately fewer managers will have to recruit and develop increasing numbers of better educated younger people (as compared to 1965), including more professional and technical employees. A review of employment and retirement policies for the increasing number of older workers will be required. Finally, help in developing methods for removing educational deficiencies at the lower end of the occupational scale, particularly for non-whites, will present a critical challenge to managers.

Use of Computers in Management Decision-Making

Perhaps by the Year 2000, computer programs will have so high a degree of artificial intelligence that there will be no need for managers. In the next decade and beyond, however, the intelligent use of computers is more likely to extend rather than replace the manager's capacities, relieving him of much routine and structured work. By enhancing the productivity of individual managers, computer systems of the Seventies will help overcome the shortage of competent managers. The increasing complexity of the managerial job, within the enterprise and especially in the realm of the enterprise's interactions with its external environment, will require all the support managers can extract from computers and related management science techniques. Accounting, inventory control, production scheduling and control, marketing, purchasing, customer ordering and shipping, among others, have all benefited from computer applications. There will be further extensions in these areas.

The development of data banks which permit the building of realistic models of relationships among the areas mentioned above will help managers to simulate decision alternatives, narrowing the range from which informed managerial judgment must choose. As one goes higher in the managerial ranks, however, the problems for decision become less structured. This consideration led many of the participants at a 1966 Sloan School conference on the impact of computers on management to conclude that "in the Year 2000, managers in man-machine systems will still be dealing with ill-structured problems."[5]

Computerized management information systems have already helped to integrate various functions and branches of the enterprise, but the "total management information system," mentioned so often in recent literature but not yet realized, may emerge within the next decade. Apart from the technical problems of designing a system to cover a large enterprise, there is the critical question of how the system will be designed to provide information at different points in the organization. Simply stated, who will have access to what information, and when? This question is related to the contrasting managerial philosophies which Douglas McGregor called Theory X and Theory Y in his book, *The Human Side of Enterprise*.[6] A top management which accepts Theory X assumptions (management by centralized direction and control) will probably be able to exercise tight control through a computerized total management information system. But a Theory Y management, concerned about developing subordinate managers through integration and self-control, will suggest that a computerized total management information system be designed to provide data for subordinate managers so that they can monitor their own progress toward organizational objectives and take corrective action before their superiors order them to do so. As Professor Jay W. Forrester put it in summing up his impressions of the conference on computer impacts mentioned earlier: "It appears that we can use computers and information technology to create more confinement or more freedom."[7] Top managers should have little difficulty deciding which approach will attract and motivate the better educated, professionally trained people who will appear in greater numbers in the 1975 labor force.

If computers free managers of a considerable amount of the routine, structured parts of their work, managers will, I believe, have more time for the ill-structured problems.

Areas of managerial activity of an ill-structured nature include the establishment of organizational objectives, the selection, development, and motivation of subordinates,[8] and the improvement of constructive relations with non-managerial employees and their unions. More attention to the interaction of the enterprise with federal, state, and local governments and with the community from which it draws both employees and public support will be necessary. These aspects of the managerial job, because they are difficult to define in advance, will require broadly trained people who are sensitive to social as well as technical changes.

The Urban Crisis: Its Significance for Management

When Senator Edward Kennedy finally spoke publicly after the assassination of his second brother, he said in a speech to the Worcester (Mass.) Chamber of Commerce: "Guns and gas are being stockpiled against crime and riots — bad schools and housing, no jobs and an inadequate passion for justice — these are being neglected." Some managers feel that these problems are best left to politicians and to governments. This feeling is shared by critics of business from the left, who contend that government action is the only answer. In contrast, an increasing number of businessmen are becoming more and more involved in trying to deal with some of these "basic causes." The view that "corporations do the most good for society when they just stick to business and maximize their profits" is no longer so adamantly defended by corporate leaders.[9] In the decade ahead, managers will become more involved in urban problems, including supporting the kind of business-government partnership that has evolved in some of our recent federal and local manpower training programs. There is no way to avoid this commitment, or to escape the consequences of the urban crisis.

Last May, the challenge was presented to management in these words:

> Today, there is another great social change now aflame in which business has an unperformed social responsibility — one as inescapable, I believe, as the responsibility for operating at a profit. I refer to that concerning the natural aspirations of those who call themselves the black minority, and I include within the problem the natural aspirations of those in other minority groups — not excluding the minority of the white race who also need training, better education, more adequate housing and more real opportunities to exercise their inherent capacities to make their own way in our busy, highly competitive American environment.[10]

Perhaps surprisingly, this is not a statement by a social critic of management, unless you would so characterize Roger M. Blough, Chairman of the Board of the United States Steel Corporation.

The manpower decisions which managers will face in the next decade will not be greatly different than they are today. The problems mentioned by Senator Kennedy and Mr. Blough will not be solved tomorrow. Migration from the South to northern cities is likely to continue. More children will be born under the handicaps of the ghetto. And, unless more is done to expand job opportunities for Negroes, high rates of teenage and young adult unemployment will persist.

Within the past year or two, managers have become actively involved through their companies in the hiring and training of the hard-core unemployed, the so-called "disadvantaged." Currently, industry is addressing the problem under government-supported and business-run programs, such as the National Alliance of Businessmen's "Job Opportunities in the Business Sector," headed by Henry Ford II. There will be further efforts, possibly with either direct government subsidy or tax credits to compensate for the added training and associated costs incurred in hiring people lacking minimum qualifications.

But the task of supervisors and managers does not end with just hiring and minimal training. A variety of decisions will have to be made beyond this initial phase. How much remedial education should be provided? Will standards of performance and discipline be relaxed until the disadvantaged are fully productive? What will this require in the training of supervisors and middle managers, and in communication with regular employees who may resent what appears to them to be pampering and perhaps reverse discrimination? And what about upgrading to better jobs? In facing up to these questions, managers may have to revise their preconceptions. No business leader has made this point more lucidly than Virgil E. Boyd, President of the Chrysler Corporation, in a speech in Detroit last June.[11]

> I thought I knew what "hard core" meant, until we became involved in this area. I was wrong. Hard core refers not to those without steady jobs, but to those who are not equipped for any job. Not the unemployed, but the unemployable — those who are unable to fill out even a simple job application. . . These people who have been pushed into the backwaters of our society can't even read simple words such as "in" and "out" signs on a door. It comes right down to blackboard drills, teaching letters that spell common colors, so they can read the instruction card that tells them to put a blue or a green seat belt or a steering wheel on a car as it comes down the assembly line. It entails teaching simple addition, so that they can count boxes of parts they take off a supplier's truck.
>
> And it goes much deeper than that. For example, some of these people signed on for job training — with an "X" of course — but failed to show up. And many of those who did report were very late. . . Naturally, a lot of people in my company — just as in many other companies — quietly nodded their heads and reaffirmed everything that they had always known to be true. They were more than ever convinced that all the people who aren't working just don't want to work. . . . But those of us who reacted to the demands for help from industry had made a commitment, an agreement with the government, and we intended to meet it. So we set out to find what really was wrong.
>
> We started by sending people out to find out why all those X's never showed up for work. The answer, in many cases, was childishly simple. If you can't read, how do you know what it says on the destination signs of the many buses that go by on a given busy street? . . . It didn't take long to establish another fact — only one in five owned an alarm clock. Why? Because they'd never had to be any particular place at any particular time before. So we took them into the plants and showed them men, just like themselves, who owned cars, and clothes, and houses, and that they owned them because these men lived within the rules of an industrial society and showed up for work, on time, every day.
>
> And this is the point at which some of our established, competent people began to revise those things which they knew to be true. They changed their thinking because once these hard core people knew how, and why, to come to work, their attendance and tardiness record was *500 per cent better* than the average of all our employees. . . Further, we found that while the majority of the hard core people had only a third to fourth grade reading ability, they also fell within a very acceptable range of I.Q. And given sufficient motivation and direction, they performed at the average level within a relatively few weeks.

Mr. Boyd concluded:

> Perhaps the possibility of these results with the unemployables should have been obvious to us all along. But it wasn't, and we have made an important discovery, and a change in attitude that is critically important to the resolution of the urban crisis. We have recognized that it is not only possible but definitely to our advantage to help the chronically unemployed, and that with a lot of help, and some patience, they will help themselves.[12]

The next decade will bring such discoveries to many managers. The involvement which initiates these discoveries will be a terribly important component of the solution of our urban crisis.

Speaking to a group of Detroit businessmen, a black militant leader, Frank Ditto, is reported to have said :"If you cats can't do it, it's never going to get done."[13] Whether private firms can do it will depend not only on their increased commitment, but also on the capacity of the economy to generate enough (increasing) demand to provide the job opportunities which are needed. A general unemployment rate around 3.5 to 4.0 per cent means very tight labor markets for most adult male members of the labor force (2.1 per cent for white males 20 years of age and over in 1967). But it also means unemployment rates of double this for non-whites (4.3 per cent for the same age group), and very high rates for teenagers. Among the young men under 20 years of age in the labor force, the unemployment rate of non-whites was double that of whites in 1967; 26.5 per cent of the non-white teen age labor force was unemployed.[14] This situation persisted while the number of employed Americans increased by over 1.5 million from 1966 through 1967 to a total of nearly 77.4 million employees in civilian jobs.

With the further expansion and younger composition of our labor force in the next decade, we will need public policies that support continued economic growth and keep unemployment rates below the 4 per cent level. We cannot tolerate the 6 per cent unemployment rates which prevailed on the average in 1958 and again in 1961. If public policy decisions are not committed to this objective, then we shall see higher rates of unemployment in the next decade, and the number of impoverished families in the United States (those with earnings less than $3,000 a year) will continue to be as high as 5 million. With unemployment falling more heavily on non-whites than on whites, the consequences for continued urban unrest and protest are worth pondering. The costs of the urban crisis will be met one way or another, and decisions by management leaders will be computed in the costs and the benefits.

Expanding Role of the Multi-National Corporation

The fourth and final area of management decisions in the next decade involves the expanding role of the multi-national corporataion. Just as management faces social and technical changes which will affect its decisions within the American society into the late 1970's, so it also looks abroad and sees new opportunities as well as new problems in other societies. These opportunities and problems, much as on the domestic front, will involve to a large extent the utilization of people.

Even though many multi-national corporations have headquarters in the United States, some of their international operations have nationals of other countries in top management positions. The president of IBM World Trade in New York, for example, is a Frenchman. These multi-national firms have also developed managerial talent for their operations abroad. This has led another Frenchman, Jean Jacques Servan-Schreiber, author of the French best-seller translated and published here this year as *The American Challenge,* to analyze the secret of American business success in Western Europe as due not to the "technological gap," but to "human factors — the ability to adapt easily, flexibility of organizations, the creative power of teamwork . . . Beyond any single explanation, each of which has an element of truth, the secret lies in the confidence of the society in its citizens . . . *What counts is the determination to liberate initiative and show confidence in man at every level.*"[15]

Perhaps this is not true of every American enterprise, but a growing number of managers in the United States are turning to those managerial philosophies and organizational structures which emphasize the development of people and their initiative in the achievement of organizational objectives. If this view is correct, and it enjoys substantial support from behavioral science research, then American leadership of multi-national corporations in the next decade will have a comparative advantage. It is possible to borrow technology, but it is more difficult to emulate the intangibles of managerial competence and leadership.[16]

At the same time, American managers working with nationals of other countries in international operation abroad have an opportunity to raise the level of competence of the nationals they employ, a competence which will help the American multi-national company survive some of the understandable nationalistic urges of the host country by helping build the country's own human resources. The American firm operating abroad cannot ignore the foreign educational systems, which are a prime source of future managers. The firm will increasingly be called upon to assist in the upgrading and expansion of those systems, particularly in the new schools of management that are springing up not only in Western Europe but also in many developing countries. New management schools have occasionally had the help of American management schools also, as in the case of the Sloan School's assistance to the Indian Institute of Management in Calcutta.

The red tape and frustrations involved in direct investment in less-developed countries are well known. American managers in the next decade will be required to decide which national partners to approach on joint ventures, what degree of control to exercise, and how managerial responsibilities are to be shared.[17] Beyond this, the multi-national corporation in the next decade will find itself "a world enterprise," generating tensions in very nationalistic nations, and, in the words of the President of the Pfizer Company, becoming "agents of change, socially, economically and culturally."[18]

To the extent that American managers are involved in multi-national operations, their commitment to the *development* of people rather than exclusively to the *direction* of people will ease the problem of their acceptance as "agents of change." They will listen and understand first, then act. They will learn the language, work to understand the culture, and develop relations with people in society at large as well as in the world of business. They cannot remain in American "islands" abroad.

Concluding Observations

The four areas of management decisions in the next decade discussed above are not all-inclusive. They are, however, among the most important. Furthermore, there is a theme common to all of them: the major challenge for management is better utilization of people, utilization of the young and better-educated members of the labor force, more effective use of management talent by aiding rather than replacing managers with computers, utilization of the untapped resources of the "disadvantaged," and the development of nationals of other countries through the multi-national corporation.

In an address to the 1968 National Conference of the British Institute of Management last March, under the title, "Education for Management and Technology in the 70's — An American Forecast," President Howard W. Johnson of M.I.T. articulated the central theme in these words:

> Societies will be strong economically in proportion to their management systems, their ability to harness technology in the service of the market, including the individual but also societal needs — for education, transportation, housing, health, adequate food, clean air and water. The leadership of this management system demands rare and imaginative men, and I am persuaded that the corporate task of the 70's will be to provide the climate in which such men are nurtured and their abilities brought to full flower within the corporate frame. The world is changing with such speed that only the adaptive and innovative can keep the pace.

Servan-Schreiber has phrased it this way: "All clichés to the contrary, American society wages much more on human intelligence than it wastes on gadgets . . . this wager on man is the origin of America's new dynamism."[19] The managerial decisions discussed above will be important in determining whether this statement can still be made at the end of the next decade.

Notes and References

1. See Kahn (4), p. 25.
2. See Bell (2).
3. American Foundation for Management Research, Hamilton, N.Y., 1968.
4. The usual assumptions about the continuation of past economic, employment, and productivity trends were made in preparing these projections. It was also assumed that the Vietnam War would end by January 1, 1970, and that defense expenditures would drop to the pre-war level. *Manpower Report of the President* (5) contains some of this information.
5. See Myers (9), p. 14.
6. See McGregor (6).
7. See Myers (9), p. 276.
8. A recent Sloan School thesis reports that five chief executives of five different organizations had 64 per cent of all their interpersonal contacts with their own subordinates. See Mintzberg (8).
9. See Albrook (1).
10. "The Public Life of Private Business," address at Annual Meeting, Iron and Steel Institute, New York, May 23, 1968.
11. The full, unpublished text was made available to me by the Public Relations Department of the Chrysler Corporation. Shorter excerpts appeared in the *New York Times,* June 11, 1968, p. 54.
12. For a comprehensive review of other business efforts, see (3).
13. Quoted in *Business Week,* February 3, 1968, p. 59.
14. See (5), Table A-5, p. 226.
15. Servan-Schreiber also notes that "a century ago, (de) Toqueville saw this essential, indeed fundamental, characteristic of the New World." See (10), pp. 252, 266.
16. Robert S. McNamara says in his new book: "In my view, the technological gap was misnamed. It is not so much a technological gap as it is a managerial gap." See (7).
17. See Tomlinson (11). This study dealt with British joint-ventures but its findings are broadly applicable.
18. From "The Multinational Company," address given by John J. Powers, Jr. at the Semi-Annual Meeting of the Manufacturing Chemists' Association, New York, November 21, 1967.
19. See Servan-Schreiber (10), p. 253.

---

1. Albrook, R. C. "Business Wrestles with Its Social Conscience," *Fortune* (August 1968), 89–91 ff.
2. Bell, D. "The Year 2000 — The Trajectory of an Idea," *Daedalus,* 96, 3 (Summer 1967), 639–655.
3. "Dealing the Negro In," *Business Week,* Special Report (May 1968), 64–68 ff.
4. Kahn, H., and A. J. Wiener. *The Year 2000.* New York: Macmillan, 1967.
5. *Manpower Report of the President,* April 1968. Washington: GPO, 1968.

6. McGregor, D. M. *The Human Side of Enterprise.* New York: McGraw-Hill, 1960.

7. McNamara, R. S. *The Essence of Security: Reflections in Office.* New York: Harper & Row, 1968.

8. Mintzberg, H. "The Manager at Work — Determination of His Activities, Functions, and Programs by Structural Observation." Unpublished doctoral thesis. Cambridge, Mass.: MIT Sloan School of Management, 1968.

9. Myers, C. A. (ed.). *The Impact of Computers on Management.* Cambridge, Mass.: MIT Press, 1967.

10. Servan-Schreiber, J. J. *The American Challenge.* New York: Atheneum, 1968.

11. Tomlinson, J. W. "A Model of the Joint-Venture Decision Process in International Business." Unpublished doctoral thesis. Cambridge, Mass.: MIT Sloan School of Management, 1968.

B. GOAL AND VALUE SYSTEMS

The notion of organizational goals as variables rather than constants is developed by Thompson and McEwen (Selection 5). The setting of goals, which defines for the organization its major purposes, is a necessary and recurring problem facing any organization. The nature of this problem is perceived as a question of what the society, or elements within it, wants done or can be persuaded to support. The strategies that organizations might adopt for coming to terms with their environments are also discussed. The adjustments to the environment, in an awkward or responsive manner, will be important in determining the organization's degree of prosperity or even survival.

Thompson and McEwen analyzed the interface between organizational goals and environment. Now we find Tannenbaum and Davis (Selection 6) evaluating the interface between organizations and man. Their frame of reference is the differences, changes, and congruencies in values — both within organizations and within man. This reading serves several purposes. First, it defines the nature of man as conceived in the industrial humanism movement. Second, it contrasts "traditional" values with new "emerging" values — a subject for lively discussion and stimulating thought. Third, it provides the philosophic foundation for many of the strategies, techniques, practices, and systems of management discussed in the following articles. Finally, it points up, through the presentation of actual examples and case studies, the transition in values.

5

Organizational Goals and Environment: Goal-Setting as an Interaction Process

JAMES D. THOMPSON
University of Pittsburgh

WILLIAM J. MCEWEN
State University of New York

In the analysis of complex organizations the definition of organizational goals is commonly utilized as a standard for appraising organizational performance. In many such analyses the goals of the organization are often viewed as a constant. Thus a wide variety of data, such as official documents, work activity records, organizational output, or statements by organizational spokesmen, may provide the basis for the definition of goals. Once this definition has been accomplished, interest in goals as a dynamic aspect of organizational activity frequently ends.

It is possible, however, to view the setting of goals (i.e., major organizational purposes) not as a static element but as a necessary and recurring problem facing any organization, whether it is governmental, military, business, educational, medical, religious, or other type.

This perspective appears appropriate in developing the two major lines of the present analysis. The first of these is to emphasize the interdependence of complex organizations within the larger society and the consequences this has for organizational goal-setting. The second is to emphasize the similarities of goal-setting *processes* in organizations with manifestly different goals. The present analysis is offered to supplement recent studies of organizational operations.[1]

It is postulated that goal-setting behavior is *purposive* but not necessarily *rational;* we assume that goals may be determined by accident, i.e., by blundering of members of the organization and, contrariwise, that the most calculated and careful determination of goals may be negated by developments outside the control of organization members. The goal-setting prob-

Taken and adapted from *American Sociological Review,* Vol. 23, No. 1, Feb. 1958, pp. 23–31. Used by permission.

lem as discussed here is essentially determining a relationship of the organization to the larger society, which in turn becomes a question of what the society (or elements within it) wants done or can be persuaded to support.

Goals as Dynamic Variables

Because the setting of goals is essentially a problem of defining desired relationships between an organization and its environment, change in either requires review and perhaps alteration of goals. Even where the most abstract statement of goals remains constant, application requires redefinition or interpretation as changes occur in the organization, the environment, or both.

The corporation, for example, faces changing markets and develops staff specialists with responsibility for continuous study and projection of market changes and product appeal. The governmental agency, its legislative mandate notwithstanding, has need to reformulate or reinterpret its goals as other agencies are created and dissolved, as the population changes, or as non-governmental organizations appear to do the same job or to compete. The school and the university may have unchanging abstract goals but the clientele, the needs of pupils or students, and the techniques of teaching change and bring with them redefinition and reinterpretation of those objectives. The hospital has been faced with problems requiring an expansion of goals to include consideration of preventive medicine, public health practices, and the degree to which the hospital should extend its activities out into the community. The mental hospital and the prison are changing their objectives from primary emphasis on custody to a stress on therapy. Even the church alters its pragmatic objectives as changes in the society call for new forms of social ethics, and as government and organized philanthropy take over some of the activities formerly left to organized religion.[2]

Reappraisal of goals thus appears to be a recurrent problem for large organization, albeit a more constant problem in an unstable environment than in a stable one. Reappraisal of goals likewise appears to be more difficult as the "product" of the enterprise becomes less tangible and more difficult to measure objectively. The manufacturing firm has a relatively ready index of the acceptability of its product in sales figures; while poor sales may indicate inferior quality rather than public distaste for the commodity itself, sales totals frequently are supplemented by trade association statistics indicating the firm's "share of the market." Thus within a matter of weeks, a manufacturing firm may be able to reappraise its decision to enter the "widget" market and may therefore begin deciding how it can get out of that market with the least cost.

The governmental enterprise may have similar indicators of the acceptability of its goals if it is involved in producing an item such as electricity, but where its activity is oriented to a less tangible purpose such as maintaining favorable relations with foreign nations, the indices of effective operation are likely to be less precise and the vagaries more numerous. The degree to which a government satisfies its clientele may be reflected periodically in elections, but despite the claims of party officials, it seldom is clear just what the mandate of the people is with reference to any particular governmental enterprise. In addition, the public is not always steadfast in its mandate.

The university perhaps has even greater difficulties in evaluating its environmental situation through response to its output. Its range of "products" is enormous, extending from astronomers to zoologists. The test of a competent specialist is not always standardized and may be changing, and the university's success in turning out "educated" people is judged by many and often conflicting standards. The university's product is in process for four or more years and when it is placed on the "market" it can be only imperfectly judged. Vocational placement statistics may give some indication of the university's success in its objectives, but initial placement is no guarantee of performance at a later date. Furthermore, performance in an occupation is only one of several abilities that the university is supposed to produce in its students. Finally, any particular department of the university may find that its reputation lags far behind its performance. A "good" department may work for years before its reputation becomes "good" and a downhill department may coast for several years before the fact is realized by the professional world.

In sum, the goals of an organization, which determine the kinds of goods or services it produces and offers to the environment, often are subject to peculiar difficulties of reappraisal. Where the purpose calls for an easily identified, readily measured product, reappraisal and readjustment of goals may be accomplished rapidly. But as goals call for increasingly intangible, difficult-to-measure products, society finds it more difficult to determine and reflect its acceptability of that product, and the signals that indicate unacceptable goals are less effective and perhaps longer in coming.

Environmental Controls Over Goals

A continuing situation of necessary interaction between an organization and its environment introduces an element of environmental control into the organization. While the motives of personnel, including goal-setting officers, may be profits, prestige, votes, or the salvation of souls, their efforts must produce something useful or acceptable to at least a part of the organizational environment to win continued support.[3]

In the simpler society social control over productive activities may be exercised rather informally and directly through such means as gossip and ridicule. As a society becomes more complex and its productive activities more deliberately organized, social controls are increasingly exercised through such formal devices as contracts, legal codes, and governmental regulations. The stability of expectations provided by these devices is arrived at through interaction, and often through the exercise of power in interaction.

It is possible to conceive of a continuum of organizational power in environmental relations, ranging from the organization that dominates its environmental relations to one completely dominated by its environment. Few organizations approach their extreme. Certain gigantic industrial enterprises, such as the *Zaibatsu* in Japan or the old Standard Oil Trust in America, have approached the dominance-over-environment position at one time, but this position eventually brought about "countervailing powers."[4] Perhaps the nearest approximation to the completely powerless organization is the commuter transit system, which may be unable to cover its costs but nevertheless is regarded as a necessary utility and cannot get permission to quit business. Most complex organizations, falling somewhere between the extremes of the power continuum, must adopt strategies for coming to terms with their environments. This is not to imply that such strategies are necessarily chosen by rational or deliberate processes. An organization can survive so long as it adjusts to its situation; whether the process of adjustment is awkward or nimble becomes important in determining the organization's degree of prosperity.

However arrived at, strategies for dealing with the organizational environment may be broadly classified as either *competitive* or *co-operative*. Both appear to be important in a complex society — of the "free enterprise" type or other.[5] Both provide a measure of environmental control over organizations by providing for "outsiders" to enter into or limit organizational decision process.

The decision process may be viewed as a series of activities, conscious or not, culminating in a choice among alternatives. For purposes of this paper we view the decision-making process as consisting of the following activities:

1. Recognizing an occasion for decision, i.e., a need or an opportunity.
2. Analysis of the existing situation.
3. Identification of alternative courses of action.
4. Assessment of the probable consequences of each alternative.
5. Choice from among alternatives.[6]

The following discussion suggests that the potential power of an outsider increases the earlier he enters into the decision process,[7] and that competition and three sub-types of co-operative strategy — *bargaining, co-optation,* and *coalition* — differ in this respect. It is therefore possible to order these forms of interaction in terms of the degree to which they provide for environmental control over organizational goal-setting decisions.

Competition

The term competition implies an element of rivalry. For present purposes competition refers to that form of rivalry between two or more organizations which is mediated by a third party. In the case of the manufacturing firm the third party may be the customer, the supplier, the potential or present member of the labor force, or others. In the case of the governmental bureau, the third party through whom competition takes place may be the legislative committee, the budget bureau, or the chief executive, as well as potential clientele and potential members of the bureau.

The complexity of competition in a heterogeneous society is much greater than customary usage (with economic overtones) often suggests. Society judges the enterprise not only by the finished product but also in terms of the desirability of applying resources to that purpose. Even the organization that enjoys a product monopoly must compete for society's support. From the society it must obtain resources — personnel, finances, and materials — as well as customers or clientele. In the business sphere of a "free enterprise" economy this competition for resources and customers usually takes place in the market, but in times of crisis the society may exercise more direct controls, such as rationing or the establishment of priorities during a war. The monopoly competes with enterprises having different purposes or goals but using similar raw materials; it competes with many other enterprises, for human skills and loyalties, and it competes with many other activities for support in the money markets.

The university, customarily a non-profit organization, competes as eagerly as any business firm, although perhaps more subtly.[8] Virtually every university seeks, if not more students, better-qualified students. Publicly supported universities compete at annual budget sessions with other governmental enterprises for shares in tax revenues. Endowed universities must compete for gifts and bequests, not only with other universities but also with museums, charities, zoos, and similar non-profit enterprises. The American university is only one of many organizations competing for foundation support, and it competes with other universities and with other types of organizations for faculty.

The public school system, perhaps one of our most pervasive forms of near-monopoly, not only competes with other governmental units for funds and with different types of organizations for teachers, but current programs espoused by professional educators often compete in a very real way with a public conception of the nature of education, e.g., as the three R's, devoid of "frills."

The hospital may compete with the mid-wife, the faith-healer, the "quack" and the patent-medicine manufacturer, as well as with neighboring hospitals, despite the fact that general hospitals do not "advertise" and are not usually recognized as competitive.

Competition is thus a complicated network of relationships. It includes scrambling for resources as well as for customers or clients, and in a complex society it includes rivalry for potential members and their loyalties. In each case a third party makes a choice among alternatives, two or more organizations attempt to influence that choice through some type of "appeal" or offering, and choice by the third party is a "vote" of support for one of the competing organizations and a denial of support to the others involved.

Competition, then, is one process whereby the organization's choice of goals is partially controlled by the environment. It tends to prevent unilateral or arbitrary choice of organizational goals, or to correct such a choice if one is made. Competition for society's support is an important means of eliminating not only inefficient organizations but also those that seek to provide goods or services the environment is not willing to accept.

Bargaining

The term bargaining, as used here, refers to the negotiation of an agreement for the exchange of goods or services between two or more organizations. Even where fairly stable and dependable expectations have been built up with important elements of the organizational environment — with suppliers, distributors, legislators, workers and so on — the organization cannot assume that these relationships will continue. Periodic review of these relationships must be accomplished, and an important means for this is bargaining, whereby each organization, through negotiation, arrives at a decision about future behavior satisfactory to the others involved.

The need for periodic adjustment of relationships is demonstrated most dramatically in collective bargaining between labor and industrial management, in which the bases for continued support by organization members are reviewed.[9] But bargaining occurs in other important, if less dramatic, areas of organizational endeavor. The business firm must bargain with its agents or distributors, and while this may appear at times to be one-sided and hence not much of a bargain, still even a long-standing agency agreement may be severed by competitive offers unless the agent's level of satisfaction is maintained through periodic review.[10] Where suppliers are required to install new equipment to handle the peculiar demands of an organization, bargaining between the two is not unusual.

The university likewise must bargain.[11] It may compete for free or unrestricted funds, but often it must compromise that ideal by bargaining away the name of a building or of a library collection, or by the conferring of an honorary degree. Graduate students and faculty members may be given financial or other concessions through bargaining, in order to prevent their loss to other institutions.

The governmental organization may also find bargaining expedient.[12] The police department, for example, may overlook certain violations of statutes in order to gain the support of minor violators who have channels of information not otherwise open to department members. Concessions to those who "turn state's evidence" are not unusual. Similarly a department of state may forego or postpone recognition of a foreign power in order to gain support for other aspects of its policy, and a governmental agency may relinquish certain activities in order to gain budget bureau approval of more important goals.

While bargaining may focus on resources rather than explicitly on goals, the fact remains that it is improbable that a goal can be effective unless it is at least partially implemented. To the extent that bargaining sets limits on the amount of resources available or the ways they may be employed, it effectively sets limits on choice of goals. Hence bargaining, like competition, results in environmental control over organizational goals and reduces the probability of arbitrary, unilateral goal-setting.

Unlike competition, however, bargaining involves direct interaction with other organizations in the environment, rather than with a third party. Bargaining appears, therefore, to invade the actual decision process. To the extent that the second party's support is necessary he is in a position to exercise a veto over final choice of alternative goals, and hence takes part in the decision.

Co-optation

Co-optation has been defined as the process of absorbing new elements into the leadership or policy-determining structure of an organization as a means of averting threats to its stability or existence.[13] Co-optation makes still further inroads on the process of deciding goals; not only must the final choice be acceptable to the co-opted party or organization, but to the extent that co-optation is effective it places the representative of an "outsider" in a position to determine the occasion for a goal decision, to participate in analyzing the existing situation, to suggest alternatives, and to take part in the deliberation of consequences.

The term co-optation has only recently been given currency in this country, but the phenomenon it describes is neither new nor unimportant. The acceptance on a corporation's board of directors of representatives of banks or other financial institutions is a time-honored custom among firms that have large financial obligations or that may in the future want access to financial resources. The state university may find it expedient (if not mandatory) to place legislators on its board of trustees, and the endowed college may find that whereas the honorary degree brings forth a token gift, membership on the board may result in a more substantial bequest. The local medical society often plays a decisive role in hospital goal-setting, since the support of professional medical practitioners is urgently necessary for the hospital.

From the standpoint of society, however, co-optation is more than an expediency. By giving a potential supporter a position of power and often of responsibility in the organization, the organization gains his awareness and understanding of the problems it faces. A business advisory council may be an effective educational device for a government, and a White House conference on education may mobilize "grass roots" support in a thousand localities, both by focusing attention on the problem area and by giving key people a sense of participation in goal deliberation.

Moreover, by providing overlapping memberships, co-optation is an important social device for increasing the likelihood that organizations related to one another in complicated ways will in fact find compatible goals. By thus reducing the possibilities of antithetical actions by two or more organizations, co-optation aids in the integration of the heterogeneous parts of a complex society. By the same token, co-optation further limits the opportunity for one organization to choose its goals arbitrarily or unilaterally.

Coalition

As used here, the term coalition refers to a combination of two or more organizations for a common purpose. Coalition appears to be the ultimate or extreme form of environmental conditioning of organizational goals.[14] A coalition may be unstable, but to the extent that it is operative, two or more organizations act as one with respect to certain goals. Coalition is a means widely used when two or more enterprises wish to pursue a goal calling for more support, especially for more resources, than any one of them is able to marshal unaided. American business firms frequently resort to coalition for purposes of research or product promotion and for the construction of such gigantic facilities as dams or atomic reactors.[15]

Coalition is not uncommon among educational organizations. Universities have established joint operations in such areas as nuclear research, archaeological research, and even social science research. Many smaller colleges have banded together for fund-raising purposes. The consolidation of public school districts in another form of coalition (if not merger), and the fact that it does represent a sharing or "invasion" of goal-setting power is reflected in some of the bitter resistance to consolidation in tradition-oriented localities.

Coalition requires a commitment for joint decision of future activities and thus places limits on unilateral or arbitrary decisions. Furthermore, inability of an organization to find partners in a coalition venture automatically prevents pursuit of that objective, and is therefore also a form of social control. If the collective judgment is that a proposal is unworkable, a possible disaster may be escaped and unproductive allocation of resources avoided. . .

Notes

1. Among recent materials that treat organizational goal-setting are Kenneth E. Boulding, *The Organizational Revolution,* New York: Harper and Brothers, 1953; Robert A. Dahl and Charles E. Lindblom, *Politics, Economics, and Welfare,* New York: Harper and Brothers, 1953; and John K. Galbraith, *American Capitalism: The Concept of Countervailing Power,* Boston: Houghton Mifflin, 1952.

2. For pertinent studies of various organizational types see Burton R. Clark, *Adult Education in Transition,* Berkeley and Los Angeles: University of California Press, 1956; Temple Burling, Edith M. Lentz, and Robert N. Wilson, *The Give and Take in Hospitals,* New York: G. P. Putnam's Sons, 1956, especially pp. 3–10; Lloyd E. Ohlin, *Sociology and the Field of Corrections,* New York: Russell Sage Foundation, 1956, pp. 13–18; Liston Pope, *Millhands and Preachers,* New Haven: Yale University Press, 1942; Charles Y. Glock and Benjamin B. Ringer, "Church Policy and the Attitudes of Ministers and Parishioners on Social Issues," *American Sociological Review,* 21 (April, 1956), pp. 148–156. For a similar analysis in the field of philanthropy, see J. R. Seeley, B. H. Junker, R. W. Jones, Jr., and others, *Community Chest: A Case Study in Philanthropy,* Toronto: University of Toronto Press, 1957, especially Chapters 2 and 5.

3. This statement would seem to exclude antisocial organizations, such as crime syndicates. A detailed analysis of such organizations would be useful for many purposes; meanwhile it would appear necessary for them to acquire a clientele, suppliers, and others, in spite of the fact that their methods at times may be somewhat unique.

4. For the *Zaibatsu* case see Japan Council, *The Control of Industry in Japan,* Tokyo: Institute of Political and Economic Research, 1953; and Edwin O. Reischauer, *The United States and Japan,* Cambridge: Harvard University Press, 1954, pp. 87–97.

5. For evidence on Russia see David Granick, *Management of the Industrial Firm in the U.S.S.R.,* New York: Columbia University Press, 1954; and Joseph S. Berliner, "Informal Organization of the Soviet Firm," *Quarterly Journal of Economics,* 66 (August, 1952), pp. 353–365.

6. This particular breakdown is taken from Edward H. Litchfield, "Notes on a General Theory of Administration," *Administrative Science Quarterly,* 1 (June 1956), pp. 3–29. We are also indebted to Robert Tannenbaum and Fred Massarik who, by breaking the decision-making process into three steps, show that subordinates can take part in the "manager's decision" even when the manager makes the final choice. See "Participation by Subordinates in the Managerial Decision-Making Process," *Canadian Journal of Economics and Political Science,* 16 (August, 1949), pp. 410–418.

7. Robert K. Merton makes a similar point regarding the role of the intellectual in public bureaucracy. See his *Social Theory and Social Structure,* Glencoe: The Free Press, 1949, Chapter VI.

8. See Logan Wilson, *The Academic Man,* New York: Oxford University Press, 1942, especially Chapter IX. Also see Warren G. Bennis, "The Effect on

Academic Goods of Their Market," *American Journal of Sociology,* 62 (July, 1956), pp. 28–33.

9. For an account of this on a daily basis see Melville Dalton, "Unofficial Union-Management Relations," *American Sociological Review,* 15 (October, 1950), pp. 611–619.

10. See Valentine F. Ridgway, "Administration of Manufacturer-Dealer Systems," *Administrative Science Quarterly,* 1 (March, 1957), pp. 464–483.

11. Wilson, *op. cit.,* Chapters VII and VIII.

12. For an interesting study of governmental bargaining see William J. Gore, "Administrative Decision-Making in Federal Field Offices," *Public Administration Review,* 16 (Autumn, 1956), pp. 281–291.

13. Philip Selznick, *TVA and the Grass Roots,* Berkeley and Los Angeles: University of California Press, 1949.

14. Coalition may involve joint action toward only limited aspects of the goals of each member. It may involve the complete commitment of each member for a specific period of time or indefinitely. In either case the ultimate power to withdraw is retained by the members. We thus distinguish coalition from merger, in which two or more organizations are fused permanently. In merger one or all of the original parts may lose their identity. Goal-setting in such a situation, of course, is no longer subject to inter-organizational constraints among the components.

15. See "The Joint Venture Is an Effective Approach to Major Engineering Projects," *New York Times,* July 14, 1957, Section 3, p. 1 F.

6

Values, Man and Organizations

ROBERT TANNENBAUM
University of California, Los Angeles

SHELDON A. DAVIS
TRW Systems

> . . . we are today in a period when the development of theory within the social sciences will permit innovations which are at present inconceivable. Among these will be dramatic changes in the organization and management of economic enterprise. The capacities of the average human being for creativity, for growth, for collaboration, for productivity (in the full sense of the term) are far greater than we have recognized . . . it is possible that the next half century will bring the most dramatic social changes in human history.[1]

For those concerned with organization theory and with organizational development work, this is an exciting and challenging time. Probably never before have the issues at the interface between changing organizations and maturing man been so apparent, so compelling, and of such potentially critical relevance to both. And to a considerable extent, the sparks at the interface reflect differences in values both within organizations and within man — human values which are coming loose from their moorings, whose functional relevance is being re-examined and tested, and which are without question in transition.

Many organizations today, particularly those at the leading edge of technology, are faced with ferment and flux. In increasing instances, the bureaucratic model — with its emphasis on relatively rigid structure, well-defined functional specialization, direction and control exercised through a formal hierarchy of authority, fixed systems of rights, duties, and procedures, and relative impersonality of human relationships — is responding inadequately to the demands placed upon it from the outside and from within the organization. There is increasing need for experimentation, for learning from experience, for flexibility and adaptability, and for growth. There is a need for greater inventiveness and creativity, and a need for collaboration among

Taken and adapted from *Industrial Management Review,* Vol. 10, No. 2, Winter 1969, pp. 69–80.

individuals and groups. Greater job mobility and the effective use of temporary systems seem essential. An environment must be created in which people will be more fully utilized and challenged and in which people can grow as human beings.

In his recent books, *Changing Organizations,* Warren Bennis has pointed out that the bureaucratic form of organization "is becoming less and less effective, that it is hopelessly out of joint with contemporary realities, and that new shapes, patterns, and models . . . are emerging which promise drastic changes in the conduct of the corporation and in managerial practices in general."[2] At least one of the newer models, the one with which our recent experience is most closely connected, is organic and systems-oriented. We feel that, for the present at least, this model is one which can suggest highly useful responses to the newer demands facing organizations.

At this historical juncture, it is not just organizations which are in flux. Man, perhaps to an extent greater than ever before, is coming alive; he is ceasing to be an object to be used, and is increasingly asserting himself, his complexity, and his importance. Not quite understanding why or how, he is moving slowly but ever close to the center of the universe.

The factors underlying man's emergence are complex and interrelated. They include higher levels of educational attainment, an increased availability of technology which both frees man from the burdens of physical and routine labor and makes him more dependent on society, an increasing rate of change affecting his environment which both threatens and challenges him, and higher levels of affluence which open up opportunities for a variety and depth of experiences never before so generally available.

The evidences of this trend are many. They are to be found, for example, in the gropings within many religions for more viable modes and values. They are to be found in the potent thrusts for independence of minorities everywhere, and in the challenges of our youth who find our values phony and often materialistically centered. They are to be found in the involvement of so many people in psychotherapy, in sensitivity training, and in self-expression activities in the arts and elsewhere. They are also to be found in the continuing and growing interest in writings and ideas in the general direction of the humanistic-existential orientation to man.

Organizations are questioning and moving away from the bureaucratic model, in part because man is asserting his individuality and his centrality, in part because of growing dissatisfaction with the personally constraining impact of bureaucracies. In this flux, organizations and man must find a way with each other. In our view, this way will be found through changing values — values which can hopefully serve the needs for effectiveness and survival of organizations and the needs for individuality and growth of emergent man. Those concerned with organization theory and with organizational development have, in our judgment, a most important role to play in this quest.

Values in Transition

Deeply impressed with the managerial and organizational implications of the increasing accumulation of knowledge about human behavior, Professor Douglas McGregor formulated his assumptions of Theory Y.[3] According to him, these assumptions were essentially his interpretations, based upon the newer knowledge and on his extensive experience, of the nature of man and of man's motivation. In our view, McGregor was overly cautious and tentative in calling the Theory Y tenets "assumptions" and in limiting them to being his "interpretations." In trying to be "scientific," he seemed reluctant in his writing to assert explicitly as *values* those elements (including the Theory Y assumptions) which so much affected his organizational theory and practice. He was not alone in his reluctance. Perhaps the most pervasive common characteristic among people in laboratory training and in organizational development work is their values, and yet, while organizational development academicians and practitioners are generally aware of their shared values and while these values implicitly guide much of what they do, they too have usually been reluctant to make them explicit.

We want here not only to own our values but also to state them openly. These values are consistent with McGregor's assumptions and in some instances go beyond his. They are not scientifically derived nor are they new, but they are compatible with relevant "findings" emerging in the behavioral sciences. They are deeply rooted in the nature of man and are therefore basically humanistic. As previously suggested, many of the values underlying the bureaucratic model and its typical implementation have been consistent with the nature of man, with the result that he has not been fully utilized, his motivation has been reduced, his growth as a person stunted, and his spirit deadened. These outcomes sorely trouble us, for we believe organizations can in the fullest sense serve man as well as themselves.

Growing evidence strongly suggests that humanistic values not only resonate with an increasing number of people in today's world, but also are highly consistent with the effective functioning of organizations built on the newer organic model. As we discuss a number of these values, we will provide some face validity for their viability by illustrating them with cases or experiences taken from our involvements with or knowledge of a number of organizations which recently have been experimenting with the interface between the organizational and humanistic frontiers described above. The illustrations come primarily from TRW Systems, with which we have had a continuing collaboration for more than four years. Other organizations with which one or both of us have been involved include Aluminium Company of Canada, Ltd., U.S. Department of State, and the Organizational Behavior Group of Case Institute of Technology.

We clearly recognize that the values to which we hold are not absolutes, that they represent directions rather than final goals. We also recognize that the degree of their short-run application often depends upon the people and other variables involved. We feel that we are now in a period of transition, sometimes slow and sometimes rapid, involving a movement away from older, less personally meaningful and organizationally relevant values toward these newer values.

Away from a View of Man as Essentially Bad Toward a View of Him as Basically Good

At his core, man is not inherently evil, lazy, destructive, hurtful, irresponsible, narrowly self-centered, and the like. The life experiences which he has, including his relationships with other people and the impact on him of the organizations with which he associates, can and often do move him in these directions. On the other hand, his more central inclination toward the good is reflected in his behavior as an infant, in his centuries-long evolution of ethical and religious precepts, and in the directions of his strivings and growth as a result of experiences such as those in psychotherapy and sensitivity training. Essentially man is internally motivated toward positive personal and social ends; the extent to which he is not motivated results from a process of demotivation generated by his relationships and/or environment.

We have been impressed with the degree to which the fairly pervasive cultural assumption of man's badness has led to organizational forms and practices designed to control, limit, push, check upon, inhibit, and punish. We are also increasingly challenged by the changes in behavior resulting from a growing number of experiments with organizational forms and practices rooted in the view of man as basically good.

Within an organization it is readily apparent to both members and perceptive visitors whether or not there is, in general, an atmosphere of respect for the individual as a person. Are people treated arbitrarily? Are there sinister coups taking place? How much of the time and energy of the members of the organization is devoted to constructive problem solving rather than to playing games with each other, backbiting, politicking, destructive competition, and other dysfunctional behavior? How does management handle problems such as the keeping of time records? (Some organizations do not have time clocks and yet report that employees generally do not abuse this kind of a system.) One of the authors can remember a chain of retail stores which fired a stock clerk because he had shifty eyes, although he was one of the best stock boys in that chain. There are all kinds of negative assumptions about man behind such an incredible action.

> For a long period of time, two senior engineers, Taylor and Durant, had real difficulty in working together. Each had a negative view of the other; mutual respect was lacking. Such attitudes resulted in their avoiding each other even though their technical disciplines were closely related. A point in time was reached when Taylor sorely needed help from Durant. Caught

up in his own negative feelings, however, he clearly was not about to ask Durant for help. Fortunately, two of Taylor's colleagues who did not share his feelings prodded him into asking Durant to work with him on the problem. Durant responded most positively, and brought along two of his colleagues the next day to study the problem in detail. He then continued to remain involved with Taylor until the latter's problem was solved. Only a stereotype had kept these men apart; Taylor's eventual willingness to approach Durant opened the door to constructive problem solving.

Away from Avoidance or Negative Evaluation of Individuals Toward Confirming Them as Human Beings

One desire frequently expressed by people with whom we consult is: "I wish I knew where I stand with my boss (with this organization) (with my colleagues) (with my subordinates). I'd really like to know what they think of me personally." We are not referring to the excessively neurotic needs of some persons for attention and response, but rather to the much more pervasive and basic need to know that one's existence makes a difference to others.

Feedback that is given is generally negative in character and often destructive of the individual instead of being focused on the perceived shortcomings of a given performance. It seems to be exceedingly difficult for most of us to give positive feedback to others — and, more specifically, to express genuine feelings of affection and caring.

When people are seen as bad, they need to be disciplined and corrected on the issue only; when they are seen as good, they need to be confirmed. Avoidance and negative evaluation can lead individuals to be cautious, guarded, defensive. Confirmation can lead to personal release, confidence, and enhancement.

A senior executive reported to one of us that he did not get nearly as much feedback as he wanted about how people thought about him as a person and whether or not they cared for him. He reported that one of the most meaningful things that had happened to him in this regard occurred when the person he reported to put his arm around him briefly at the end of a working session, patted him on the shoulder, and said, "Keep up the good work," communicating a great deal of warmth and positive feelings towards the person through this behavior. This event had taken place two years ago and lasted about five seconds, yet it was still fresh in the senior executive's memory and obviously has had a great deal of personal meaning for him. In our culture, most of us are grossly undernourished and have strong need for the personal caring of others.

Away from a View of Individuals as Fixed Toward Seeing Them as Being in Process

The traditional view of individuals is that they can be defined in terms of given interests, knowledge, skills, and personality characteristics: they can gain new knowledge, acquire additional skills, and even at times change their interests, but it is rare that people really change. This view, when buttressed by related organizational attitudes and modes, insures a relative fixity of individuals, with crippling effects. The value to which we hold is that people can constantly be in flux, groping, questing, testing, experimenting, and growing. We are struck by the tremendous untapped potential in most individuals yearning for discovery and release. Individuals may rarely change in core attributes, but the range of alternatives for choice can be widened, and the ability to learn how to learn more about self can be enhanced.

Organizations at times question whether it is their responsibility to foster individual growth. Whether or not it is, we believe that for most organizations, especially those desiring long-term survival through adaptability, innovation, and change, it is an increasing necessity. Further, evidence suggests that to have people in process requires a growth-enhancing environment. Personal growth requires healthy organizations. This value, then, carries with it great implications for work in organizational development. In organizations, people continuously experience interpersonal difficulties in relating to the other people with whom they must work. Some reasons for the difficulties are that people listen very badly to each other, attribute things of a negative nature to another person, and make all kinds of paranoid assumptions, with the result that communication breaks down rather severely.

There have been many instances within TRW Systems of people, who, in the eyes of others around them, produce some fairly significant changes in their own behavior. Most of these changes have been reported quite positively. In some cases there have been rather dramatic changes with respect to how a person faces certain kinds of problems — how he handles conflicts, how he conducts staff meetings. In those cases an individual who is perceived as having changed quite often reports that these changes are personally rewarding, that he feels better about himself and more optimistic and expansive about life.

TRW Systems is committed to a continuation and improvement of its Career Development program, which places considerable emphasis on the personal and professional growth of its members. Although the original commitment was perhaps largely based on faith, experience gained in recent years strongly suggests that one of the most productive investments the organization can make is in the continuing growth of its members and in the health of the environment in which they work.

Away from Resisting and Fearing Individual Differences Toward Accepting and Utilizing Them

The pervasive and long-standing view of man as bad takes on even more serious implications when individual differences among men appear — differences in race, religion, personality (including personal style), specialties, and personal perceptions (definitions of truth or reality). A bad man poses sufficient problems but a strange bad man often becomes impossible.

Organizations and individuals are frequently threatened by what they consider questioning of or challenge to their existing values and modes, represented by the presence of alternative possibilities. And they choose to avoid the challenge and the related and expected conflicts, discomforts, and the like, which might follow. As a result, they achieve drabness, a lack of creativity, and a false sense of peace and security. We firmly believe that the existence of differences can be highly functional. There is no single truth, no one right way, no chosen people. It is at the interface of differences that ferment occurs and that the potential for creativity exists. Furthermore, for an organization to deny to itself (in the name of "harmony" or some similar shibboleth) the availability of productive resources simply because they do not conform to an irrelevant criterion is nothing short of madness. To utilize differences creatively is rarely easy, but our experience tells us that the gains far outweigh the costs.

In the play "Right You Are," Pirandello makes the point that truth in a particular human situation is a collection of what each individual in the situation sees. Each person will see different facets of the same event. In a positive sense, this would lead us to value seeing all the various facets of an issue or problem as they unfold in the eyes of all the beholders and to place a positive value on our interdependence with others, particularly in situations where each of us can have only part of the answer or see part of the reality.

> An organization recently faced the problem of filling a key position. The man whose responsibility it was to fill the position sat down with five or six people who, due to their various functional roles, would have a great deal of interaction with the person in that position and with his organization. The man asked them to help him identify logical candidates. The group very quickly identified a number of people who ought to be considered and the two or three who were the most logical candidates. Then the group went beyond the stated agenda and came up with a rather creative new organizational notion, which was subsequently implemented and proved to be very desirable. After this took place, the executive, who had called the meeting in order to get help for the decision he had to make, reported that it was very clear to him that doing the job became much easier by getting everyone together to share their varying perceptions. This meant that he had more relevant data available to him in making his decision. Furthermore, the creative organizational concept only came about as a result of the meeting's having taken place.

In most organizations persons and groups with markedly different training, experience, points of view, and modes of operating frequently bump into each other. Project managers face functional performers, mechanical engineers face electrical engineers, designers face hardware specialists, basic researchers face action-oriented engineers, financial specialists face starry-eyed innovators. Each needs to understand and respect the world of the other, and organizations should place a high value upon and do much to facilitate the working through of the differences which come into sharp focus at interfaces such as these.

Away from Utilizing an Individual Primarily with Reference to His Job Description Toward Viewing Him as a Whole Person

People get pigeon-holed very easily, with job description (or expectations of job performance) typically becoming the pigeon hole. A cost accountant is hired, and from then on he is seen and dealt with as a cost accountant. Our view is that people generally have much more to contribute and to develop than just what is expected of them in their specific positions. Whole persons, not parts of persons, are hired and available for contribution. The organizational challenge is to recognize this fact and discover ways to provide outlets for the rich, varied, and often untapped resources available to them.

One of many personal examples that could be cited within TRW Systems is that of a person trained as a theoretical physicist. Having pursued this profession for many years, he is now effectively serving also as a part-time behavioral science consultant (a third-party process facilitator) to the personnel organization within the company. This is an activity for which he had no previous formal training until a new-found interest began asserting itself. The organization has supported him in this interest, has made a relevant learning opportunity available to him, and has opened the door to his performing an additional function within the organization.

An organizational example involves the question of charters that are defined for particular sub-elements of the organization: divisions, staffs, labs, etc. What are their functions? What are they supposed to do? To state the extreme, an organizational unit can have very sharply defined charters so that each person in it knows exactly what he is supposed to do and not do. This can lead to very clean functional relationships. Another approach, however, is to say that the *core* of the charter will be very clear with discrete responsibilities identified, but the outer edges (where one charter interacts with others) will not be sharply defined and will deliberately overlap and interweave with other charters. The latter approach assumes that there is a potential synergy within an organization which people can move toward fully actualizing if they can be constructive and creative in their interpersonal and intergroup relations. Very different charters are produced in this case, with very different outcomes. Such charters must, by definition, not be clean and sharply described, or the innovative and coordinated outcomes that might come about by having people working across charter boundaries will not occur.

Away from Walling-Off the Expression of Feelings Toward Making Possible Both Appropriate Expression and Effective Use

In our culture, there is a pervasive fear of feelings. From early childhood, children are taught to hide, repress, or deny the existence of their feelings, and their learnings are reinforced as they grow older. People are concerned about "losing control," and organizations seek rational, proper, task-oriented behavior, which emphasizes head-level as opposed to gut-level behavior. But organizations also seek high motivation, high morale, loyalty, team work, commitment, and creativity, all of which, if they are more than words, stem from personal feelings. Further, an individual cannot be a whole person if he is prevented from using or divorced from his feelings. And the energy dissipated in repression of feelings is lost to more productive endeavors.

We appreciate and are not afraid of feelings, and strongly believe that organizations will increasingly discover that they have a reservoir of untapped resources available to them in the feelings of their members, that the repression of feelings in the past has been more costly, both to them and to their members, than they ever thought possible.

One of the relevant questions to ask within an organization is how well problems stay solved once they are apparently solved. If the feelings involved in such problems are not directly dealt with and worked through, the problem usually does not remain solved for very long. For example, if two subordinates are fighting about something, their supervisor can either intervene and make the decision for them or arbitrate. Both methods can solve the immediate difficulty, but the fundamental problem will most likely again occur in some other situation or at some other time. The supervisor has dealt only with the symptoms of the real problem.

The direct expression of feelings, no matter what they are, does typically take place somewhere along the line, but usually not in the relevant face-to-face relationship. A person will attend a staff meeting and experience a great deal of frustration with the meeting as a whole or with the behavior of one or more persons in it. He will then talk about his feelings with another colleague outside the meeting or bring them home and discuss them with or displace them on his wife or children, rather than talking about them in the meeting where such behavior might make an important difference. To aid communication of feelings, participants at a given staff meeting could decide that one of the agenda items will be: "How do we feel about this meeting; how is it going; how can it be improved?" They could then talk face-to-face with each other while the feeling is immediately relevant to the effective functioning of the staff group. The outcomes of the face-to-face confrontation can be far more constructive than the "dealing-with symptoms" approach.

Away from Maskmanship and Game-Playing Toward Authentic Behavior

Deeply rooted in existing organizational lore is a belief in the necessity or efficacy of being what one is not, both as an individual and as a group. Strategy and out-maneuvering are valued. Using diplomacy, wearing masks, not saying what one thinks or expressing what one feels, creating an image — these and other deceptive modes are widely utilized. As a result, in many interpersonal and intergroup relations, mask faces mask, image faces image, and much energy is employed in dealing with the other person's game. That which is much more basically relevant to the given relationship is often completely avoided in the transaction.

To be that which one (individual or group) truly is — to be authentic — is a central value to us. Honesty, directness, and congruence, if widely practiced, create an organizational atmosphere in which energies get focused on the real problems rather than on game-playing and in which individuals and groups can genuinely and meaningfully encounter each other.

Recently, two supervisors of separate units within an organization got together to resolve a problem that affected both of them. At one point in their discussion, which had gone on for some time and was proving not to be very fruitful, one of them happened to mention that he had recently attended a sensitivity training laboratory conducted by the company. At that point, the other one mentioned that sometime back he had also attended a laboratory. They both quickly decided "to cut out the crap," stop the game they were playing, and really try to solve the problem they had come to face. Within a very short period of time, they dramatically went from a very typical organizational mode of being very closed, wearing masks, and trying to outmaneuver each other, to a mode of being open and direct. They found that the second mode took less energy and that they solved the problem in much less time and were able to keep it solved. But, somehow, at least one of them had not felt safe in taking off his mask until he learned that the other had also gone through a T Group.

When people experience difficulty with others in organizations, they quite often attribute the difficulty to the fact that the other person or group is not trustworthy. This attitude, of course, justifies their behavior in dealing with the other. On numerous occasions within TRW Systems, groups or individuals who are experiencing distrust are brought together and helped to articulate how they feel about each other. When the fact that "I do not trust you" is out on the table, and only then, can it be dealt with. Interestingly, it turns out that when the feeling is exposed and worked through, there are not really very many fundamentally untrustworthy people. There certainly are all kinds of people continuously doing things that create feelings of mistrust in others. But these feelings and the behavior that triggers them are rarely explored in an effort to work them through. Instead, the mistrust escalates, continues to influence the behavior of both parties, and becomes self-fulfilling. Once the locked-in situation is broken through and the people involved really start talking to each other authentically, however, trust issues, about which people can be very pessimistic, become quite workable. This has happened many, many times in organizational development efforts at TRW Systems.

Away from Use of Status for Maintaining Power and Personal Prestige Toward Use of Status for Organizationally Relevant Purposes

In organizations, particularly large ones, status and symbols of status can play an important role. In too many instances, however, they are used for narrowly personal ends, both to hide behind and to maintain the aura of power and prestige. One result is that dysfunctional walls are built and communication flow suffers.

We believe that status must always be organizationally (functionally) relevant. Some people know more than others, some can do things others cannot do, some carry more responsibility than others. It is often useful for status to be attached to these differences, but such status must be used by its holder to further rather than to wall off the performance of the function out of which the status arises. An organization must be constantly alert to the role that status plays in its functioning.

It is relatively easy to perceive how status symbols are used within an organization, how relatively functional or dysfunctional they are. In some organizations, name-dropping is one of the primary weapons for accomplishing something. A person can go to a colleague with whom he is having a quarrel about what should be done and mention that he had a chat with the president of the organization yesterday. He then gets agreement. He may or may not have talked with the president, he may or may not have quoted him correctly; but he is begging the question by using a power figure in order to convince the other person to do it his way. In other organizations, we have observed that people very rarely work a problem by invoking the name of a senior executive, and that, in fact, those who do name-drop are quickly and openly called to task.

At TRW Systems, with only minor exceptions, middle- and top-level executives, as well as key scientists and engineers, are typically available for consultation with anyone in the organization on matters of functional relevance to the organization. There is no need to use titles, to "follow the organization chart," to obtain permission for the consultation from one's boss or to report the results to him afterwards. As a result, those who can really help are sought out, and problems tend to get worked at the point of interface between need on the one hand and knowledge, experience, and expertise on the other.

Away from Distrusting People Toward Trusting Them

A corollary of the view that man is basically bad is the view that he cannot be trusted. And if he cannot be trusted, he must be carefully watched. In our judgment, many traditional organizational forms exist, at least in part, because of distrust. Close supervision, managerial controls, guarding, security, sign-outs, carry with them to some extent the implication of distrust.

The increasing evidence available to us strongly suggests that distrusting people often becomes a self-confirming hypothesis — distrusting another leads to behavior consciously or unconsciously designed by the person or group not trusted to "prove" the validity of the distrust. Distrust begets distrust. On the other hand, the evidence also suggests that trust begets trust; when people are trusted, they often respond in ways to merit or justify that trust.

Where distrust exists, people are usually seen as having to be motivated "from the outside in," as being responsive only to outside pressure. But when trust exists, people are seen as being motivated "from the inside out," as being at least potentially self-directing entities. One motivational device often used in the outside-in approach involves the inculcation of guilt. Rooted in the Protestant ethic, this device confronts the individual with "shoulds," "oughts," or "musts" as reasons for behaving in a given way. Failure to comply means some external standard has not been met. The individual has thus done wrong, and he is made to feel guilty. The more trustful, inside-out approach makes it possible for the individual to do things because they make sense to him, because they have functional relevance. If the behavior does not succeed, the experience is viewed in positive terms as an opportunity to learn rather than negatively as a reason for punishment and guilt.

Organizations which trust go far to provide individuals and groups with considerable freedom for self-directed action backed up by the experience-based belief that this managerial value will generate the assumption of responsibility for the exercise of that freedom.

> In California, going back about 27 years, a forward-looking director of one of our state prisons got the idea of a "prison without walls." He developed and received support for an experiment that involved bringing prisoners to the institution where correctional officers, at that time called guards, carried no guns or billy clubs. There were no guards in the towers or on the walls. The incoming prisoners were shown that the gate was not locked. Under this newer organizational behavior, escape rates decreased, and the experiment has become a model for many prisons in this country and abroad.
>
> An organizational family embarked upon a two-day team-development lab shortly after the conclusion was reached from assessment data that the

partial failure of a space vehicle had resulted from the non-functioning of a subsystem developed by this team. At the outset of the lab, an aura of depression was present but there was no evidence that the team had been chastised by higher management for the failure. Further, in strong contrast with what most likely would have been the case if they had faced a load of guilt generated from the outside, there was no evidence of mutual destructive criticism and recriminations. Instead, the team was able in time to turn its attention to a diagnosis of possible reasons for the failure and to action steps which might be taken to avoid a similar outcome in the future.

During a discussion which took place between the head of an organization and one of his subordinates (relating to goals and objectives for that subordinate for the coming year), the supervisor said that one of the things he felt very positive about with respect to that particular subordinate was the way he seemed to be defining his own set of responsibilities. This comment demonstrated the large degree of trust that was placed in the subordinates of this particular supervisor. While the supervisor certainly made it clear to this individual that there were some specific things expected of him, he consciously created a large degree of freedom within which the subordinate would be able to determine for himself how he should spend his time, what priorities he ought to have, what his function should be. This is in great contrast to other organizations which define very clearly and elaborately what they expect from people. Two very different sets of assumptions about people underlie these two approaches.

Away from Avoiding Facing Others with Relevant Data Toward Making Appropriate Confrontation

This value trend is closely related to the one of "from maskmanship toward authenticity," and its implementation is often tied to moving "from distrust toward trust."

In many organizations today there is an unwillingness to "level" with people, particularly with respect to matters which have personal implications. In merit reviews, the "touchy" matters are avoided. Often, incompetent or unneeded employees are retained much longer than is justified either from the organization's or their own point of view. Feelings toward another accumulate and at times fester, but they remain unexpressed. "Even one's best friends won't tell him."

Confrontation fails to take place because "I don't want to hurt Joe," although in fact the non-confronter may be concerned about being hurt himself. We feel that a real absurdity is involved here. While it is widely believed that to "level" is to hurt and, at times, destroy the other, the opposite may often be the case. Being left to live in a "fool's paradise" or being permitted to continue with false illusions about self is often highly hurtful and even destructive. Being honestly confronted in a context of mutual trust and caring is an essential requirement for personal growth. In an organizational setting, it is also an important aspect of "working the problem."

A quite dramatic example of confrontation and its impact occurred in a sensitivity training laboratory when one executive giving feedback to a colleague said to him that he and others within the organization perceived him as being ruthless. This came as a tremendous jolt to the person receiving the feedback. He had absolutely no perception of himself as ruthless and no idea that he was doing things which would cause others to feel that way about him. The confrontation was an upending experience for him. As a result, he later began to explore with many people in the organization what their relationship with him was like and made some quite marked changes in his behavior after getting additional data which tended to confirm what he had recently heard. In the absence of these data (previously withheld because people might not want to hurt him), he was indeed living in a fool's paradise. A great deal of energy was expended by other people in dealing with his "ruthlessness," and a considerable amount of avoidance took place, greatly influencing the productivity of everyone. Once this problem was exposed and worked through, this energy became available for more productive purposes.

Away from Avoidance of Risk-Taking Toward Willingness to Risk

A widely discernible attribute of large numbers of individuals and groups in organizations today is the unwillingness to risk, to put one's self or the group on the line. Much of this reluctance stems from not being trusted, with the resulting fear of the consequences expected to follow close upon the making of an error. It often seems that only a reasonable guarantee of success will free an individual or group to take a chance. Such a stance leads to conformity, to a repetition of the past, to excessive caution and defensiveness. We feel that risk-taking is an essential quality in adaptable, growthful organizations; taking a chance is necessary for creativity and change. Also, individuals and groups do learn by making mistakes. Risk-taking involves being willing "to take the monkey on my back," and it takes courage to do so. It also takes courage and ingenuity on the part of the organization to foster such behavior.

At TRW Systems, the president and many of the senior executives were until recently located on the fifth floor of one of the organization's buildings, and part of the language of the organization was "the fifth floor," meaning that place where many of the power figures resided. This phrase was used quite often in discussion: "The fifth floor feels that we should —." In working with groups one or two levels below the top executives to explore what they might do about some of the frustrations they were experiencing in getting their jobs done, one of the things that dominated the early discussions was the wish that somehow "the fifth floor" would straighten things out. For example, a group of engineers of one division was having problems with a group of engineers of another division, and they stated that "the fifth floor" (or at least one of its executives) ought to go over to the people in the other division and somehow "give them the word." After a while, however, they began to realize that it really was not very fruitful or productive to talk about what they wished someone else would do, and they began to face the problem of what they could do about the situation directly.

The discussion then became quite constructive and creative, and a number of new action items were developed and later successfully implemented — even though there was no assurance of successful outcomes at the time the action items were decided upon.

Away from a View of Process Work as Being Unproductive Effort Toward Seeing It as Essential to Effective Task Accomplishment

In the past and often in the present, productive effort has been seen as that which focused directly on the production of goods and services. Little attention has been paid to the processes by which such effort takes place; to do so has often been viewed as a waste of time. Increasingly, however, the relevance to task accomplishment of such activities as team maintenance and development, diagnosis and working through of interpersonal and intergroup communication barriers, confrontation efforts for resolution of organizationally dysfunctional personal and interpersonal hangups, and assessment and improvement of existing modes of decision making is being recognized. And, in fact, we harbor growing doubts with respect to the continued usefulness of the notion of a task-process dichotomy. It seems to us that there are many activities which can make contributions to task accomplishment and that the choice from among these is essentially an economic one.

Within TRW Systems, proposals are constantly being written in the hope of obtaining new projects from the Department of Defense, NASA, and others. These proposals are done under very tight time constraints. What quite often happens is that the request for the proposal is received from the customer and read very quickly by the principals involved. Everybody then charges off and starts working on the proposal because of the keenly felt time pressure. Recently, on a very major proposal, the proposal manager decided that the first thing he should do was to spend a couple of days (out of a three-month period of available time) meeting with the principals involved. In this meeting, they would not do any writing of the proposal but would talk about how they were going to proceed, make sure they were all making the same assumptions about who would be working on which subsystem, how they would handle critical interfaces, how they would handle critical choice points during the proposal period, and so on. Many of the principals went to the meeting with a great deal of skepticism, if not impatience. They wanted to get "on with the job," which to them meant writing the proposal. Spending a couple of days talking about "how we're going to do things" was not defined by them as productive work.

After the meeting, and after the proposal had been written and delivered to the customer, a critique was held on the process used. Those involved in general reported very favorably on the effects of the meeting which took place at the beginning of the proposal-writing cycle. They reported things such as: "The effect of having spent a couple of days as we did meant that at that point we then charged off and started actually writing the proposal, we were able to function as if we had already been working together for perhaps two months. We were much more effective with each other and much more efficient, so that in the final analysis, it was time well spent." By giving attention to their ways of getting work done, they clearly had facilitated their ability to function well as a team.

Away from a Primary Emphasis on Competition Toward a Much Greater Emphasis on Collaboration

A pervasive value in the organizational milieu is competition. Competition is based on the assumption that desirable resources are limited in quantity and that individuals or groups can be effectively motivated through competing against one another for the possession of these resources. But competition can often set man against man and group against group in dysfunctional behavior, including a shift of objectives from obtaining the limited resource to blocking or destroying the competitor. Competition inevitably results in winners and losers, and at least some of the hidden costs of losing can be rather high in systemic terms.

Collaboration, on the other hand, is based on the assumption that the desirable limited resources can be shared among the participants in a mutually satisfactory manner and, even more important, that it is possible to increase the quantity of the resources themselves.

As organizational work becomes more highly specialized and complex, with its accomplishment depending more and more on the effective interaction of individuals and groups, and as the organic or systems views of organizational functioning become more widely understood, the viability of collaboration as an organizational mode becomes ever clearer. Individuals and groups are often highly interdependent, and such interdependency needs to be facilitated through collaborative behavior rather than walled off through competition. At the same time, collaborative behavior must come to be viewed as reflecting strength rather than weakness.

In organizations which have a high degree of interdependency, one of the problems people run into regarding the handling of this interdependency is that they look for simple solutions to complex problems. Simple solutions do not produce very good results because they deal with the symptoms rather than with the real problems.

A major reorganization recently took place within TRW Systems. The president of the organization sketched out the broad, general directions of the reorganization, specifying details only in one or two instances. He assigned to a large number of working committees the development of the details of the new organization. The initial reaction of some people was that these were things that the president himself should be deciding. The president, however, did not feel he had enough detailed understanding and knowledge to come up with many of the appropriate answers. He felt strongly that those who had the knowledge should develop the answers. This was an explicit, conscious recognition on his part of the fact that he did indeed need very important inputs from other people in order to effect the changes he was interested in making. These working committees turned out to be very effective. As a result of the president's approach, the reorganization proceeded with far less disruption and resistance than is typically the case in major reorganizations.

Another example involved a major staff function which was experiencing a great deal of difficulty with other parts of the organization. The unit having the trouble made the initial decision to conduct briefings throughout the organization to explain what they were really trying to accomplish, how they were organized, what requirements they had to meet for outside customers, and so on. They felt that their job would be easier if they could solicit better understanding. What actually took place was quite different. Instead of conducting briefings to convince the "heathen," the people in this unit revised their plan and met with some key people from other parts of the company who had to deal with them to ask what the unit was doing that was creating problems at the interface. After receiving a great deal of fairly specific data, the unit and the people with whom they consulted developed joint collaborative action items for dealing with the problems. This way of approaching the problem quickly turned interfaces that had been very negative and very hostile into ones that were relatively cooperative. The change in attitude on both sides of the interface provided a positive base for working toward satisfactory solutions to the problems.

Some Implications of These Values in Transition

Many people would agree with the value trends stated in this paper and indeed claim that they use these guidelines in running their own organizations. However, there is often quite a gap between saying that you believe in these values and actually practicing them in meaningful, important ways. In many organizations, for example, there is a management-by-objectives process which has been installed and used for several years — an approach which can involve the implementation of some of the values stated earlier in this paper. If, however, one closely examines how this process takes place in many organizations, it is in fact a very mechanical one, one which is used very defensively in some cases. What emerges is a statement of objectives which has obtained for the boss what he really wants, and, at the end of the year, protects the subordinate if he does not do everything that his boss thought he might do. It becomes a "Pearl Harbor file." The point that needs emphasis is that the payoff in implementing these values by techniques is not in the techniques themselves but in how they are applied and in what meaning their use has for the people involved.

To us, the implementation of these values clearly involves a bias regarding organizational development efforts. Believing that people have vast amounts of untapped potential and the capability and desire to grow, to engage in meaningful collaborative relationships, to be creative in organizational contexts, and to be more authentic, we feel that the most effective change interventions are therapeutic in nature. Such interventions focus directly on the hangups, both personal and organizational, that block a person from realizing his potential. We are referring to interventions which assist a person in breaking through the neurotic barriers in himself, in others around him, and in the ongoing culture.

We place a strong emphasis on increasing the sanity of the individuals in the organization and of the organization itself. By this we mean putting the individuals and the organization more in touch with the realities existing within themselves and around them. With respect to the individual, this involves his understanding the consequences of his behavior. How do people feel about him? How do they react to him? Do they trust him? With respect to the organization, it involves a critical examination of its culture and what that culture produces: the norms, the values, the decision-making processes, the general environment that it has created and maintained over a period of time.

There are obviously other biases and alternatives available to someone approaching organizational development work. One could concentrate on structural interventions: How should we organize? What kind of charters should people in various functional units have? The bias we are stating does not mean that structure, function, and charters are irrelevant, but that they are less important and have considerably less leverage in the early stages of organizational development efforts than working with the individuals and groups in a therapeutic manner. Furthermore, as an individual becomes more authentic and interpersonally competent, he becomes far more capable of creative problem-solving. He and his associates have within them more resources for dealing with questions of structure, charters, and operating procedures, in more relevant and creative ways, than does someone from outside their system. Such therapeutic devices include the full range of laboratory methods usually identified with the NTL Institute: sensitivity training, team building, intergroup relationship building, and so on. They also include individual and group counseling within the organization, and the voluntary involvement of individuals in various forms of psychotherapy outside the organization.

In order to achieve a movement towards authenticity, focus must be placed on developing the whole person and in doing this in an organic way. The program cannot be something you crank people through; it must be tailored in a variety of ways to individual needs as they are expressed and identified. In time, therapy and individual growth (becoming more in touch with your own realities) becomes values in and of themselves. And as people become less demotivated and move toward authenticity, they clearly demonstrate that they have the ability to be creative about organization matters, and this too becomes a value shared within the organization. Once these values are introduced and people move towards them, the movement in and of itself will contain many forces that make for change and open up new possibilities in an organization. For example, as relationships become more trustworthy, as people are given more responsibility, as competition gives way to collaboration, people experience a freeing up. They are more apt to challenge all the given surroundings, to test the limits, to try new solutions, and to rock the boat. This can be an exciting and productive change, but it can also be troublesome, and a variety of responses to it must be expected.

Therapeutic efforts are long-term efforts. Movement towards greater authenticity, which leads to an organization's culture becoming more positive, creative, and growthful, is something that takes a great deal of time and a great deal of energy. In this kind of approach to organizational development, there is more ambiguity and less stability than in other approaches that might be taken. Patience, persistence, and confidence are essential through time if significant change is to occur and be maintained.

For the organizational development effort to have some kind of permanency, it is very important that it becomes an integral part of the line organization and its mode of operating. Many of the people involved in introducing change in organizations are in staff positions, typically in personnel. If, over time, the effort continues to be mainly one carried out by staff people, it is that much more tenuous. Somehow the total organization must be involved, particularly those people with line responsibility for the organization's success and for its future. They must assimilate the effort and make it a part of their own behavior within the organization. In other words, those people who have the greatest direct impact on and responsibility for creating, maintaining, and changing the culture of an organization must assume direct ownership of the change effort.

In the transition and beyond it, these changes can produce problems for the organization in confronting the outside world with its traditional values. For example, do you tell the truth to your customers when you are experiencing problems building a product for them, or do you continue to them that everything is going along fine? For the individual, there can be problems in other relationships around him, such as within his family at home. We do not as yet have good methods developed for dealing with these conflicts, but we can certainly say that they will take place and will have to be worked out.

As previously stated, the Career Development program at TRW Systems, now in its fifth year of operation, is an effort in which both authors have been deeply involved. We feel it is one of the more promising examples of large-scale, long-term, systematic efforts to help people move toward the values we have outlined.

One question that is constantly raised about efforts such as the Career Development program at TRW Systems relates to assessing their impact. How does one know there has been a real payoff for the organization and its members? Some behavioral scientists have devised rather elaborate, mechanical tools in order to answer this question. We feel that the values themselves suggest the most relevant kind of measurement. The people involved have the capacity to determine the relevance and significance to them and to their organizational units of what they are doing. Within TRW Systems, a very pragmatic approach is taken. Questions are asked such as: Do we feel this has been useful? Are these kinds of problems easier to resolve? Are there less hidden agenda now? Do we deal more quickly and effectively with troublesome intergroup problems? The payoff is primarily discussed in qualitative terms, and we feel this is appropriate. It does not mean that quantitative judgments are not possible, but to insist on reducing the human condition to numbers, or to believe that it can be done, is madness.

The role of the person introducing change (whether he is staff or in the line) is a very tough, difficult, and, at times, lonely one. He personally must be as congruent as he can with the values we have discussed. If people perceive him to be outside the system of change, they should and will reject him. He must be willing and able to become involved as a person, not merely as the expert who will fix everybody else up. He, too, must be in process. This is rewarding, but also very difficult.

Introducing change into a social system almost always involves some level of resistance to that change. Accepting the values we have described means that one will not be fully satisfied with the here and now because the limits of man's potential have certainly not been reached. All we know for sure is that the potential is vast. Never accepting the status quo is a rather lonely position to take. In effect, as one of our colleagues has put it, you are constantly saying to yourself, "Fifty million Frenchmen are wrong!" From your own experience we know that this attitude can produce moments when one doubts one's sanity: "How come nobody else seems to feel the way I do, or to care about making things better, or to believe that it is possible to seek improvements?" Somehow, these moments must be worked through, courage must be drawn upon, and new actions must follow.

We are struck with and saddened by the large amounts of frustration, feelings of inadequacy, insecurity, and fear that seem to permeate groups of behavioral science practitioners when they meet for seminars or workshops. Belief in these values must lead to a bias towards optimism about the human condition. "Man does have the potential to create a better world, and I have the potential to contribute to that effort." But in addition to this bias towards optimism, there has to be a recognition of the fundamental fact that we will continuously have to deal with resistance to change, including resistances within ourselves. People are not standing in line outside our doors asking to be freed up, liberated, and upended. Cultures are not saying: "Change us, we can no longer cope, we are unstable." Commitment to trying to implement these values as well as we can is not commitment to an easy, safe existence. At times, we can be bone weary of confrontation, questioning, probing, and devil's-advocating. We can have delightful fantasies of copping out on the whole mess and living on some island. We can be fed up with and frightened by facing someone's anger when we are confronting him with what is going on around him. We can be worn out from the continuous effort to stretch ourselves as we try to move towards living these values to the fullest.

On the other hand, the rewards we experience can be precious, real, and profound. They can have important meaning for us individually, for those with whom we work, and for our organizations. Ultimately, what we stand for can make for a better world — and we deeply know that this is what keeps us going.

Notes

1. McGregor, D. M., *The Professional Manager.* New York, McGraw-Hill, 1967, p. 244.
2. Bennis, W. G., *Changing Organizations,* New York, McGraw-Hill, 1966, p. 4.
3. See p. 157.

PART THREE

Types of Management Systems

Just as the nature of organizational life is affected by external forces, it is also affected by the executive's conscious, and occasionally unconscious, motivation. Basic assumptions and attitudes held by executives and managers are acted upon and find expression in a variety of organizational designs and climates.

Part Three includes three typologies — contrasting differing sets of managerial assumptions about people, differing organizational systems, and differing constellations of managerial behavior.

In Selection 7, we return to the writings of Douglas McGregor — which served as a philosophic base for the Tannenbaum and Davis selection. The beliefs influencing the types of management systems applied in organizations were developed by McGregor under two sets of propositions — "Theory X" and "Theory Y." In his last published work,[1] McGregor clarified his meaning:

> Theory X and Theory Y are *not* managerial strategies. They are underlying beliefs about the nature of man that *influence* managers to adopt one strategy rather than another. In fact, depending upon other characteristics of the manager's view of reality and upon the particular situation in which he finds himself, a manager who holds the beliefs that I call Theory X could adopt a considerable array of strategies, some of which would be typically called "hard" and some of which would be called "soft."
>
> The same is true with respect to Theory Y. . . . The belief that man is essentially like a machine that is set into action by the application of external forces differs in more than degree from the belief that man is an organic system whose behavior is affected not only by external forces but by intrinsic ones. Theory X and Theory Y are not polar opposites; they do not lie at extremes of a scale. They are simply *different* cosmologies.

It is clear from McGregor (Selection 7) that he was influenced by Abraham Maslow, whose early writing on the "hierarchy of needs" is included in Part Four. McGregor may have been influ-

[1] Douglas McGregor in *The Professional Manager,* ed. Warren G. Bennis and Caroline McGregor, McGraw-Hill Book Company, 1967, pp. 79–80.

enced also by the theory of human needs set forth by Walter Langer.[2]

Whereas McGregor conceptualizes basic human values as the foundation for the type of management system in operation, we find Burns and Stalker (Selection 8) outlining the type of organization system which might be most adaptable under different rates of technical and market change. They present two contrasting forms of management systems — the mechanistic system and the organic system. Their underlying proposition is that either form may be "rational" for the organization. Thus, they contend there is no universally correct management system. Rather, the mechanistic management system may be appropriate to stable conditions; the organic management system may be more appropriate to changing conditions. However, since "change" is becoming the rule rather than the exception, the logical prescription may be that organizations should be shifting toward organic systems.

The third article in Part Three emphasizes the historical evolution of managerial practice in terms of four models of organizational behavior. Davis (Selection 9) asserts that each successive model serves needs of an increasingly high order and is increasingly democratic in character. These relationships may be shown schematically as follows:

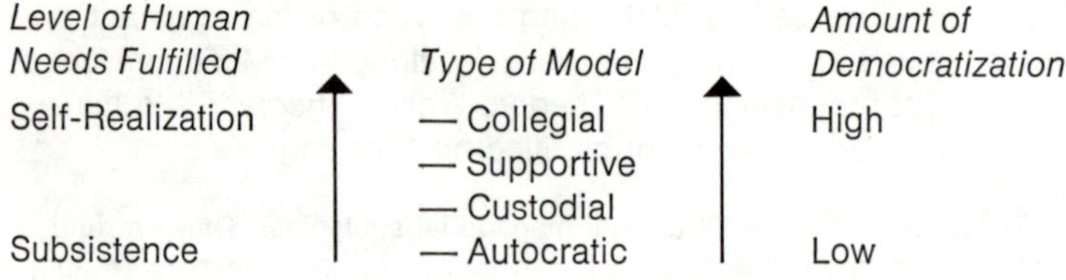

Davis concludes that the transition toward more democratic models of organizational behavior is required both by the nature of technology and market change (as discussed by Burns and Stalker), and the nature of the need structure of humans (as discussed by McGregor).

[2] See Walter C. Langer, *Psychology and Human Living,* Appleton-Century-Crofts, 1943.

7

The Human Side of Enterprise

Douglas Murray McGregor
Massachusetts Institute of Technology

It has become trite to say that industry has the fundamental know-how to utilize physical science and technology for the material benefit of mankind, and that we must now learn how to utilize the social sciences to make our human organizations truly effective.

To a degree, the social sciences today are in a position like that of the physical sciences with respect to atomic energy in the thirties. We know that past conceptions of the nature of man are inadequate and, in many ways, incorrect. We are becoming quite certain that, under proper conditions, unimagined resources of creative human energy could become available within the organizational setting.

We cannot tell industrial management how to apply this new knowledge in simple, economic ways. We know it will require years of exploration, much costly development, research, and a substantial amount of creative imagination on the part of management to discover how to apply this growing knowledge to the organization of human effort in industry.

Management's Task: The Conventional View

The conventional conception of management's task in harnessing human energy to organizational requirements can be stated broadly in terms of three propositions. In order to avoid the complications introduced by a label, let us call this set of propositions "Theory X":

1. Management is responsible for organizing the elements of productive enterprise — money, materials, equipment, people — in the interest of economic ends.
2. With respect to people, this is a process of directing their efforts, motivating them, controlling their actions, modifying their behavior to fit the needs of the organization.
3. Without this active intervention by management, people would be passive — even resistant — to organizational needs. They must therefore be

Reprinted by permission of the publisher from *Management Review*, Nov. 1957, pp. 22–28, 88–92.

persuaded, rewarded, punished, controlled — their activities must be directed. This is management's task. We often sum it up by saying that management consists of getting things done through other people.

4. The average man is by nature indolent — he works as little as possible.
5. He lacks ambition, dislikes responsibility, prefers to be led.
6. He is inherently self-centered, indifferent to organizational needs.
7. He is by nature resistant to change.
8. He is gullible, not very bright, the ready dupe of the charlatan and the demagogue.

The human side of economic enterprise today is fashioned from propositions and beliefs such as these. Conventional organization structures and managerial policies, practices, and programs reflect these assumptions.

In accomplishing its task — with these assumptions as guides — management has conceived of a range of possibilities.

At one extreme, management can be "hard" or "strong." The methods for directing behavior involve coercion and threat (usually disguised), close supervision, tight controls over behavior. At the other extreme, management can be "soft" or "weak." The methods for directing behavior involve being permissive, satisfying people's demands, achieving harmony. Then they will be tractable, accept direction.

This range has been fairly completely explored during the past half century, and management has learned some things from the exploration. There are difficulties in the "hard" approach. Force breeds counter-forces: restriction of output, antagonism, militant unionism, subtle but effective sabotage of management objectives. This "hard" approach is especially difficult during times of full employment.

There are also difficulties in the "soft" approach. It leads frequently to the abdication of management — to harmony, perhaps, but to indifferent performance. People take advantage of the soft approach. They continually expect more, but they give less and less.

Currently, the popular theme is "firm but fair." This is an attempt to gain the advantages of both the hard and the soft approaches. It is reminiscent of Teddy Roosevelt's "speak softly and carry a big stick."

Is the Conventional View Correct?

The findings which are beginning to emerge from the social sciences challenge this whole set of beliefs about man and human nature and about the task of management. The evidence is far from conclusive, certainly, but it is suggestive. It comes from the laboratory, the clinic, the schoolroom, the home, and even to a limited extent from industry itself.

The social scientist does not deny that human behavior in industrial organization today is approximately what management perceives it to be.

He has, in fact, observed it and studied it fairly extensively. But he is pretty sure that this behavior is *not* a consequence of man's inherent nature. It is a consequence rather of the nature of industrial organizations, of management philosophy, policy, and practice. The conventional approach of Theory X is based on mistaken notions of what is cause and what is effect.

Perhaps the best way to indicate why the conventional approach of management is inadequate is to consider the subject of motivation.

Physiological Needs

Man is a wanting animal — as soon as one of his needs is satisfied, another appears in its place. This process is unending. It continues from birth to death.

Man's needs are organized in a series of levels — a hierarchy of importance. At the lowest level, but pre-eminent in importance when they are thwarted, are his *physiological needs.* Man lives for bread alone, when there is no bread. Unless the circumstances are unusual, his needs for love, for status, for recognition are inoperative when his stomach has been empty for a while. But when he eats regularly and adequately, hunger ceases to be an important motivation. The same is true of the other physiological needs of man — for rest, exercise, shelter, protection from the elements.

A satisfied need is not a motivator of behavior! This is a fact of profound significance that is regularly ignored in the conventional approach to the management of people. Consider your own need for air: Except as you are deprived of it, it has no appreciable motivating effect upon your behavior.

Safety Needs

When the physiological needs are reasonably satisfied, needs at the next higher level begin to dominate man's behavior — to motivate him. These are called *safety needs.* They are needs for protection against danger, threat, deprivation. Some people mistakenly refer to these as needs for security. However, unless man is in a dependent relationship where he fears arbitrary deprivation, he does not demand security. The need is for the "fairest possible break." When he is confident of this, he is more than willing to take risks. But when he feels threatened or dependent, his greatest need is for guarantees, for protection, for security.

The fact needs little emphasis that, since every industrial employee is in a dependent relationship, safety needs may assume considerable importance. Arbitrary management actions, behavior which arouses uncertainty with respect to continued employment or which reflects favoritism or discrimination, unpredictable administration of policy — these can be powerful motivators of the safety needs in the employment relationship *at every level,* from worker to vice president.

Social Needs

When man's physiological needs are satisfied and he is no longer fearful about his physical welfare, his *social needs* become important motivators of his behavior — needs for belonging, for association, for acceptance by his fellows, for giving and receiving friendship and love.

Management knows today of the existence of these needs, but it often assumes quite wrongly that they represent a threat to the organization. Many studies have demonstrated that the tightly knit, cohesive work group may, under proper conditions, be far more effective than an equal number of separate individuals in achieving organizational goals.

Yet management, fearing group hostility to its own objectives, often goes to considerable lengths to control and direct human efforts in ways that are inimical to the natural "groupiness" of human beings. When man's social needs — and perhaps his safety needs, too — are thus thwarted, he behaves in ways which tend to defeat organizational objectives. He becomes resistant, antagonistic, uncooperative. But this behavior is a consequence, not a cause.

Ego Needs

Above the social needs — in the sense that they do not become motivators until lower needs are reasonably satisfied — are the needs of greatest significance to management and to man himself. They are the *egoistic needs,* and they are two kinds:

1. Those needs that relate to one's self-esteem — needs for self-confidence, for independence, for achievement, for competence, for knowledge.
2. Those needs that relate to one's reputation — needs for status, for recognition, for appreciation, for the deserved respect of one's fellows.

Unlike the lower needs, these are rarely satisfied; man seeks indefinitely for more satisfaction of these needs once they have become important to him. But they do not appear in any significant way until physiological, safety, and social needs are all reasonably satisfied.

The typical industrial organization offers few opportunities for the satisfaction of these egoistic needs to people at lower levels in the hierarchy. The conventional methods of organizing work, particularly in mass-production industries, give little heed to these aspects of human motivation. If the practices of scientific management were deliberately calculated to thwart these needs, they could hardly accomplish this purpose better they they do.

Self-Fulfillment Needs

Finally — a capstone, as it were, on the hierarchy of man's needs — there are what we may call the *needs for self-fulfillment.* These are the needs for realizing one's own potentialities, for continued self-development, for being creative in the broadest sense of that term.

It is clear that the conditions of modern life give only limited opportunity for these relatively weak needs to obtain expression. The deprivation most people experience with respect to other lower-level needs diverts their energies into the struggle to satisfy *those* needs, and the needs for self-fulfillment remain dormant.

Management and Motivation

We recognize readily enough that a man suffering from a severe dietary deficiency is sick. The deprivation of physiological needs has behavioral consequences. The same is true — although less well recognized — of deprivation of higher-level needs. The man whose needs for safety, association, independence, or status are thwarted is sick just as surely as the man who has rickets. And his sickness will have behavioral consequences. We will be mistaken if we attribute his resultant passivity, his hostility, his refusal to accept responsibility to his inherent "human nature." These forms of behavior are *symptoms* of illness — of deprivation of his social and egoistic needs.

The man whose lower-level needs are satisfied is not motivated to satisfy those needs any longer. For practical purposes they exist no longer. Management often asks, "Why aren't people more productive? We pay good wages, provide good working conditions, have excellent fringe benefits and steady employment. Yet people do not seem to be willing to put forth more than minimum effort."

The fact that management has provided for these physiological and safety needs has shifted the motivational emphasis to the social and perhaps to the egoistic needs. Unless there are opportunities *at work* to satisfy these higher-level needs, people will be deprived; and their behavior will reflect this deprivation. Under such conditions, if management continues to focus its attention on physiological needs, its efforts are bound to be ineffective.

People *will* make insistent demands for more money under these conditions. It becomes more important than ever to buy the material goods and services which can provide limited satisfaction of the thwarted needs. Although money has only limited value in satisfying many higher-level needs, it can become the focus of interest if it is the *only* means available.

The Carrot-and-Stick Approach

The carrot-and-stick theory of motivation (like Newtonian physical theory) works reasonably well under certain circumstances. The *means* for satisfying man's physiological and (within limits) his safety needs can be provided or withheld by management. Employment itself is such a means, and so are wages, working conditions, and benefits. By these means the individual can be controlled so long as he is struggling for subsistence.

But the carrot-and-stick theory does not work at all once man has reached an adequate subsistence level and is motivated primarily by higher needs. Management cannot provide a man with self-respect, or with the respect of his fellows, or with the satisfaction of needs for self-fulfillment. It can create such conditions that he is encouraged and enabled to seek such satisfactions for *himself,* or it can thwart him by failing to create those conditions.

But this creation of conditions is not "control." It is not a good device for directing behavior. And so management finds itself in an odd position. The high standard of living created by our modern technological know-how provides quite adequately for the satisfaction of physiological and safety needs. The only significant exception is where management practices have not created confidence in a "fair break" — and thus where safety needs are thwarted. But by making possible the satisfaction of low-level needs, management has deprived itself of the ability to use as motivators the devices on which conventional theory has taught it to rely — rewards, promises, incentives, or threats and other coercive devices.

The philosophy of management by direction and control — *regardless of whether it is hard or soft* — is inadequate to motivate because the human needs on which this approach relies are today unimportant motivators of behavior. Direction and control are essentially useless in motivating people whose important needs are social and egoistic. Both the hard and the soft approach fail today because they are simply irrelevant to the situation.

People, deprived of opportunities to satisfy at work the needs which are now important to them, behave exactly as we might predict — with indolence, passivity, resistance to change, lack of responsibility, willingness to follow the demagogue, unreasonable demands for economic benefits. It would seem that we are caught in a web of our own weaving.

A New Theory of Management

For these and many other reasons, we require a different theory of the task of managing people based on more adequate assumptions about human nature and human motivation. I am going to be so bold as to suggest the broad dimensions of such a theory. Call it "Theory Y," if you will.

1. Management is responsible for organizing the elements of productive enterprise — money, materials, equipment, people — in the interest of economic ends.
2. People are *not* by nature passive or resistant to organizational needs. They have become so as a result of experience in organizations.
3. The motivation, the potential for development, the capacity for assuming responsibility, the readiness to direct behavior toward organizational goals are all present in people. Management does not put them there. It is a responsibility of management to make it possible for people to recognize and develop these human characteristics for themselves.
4. The essential task of management is to arrange organizational conditions and methods of operation so that people can achieve their own goals *best* by directing *their own* efforts toward organizational objectives.

This is a process primarily of creating opportunities, releasing potential, removing obstacles, encouraging growth, providing guidance. It is what Peter Drucker has called "management by objectives" in contrast to "management by control." It does *not* involve the abdication of management, the absence of leadership, the lowering of standards, or the other characteristics usually associated with the "soft" approach under Theory X.

Some Difficulties

It is no more possible to create an organization today which will be a full, effective application of this theory than it was to build an atomic power plant in 1945. There are many formidable obstacles to overcome.

The conditions imposed by conventional organization theory and by the approach of scientific management for the past half century have tied men to limited jobs which do not utilize their capabilities, have discouraged the acceptance of responsibility, have encouraged passivity, have eliminated meaning from work. Man's habits, attitudes, expectations — his whole conception of membership in an industrial organization — have been conditioned by his experience under these circumstances.

People today are accustomed to being directed, manipulated, controlled in industrial organizations and to finding satisfaction for their social, egoistic, and self-fulfillment needs away from the job. This is true of much of management as well as of workers. Genuine "industrial citizenship" — to borrow again a term from Drucker — is a remote and unrealistic idea, the meaning of which has not even been considered by most members of industrial organizations.

Another way of saying this is that Theory X places exclusive reliance upon external control of human behavior, while Theory Y relies heavily on self-control and self-direction. It is worth noting that this difference is the difference between treating people as children and treating them as mature adults. After generations of the former, we cannot expect to shift to the latter overnight.

Steps in the Right Direction

Before we are overwhelmed by the obstacles, let us remember that the application of theory is always slow. Progress is usually achieved in small steps. Some innovative ideas which are entirely consistent with Theory Y are today being applied with some success.

Decentralization and Delegation

These are ways of freeing people from the too-close control of conventional organization, giving them a degree of freedom to direct their own activities, to assume responsibility, and, importantly, to satisfy their egoistic needs. In this connection, the flat organization of Sears, Roebuck and Company provides an interesting example. It forces "management by objectives," since it enlarges the number of people reporting to a manager until he cannot direct and control them in the conventional manner.

Job Enlargement

This concept, pioneered by I.B.M. and Detroit Edison, is quite consistent with Theory Y. It encourages the acceptance of responsibility at the bottom of the organization; it provides opportunities for satisfying social and egoistic needs. In fact, the reorganization of work at the factory level offers one of the more challenging opportunities for innovation consistent with Theory Y.

Participation and Consultative Management

Under proper conditions, participation and consultative management provide encouragement to people to direct their creative energies toward organizational objectives, give them some voice in decisions that affect them, provide significant opportunities for the satisfaction of social and egoistic needs. The Scanlon Plan is the outstanding embodiment of these ideas in practice.

Performance Appraisal

Even a cursory examination of conventional programs of performance appraisal within the ranks of management will reveal how completely consistent they are with Theory X. In fact, most such programs tend to treat the individual as though he were a product under inspection on the assembly line.

A few companies — among them General Mills, Ansul Chemical, and General Electric — have been experimenting with approaches which involve the individual in setting "targets" or objectives *for himself* and in a *self*-evaluation of performance semiannually or annually. Of course, the superior plays an important leadership role in this process — one, in fact, which demands substantially more competence than the conventional approach. The role is, however, considerably more congenial to many managers than the role of "judge" or "inspector" which is usually forced upon them. Above all, the individual is encouraged to take a greater responsibility for planning and appraising his own contribution to organizational objectives, and the accompanying effects on egoistic and self-fulfillment needs are substantial.

Applying the Ideas

The not infrequent failure of such ideas as these to work as well as expected is often attributable to the fact that a management has "bought the idea" but applied it within the framework of Theory X and its assumptions.

Delegation is not an effective way of exercising management by control. Participation becomes a farce when it is applied as a sales gimmick or a device for kidding people into thinking they are important. Only the management that has confidence in human capacities and is itself directed toward organizational objectives rather than toward the preservation of personal power can grasp the implications of this emerging theory. Such management will find and apply successfully other innovative ideas as we move slowly toward the full implementation of a theory like Y.

The Human Side of Enterprise

It is quite possible for us to realize substantial improvements in the effectiveness of industrial organizations during the next decade or two. The social sciences can contribute much to such developments; we are only beginning to grasp the implications of the growing body of knowledge in these fields. But if this conviction is to become a reality instead of a pious hope, we will need to view the process much as we view the process of releasing the energy of the atom for constructive human ends — as a slow, costly, sometimes discouraging approach toward a goal which would seem to many to be quite unrealistic.

The ingenuity and the perseverance of industrial management in the pursuit of economic ends have changed many scientific and technological dreams into commonplace realities. It is now becoming clear that the application of these same talents to the human side of enterprise will not only enhance substantially these materialistic achievements, but will bring us one step closer to "the good society."

8

Mechanistic and Organic Systems

Tom Burns
University of Edinburgh

G. M. Stalker
University of Edinburgh

We are now at the point at which we may set down the outline of the two management systems which represent for us the two polar extremities of the forms which such systems can take when they are adapted to a specific rate of technical and commercial change. The case we have tried to establish from the literature, as from our research experience exhibited in the last chapter, is that the different forms assumed by a working organization do exist objectively and are not merely interpretations offered by observers of different schools.

Both types represent a "rational" form of organization, in that they may both, in our experience, be explicitly and deliberately created and maintained to exploit the human resources of a concern in the most efficient manner feasible in the circumstances of the concern. Not surprisingly, however, each exhibits characteristics which have been hitherto associated with different kinds of interpretation. For it is our contention that empirical findings have usually been classified according to sociological ideology rather than according to the functional specificity of the working organization to its task and the conditions confronting it.

We have tried to argue that these are two formally contrasted forms of management system. These we shall call the mechanistic and organic forms.

A *mechanistic* management system is appropriate to stable conditions. It is characterized by:

(a) the specialized differentiation of functional tasks into which the problems and tasks facing the concern as a whole are broken down;
(b) the abstract nature of each individual task, which is pursued with techniques and purposes more or less distinct from those of the concern as a whole; i.e., the functionaries tend to pursue the technical improvement of means, rather than the accomplishment of the ends of the concern;

Taken and adapted from Tom Burns and G. M. Stalker, *The Management of Innovation,* London: Tavistock Publications, 1961, pp. 119–125. Used by permission.

(c) the reconciliation, for each level in the hierarchy, of these distinct performances by the immediate superiors, who are also, in turn, responsible for seeing that each is relevant in his own special part of the main task.
(d) the precise definition of rights and obligations and technical methods attached to each functional role;
(e) the translation of rights and obligations and methods into the responsibilities of a functional position;
(f) hierarchic structure of control, authority and communication;
(g) a reinforcement of the hierarchic structure by the location of knowledge of actualities exclusively at the top of the hierarchy, where the final reconciliation of distinct tasks and assessment of relevance is made;[1]
(h) a tendency for interaction between members of the concern to be vertical, i.e., between superior and subordinate;
(i) a tendency for operations and working behaviour to be governed by the instructions and decisions issued by superiors;
(j) insistence on loyalty to the concern and obedience to superiors as a condition of membership;
(k) a greater importance and prestige attaching to internal (local) than to general (cosmopolitan) knowledge, experience, and skill.

The *organic* form is appropriate to changing conditions which give rise constantly to fresh problems and unforeseen requirements for action which cannot be broken down or distributed automatically arising from the functional roles defined within a hierarchic structure. It is characterized by:

(a) the contributive nature of special knowledge and experience to the common task of the concern;
(b) the "realistic" nature of the individual task, which is seen as set by the total situation of the concern;
(c) the adjustment and continual re-definition of individual tasks through interaction with others;
(d) the shedding of "responsibility" as a limited field of rights, obligations and methods. (Problems may not be posted upwards, downwards or sideways as being someone else's responsibility);
(e) the spread of commitment to the concern beyond any technical definition;
(f) a network structure of control, authority, and communication. The sanctions which apply to the individual's conduct in his working role derive more from presumed community of interest with the rest of the working organization in the survival and growth of the firm, and less from a contractual relationship between himself and a non-personal corporation, represented for him by an immediate superior;
(g) omniscience no longer imputed to the head of the concern; knowledge about the technical or commercial nature of the here and now task may

be located anywhere in the network; this location becoming the *ad hoc* centre of control authority and communication;

(h) a lateral rather than a vertical direction of communication through the organization, communication between people of different rank, also, resembling consultation rather than command;

(i) a content of communication which consists of information and advice rather than instructions and decisions;

(j) commitment to the concern's tasks and to the "technological ethos" of material progress and expansion is more highly valued than loyalty and obedience;

(k) importance and prestige attach to affiliations and expertise valid in the industrial and technical and commercial milieux external to the firm.

One important corollary to be attached to this account is that while organic systems are not hierarchic in the same sense as are mechanistic, they remain stratified. Positions are differentiated according to seniority— i.e., greater expertise. The lead in joint decisions is frequently taken by seniors, but it is an essential presumption of the organic system that the lead, i.e. "authority," is taken by whoever shows himself most informed and capable, i.e., the "best authority." The location of authority is settled by consensus.

A second observation is that the area of commitment to the concern— the extent to which the individual yields himself as a resource to be used by the working organization—is far more extensive in organic than in mechanistic systems. Commitment, in fact, is expected to approach that of the professional scientist to his work, and frequently does. One further consequence of this is that it becomes far less feasible to distinguish "informal" from "formal" organization.

Thirdly, the emptying out of significance from the hierarchic command system, by which co-operation is ensured and which serves to monitor the working organization under a mechanistic system, is countered by the development of shared beliefs about the values and goals of the concern. The growth and accretion of institutionalized values, beliefs, and conduct, in the form of commitments, ideology, and manners, around an image of the concern in its industrial and commercial setting make good the loss of formal structure.

Finally, the two forms of system represent a polarity, not a dichotomy; there are, as we have tried to show, intermediate stages between the extremities empirically known to us. Also, the relation of one form to the other is elastic, so that a concern oscillating between relative stability and relative change may also oscillate between the two forms. A concern may (and frequently does) operate with a management system which includes both types.

The organic form, by departing from the familiar clarity and fixity of the hierarchic structure, is often experienced by the individual manager as an uneasy, embarrassed, or chronically anxious quest for knowledge about what he should be doing, or what is expected of him, and similar apprehensiveness about what others are doing. Indeed, as we shall see later, this kind of response is necessary if the organic form of organization is to work effectively. Understandably, such anxiety finds expression in resentment when the apparent confusion besetting him is not explained. In these situations, all managers some of the time, and many managers all the time, yearn for more definition and structure.

On the other hand, some managers recognize a rationale of non-definition, a reasoned basis for the practice of those successful firms in which designation of status, function, and line of responsibility and authority has been vague or even avoided.

The desire for more definition is often in effect a wish to have the limits of one's task more neatly defined — to know what and when one doesn't have to bother about as much as to know what one does have to. It follows that the more definition is given, the more omniscient the management must be, so that no functions are left wholly or partly undischarged, no person is overburdened with undelegated responsibility, or left without the authority to do his job properly. To do this, to have all the separate functions attached to individual roles fitting together and comprehensively, to have communication between persons constantly maintained on a level adequate to the needs of each functional role, requires rules or traditions of behaviour proved over a long time and an equally fixed, stable task. The omniscience which may then be credited to the head of the concern is expressed throughout its body through the lines of command extending in a clear, explicitly titled hierarchy of officers and subordinates.

The whole mechanistic form is instinct with this twofold principle of definition and dependence which acts as the frame within which action is conceived and carried out. It works, unconsciously, almost in the smallest minutiae of daily activity. "How late is late?" The answer to this question is not to be found in the rule book, but in the superior. Late is when the boss thinks it is late. Is he the kind of man who thinks 8.00 is the time, and 8.01 is late? Does he think that 8.15 is all right occasionally if it is not a regular thing? Does he think that everyone should be allowed a 5-minutes grace after 8.00 but after that they are late?

Settling questions about how a person's job is to be done in this way is nevertheless simple, direct, and economical of effort. We shall, in a later chapter, examine more fully the nature of the protection and freedom (in other respects than his job) which this affords the individual.

One other feature of mechanistic organization needs emphasis. It is a necessary condition of its operation that the individual "works on his own," functionally isolated; he "knows his job," he is "responsible for seeing it's done." He works at a job which is in a sense artificially abstracted from the realities of the situation the concern is dealing with, the accountant "dealing with the costs side," the works manager "pushing production," and so on. As this works out in practice, the rest of the organization becomes part of the problem situation the individual has to deal with in order to perform successfully; i.e., difficulties and problems arising from work or information which has been handed over the "responsibility barrier" between two jobs or departments are regarded as "really" the responsibility of the person from whom they were received. As a design engineer put it, "When you get designers handing over designs completely to production, it's their responsibility now. And you get tennis games played with the responsibility for anything that goes wrong. What happens is that you're constantly getting unsuspected faults arising from characteristics which you didn't think important in the design. If you get to hear of these through a sales person, or a production person, or somebody to whom the design was handed over in the dim past, then, instead of being a design problem, it's an annoyance caused by that particular person, who can't do his own job — because you'd thought you were finished with that one, and you're on to something else now."

When the assumptions of the form of organization make for preoccupation with specialized tasks, the chances of career success, or of greater influence, depend rather on the relative importance which may be attached to each special function by the superior whose task it is to reconcile and control a number of them. And, indeed, to press the claims of one's job or department for a bigger share of the firm's resources is in many cases regarded as a mark of initiative, of effectiveness, and even of "loyalty to the firm's interests." The state of affairs thus engendered squares with the role of the superior, the man who can see the wood instead of just the trees, and gives it the reinforcement of the aloof detachment belonging to a court of appeal. The ordinary relationship prevailing between individual managers "in charge of" different functions is one of rivalry, a rivalry which may be rendered innocuous to the persons involved by personal friendship or the norms of sociability, but which turns discussion about the situations which constitute the real problems of the concern — how to make products more cheaply, how to sell more, how to allocate resources, whether to curtail activity in one sector, whether to risk expansion in another, and so on — into an arena of conflicting interests.

The distinctive feature of the second, organic system is the pervasiveness of the working organization as an institution. In concrete terms, this makes itself felt in a preparedness to combine with others in serving the general aims of the concern. Proportionately to the rate and extent of change, the less can the omniscience appropriate to command organizations be ascribed to the head of the organization; for executives, and even operatives, in a changing firm it is always theirs to reason why. Furthermore, the less definition can be given to status, roles, and modes of communication, the more do the activities of each member of the organization become determined by the real tasks of the firm as he sees them than by instruction and routine. The individual's job ceases to be self-contained; the only way in which "his" job can be done is by his participating continually with others in the solution of problems which are real to the firm, and put in a language of requirements and activities meaningful to them all. Such methods of working put much heavier demands on the individual. . . .

We have endeavoured to stress the appropriateness of each system to its own specific set of conditions. Equally, we desire to avoid the suggestion that either system is superior under all circumstances to the other. In particular, nothing in our experience justifies the assumption that mechanistic systems should be superseded by organic in conditions of stability.[2] The beginning of administrative wisdom is the awareness that there is no one optimum type of management system.

Notes

1. This functional attribute of the head of a concern often takes on a clearly expressive aspect. It is common enough for concerns to instruct all people with whom they deal to address correspondence to the firm (i.e., to its formal head) and for all outgoing letters and orders to be signed by the head of the concern. Similarly, the printed letter heading used by Government departments carries instructions for the replies to be addressed to the Secretary, etc. These instructions are not always taken seriously, either by members of the organization or their correspondents, but in one company this practice was insisted upon and was taken to somewhat unusual lengths; *all* correspondence was delivered to the managing director, who would thereafter distribute excerpts to members of the staff, synthesizing their replies into the letter of reply which he eventually sent. Telephone communication was also controlled by limiting the numbers of extensions, and by monitoring incoming and outgoing calls.

2. A recent instance of this assumption is contained in H. A. Shepard's paper addressed to the Symposium on the Direction of Research Establishments, 1956. "There is much evidence to suggest that the optimal use of human resources in industrial organizations requires a different set of conditions, assumptions, and skills from those traditionally present in industry. Over the past twenty-five years, some new orientations have emerged from organizational experiments, observations and inventions. The new orientations depart radically from doctrines associated with Scientific Management and traditional bureaucratic patterns.

"The central emphases in this development are as follows:

1. Wide participation in decision-making, rather than centralized decision-making.
2. The face-to-face group, rather than the individual, as the basic unit of organization.
3. Mutual confidence, rather than authority, as the integrative force in organization.
4. The supervisor as the agent for maintaining intragroup and intergroup communication, rather than as the agent of higher authority.
5. Growth of members of the organization to greater responsibility, rather than external control of the members' performance or their tasks."

9

Evolving Models of Organizational Behavior

KEITH DAVIS
Arizona State University

The affluent society of which John Kenneth Galbraith wrote a decade ago has become even more affluent.[1] There are many reasons for this sustained improvement in productivity, and some of them are advancing technology, available resources, improved education, and a favorable economic and social system. There is, however, another reason of key significance to all of us. That reason is management, specifically the capacity of managers to develop organizational systems which respond productively to the changing conditions of society. In recent years this has meant more complex administrative systems in order to challenge and motivate employees toward better teamwork. Improvement has been made by working smarter, not harder. An increasingly sophisticated knowledge of human behavior is required; consequently, theoretical models of organizational behavior have had to grow to absorb this new knowledge. It is these evolving models of organizational behavior which I wish to discuss; then I shall draw some conclusions about their use.

The significant point about models of organizational behavior is that the model which a manager holds normally determines his perception of the organizational world about him. It leads to certain assumptions about people and certain interpretations of events he encounters. The underlying model serves as an unconscious guide to each manager's behavior. He acts as he thinks. Since his acts do affect the quality of human relations and productivity in his department, he needs to be fully aware of the trends that are occurring. If he holds to an outmoded model, his success will be limited and his job will be harder, because he will not be able to work with his people as he should.

Similarly, the model of organizational behavior which predominates among the management of an organization will affect the success of that whole organization. And at a national level the model which prevails within a country will influence the productivity and economic development of that

Taken and adapted from *Academy of Management Journal,* Vol. 11, No. 1, March 1968, pp. 27–38. Used by permission.

nation. Models of organizational behavior are a significant variable in the life of all groups.

Many models of organizational behavior have appeared during the last 100 years, and four of them are significant and different enough to merit further discussion. These are the autocratic, custodial, supportive, and collegial models. In the order mentioned, the four models represent a historical evolution of management thought. The autocratic model predominated 75 years ago. In the 1920s and 1930s it yielded ground to the more successful custodial model. In this generation the supportive model is gaining approval. It predominates in many organizations, although the custodial model probably still prevails in the whole society. Meanwhile, a number of advanced organizations are experimenting with the collegial model.

The four models are not distinct in the sense that a manager or a firm uses one and only one of them. In a week — or even a day — a manager probably applies some of all four models. On the other hand, one model tends to predominate as his habitual way of working with his people, in such a way that it leads to a particular type of teamwork and behavioral climate among his group. Similarly, one model tends to dominate the life of a whole organization, but different parts therein may still be pursuing other models. The production department may take a custodial approach, while supportive ideas are being tried in the office, and collegial ideas are practiced in the research department. The point is that one model of organizational behavior is not an adequate label to describe all that happens in an organization, but it is a convenient way to distinguish one prevailing way of life from another. By comparing these four models, we can recognize certain important distinctions among them.

The Autocratic Model

The autocratic model has its roots deep in history, and certainly it became the prevailing model early in the industrial revolution. As shown in Figure 1, this model depends on power. Those who are in command must have the power to demand, "You do this — or else," meaning that an employee will be penalized if he does not follow orders. This model takes a threatening approach, depending on negative motivation backed by power.

In an autocratic environment the managerial orientataion is formal, official authority. Authority is the tool with which management works and the context in which it thinks, because it is the organizational means by which power is applied. This authority is delegated by right of command over the people to whom it applies. In this model, management implicitly assumes that it knows what is best and that it is the employee's obligation to follow orders without question or interpretation. Management assumes

FIGURE 1

Four Models of Organizational Behavior

	Autocratic	Custodial	Supportive	Collegial
Depends on:	Power	Economic resources	Leadership	Mutual contribution
Managerial orientation:	Authority	Material rewards	Support	Integration and teamwork
Employee orientation:	Obedience	Security	Performance	Responsibility
Employee psychological result:	Personal dependency	Organizational dependency	Participation	Self-discipline
Employee needs met:	Subsistence	Maintenance	Higher-order	Self-realization
Performance result:	Minimum	Passive cooperation	Awakened drives	Enthusiasm
Morale measure:	Compliance	Satisfaction	Motivation	Commitment to task and team

Source: Adapted from Keith Davis, **Human Relations at Work: The Dynamics of Organizational Behavior** (3rd ed.; New York: McGraw-Hill, 1967), p. 480.

that employees are passive and even resistant to organizational needs. They have to be persuaded and pushed into performance, and this is management's task. Management does the thinking; the employees obey the orders. This is the "Theory X" popularized by Douglas McGregor as the conventional view of management.[2] It has its roots in history and was made explicit by Frederick W. Taylor's concepts of scientific management. Though Taylor's writings show that he had worker interests at heart, he saw those interests served best by a manager who scientifically determined what a worker should do and then saw that he did it. The worker's role was to perform as he was ordered.

Under autocratic conditions an employee's orientation is obedience. He bends to the authority of a boss — not a manager. This role causes a psychological result which in this case is employee personal dependency on his boss whose power to hire, fire, and "perspire" him is almost absolute. The boss pays relatively low wages because he gets relatively less performance from the employee. Each employee must provide subsistence needs for himself and his family; so he reluctantly gives minimum performance, but he is not motivated to give much more than that. A few men give higher performance because of internal achievement drives, because they personally like their boss, because the boss is a "natural-born leader," or because of some other fortuitous reason; but most men give only minimum performance.

When an autocratic model of organizational behavior exists, the measure of an employee's morale is usually his compliance with rules and orders.

Compliance is unprotesting assent without enthusiasm. The compliant employee takes his orders and does not talk back.

Although modern observers have an inherent tendency to condemn the autocratic model of organizational behavior, it is a useful way to accomplish work. It has been successfully applied by the empire builders of the 1800s, efficiency engineers, scientific managers, factory foremen, and others. It helped to build great railroad systems, operate giant steel mills, and produce a dynamic industrial civilization in the early 1900s.

Actually the autocratic model exists in all shades of gray, rather than the extreme black usually presented. It has been a reasonably effective way of management when there is a "benevolent autocrat" who has a genuine interest in his employees and when the role expectation of employees is autocratic leadership.[3] But these results are usually only moderate ones lacking the full potential that is available, and they are reached at considerable human costs. In addition, as explained earlier, conditions change to require new behavioral models in order to remain effective.

As managers and academicians became familiar with limitations of the autocratic model, they began to ask, "Is there a better way? Now that we have brought organizational conditions this far along, can we build on what we have in order to move one step higher on the ladder of progress?" Note that their thought was not to throw out power as undesirable, because power is needed to maintain internal unity in organizations. Rather, their thought was to build upon the foundation which existed: "Is there a better way?"

The Custodial Model

Managers soon recognized that although a compliant employee did not talk back to his boss, he certainly "thought back"! There were many things he wanted to say to his boss, and sometimes he did say them when he quit or lost his temper. The employee inside was a seething mass of insecurity, frustrations, and aggr essions toward his boss. Since he could not vent these feelings directly, sometimes he went home and vented them on his wife, family, and neighbors; so the community did not gain much out of this relationship either.

It seemed rather obvious to progressive employers that there ought to be some way to develop employee satisfactions and adjustment during production — and in fact this approach just might cause more productivity! If the employee's insecurities, frustrations, and aggressions could be dispelled, he might feel more like working. At any rate the employer could sleep better, because his conscience would be clearer.

Development of the custodial model was aided by psychologists, industrial relations specialists, and economists. Psychologists were interested in employee satisfaction and adjustment. They felt that a satisfied employee would be a better employee, and the feeling was so strong that "a happy employee" became a mild obsession in some personnel offices. The industrial relations specialists and economists favored the custodial model as a means of building employee security and stability in employment. They gave strong support to a variety of fringe benefits and group plans for security.

The custodial model originally developed in the form of employee welfare programs offered by a few progressive employees, and in its worst form it became known as employer paternalism. During the depression of the 1930s emphasis changed to economic and social security and then shortly moved toward various labor plans for security and control. During and after World War II, the main focus was on specific fringe benefits. Employers, labor unions, and government developed elaborate programs for overseeing the needs of workers.

A successful custodial approach depends on economic resources, as shown in Figure 1. An organization must have economic wealth to provide economic security, pensions, and other fringe benefits. The resulting managerial orientation is toward economic or material rewards, which are designed to make employees respond as economic men. A reciprocal employee orientation tends to develop emphasizing security.

The custodial approach gradually leads to an organizational dependency by the employee. Rather than being dependent on his boss for his weekly bread, he now depends on large organizations for his security and welfare. Perhaps more accurately stated, an organizational dependency is added atop a reduced personal dependency on his boss. This approach effectively serves an employee's maintenance needs, as presented in Herzberg's motivation-maintenance model, but it does not strongly motivate an employee.[4] The result is a passive cooperation by the employee. He is pleased to have his security; but as he grows psychologically, he also seeks more challenge and autonomy.

The natural measure of morale which developed from a custodial model was employee satisfaction. If the employee was happy, contented, and adjusted to the group, then all was well. The happiness-oriented morale survey became a popular measure of success in many organizations.

Limitations of the Custodial Model

Since the custodial model is the one which most employers are currently moving away from, its limitations will be further examined. As with the autocratic model, the custodial model exists in various shades of gray, which means that some practices are more successful than others. In most cases, however, it becomes obvious to all concerned that most employees under custodial conditions do not produce anywhere near their capacities, nor are they motivated to grow to the greater capacities of which they are capable. Though employees may be happy, most of them really do not feel fulfilled or self-actualized.

The custodial model emphasizes economic resources and the security those resources will buy, rather than emphasizing employee performance. The employee becomes psychologically preoccupied with maintaining his security and benefits, rather than with production. As a result, he does not produce much more vigorously than under the old autocratic approach. Security and contentment are necessary for a person, but they are not themselves very strong motivators.

In addition, the fringe benefits and other devices of the custodial model are mostly off-the-job. They are not directly connected with performance. The employee has to be too sick to work or too old to work in order to receive these benefits. The system becomes one of public and private paternalism in which an employee sees little connection between his rewards and his job performance and personal growth; hence he is not motivated toward performance and growth. In fact, an overzealous effort to make the worker secure and happy leads to a brand of psychological paternalism no better than earlier economic paternalism. With the psychological variety, employee needs are dispensed from the personnel department, union hall, and government bureau, rather than the company store. But in either case, dependency remains, and as Ray E. Brown observes, "Men grow stronger on workouts than on handouts. It is in the nature of people to wrestle with a challenge and rest on a crutch . . . The great desire of man is to stand on his own, and his life is one great fight against dependency. Making the individual a ward of the organization will likely make him bitter instead of better."[5]

As viewed by William H. Whyte, the employee working under custodialism becomes an "organization man" who belongs to the organization and who has "left home, spiritually as well as physically, to take the vows of organizational life."[6]

As knowledge of human behavior advanced, deficiencies in the custodial model became quite evident, and people again started to ask, "Is there a better way?" The search for a better way is not a condemnation of the custodial model as a whole; however, it is a condemnation of the assumption that custodialism is "the final answer" — the one best way to work with people in organizations. An error in reasoning occurs when a person perceives that the custodial model is so desirable that there is no need to move beyond it to something better.

The Supportive Model

The supportive model of organizational behavior has gained currency during recent years as a result of a great deal of behavioral science research as well as favorable employer experience with it. The supportive model establishes a manager in the primary role of psychological support of his employees at work, rather than in a primary role of economic support (as in the custodial model) or "power over" (as in the autocratic model). A supportive approach was first suggested in the classical experiments of Mayo and Roethlisberger at Western Electric Company in the 1930s and 1940s. They showed that a small work group is more productive and satisfied when its members perceive that they are working in a supportive environment. This interpretation was expanded by the work of Edwin A. Fleishman with supervisory "consideration" in the 1940s[7] and that of Rensis Likert and his associates with the "employee-oriented supervisor" in the 1940s and 1950s.[8] In fact, the *coup de grace* to the custodial model's dominance was administered by Likert's research which showed that the happy employee is not necessarily the most productive employee.

Likert has expressed the supportive model as the '"principle of supportive relationships" in the following words: "The leadership and other processes of the organization must be such as to ensure a maximum probability that in all interactions and all relationships with the organization each member will, in the light of his background, values, and expectations, view the experience as supportive and one which builds and maintains his sense of personal worth and importance."[9]

The supportive model, shown in Figure 1, depends on leadership instead of power or economic resources. Through leadership, management provides a behavioral climate to help each employee grow and accomplish in the interests of the organization the things of which he is capable. The leader assumes that workers are not by nature passive and resistant to organizational needs, but that they are made so by an inadequate supportive climate at work. They will take responsibility, develop a drive to contribute, and improve themselves, if management will give them half a chance. Management's orientation, therefore, is to support the employee's performance.

Since performance is supported, the employee's orientation is toward it instead of mere obedience and security. He is responding to intrinsic motivations in his job situation. His psychological result is a feeling of participation and task involvement in the organization. When referring to his organization, he may occasionally say "we," instead of always saying "they." Since his higher-order needs are better challenged, he works with more awakened drives than he did under earlier models.

The difference between custodial and supportive models is illustrated by the fact that the morale measure of supportive management is the employee's level of motivation. This measure is significantly different from the satisfaction and happiness emphasized by the custodial model. An employee who has a supportive leader is motivated to work toward organizational objectives as a means of achieving his own goals. This approach is similar to McGregor's popular "Theory Y."

The supportive model is just as applicable to the climate for managers as for operating employees. One study reports that supportive managers usually led to high motivation among their subordinate managers. Among those managers who were low in motivation, only 8 per cent had supportive managers. Their managers were mostly autocratic.[10]

It is not essential for managers to accept every assumption of the supportive model in order to move toward it, because as more is learned about it, views will change. What is essential is that modern managers in business, unions, and government do not become locked into the custodial model. They need to abandon any view that the custodial model is the final answer, so that they will be free to look ahead to improvements which are fitting to their organization in their environment.

The supportive model is only one step upward on the ladder of progress. Though it is just now coming into dominance, some firms which have the proper conditions and managerial competence are already using a collegial model of organizational behavior, which offers further opportunities for improvement.

The Collegial Model

The collegial model is still evolving, but it is beginning to take shape. It has developed from recent behavioral science research, particularly that of Likert, Katz, Kahn, and others at the University of Michigan,[11] Herzberg with regard to maintenance and motivational factors,[12] and the work of a number of people in project management and matrix organization.[13] The collegial model readily adapts to the flexible, intellectual environment of scientific and professional organizations. Working in substantially unprogrammed activities which require effective teamwork, scientific and professional employees desire the autonomy which a collegial model permits, and they respond to it well.

The collegial model depends on management's building a feeling of mutual contribution among participants in the organization, as shown in Figure 1. Each employee feels that he is contributing something worthwhile and is needed and wanted. He feels that management and others are similarly contributing, so he accepts and respects their roles in the organization. Managers are seen as joint contributors rather than bosses.

The managerial orientation is toward teamwork which will provide an integration of all contributions. Management is more of an integrating power than a commanding power. The employee response to this situation is responsibility. He produces quality work not primarily because management tells him to do so or because the inspector will catch him if he does not, but because he feels inside himself the desire to do so for many reasons. The employee psychological result, therefore, is self-discipline. Feeling responsible, the employee disciplines himself for team performance in the same way that a football team member disciplines himself in training and in game performance.

In this kind of environment an employee normally should feel some degree of fulfillment and self-realization, although the amount will be modest in some situations. The result is job enthusiasm, because he finds in the job such Herzberg motivators as achievement, growth, intrinsic work fulfillment, and recognition. His morale will be measured by his commitment to his task and his team, because he will see these as instruments for his self-actualization.

Some Conclusions About Models of Organizational Behavior

The evolving nature of models of organizational behavior makes it evident that change is the normal condition of these models. As our understanding of human behavior increases or as new social conditions develop, our organizational behavior models are also likely to change. It is a grave mistake to assume that one particular model is a "best" model which will endure for the long run. This mistake was made by some old-time managers about the autocratic model and by some humanists about the custodial model, with the result that they became psychologically locked into these models and had difficulty altering their practices when conditions demanded it. Eventually the supportive model may also fall to limited use; and as further progress is made, even the collegial model is likely to be surpassed. There is no permanently "one best model" of organizational behavior, because what is best depends upon what is known about human behavior in whatever environment and priority of objectives exist at a particular time.

A second conclusion is that the models of organizational behavior which have developed seem to be sequentially related to man's psychological hierarchy of needs. As society has climbed higher on the need hierarchy, new models of organizational behavior have been developed to serve the higher-order needs that became paramount at the time. If Maslow's need hierarchy is used for comparison, the custodial model of organizational behavior is seen as an effort to serve man's second-level security needs.[14] It moved one step above the autocratic model which was reasonably serving man's subsistence needs, but was not effectively meeting his needs for security. Similarly the supportive model is an effort to meet employees' higher-level needs, such as affiliation and esteem, which the custodial model was unable to serve. The collegial model moves even higher toward service of man's need for self-actualization.

A number of persons have assumed that emphasis on one model of organizational behavior was an automatic rejection of other models, but the comparison with man's need hierarchy *suggests that each model is built upon the accomplishments of the other.* For example, adoption of a supportive approach does not mean abandonment of custodial practices which serve necessary employee security needs. What it does mean is that custodial practices are relegated to secondary emphasis, because employees have progressed up their need structure to a condition in which higher needs predominate. In other words, the supportive model is the appropriate model to use *because* subsistence and security needs are already reasonably met by a suitable power structure and security system. If a misdirected modern manager should abandon these basic organizational needs, the system would quickly revert to a quest for a workable power structure and security system in order to provide subsistence-maintenance needs for its people.

Each model of organizational behavior in a sense outmodes its predominance by gradually satisfying certain needs, thus opening up other needs which can be better served by a more advanced model. Thus each new model is built upon the success of its predecessor. The new model simply represents a more sophisticated way of maintaining earlier need satisfactions, while opening up the probability of satisfying still higher needs.

A third conclusion suggests that the present tendency toward more democratic models of organizational behavior will continue for the longer run. This tendency seems to be required by both the nature of technology and the need structure. Harbison and Myers, in a classical study of management throughout the industrial world, conclude that advancing industrialization leads to more advanced models of organizational behavior. Specifically, authoritarian management gives way to more constitutional and democratic-participative models of management. These developments are inherent in the system; that is, the more democratic models tend to be necessary in order to manage productively an advanced industrial system.[15] Slater and Bennis also conclude that more participative and democratic models of organizational behavior inherently develop with advancing industrialization. They believe that "democracy is inevitable," because it is the only system which can successfully cope with changing demands of contemporary civilization in both business and government.[16]

Both sets of authors accurately point out that in modern, complex organizations a top manager cannot be authoritarian in the traditional sense and remain efficient, because he cannot know all that is happening in his organization. He must depend on other centers of power nearer to operating problems. In addition, educated workers are not readily motivated toward creative and intellectual duties by traditional authoritarian orders. They require higher-order need satisfactions which newer models of organizational behavior provide. Thus there does appear to be some inherent necessity for more democratic forms of organization in advanced industrial systems.

A fourth and final conclusion is that, though one model may predominate as most appropriate for general use at any point in industrial history, some appropriate uses will remain for other models. Knowledge of human behavior and skills in applying that knowledge will vary among managers. Role expectations of employees will differ depending upon cultural history. Policies and ways of life will vary among organizations. Perhaps more important, task conditions will vary. Some jobs may require routine, low-skilled, highly programmed work which will be mostly determined by higher authority and provide mostly material rewards and security (autocratic and custodial conditions). Other jobs will be unprogrammed and intellectual, requiring teamwork and self-motivation, and responding best to supportive and collegial conditions. This use of different management practices with people according to the task they are performing is called "management according to task" by Leavitt.[17]

In the final analysis, each manager's behavior will be determined by his underlying theory of organizational behavior, so it is essential for him to understand the different results achieved by different models of organizational behavior. The model used will vary with the total human and task conditions surrounding the work. The long-run tendency will be toward more supportive and collegial models because they better serve the higher-level needs of employees.

Notes

1. John Kenneth Galbraith, *The Affluent Society* (Boston, Mass.: Houghton Mifflin, 1958).

2. Douglas McGregor, "The Human Side of Enterprise," in *Proceedings of the Fifth Anniversary Convocation of the School of Industrial Management* (Cambridge, Mass.: Massachusetts Institute of Technology, April 9, 1957). Theory X and Theory Y were later popularized in Douglas McGregor, *The Human Side of Enterprise* (New York: McGraw-Hill, 1960).

3. This viewpoint is competently presented in R. N. McMurry, "The Case for Benevolent Autocracy," *Harvard Business Review* (Jan.-Feb., 1958), pp. 82–90.

4. Frederick Herzberg, Bernard Mausner, and Barbara Synderman, *The Motivation to Work* (New York: John Wiley and Sons, 1959).

5. Ray E. Brown, *Judgment in Administration* (New York: McGraw-Hill, 1966), p. 75.

6. William H. Whyte, Jr., *The Organization Man* (New York: Simon and Schuster, 1956), p. 3.

7. An early report of this research is Edwin A. Fleishman, *"Leadership Climate" and Supervisory Behavior* (Columbus, Ohio: Personnel Research Board, Ohio State University, 1951).

8. There have been many publications by the Likert group at the Survey Research Center, University of Michigan. An early basic one is Daniel Katz *et. al.*, *Productivity, Supervision and Morale in an Office Situation* (Ann Arbor, Mich.: The University of Michigan Press, 1950).

9. Rensis Likert, *New Patterns of Management* (New York: McGraw-Hill, 1961), pp. 102–103. (Italics in original.)

10. M. Scott Myers, "Conditions for Manager Motivation," *Harvard Business Review* (Jan.-Feb., 1966), p. 1. This study covered 1,344 managers at Texas Instruments, Inc.

11. Likert describes a similar model as System 4 in Rensis Likert, *The Human*

Organization: Its Management and Value (New York: McGraw-Hill, 1967), pp. 3–11.

12. Herzberg *et. al., op. cit.*

13. For example, see Keith Davis, "Mutuality in Understanding of the Program Manager's Management Role," *IEEE Transactions on Engineering Management* (Dec., 1965), pp. 117–122.

14. A. H. Maslow, "A Theory of Human Motivation," *Psychological Review* (L, 1943), 370–396.

15. Frederick Harbison and Charles A. Meyers, *Management in the Industrial World: An International Analysis* (New York: McGraw-Hill, 1959), pp. 40–67. The authors also state on page 47, "The design of systems of authority is equally as important in the modern world as the development of technology."

16. Philip E. Slater and Warren G. Bennis, "Democracy Is Inevitable," *Harvard Business Review* (March-April, 1964), pp. 51–59.

17. Harold J. Leavitt, "Management According to Task: Organizational Differentiation," *Management International* (1962), No. 1, pp. 13–22.

PART FOUR

Leadership and Group Performance

Theory and research are demonstrating a multiplicity of leadership styles: various styles, with differing consequences, are produced by diverse forces. The question to be asked is "Under what circumstances is a particular style most effective?," rather than "What leadership style is most effective?"

Reddin (Selection 10) provides a synthesis of the empirical and conceptual literature on leadership style and discusses the possible consequences of such literature for organizational effectiveness. We feel one of his main contributions is the multiple-variable model for analyzing styles of leadership under different circumstances. His interpretation of the meaning of effective leadership is a forceful one; he also reviews the alternative viewpoints. It is useful to consider the probable effectiveness of the leadership styles described in terms of the types of management systems described in Part Three.

Fiedler (Selection 11) suggests that the optimal effectiveness of leadership might depend upon the intensity with which group members interact. He presents three types of groups in terms of the work relations among members — interacting, coacting, and counteracting groups — and finds that the major task of the leader differs with each group. Subsequently, he presents a "contingency model" which postulates that group performance will depend upon ". . . the appropriate matching of leadership style and the degree of favorableness of the group situation for the leader. . . ."[1]

[1] Fred E. Fiedler, *A Theory of Leadership Effectiveness,* McGraw-Hill Book Company, 1967, p. 151.

10

The 3-D Management Style Theory: A Typology Based on Task and Relationships Orientations

W. J. Reddin
University of New Brunswick

Trainers are currently showing great interest in the classification of the typical behavior of managers. This has also occupied the attention of political and administrative scientists, sociologists and psychologists for some years. It is widely recognized that such classifications may enable organizational, group, or even personal life to be better understood and changed.

Trainers, though, have special needs. They must have a classification or a cognitive map, that is as close to reality as possible. If they use one that is not, it will be seen as too gimmicky, unreal, too academic, too soft-nosed, or simply useless.

Figure 1 shows six managerial typologies, used to varying degrees, together with their apparent basis of classification.

The Two Underlying Variables

Speaking very generally, the underlying theoretical components of four of these six psychological typologies are two fundamental personality variables which might be called Task Orientation and Relationships Orientation. These two variables go under the names shown in Figure 2.

The importance of these two underlying variables is well grounded in empirical findings, in particular the Ohio State Leadership Studies, the Michigan Leadership Studies, and the work of Bales[2] at Harvard.

Ohio State Leadership Studies

The Ohio State Leadership Studies isolated two independent factors to describe management behavior. One is initiating structure and the other is consideration. As they are independent, a score on one factor may be com-

Reproduced by special permission from the April 1967 *Training and Development Journal*.

FIGURE 1

Psychological Managerial Typologies

Author	Basis of Classification	Types
Lewin - Lippitt - White[12]	Initiation Guidance	Democratic, Laissez-Faire, Autocratic
McGregor[14]	Assumptions About the Nature of Man	Theory "X," Theory "Y"
Jennings[11]	Power Impulse, Hierarchical Orientation, Order Impulse, et al.	Abdicrat, Bureaucrat, Autocrat, Democrat, Neurocrat, Executive
Blake - Mouton[3]	Concern for Production Concern for People	1,1; 1,9; 9,1; 5,5; 9,9
Raskin[18]	Factor Analysis	Leadership Skills, Hostile Self Seeking, Dependent - Exploited, Interpersonal Orderly
Carron[4]	Consideration Scores Structure Scores	Laissez-Faire, Democratic, Autocratic, Paternalistic

FIGURE 2

Two Underlying Variables

Author	Task Orientation	Relationships Orientation
Blake - Mouton	Concern for Production	Concern for People
McGregor	Theory "X"	Theory "Y"
Carron	Structure	Consideration
Lewin - Lippitt - White	Initiation	Guidance

bined with any score on the other. It appears that a high score on both tends to correlate best with effectiveness, but that some studies show that low scores on both may lead to effectiveness. In any case, a certain minimum amount of consideration appears to be critical.

A factor analytic study by Halpin and Winer,[10] part of the Ohio State Leadership Studies, suggests that most of the individual differences in leadership performance can be explained by positing these two variables. In their study of air-crew commanders they found that these two factors together accounted for 83 per cent of the differences in leader behavior.

Michigan Leadership Studies

The Michigan Leadership Studies, based on extensive interview work, produced a continuum with production-centered at one end and employee-

FIGURE 3

Research Support for Two Underlying Variables

	Task Orientation	Relationships Orientation
Ohio State	Structure	Consideration
Michigan	Production Centered	Employee Centered
Bales	Task Leadership	Socio-Emotional Leadership
Zelditch	Task Specialist	Maintenance Specialist

centered at the other. This continuum grew, in part, out of boys' club studies. On some dimensions, democratically-conducted boys' clubs did better than clubs led in an autocratic or laissez-faire manner. While there is a great deal of evidence that the employee-centered leadership is often effective, it is clear also that production-centered leadership is sometimes just as effective.

Bales' Studies

The studies of small groups at Harvard have derived two leadership types; the Task Leader and the Social-Emotional Leader. These appear to be independent leadership types. To be high on one does not correlate with being high on the other.

This task and relationship dichotomy is a widespread social phenomenon. Zelditch[21] studied role differentiation in the basic family unit in fifty-six societies. He found that, within the family, there was a characteristic differentiation into the task specialist and maintenance specialist roles. The male adult was typically the task specialist, the female adult, the maintenance specialist.

It seems then that many studies refer to similar underlying dimensions. While each study defines the dimension in its own way, and not all posit independence, they might reasonably be presented by the terms, Task Orientation and Relationships Orientation which appear to capture the common thread of meaning.

That task and relationships orientation are fundamental and independent measures of managerial performance has high face validity. What is there that cannot be said to be part of either the manager's job or the people who inhabit the manager's environment? Many studies such as Raskin[18] support these two measures as fundamental and independent.

Definitions which appear to be broad enough to incorporate the findings, orientations, and definitions, of the studies cited are:

Task Orientation is defined as the extent to which a manager is likely to direct his own and his subordinates' efforts toward goal attainment. Those with high task orientation tend to direct more than others through planning, communicating, informing, scheduling and introducing new ideas.

Relationships Orientation is defined as the extent to which a manager is likely to have highly personal job relationships characterized by mutual trust, respect for subordinates' ideas and consideration of their feelings. Those with high relationships or orientation have good rapport with other and good two-way communication.

These definitions relate closely to Structures (S) and Consideration (C) of the "Leadership Opinion Questionnaire" (Fleishman, 1951, 1953, 1957, 1960).[5, 6, 7, 8]

The two dimensions of the "Leadership Opinion Questionnaire" are independent (r = −.01) when several studies are considered together, although higher correlations (r = −.47) have been reported on individual studies.

The Non-Normative Styles

If these variables are treated as independent and continuous, the four type typology of Latent Non-Normative styles is obtained.

No claims can be made that any one of these four styles is more effective than the other. Attempts to consider "the manager" as a single, internally undifferentiated job function have proven consistently fruitless. It is now clear that management jobs vary widely in the behavior required for successful performance. Thus, while task and relationships orientation may be powerful personality factors, any particular combination is not, in itself, effective or otherwise. Some jobs, to be performed effectively, demand a high relationships orientation and low task orientation. Some require the opposite.

In the mid 1920's, E. K. Strong, Jr.[20] attempted to develop an "executive" scale for his vocational interest blank. The scale he attempted to develop did not meet the validity standards for the Strong Vocational Interest Blank and was not used in it. Instead he successfully developed scales for produc-

FIGURE 4

Latent Styles

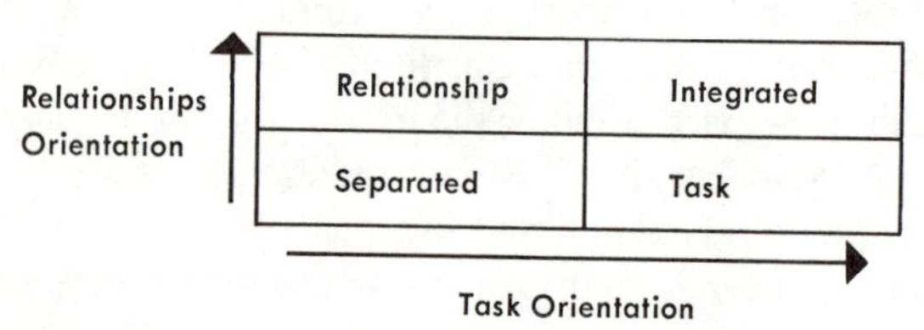

tion managers, sales managers, personnel managers and others. This supports the view that the positing of an ideal manager type may be less useful than positing the existence of several possible ideal types.

That management jobs are significantly different from one another is further supported by the finding that different jobs appear to demand or create different values in effective managers. Nash[17] points out that the economic scale of the Allport-Vernon Study of Values correlates with criteria of management effectiveness positively in a large mail order house to distinctly negatively related for public administrators (Mandell),[15] (Mandell & Adkins).[16]

An important finding (Fleishman & Peters)[9] was that the consideration and structure scores of managers in a manufacturing organization they investigated were not correlated with the effectiveness scores given by top management. Thus effectiveness, in this one organization at least, appears as an independent variable.

Anderson[1] reviewed forty-nine studies in which authoritarian and democratic leadership have been experimentally compared. He concluded that the evidence available demonstrates that neither authoritarian nor democratic leadership is consistently associated with better performance and that therefore the authoritarian — democratic construct provides an inadequate conception of leadership behavior.

All this does appear to be rather strong evidence that when speaking of managers, in general, it is inappropriate to consider that any one combination of task and relationships orientation is more likely to lead to effectiveness than another. It seems best then to treat as non-normative the four styles, created by dichotomizing the task and relationships variables.

Normative Style Typologies

Several typologies however do posit a single normatively good type. For example theory "Y" of McGregor and the 9,9 style of Blake. They each express a particular management philosophy. This arises in part because these and some other typologies are culture bound. Most of them, all North American, give some positive value to the permissive, democratic, human-relations approach. McGregor uses two types which might be simply labeled normatively as "Good" and "Bad." All this is nothing new. As Liu[13] points out, this "Good" and "Bad" classification was used in China in the 11th century and before. There were the Chun-Tzu (Virtuous Man) and Hsiao-Jen (Unworthy Person). The Confucian political philosophy used this dichotomy to classify bureaucrats:

> The virtuous ones are those loyal to the state or the sovereign, steadfast in their moral and political principles, cordial toward their colleagues, kind toward the common people, and dedicated to the Confucian ideal of government, which is to improve both the material welfare and moral well-being of society.

Liu points out that in the Chinese cultural environment, a moralistic basis was more important than a rational-legal basis for classification. This Chinese model, so obviously culture bound, leads us to look at current typologies to see to what extent they suffer from this. Obviously, most of them do.

The arguments for having a single normatively good type are many, though the notion itself is theoretically unsound. Many management style typologies are directed toward managers who appear to want to be told how to act; some of the typologies are used as identification models in the design of management development courses where having one type may facilitate the course design but not necessarily a manager's personal growth.

When the typologist bases his theoretical constructs on a particular work situation, he might be expected to posit an effective type that fits that situation. Unfortunately, however, there has been a tendency to call the particular typologies general typologies. Blake, from his work with top management in an industrial situation, has developed an effective type with a high task and relationships orientation. This may be correct for the top management in an industry in the U.S.A. but it may also be limited to it. Similarly, McGregor, in the context of his work in university administration, has produced a "Y" type with a very strong coaching supportive role. For teachers or university administrators who need not meet a payroll this type probably is the best one. It may not always be suited to industry.

The style of an effective manager in the army, the church, the civil service, and industry, may all be different. A style typology must recognize these differences if it is to be most useful. Positing a single effective style is inappropriate. A useful typology must allow that a variety of styles may be effective or ineffective depending on the situation.

Resolving The Normative Issue

If any style may be less-effective or more-effective, depending on circumstances, then each Non-Normative or Latent Style will have two behavioral counterparts, one less-effective and the other more-effective. Thus the four-style typology produced by dichotomizing the two underlying variables of task and relationships orientation, is expanded to a twelve style typology of four less-effective types, four latent types and four more-effective types.[19]

Here is a capsule description of the eight types:

Deserter

One who often displays his lack of interest in both task and relationships. He is ineffective not only because of his lack of interest but also because of his effect on morale. He may not only desert but may also hinder the performance of others through intervention or by withholding information.

FIGURE 5

The Twelve 3-D Styles

	No Orientation	Relationships Orientation	Task Orientation	Task and Relationships Orientation
Ineffective	Deserter	Missionary	Autocrat	Compromiser
Latent	Separated	Relationships	Task	Integrated
Effective	Bureaucrat	Developer	Benevolent Autocrat	Executive

Missionary

One who puts harmony and relationships above other considerations. He is ineffective because his desire to see himself and be seen as a "good person" prevents him from risking a disruption of relationships in order to get production.

Autocrat

One who puts the immediate task before all other considerations. He is ineffective in that he makes it obvious that he has no concern for relationships and has little confidence in others. While many may fear him they also dislike him and are thus motivated to work only when he applies direct pressure.

Compromiser

One who recognizes the advantages of being oriented to both task and relationships but who is incapable or unwilling to make sound decisions. Ambivalence and compromise are his stock-in-trade. The strongest influence in his decision making is the most recent or heaviest pressure. He tries to minimize immediate problems rather than maximize long term production. He attempts to keep those people who can influence his career as happy as possible.

Bureaucrat

One who is not really interested in either task or relationships but who, by simply following the rules, does not make this too obvious and thus does not let it affect morale. He is effective in that he follows the rules and maintains a mask of interest.

Developer

One who places implicit trust in people. He sees his job as primarily concerned with developing the talents of others and of providing a work atmosphere conducive to maximizing individual satisfaction and motivation. He is effective in that the work environment he creates is conducive to his

FIGURE 6

3-D Theory

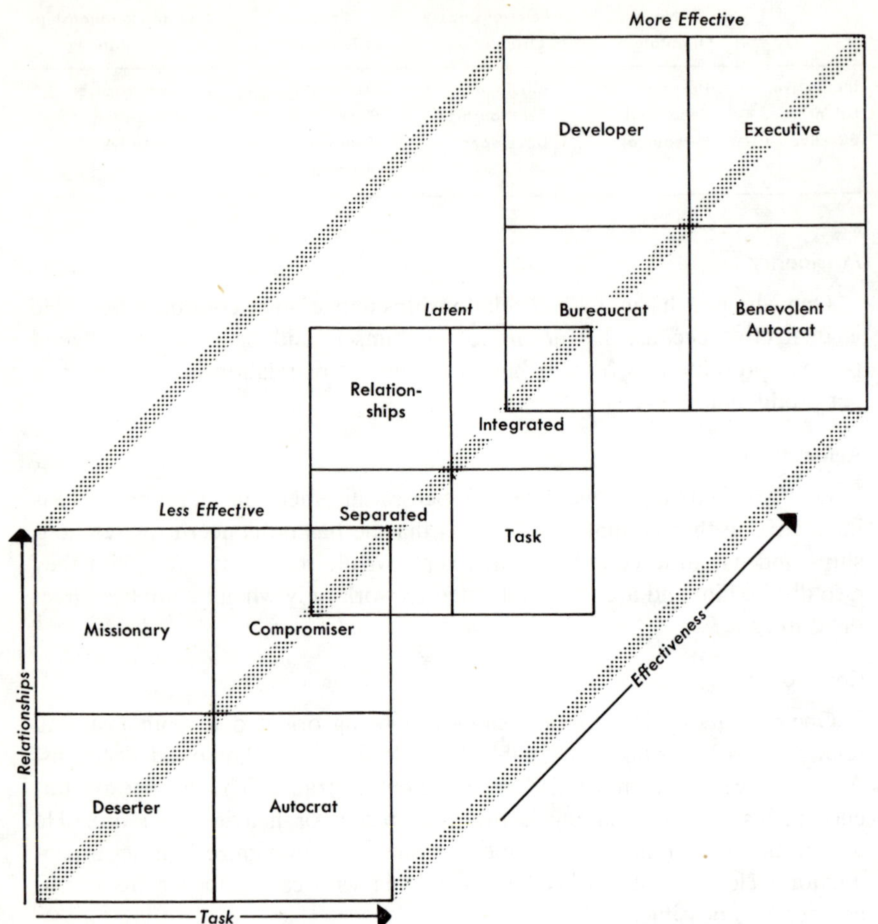

subordinates developing commitment to both himself and the job. While successful in obtaining high production, his high relationships orientation would on occasions lead him to put the personal development of others before short or long run production, even though this personal development may be unrelated to the job and the development of successors to his position.

Benevolent Autocrat

One who places implicit trust in himself and is concerned with both the immediate and long run task. He is effective in that he has a skill in inducing others to do what he wants them to do without creating enough resentment so that production might drop. He creates, with some skill, an environment which minimizes aggression toward him and which maximizes obedience to his commands.

Executive

One who sees his job as effectively maximizing the effort of others in relationship to the short and long run task. He sets high standards for production and performance and recognizes that because of individual differences and expectations that he will have to treat everyone differently. He is effective in that his commitment to both task and relationships is evident to all. This acts as a powerful motivator. His effectiveness in obtaining results with both of these dimensions also leads naturally to optimum production.

Effectiveness

The essential difference between less-effective types and more-effective types is often expressed in terms of the qualities a manager possesses. When a single effective type is posited, this amounts to a return to the trait theory of leadership. A better explanation of effectiveness would appear to lay in the extent to which a manager's style, his combination of task and relationships orientation, fits the style demands of the situation he is in. Five elements compose the style demands. Two pairs of elements are related.

Style Demands of Situation:

1. The style demands of the job.
2. The style demands of the superior:
   A. The corporate philosophy
   B. The style of the superior
3. The style demand of subordinates:
   A. The expectations of subordinates
   B. The styles of subordinates

The third dimension is thus an output variable that is a function of the appropriateness of the underlying style to the demands of the job. A separated underlying style, for instance, might prove more-effective in a job where an orientation to routine was demanded; thus, the Bureaucrat style. The same underlying style in an aggressive sales organization would probably produce Deserter-style tendencies.

Management style theories such as these have more than simply entertainment value. Once a realistic set of types of managers has been established and agreed on, industry can use it many ways, and has done so. Management appraisal is made much more effective, as is management counselling. Several tests using the 3-D theory have been developed which may be used in appraisal or counselling. The appraisal tests compare a manager's leanings to each of the eight types with that of other managers. The counselling tests allow a manager to say what he thinks is the best style behavior under various conditions; his answers are then discussed with him.

A recently-developed use is that of training and organizational change. Style models are used as the central theme of training courses. They provide a concrete framework by which behavior on such courses may be discussed. Organizational change is also facilitated as organizations too have styles which may be diagnosed, held up for inspection, and parts modified as necessary. The 3-D typology has been used in all of these ways.

In Summary

3-D Theory Distinctiveness:

- Not normative, culture-bound, or tied to single stereotype ideal national or industrial style.
- Four potentially more-effective styles.
- Effectiveness is function of match of style to situation.
- Key managerial qualities leading to effectiveness not task and relationships orientation but diagnostic skill and style flexibility.
- The five situational elements identified.
- Several observable styles included which previously have received little attention.
- Effectiveness is emphasized.
- Clear theoretical framework.

References

1. Anderson, Richard C. "Learning In Discussions, A Resume Of The Authoritarian-Democratic Studies." *Harvard Education Review,* 29 (1959), 201–215.

2. Bales, R. F. "The Equilibrium Problem in Small Groups," 111–161. In T. Parson, R. F. Bales, and E. A. Shils (eds.), *"Working Papers in the Theory of Action."* Glencoe, Ill.: Free Press, 1953.

3. Blake, R. R., J. S. Mouton. *"The Managerial Grid."* Houston: Gulf Publishing, 1964.

4. Carron, T. J. "Human Relations Training and Attitude Change: A Vector Analysis." *Personnel Psychology,* 17, 4, Winter 1964.

5. Fleishman, E. A. *Leadership Climate and Supervisory Behavior.* Columbus, Ohio: Personnel Research Board, Ohio State University, 1951.

6. Fleishman, E. A. "The Measurement of Leadership Attitudes In Industry." *Journal of Applied Psychology,* XXXVII (1953), 153–158.

7. Fleishman, E. A. "The Leadership Opinion Questionnaire." In Stogdill, R. M. and Coons, A. E. (eds.), *Leader Behavior, Its Description and Measurement.* Columbus, Ohio: Bureau of Business Research, Ohio State University, 1957.

8. Fleishman, E. A. "Manual for Administering The Leadership Opinion Questionnaire." Chicago: Science Research Associates, 1960.

9. Fleishman, E. A. and D. R. Peters. "International Values, Leadership Attitudes, and Managerial 'Success'." *Personnel Psychology,* 15, 2 (1962), 127–143.

10. Halpin, A. W. and B. J. Winer. "A Factorial Study of the Leader Behavior Descriptions." In R. M. Stogdill and A. E. Coons (eds.), *Leader Behavior: Its Description and Measurement.* Columbus, Ohio: Bureau of Business Research Monograph 88, Ohio State University, 1957.

11. Jennings, E. E. *The Executive.* New York: Harper & Row, 1962.

12. Lewin, K., R. Lippitt, and R. K. White. "Patterns of Aggressive Behavior in Experimentally Created 'Social Climates'." *Journal of Social Psychology,* 10 (1939), 271–279.

13. Liu, James T. C. "Eleventh-Century Chinese Bureaucrats: Some Historical Classifications and Behavioral Types." *Administrative Science Quarterly,* 4, 2 (1959), 207–226.

14. McGregor, D. *The Human Side of Enterprise.* New York: McGraw-Hill, 1960.

15. Mandell, M. M. "The Selection of Executives." In Dooher, M. J. and E. Marting (eds.), *The Selection of Management Personnel,* I and II. New York: American Management Association, 1957.

16. Mandell, M. M. and D. C. Adkins. "The Validity of Written Tests for The Selection of Administrative Personnel." *Educational and Psychological Measurement,* VI (1946), 293–312.

17. Nash, A. N. "Vocational Interests of Effective Managers: A Review of the Literature." *Personnel Psychology,* 18, 1 (1965), 21–37.

18. Raskin, A., J. K. Boruchow, and R. Golob. "The Concept of Task Versus Person Orientation in Nursing." *Journal of Applied Psychology,* 49, 3 (1965), 182–187.

19. Reddin, W. J. "The Tri-Dimensional Grid." *Training Directors Journal,* 18, 7 (July 1964), 9–18 (an early formulation).

20. Strong, E. K., Jr. "Vocational Guidance of Executive." *Journal of Applied Psychology,* XI (1927), 331–347.

21. Zelditch, M. "Role Differentiation in the Nuclear Family: A Comparative Study." In T. Parsons, R. E. Bales et al. (eds.), "Family Socialization, and Interaction Process." Glencoe, Ill.: Free Press, 1955.

11

Interacting, Coacting, and Counteracting Groups

Fred E. Fiedler
University of Illinois

The first classification which appears important is of the internal work relations among the members. A small group is generally defined as a set of individuals in face-to-face interaction who perceive each other as interrelated, or as reciprocally affecting each other, and who pursue a shared goal.

These groups vary, however, in the intensity and degree to which the members interact. Roby and Lanzetta suggested — in 1958 — one classification of group tasks which differentiates between groups whose members work "in series" and whose members work "in parallel." In the former, the work of one member is directly dependent upon the completion of work by another. Thus, the riveter cannot perform his job until his coworker has supplied him with the properly heated rivet. In the parallel task, two men perform their jobs at the same time. The work of one salesman in a store does not directly depend upon the performance of another.

The present classification presents a very similar schema, which focuses on the group rather than on the task alone and extends the Roby and Lanzetta scheme. We are here classifying groups first in terms of the work relations among members, namely into *interacting, coacting,* or *counteracting* groups.

Interacting Groups

These groups, as already indicated, require the close coordination of several team members in the performance of the primary task. The ability of one man to perform his job may depend upon the fact that another has first completed his share of the task. This is illustrated by a basketball team which requires men to get and pass the ball to others who are in a position to shoot a basket. Many tasks also require the close and simultaneous coordination of two or more men. One man, by himself, cannot move a piano or play a quartet. One man, by himself, cannot run a destroyer. A tank crew requires a series of interrelated activities, such as maneuvering the tank, loading, aiming, and firing the gun, as well as maintaining the equipment. Most of these functions are interdependent to the point where failure on the part of one crew member spells failure for the entire team. Similarly, in the management of a business organization, departments concerned with purchasing, production, advertising, and sales must closely coordinate their work if the enterprise is to succeed.

One major task of the leader in interacting groups consists of coordinating the various task functions or the group's activities so that the work flows smoothly and without interruption, or so that men working together can do so harmoniously and without getting into each other's way. The leader's job is one of directing, channeling, guiding, refereeing, timing, and coordinating the group members' work.

The hallmark of the interacting group is the interdependence of group members. It is generally difficult in these groups to assign credit for good team performance to any one member of the group. It may be possible to identify a team member who failed to perform his assigned job and therefore prevented his group from completing the task successfully. However, it is not easily possible in such teams to identify the degree to which a particular group member directly contributed to success. Each man must do his part if the team is to be successful, and the group is generally rewarded as a group or else the leader alone is rewarded.

Coacting Groups

These groups also work together on a common task. However, each of the group members does his job relatively independently of other team members. The characteristic pattern in such groups is that each group member is on his own, and his performance depends on his own ability, skill, and motivation. His reward, not infrequently, is computed on a piecework basis in a production job or on a commission basis in sales work. The group product is typically the sum of the individual performance scores. Thus, the effectiveness of a department in a store is computed as the sum of the sales made by each clerk, and the score of a bowling team or a rifle marksmanship team is the sum of each member's scores. While it is true that each individual member will be affected by the moral and logistic support which he receives from his group, his own performance is relatively independent of that of others within his group. Not infrequently such a team situation leads to rivalry and competition among group members, which serves as a motivating force for better individual performance.

The leader's function in groups of this nature is clearly different from that required of the interacting group's leader. He has little need to coordinate group action or to develop team training and motivation for cooperative team activities. His major purposes are the development of individual group-member motivation and the individual training which will enable each member to perform up to his ability, and the prevention of destructive rivalries and competition. We may here subdivide the leader's functions into a number of separate major categories: (1) the leader as the coach and trainer of the group members or as the adviser and consultant; (2) the leader as the quasi-therapeutic, anxiety-reducing agent who gives emotional support and tension relief to his members; and finally, (3) the leader as the supervisor, evaluator, or spokesman of the group. All these functions may, of course, be performed by the same leader, and certain combinations may be essential if the group is to survive and perform its work.

Counteracting Groups

The third category of groups consists of individuals who are working together for the purpose of negotiating and reconciling conflicting opinions and purposes. These groups are typically engaged in negotiation and bargaining processes, with some members representing one point of view and others an opposing or, at least, divergent point of view. Each individual member, to a greater or lesser extent, works toward achieving his own or his party's ends at the expense of the other.

In some respects it may seem a contradiction in terms to speak here of a group. The goal is, in one sense, not shared by all members of the team since each subgroup typically seeks to "win" over the other side. There are, thus, at least two goals within such groups, and the specific aims are not shared by all members. Nevertheless, it is also true that all members share the task of reaching a common decision or a common goal, namely, that of reaching an acceptable accommodation if not a mutually satisfactory solution. Moreover, the members of the group are usually quite aware of the importance of interacting, communicating, and cooperating if a creative solution is to emerge from the interaction. The criterion of performance here is not the productivity of the individual, nor necessarily the satisfaction of the participants. Rather, it is the degree to which the constituents of the group members will find the solution acceptable and satisfactory. As McGrath's excellent analysis of 1963 pointed out, the primary loyalty of the group member may be to his outside constituency, to the reference group which he represents. He is, at the same time, bound to work closely and effectively with other members in the negotiation group because a solution can be satisfactory to his own group only when it is also satisfactory to the other party of the bargaining or negotiating process. Frequently the issues are further complicated by the necessity to satisfy still a third impartial group such as the public interest, the legislature, or a court of law.

The leader of the counteracting group, that is, the moderator or negotiator, has a task which again differs from that of the interacting or coacting group's leader. It is the leader's job to maintain the group, to facilitate communication and mutual understanding, and to establish a climate conducive to the development of creative solutions to the conflict, namely, to influence the group toward effective performance.

Figure 1 schematically indicates the approximate places on several continua which interacting, coacting and counteracting groups occupy. This figure shows that the relations among group members, and between group members and leaders, differ in these three types of groups and that the demands on the leader will likewise differ in these three situations. Most groups are a mixture of all three types, although one feature generally predominates. Most leaders of interacting or coacting task groups must at times reconcile differences among group members, and most groups perform some interacting and some coacting tasks.

FIGURE 1

Schematic Comparison of Interacting, Coacting, and
Counteracting Groups in Three Dimensions

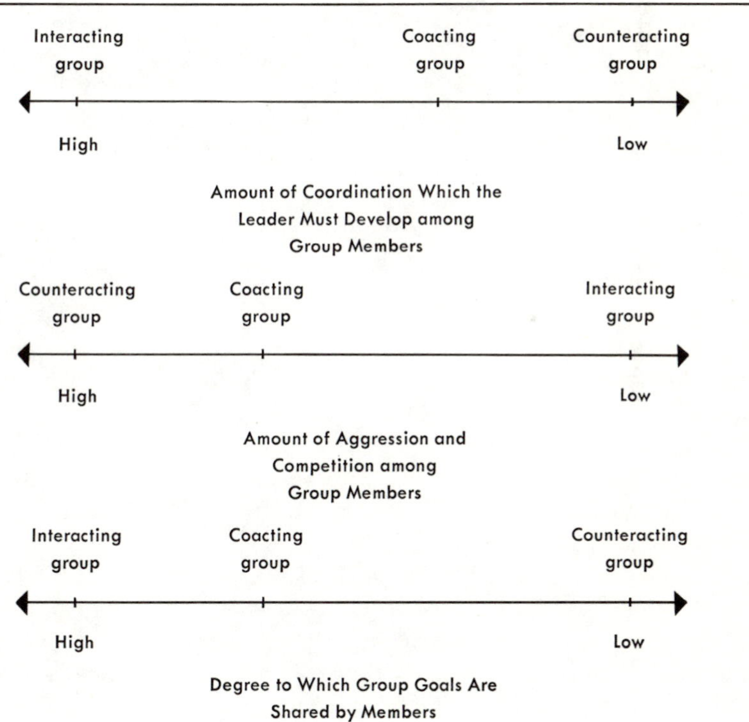

PART FIVE

Motivation

In human behavior, the basic motivators are needs — which the individual is compelled, by inner urges, to try to satisfy. In Part Five, Hunt and Hill (Selection 12) summarize the models of motivation developed by Herzberg and Vroom and Maslow. They conclude that the Vroom model has the greatest utility for organizational research, but caution us not to accept their conclusion as "final." Herzberg's (Selection 13) and Vroom's models are primarily applied models concerned with motivation in organizations. Maslow (Selection 14), on the other hand, presents a generalized model of human motivation — one not intended to explain motivation within any particular institutional setting. Kelly, however, has commented: "Maslow's theory of human motivation is the most widely taught view of motivation in North American business schools and provides the theoretical framework for much organization theory."[1]

Hunt and Hill's analysis, the representative article by Herzberg, and the early essay by Maslow complement one another. First, they exemplify the possibility of approaching a common subject in different ways. Thus, the "best" approach probably should be evaluated with respect to the purposes to be served by the model. Second, the analysis, article, and essay demonstrate that a variety of research techniques can be used in the study of motivation.

[1] Joe Kelly, *Organizational Behavior,* Richard D. Irwin, Inc., and Dorsey Press, 1969, p. 176.

12

The New Look in Motivation Theory for Organizational Research

J. G. HUNT
Southern Illinois University

J. W. HILL
Southern Illinois University

During the last few years the treatment of motivation with respect to industrial and other formal organizations has more often than not been in terms of models by Maslow or Herzberg.[1] Where theories are apparently so thoroughly accepted, one naturally assumes a fairly substantial amount of data leading to empirical verification. However, as we shall show, there is relatively little empirical evidence concerning Maslow's theory; and while there are many studies bearing on Herzberg's theory, it remains controversial. After comparing these two approaches and reviewing their present status, we will describe a newer motivation theory developed by Vroom, which is similar to those developed by Atkinson *et al.* and Edwards in experimental psychology, and Peak, Rosenberg and Fishbein in social psychology.[2] It is our contention, on both theoretical and empirical grounds, that Vroom's theory, more than Maslow's or Herzberg's, is in line with the thinking of contemporary psychologists and industrial sociologists and is the best yet developed for organizational use.

The Maslow Model

Maslow's theory hypothesizes five broad classes of needs arranged in hierarchical levels of prepotency so that when one need level is satisfied, the next level is activated. The levels are: (1) physiological needs; (2) security or safety needs; (3) social, belonging, or membership needs; (4) esteem needs further subdivided into esteem of others and self-esteem including autonomy; and (5) self-actualization or self-fulfillment needs.

Taken and adapted from *Human Organization,* Vol. 28, No. 2, Summer 1969, pp. 100–109. Used by permission.

The original papers present very little empirical evidence in support of the theory and no research at all that tests the model in its entirety. Indeed, Maslow argues that the theory is primarily a framework for future research. He also discusses at length some of the limitations of the model and readily admits that these needs may be unconscious rather than conscious. While Maslow discusses his model and its limitations in detail, a widely publicized paper by McGregor gives the impression that the model can be accepted without question and also that it is fairly easy to apply.[3] In truth, the model is difficult to test, which is probably why there are so few empirical studies to either prove or refute the theory.

Porter provides the most empirical data concerning the model.[4] At the conscious level he measures all except the physiological needs. His samples are based only on managers, but they cover different managerial levels in a wide range of business organizations in the United States and thirteen other countries. Porter's studies have a number of interesting findings, but here we are primarily concerned with two: (1) in the United States and Britain (but not in the other twelve countries) there tends to be a hierarchical satisfaction of needs as Maslow hypothesizes; and (2) regardless of country or managerial level there is a tendency for those needs which managers feel are most important to be least satisfied.

A study by Beer of female clerks provides additional data concerning the model.[5] He examines the relationship between participative and considerate or human relations-oriented supervisory leadership styles and satisfaction of needs. He also goes one step further and argues that need satisfaction, as such, does not necessarily lead to motivation. Rather, motivation results only from need satisfaction which occurs in the process of task-oriented work. He reasons that a participative leadership style should meet this condition since it presumably allows for the satisfaction of the higher order needs (self-actualization, autonomy, and esteem). Beer found that the workers forced to arrange needs in a hierarchy (as required by his ranking method) tend to arrange them as predicted by Maslow. He also found that self-actualization, autonomy and social needs were most important while esteem and security needs were least important, although his method (unlike Porter's) did not allow a consideration of the relationship between importance and need satisfaction. Interestingly enough, there was no significant relationship between need satisfaction and Beer's measure of motivation nor between any of the leadership style dimensions and motivation. There were, however, significant relationships between leadership style dimensions and need satisfaction. Beer concludes that the model has questionable usefulness for a theory of industrial motivation although it may provide a fairly reliable measurement of the *a priori* needs of industrial workers.

We have found only three studies that systematically consider the Maslow theory in terms of performance.[6]

The first of these, by Clark, attempts to fit a number of empirical studies conducted for different purposes into a framework which provides for progressive activation and satisfaction of needs at each of the hierarchical levels. The findings are used to make predictions concerning productivity, absenteeism, and turnover as each need level is activated and then satisfied. While the article does not explicitly test the Maslow model, it is highly suggestive in terms of hypotheses for future research that might relate the theory to work group performance.

A second study, by Lawler and Porter, correlates satisfaction of managers' needs (except physiological) with rankings of their performance by superiors and peers. All correlations are significant but low, ranging from .16 to .30. Lawler and Porter conclude that satisfaction of higher order needs is more closely related to performance than satisfaction of lower order needs. However, the differences are not very great and they are not tested for significance. For example, correlations of superior ratings for the lower order security and social needs are .21 and .23 while for the higher order esteem, autonomy, and self-actualization needs they are .24, .18, and .30. Peer correlations are similar. Thus, unlike Lawler and Porter, we conclude that in this study the correlations for lower order needs are about the same as for higher order needs.

A more recent Porter and Lawler investigation seems to provide additional support for their earlier findings by showing that higher order needs accounted for more relationships significant at the .01 level than lower order needs. However, they do not report correlations between these needs and performance and so we cannot evaluate their conclusion as we did for their earlier study.

The Herzberg Model

A second frequently mentioned motivational model is that proposed by Herzberg and his associates in 1959.[7] They used a semi-structured interview technique to get respondents to recall events experienced at work which resulted in a marked improvement or a marked reduction in their job satisfaction. Interviewees were also asked, among other things, how their feelings of satisfaction or dissatisfaction affected their work performance, personal relationships, and well-being. Content analysis of the interviews suggested that certain job characteristics led to job satisfaction, while *different* job characteristics led to job dissatisfaction. For instance, job achievement was related to satisfaction while working conditions were related to dissatisfaction. Poor conditions led to dissatisfaction, but good conditions did not necessarily lead to satisfaction. Thus, satisfaction and dissatisfaction are not simple opposites. Hence a two-factor theory of satisfaction is needed.

The job content characteristics which produced satisfaction were called "motivators" by Herzberg and his associates because they satisfied the individual's need for self-actualization at work. The job environment characteristics which led to dissatisfaction were called "hygienes" because they were work-supporting or contextual rather than task-determined and hence were analogous to the "preventative" or "environmental" factors recognized in medicine. According to this dichotomy, motivators include achievement, recognition, advancement, possibility of growth, responsibility, and work itself. Hygienes, on the other hand, include salary; interpersonal relations with superiors, subordinates, and peers; technical supervision; company policy and administration; personal life; working conditions; status; and job security.

There is considerable empirical evidence for this theory. Herzberg himself, in a summary of research through early 1966, includes ten studies of seventeen populations which used essentially the same method as his original study.[8] In addition, he reviews twenty more studies which used a variety of methodologies to test the two-factor theory. Of the studies included in his review, those using his critical incident method generally confirm the theory. Those using other methods give less clear results, which Herzberg acknowledges but attempts to dismiss for methodological reasons. At least nine other studies, most of which have appeared since Herzberg's 1966 review, raise even more doubts about the theory.[9]

While it is beyond the scope of the present article to consider these studies in detail, they raise serious questions as to whether the factors leading to satisfaction and dissatisfaction are really different from each other. A number of the studies show that certain job dimensions appear to be more important for *both* satisfaction and dissatisfaction. Dunnette, Campbell, and Hakel for example, conclude from these and also from their own studies that Herzberg is shackled to his method and that achievement, recognition, and responsibility seem important for both satisfaction *and* dissatisfaction while such dimensions as security, salary, and working conditions are less important.[10] They also raise by implication an issue concerning Herzberg's methodology which deserves further comment. That is, if data are analyzed in terms of percentage differences between groups, one result is obtained; if they are analyzed in terms of ranks within groups, another result occurs. The first type of analysis is appropriate for identifying factors which account for differences between events (as Herzberg did in his original hypothesis). The second type of analysis is appropriate if we want to know the most important factors within the event categories (which is what Herzberg claims he was doing). Analyzing the findings of Dunnette and his colleagues by the first method, we confirm Herzberg's theory; but if we rank the findings within categories, as Dunnette *et al.* also did, we find no confirmation. If we want to know whether "achievement" is important in job satisfaction we must look at its relative rank among other factors mentioned in the events leading to satisfaction, not whether it is mentioned a greater percentage of the time in satisfying events than in dissatisfying events. This distinction in analytical methods was discussed several years ago by Viteles and even earlier by Kornhauser.[11]

We conclude that any meaningful discussion of Herzberg's theory must recognize recent negative evidence even though the model seems to make a great deal of intuitive sense. Much the same can be said of Maslow's theory.

Further Considerations in Using the Maslow and Herzberg Theories

Putting aside for the moment the empirical considerations presented by the two models, it is instructive to compare them at the conceptual level suggested in Figure 1. While the figure shows obvious similarities between the Maslow and Herzberg models, there are important differences as well. Where Maslow assumes that any need can be a motivator if it is relatively unsatisfied, Herzberg argues that only the higher order needs serve as motivators and that a worker can have unsatisfied needs in both the hygiene and

FIGURE 1

Maslow's Need-Priority Model Compared with Herzberg's Motivation-Hygiene Model

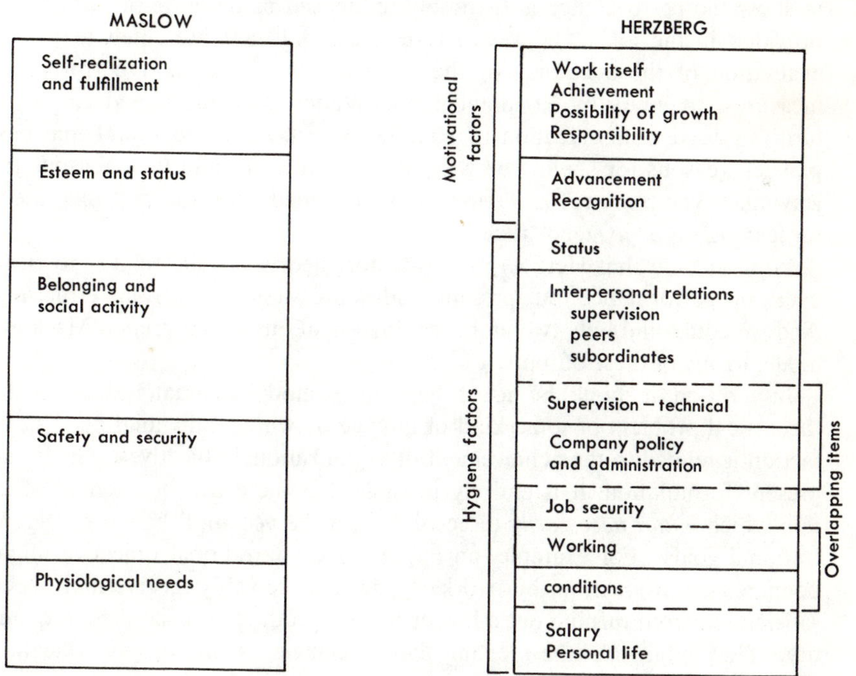

Adapted from K. Davis, *Human Relations at Work*, New York, McGraw-Hill, 1967, p. 37.

motivator areas simultaneously. One might argue that the reason higher order needs are motivators is that lower order needs have essentially been satisfied. However, Herzberg presents some evidence that even in relatively low level blue-collar and service jobs, where presumably lower order needs are less well-satisfied, the higher order needs are still the only ones seen by the workers as motivators.[12]

Another important consideration is the relationship of these models to the accomplishment of organizational objectives. Even if there were unequivocal empirical support for the theories, there is need to translate the findings into usable incentives for promoting such objectives as superior performance, lower turnover, lower absenteeism, etc. If not, they are of little use to industrial organizations. As indicated earlier, there is relatively little evidence empirically relating Maslow's model to performance, or even to psychological well-being. Furthermore, the one Lawler and Porter study seems to show that satisfaction of higher and lower order needs are about equally related to performance, although their later investigation suggests that the former are more strongly related to performance than the latter. But we cannot tell for sure because correlations and differences between correlations are not reported.

Similarly, although Herzberg asked his respondents for effects of job events on their performance, he reports only two studies which attempt to measure performance independent of the respondent's estimate. These seem to show the performance is favorably influenced as more "motivators" are provided in the job.[13] However, insufficient data are presented to permit evaluation of the adequacy of the experimental design and performance measures. A study by Friedlander and Walton that considered employee turnover used a modification of Herzberg's technique and found that employees' reasons for staying on the job were different than their reasons for leaving.[14] The reasons for staying would be called "motivators" while those for leaving were "hygiene" factors.

We conclude that Herzberg's two-factor theory *may* be related to turnover and performance; but present studies are subject to serious criticisms. And we could find only two empirical investigations which related Maslow's model to any of these outputs.

In addition, it should be noted that neither model adequately handles the theoretical problem of some kind of linkage by which individual need satisfaction is related to the achievement of organizational objectives. Given the present formulation, it is entirely possible that there can be need satisfaction which is *not necessarily* directed toward the accomplishment of organizational goals. For example, an important organizational objective might be increased production, but workers might conceivably receive more need satisfaction from turning out a higher quality product at a sacrifice in quantity. They might also be meeting their social needs through identification with a work group with strong sanctions against "rate busting."

Finally, neither of these theories as they stand can really handle the problem of individual differences in motivation. Maslow, for example, explains that his model may not hold for persons with particular experiences. His theory is therefore nonpredictive because data that do not support it can be interpreted in terms of individual differences in previous need gratification leading to greater or lesser prepotency of a given need-category.[15] Herzberg, in similar fashion, describes seven types of people differentiated by the extent to which they are motivator or hygiene seekers, or some combination of the two, although he never relates these differences empirically to actual job performance. We turn then to a model which explicitly recognizes these issues and appears to offer great potential for understanding motivation in organizations.

The Vroom Model

Brayfield and Crockett as long ago as 1955 suggested an explicit theoretical linkage betwen satisfaction, motivation and the organizational goal of productivity. They said:

> It makes sense to us to assume that individuals are motivated to achieve certain environmental goals and that the achievement of these goals results in satisfaction. Productivity is seldom a goal in itself but is more commonly a means to goal attainment. Therefore, . . . we might expect high satisfaction and high productivity to occur together when productivity is perceived as a path to certain important goals and when these goals are achieved.[16]

Georgopoulas, Mahoney and Jones provide some early empirical support for this notion in their test of the "path-goal hypothesis."[17] Essentially, they argue that an individual's motivation to produce at a given level depends upon his particular needs as reflected in the goals toward which he is moving *and* his perception of the relative usefulness of productivity behavior as a path to attainment of these goals. They qualify this, however, by saying that the need must be sufficiently high, no other economical paths must be available to the individual, and there must be a lack of restraining practices.

More recently, Vroom has developed a motivational model which extends the above concepts and is also related to earlier work of experimental and social psychologists.[18] He defines motivation as a "process governing choices, made by persons or lower organisms, among alternative forms of voluntary activity."[19] The concept is incorporated in Figure 2, which depicts Vroom's model graphically. Here, the individual is shown as a role occupant faced with a set of alternative "first-level outcomes." His preference choice among these first-level outcomes is determined by their expected relationship to possible "second-level outcomes."

FIGURE 2

Vroom's Motivational Model

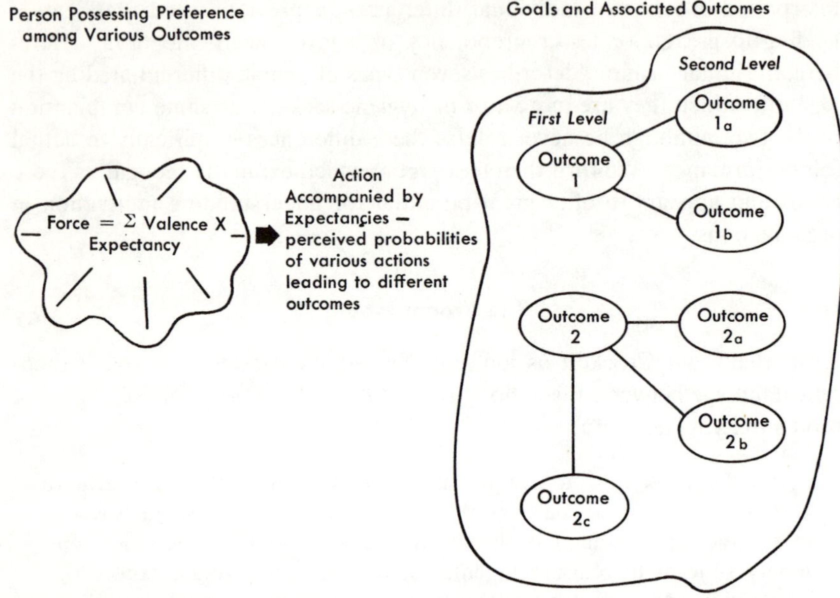

Adapted from M. D. Dunnette, "The Motives of Industrial Managers," *Organizational Behavior and Human Performance*, Vol. 2, 1967, p. 178. (Copyright, Academic Press, Inc.)

Two concepts are introduced to explain the precise method of determining preferences for these first-level outcomes. These concepts are *valence* and *instrumentality*. Valence refers to the strength of an individual's desire for a particular outcome. Instrumentality indicates an individual's perception of the relationship between a first-level outcome and a second-level outcome or, in other words, the extent to which a first-level outcome is seen as leading to the accomplishment of a second-level outcome.

Valence is measured by instructing workers to rank important individual goals in order of their desirability, or they may rate goals on Likert-type scales. Instrumentality can be measured by rating scales which involve perceived differences in the direction and strength of relationships between various first- and second-level outcomes. Important goals of industrial workers often cited in the empirical behavioral science literature are promotion, pay, pleasant working conditions and job security. The goals can be ranked by individual workers in terms of their desirability. The resulting scores are measures of valence.

In addition, each individual can be instructed to indicate on an appropriate scale the likelihood that a certain job behavior, e.g., high productivity, will lead to each of the four goals described. This score is the instrumental relationship between productivity and a specified goal. Obviously there are alternative methods of measurement available for the concepts; we will leave these for a more detailed discussion later.

Vroom expresses the valence of a first-level outcome to a person "as a monotonically increasing function of an algebraic sum of the products of the valences of all [second-level] outcomes and his conceptions of its instrumentality for the attainment of the [second-level] outcomes."[20]

For example, assume that an individual desires promotion and feels that superior performance is a very strong factor in achieving that goal. His first-level outcomes are then superior, average, or poor performance. His second-level outcome is promotion. The first-level outcome of high performance thus acquires a positive valence by virtue of its expected relationship to the preferred second-level outcome of promotion. Assuming no negative second-level outcomes associated with high performance and no other first-level outcomes that contribute to promotion, we expect motivation toward superior performance because promotion is important and superior performance is seen as instrumental in its accomplishment. Or, to put it in Vroom's terms, performance varies directly with the product of the valence of the reward (promotion) and the perceived instrumentality of performance for the attainment of the reward.

An additional concept in Vroom's theory is *expectancy.* This is a belief concerning the likelihood that a particular action or effort will be followed by a particular first-level outcome and can be expressed as a subjective probability ranging from 0 to 1. Expectancy differs from instrumentality in that it relates *efforts* to first-level outcomes where instrumentality relates first- and second-level outcomes to each other. Vroom ties this concept to his previous one by stating, "the force on a person to perform an [action] is a monotonically increasing function of the algebraic sum of the products of the valences of all [first-level] outcomes and the strength of his expectancies that the [action] will be followed by the attainment of these outcomes."[21] "Force" here is similar to our concept of motivation.

This motivational model, unlike those discussed earlier, emphasizes individual differences in motivation and makes possible the examination of very explicit relationships between motivation and the accomplishment of organizational goals, whatever these goals may be. Thus instead of assuming that satisfaction of a specific need is likely to influence organizational objectives in a certain way, we can find out how important to the employees are the various second-level outcomes (worker goals), the instrumentality of various first-level outcomes (organizational objectives) for their attainment, and the expectancies that are held with respect to the employees' ability to influence the first-level outcomes.

Empirical Tests of Vroom's Model

Vroom has already shown how his model can integrate many of the empirical findings in the literature on motivation in organizations.[22] However, because it is a relatively recent development, empirical tests of the model itself are just beginning to appear. Here we shall consider four such investigations.

In the first study, Vroom is concerned with predicting the organizational choices of graduating college students on the basis of their instrumentality-goal index scores.[23] These scores reflect the extent to which membership in an organization was perceived by the student as being related to the acquisition of desired goals. According to the theory, the chosen organization should be the one with the highest instrumentality-goal index. Ratings were used to obtain preferences for fifteen different goals and the extent to which these goals could be attained through membership in three different organizations. These two ratings were thus measures of the valences of second-level outcomes and the instrumentality of organized membership for attainment of these outcomes, respectively. The instrumentality-goal index was the correlation between these two measures. But Vroom's theory also involves consideration of expectancy, i.e., how probable is it that the student can become a member of a particular organization. The choice is not his alone but depends upon whether he is acceptable to the organization. A rough measure of expectancy in this study was whether or not the student had received an offer by the organization. If he had received an offer, expectancy would be high; if not, it would be low. The results show that, considering only organizations from which offers of employment were actually received, 76 percent of the students chose the organization with the highest instrumentality-goal index score. The evidence thus strongly supports Vroom's theory.

The next study, by Galbraith and Cummings, utilizes the model to predict the productivity of operative workers.[24] Graphic rating scales were used to measure the instrumentality of performance for five goals — money, fringe benefits, promotion, supervisor's support, and group acceptance. Similar ratings were used for measuring the desirability of each of the goals for the worker. The authors anticipated that a worker's expectation that he could produce at a high level would have a probability of one because the jobs were independent and productivity was a function of the worker's own effort independent of other human or machine pacing. Figure 3 outlines the research design.

Multiple regression analysis showed that productivity was significantly related positively to the instrumentality-goal interactions for supervisor support and money, and there was an almost significant ($p < .10$) relationship with group acceptance. The other factors did not approach significance and the authors explain this lack of significance in terms of the situational con-

FIGURE 3

Individual Goals and Productivity as Measured by Vroom's Model in One Industrial Plant

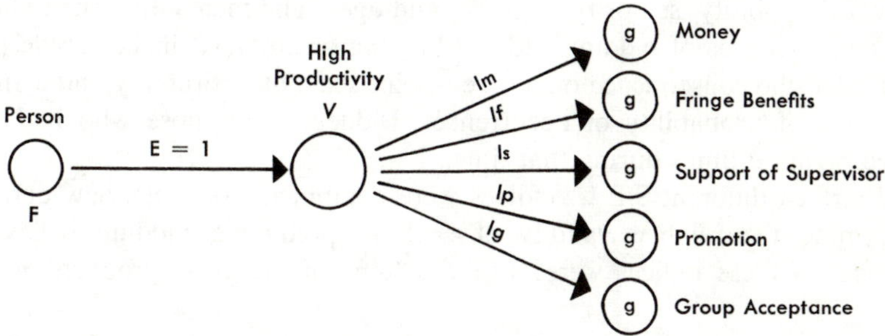

g = Desirability of a particular outcome (rating)
I = Instrumentality of production for particular outcome (rating of relationship)
E = Expectancy (= 1 here because worker sets own pace and is assumed to be capable of high productivity)
V = (Valence) the sum of the cross products of instrumentality and g
F = (Force) expectancy times the valence of productivity
Productivity = Objective measures of amount of production in relation to the production standard

Based on data from J. Galbraith and L. L. Cummings. See Reference 23.

text. That is, fringe benefits were dependent not so much on productivity as on a union/management contract, and promotion was based primarily on seniority. Thus the instrumentality of productivity for the attainment of these goals was low and the model would predict no relationship.

The Galbraith and Cummings study thus supports Vroom's contention that motivation is related to productivity in those situations where the acquisition of desired goals is dependent upon the individual's production and not when desired outcomes are contingent on other factors.

A third study is that of Hill relating a model similar to Vroom's to behavior in a utility company.[25] Hill's model is based upon Edward's subjective expected utility maximization theory of decision making.[26] Here one given a choice between alternatives A and/or B will select that alternative which maximizes his subjective expected utility or expected value. If the outcomes associated with action A are more desirable than those associated with B, and their probability of occurrence is greater than or equal to those associated with B, then an individual will choose behavior A over behavior B. The basic concepts are subjective expectation and subjective utility or valence. Expectation and utility are multiplicatively related and can be measured by the same techniques used to test Vroom's theory. Where a relationship is found between Subjective Expected Utility (S.E.U.) and overt behavior, it can be interpreted as support for Vroom.

The behavior considered in Hill's study is that of job bidding. This behavior is encountered in organizations that post descriptions of job openings on employee bulletin boards and encourage qualified employees to "bid" (apply) for them. Here records were kept of the number of bids made over a three-year period by groups of semi-skilled electrical repairmen matched in learning ability, seniority in grade, and age. The men were asked about the consequences of bidding and not bidding on the next higher grade job, and rated the consequence on a seven-point scale of desirability and a similar scale of probability of occurrence. Bidders were those who had bid three or more times during that time.

Fourteen different S.E.U. indices were computed from interview data to determine the relative validity of each in predicting bidding behavior. Typical of these indices were: (1) the sums of the cross products of expectation and utility for the positive consequences of bidding ($\Sigma\ \overset{+}{\text{S.E.U.}}$); (2) the same score for the negative consequences of bidding ($\Sigma\ \overset{-}{\text{S.E.U.}}$); and (3) the cross products of the *mean* expectation and utility scores for positive and negative consequences $\left(\frac{\Sigma\ \overset{+}{\text{S.E.U.}}}{\text{N}}, \frac{\Sigma\ \overset{-}{\text{S.E.U.}}}{\text{N}}\right)$. In addition to these S.E.U. indices, two traditional attitudinal and motivational measures were used. Semantic Differential scales measured each subject's respective evaluation of bidding and the next higher grade job and each subject's Need for Achievement was obtained.[27]

It was hypothesized that: (1) there would be a positive correlation between the S.E.U. indices and bidding; and (2) the S.E.U. indices would be more highly related to bidding behavior than the traditional measures.

We do not discuss relationships for all of the indices here but do not consider results for one of the more comprehensive indices and those from multiple regression analysis. This index is the algebraic sum of the cross products of the positive and negative consequences of bidding minus the same score for not bidding for each individual. The correlation of this index with bidding was .26, $p < .05$ for a one-tailed test. The correlations between the two Semantic Differential scales and bidding were $-.09$ and $-.25$, respectively. Neither of these is significant for a one-tailed test predicting a positive correlation. The correlation between Need for Achievement and bidding was a nonsignificant .17. A multiple regression analysis determined the relative contribution of the S.E.U. indices to the prediction of bidding. A variable was selected for analysis on the basis of its relationship to the criterion and its intercorrelation with the other predictors. The multiple correlation for bidding and seven selected variables was .61, $p < .05$. This correlation included four S.E.U. indices, all of which had higher beta weights than the Semantic Differentials or Need for Achievement. Thus these variables accounted for more variance in the criterion than did the traditional attitudinal and motivational measures. Both hypotheses were therefore confirmed. This study adds support to the usefulness of this type of model in the study of motivation.

Finally, Lawler and Porter report a study that attempts to relate managerial attitudes to job performance rankings by superiors and peers.[28] In it, 154 managers from five different organizations completed questionnaires concerning seven kinds of rewards, and their expectations that different kinds of behavior would lead to these rewards. The expectations and the ratings of the importance of instrumentality and valence, respectively, were combined multiplicatively to yield multiple correlations which were significantly related to supervisor and peer rankings of the manager's effort to perform his job well. The correlations were higher with effort to perform the job than with the rankings of job performance. Lawler and Porter predicted this result because they reasoned that job performance is influenced by variables other than motivation — e.g., by ability and role perceptions. Of course, Vroom's model is not a behavioral theory but one of motivation only. Motivation is not going to improve performance if ability is low or role perceptions are inaccurate. Vroom's model explains how goals influence effort and that is exactly the relationship found by Lawler and Porter.

Conclusion

Taken together, the four studies discussed in the previous section seem to show that Vroom's model holds great promise for predicting behavior in organizations. There still remain some unanswered questions. We do not know all of the goals that have positive valence in a work situation. We do not know how much of a difference in force is necessary before one kind of outcome is chosen over another. Nor do we know what combination of measures yields the best prediction in a given situation. The answers to these and other questions await further research.

One more point should perhaps be made concerning the four studies and their measurement of Vroom's concepts. While it is true that all of them used subjective measures, the model can in fact be tested with more objective devices. Instrumentality can be inferred from organization practices, expectations can be manipulated by instructions, and goals can be inferred from observed approach and avoidance behaviors. Of course, all of these techniques require assumptions concerning their relationship to the worker's subjective perceptions of the situation; but the model is certainly not bound to the methods of measurement used so far. In fact, Vroom specifies in considerable detail the different kinds of techniques that might be used to test his model.[29]

More work must be done before we can make any statements concerning the overall validity of Vroom's model. But the rigor of his formulation, the relative ease of making the concepts operational, and the model's emphasis on individual differences show considerable promise. We are also encouraged by the results of relatively sophisticated studies testing the theory. We believe it is time for those interested in organizational behavior to take a more thoroughly scientific look at this very complex subject of industrial motivation, and Vroom's model seems a big step in that direction.

Notes

1. A. H. Maslow, *Motivation and Personality,* Harper and Row, New York; 1954; "A Theory of Human Motivation," *Psychological Review,* Vol. 50, 1943, pp. 370–396; and *Eupsychian Management,* Homewood, Illinois, Irwin-Dorsey, 1965; F. Herzberg, B. Mausner, and B. B. Snyderman, *The Motivation to Work,* Wiley, New York, 1959; and F. Herzberg, *Work and the Nature of Man,* World Publishing Co., Cleveland, Ohio, 1966, pp. 130–131. V. H. Vroom, *Work and Motivation,* Wiley, New York, 1964.

2. J. W. Atkinson, J. R. Bastian, R. W. Earl, and G. H. Litwin, "The Achievement Motive, Goal Setting, and Probability Preferences," *Journal of Abnormal and Social Psychology,* Vol. 60, 1960, pp. 27–36; W. Edwards, "Behavioral Decision Theory," *Annual Review of Psychology,* Annual Reviews Inc., Palo Alto, California, 1961, pp. 473–499; H. Peak, "Attitude and Motivation," *Nebraska Symposium on Motivation,* University of Nebraska Press, Lincoln, Nebraska, 1955, pp. 148–184; M. Rosenberg, "Cognitive Structure and Attitudinal Affect," *Journal of Abnormal and Social Psychology,* Vol. 53, 1956, pp. 367–372; M. Fishbein, "An Operational Definition of Belief and Attitude," *Human Relations,* Vol. 15, 1962, pp. 35–43.

3. D. McGregor, "Adventure in Thought and Action," *Proceedings of the Fifth Anniversary Convocation of the School of Industrial Management, Massachusetts Institute of Technology,* Massachusetts Institute of Technology, Cambridge, Massachusetts, 1957, pp. 23–30.

4. L. W. Porter, *Organizational Patterns of Managerial Job Attitudes,* American Foundation for Management Research, New York, 1964. See also M. Haire, E. Ghiselli and L. W. Porter, *Managerial Thinking: An International Study,* Wiley, New York, 1966, especially chapters 4 and 5.

5. M. Beer, *Leadership, Employee Needs, and Motivation,* Bureau of Business Research, Ohio State University, Columbus, Ohio, 1966.

6. J. V. Clark, "Motivation in Work Groups: A Tentative View," *Human Organization,* Vol. 19, 1960, pp. 199–208. E. E. Lawler and L. W. Porter, "The Effect of Performance on Job Satisfaction," *Industrial Relations,* Vol. 7, No. 1, 1967, pp. 20–28. L. W. Porter and E. E. Lawler, *Managerial Attitudes and Performance,* Irwin-Dorsey, Homewood, Illinois, 1968, pp. 148, 150.

7. Herzberg, Mausner and Snyderman, *op. cit.*

8. Herzberg, *op. cit.,* chapters 7, 8. See also K. Davis, *Human Relations at Work* (Third Edition) McGraw-Hill, New York, 1967, pp. 32–36; and R. J. Burke, "Are Herzberg's Motivators and Hygienes Undimensional?" *Journal of Applied Psychology,* Vol. 50, 1966, pp. 217–321.

9. For a review of six of these studies as well as a report on their own similar

findings see M. D. Dunnette, J. P. Campbell, and M. D. Hakel, "Factors Contributing to Job Satisfaction and Job Dissatisfaction in Six Occupational Groups," *Organizational Behavior and Human Performance,* Vol. 2, 1967, pp. 143–174. See also C. L. Hulin and P. A. Smith, "An Empirical Investigation of Two Implications of the Two-Factor Theory of Job Satisfaction," *Journal of Applied Psychology,* Vol. 51, 1967, pp. 396–402; C. A. Lindsay, E. Marks, and L. Gorlow, "The Herzberg Theory: A Critique and Reformulation," *Journal of Applied Psychology,* Vol. 51, 1967, pp. 330–339. This latter study and one by J. R. Hinrichs and L. A. Mischkind, "Empirical and Theoretical Limitations of the Two-Factor Hypothesis of Job Satisfaction," *Journal of Applied Psychology,* Vol. 51, 1967, pp. 191–200, are especially useful for suggesting possible reformulations and extensions of the theory which may help overcome some of the objections voiced in the studies mentioned above.

10. Dunnette, Campbell and Hakell, *op. cit.,* pp. 169–173.

11. M. S. Viteles, *Motivation and Morale in Industry,* Norton, New York, 1953, chapter 14: A. Kornhauser, "Psychological Studies of Employee Attitudes," *Journal of Consulting Psychology,* Vol. 8, 1944, pp. 127–143.

12. Herzberg, *op. cit.,* Chapters 7–9.

13. Herzberg, *op. cit.,* Chapter 8.

14. F. Friedlander and E. Walton, "Positive and Negative Motivations Toward Work," *Administrative Science Quarterly,* Vol. 9, 1964, pp. 194–207.

15. It should be noted that the Porter and Lawler research reported above extends the Maslow model by providing an explicit linkage between need satisfaction and performance and also implicitly recognizes individual motivational differences. To do these things, their research makes use of the Vroomian concepts discussed in the next section.

16. A. H. Brayfield and W. H. Crockett, "Employee Attitudes and Employee Performance," *Psychological Bulletin,* Vol. 52, 1955, p. 416.

17. B. S. Georgopoulas, G. M. Mahoney, and N. W. Jones, "A Path-Goal Approach to Productivity," *Journal of Applied Psychology,* Vol. 41, 1957, pp. 345–353.

18. This section is based especially on discussions in Vroom, *op. cit.,* Chapters 2 and 7. See also J. Galbraith and L. L. Cummings, "An Empirical Investigation of the Motivational Determinants of Task Performance: Interactive Effects between Instrumentality–Valence and Motivation–Ability," *Organizational Behavior and Human Performance,* Vol. 2, 1967, pp. 237–257.

19. Vroom, *op. cit.,* p. 6.

20. Vroom, *op. cit.,* p. 17.

21. Vroom, *op. cit.,* p. 18.

22. Vroom, *op. cit.*

23. V. H. Vroom, "Organizational Choice: A Study of Pre- and Postdecision Processes," *Organizational Behavior and Human Performance,* Vol. 1, 1966, pp. 212–225.

24. Galbraith and Cummings, *op. cit.,* pp. 237–257.

25. J. W. Hill, "An Application of Decision Theory to Complex Industrial Behavior," unpublished dissertation, Wayne State University, Detroit, Michigan, 1965.

26. Edwards, *op. cit.,* pp. 473–499.

27. For discussions of these measures see C. Osgood, G. Suci, and P. Tannenbaum, *The Measurement of Meaning,* University of Illinois Press, Urbana, Ill., 1957; A. L. Edwards, *Personal Preference Schedule Manual,* Psychological Corporation, New York, 1959.

28. E. E. Lawler and L. W. Porter, "Antecedent Attitudes of Effective Managerial Performance," *Organizational Behavior and Human Performance,* Vol. 2, 1967, pp. 122–142.

29. Vroom, *Work and Motivation, op. cit.,* Chapter 2.

13

The Motivation–Hygiene Concept and Problems of Manpower

FREDERICK HERZBERG
Western Reserve University

I wish to preface my remarks in this article with a disclaimer of competence in the field of manpower. My research and contemplative efforts are more directly related to an equally large and protean problem, that of industrial mental health. From my investigations in the latter area, I have formulated a general theory of mental health, and a specific application to job attitudes that may have a bearing on certain aspects of "manpower" questions.

I apologize to the reader who already has familiarity with the Motivation-Hygiene theory of job attitudes for occupying the next few pages with a repetition of data and comments which have appeared a number of times elsewhere. I must lay the groundwork for my thoughts on "manpower" by first presenting my theory of job attitudes, without which I have very little excuse for accepting the invitation to contribute to this issue.

The Motivation-Hygiene theory of job attitudes began with a depth interview study of over 200 engineers and accountants representing Pittsburgh industry (10). These interviews probed sequences of events in the work lives of the respondents to determine the factors that were involved in their feeling exceptionally happy and conversely exceptionally unhappy with their jobs. From a review and an analysis of previous publications in the general area of job attitudes, a two-factor hypothesis was formulated to guide the original investigation. This hypothesis suggested that the factors involved in producing job satisfaction were separate and distinct from the factors that led to job dissatisfaction. Since separate factors needed to be considered depending on whether job satisfaction or job dissatisfaction was involved, it followed that these two feelings were not the obverse of each other. The opposite of job satisfaction would not be job dissatisfaction, but rather *no* job satisfaction; and similarly the opposite of job dissatisfaction is *no* job dissatisfaction — not job satisfaction. The statement of the

Reprinted by permission from the Jan.–Feb. 1964 issue of *Personnel Administration*.

concept is awkward and may appear at first to be a semantic ruse, but there is more than a play with words when it comes to understanding the behavior of people on jobs. The fact that job satisfaction is made up of two unipolar traits is not a unique occurrence. The difficulty of establishing a zero point in psychology with the procedural necessity of using instead a bench mark (mean of a population) from which to start our measurement, has led to the conception that psychological traits are bipolar. Empirical investigations, however, have cast some shadows on the assumptions of bipolarity; one timely example is a study of conformity and non-conformity, where they were shown not to be opposites, but rather two separate unipolar traits (3).

Methodology

Before proceeding to the major results of the original study, three comments on methodology are in order. The investigation of attitudes is plagued with many problems, least of which is the measurement phase, although it is measurement to which psychologists have hitched their scientific integrity. First of all, if I am to assess a person's feeling about something, how do I know he has a feeling? Too often we rely on his say so, even though opinion polling is replete with instances in which respondents gladly respond with all shades of feeling when in reality they have never thought of the issue and are devoid of any practical affect. They respond to respond and we become deceived into believing that they are revealing feelings or attitudes. Secondly, assuming the respondent does have genuine feelings regarding the subject under investigation, are his answers indicative of his feelings; or are they rationalizations, displacements from other factors which are for many reasons less easy to express, coin of the realm expressions for his particular job classification, etc.? Those who have had experience with job morale surveys recognize these ghosts and unfortunately some have contributed to the haunting of companies. Thirdly, how do you equate feelings? If two persons state that they are happy with their jobs, how do you know they are equally happy? We can develop scales, but in truth we are only satisfying our penchant for rulers which do not get inside the experience and measure the phenomenological reality, but rather have significance wholly within our devices.

To meet these objections, the methodology of the original study was formulated. It included a study of changes in job attitudes in the hope that if attitudes change there is more likelihood that an attitude exists. Further, it focused on experiences in the lives of the respondents which contained substantive data that could be analyzed apart from the interpretations of the respondents. Finally, rather than attempt to measure degree of feeling, it focused on peak experiences and contrasted negative peaks with positive peaks; without being concerned with the equality of the peaks. Briefly, we asked our respondents to describe periods in their lives when they were exceedingly happy and unhappy with their jobs. Each respondent gave as many "sequences of events" as he could which met certain criteria including a marked change in feeling, a beginning and an end, and contained some substantive description other than feelings and interpretations.

A rational analysis of the "sequences of events" led to the results shown in the accompanying chart. For a more complete description of the methodology as well as the results, see *The Motivation to Work* (10).

The proposed hypothesis appears verified. The factors on the right that led to satisfaction (achievement, recognition for achievement, intrinsic interest in the work, responsibility, and advancement) are mostly unipolar; that is, they contribute very little to job dissatisfaction. Conversely, the dissatisfiers (company policy and administrative practices, supervision, interpersonal relationships, working conditions, and salary) contribute very little to job satisfaction.

Satisfiers and Dissatisfiers

What is the explanation for such results? Do the two sets of factors have two separate themes? It appears so, for the factors on the right all seem to describe man's relationship to what he does, to his job content, achievement on a task, recognition for task achievement, the nature of the task, responsibility for a task, and professional advancement or growth in task capability.

What is the central theme for the dissatisfiers? Restating the factors as the kind of administration and supervision received in doing the job, the nature of interpersonal relationships and working conditions that surround the job, and the amount of salary that accrues to the individual for doing his job, suggest the distinction with the "satisfier" factors. Rather than describing man's relationship to what he does, the "dissatisfier" factors describe his relationship to the context or environment in which he does his job. One cluster of factors relates to what the person does and the other to the situation in which he does it.

As usual with any new theory, a new jargon is invented, perhaps to add some fictitious uniqueness to the theory, although I prefer to think that these new terms better convey the meaning of the theory. Because the factors on the left serve primarily as preventatives, that is to prevent job dissatisfaction, and because they also deal with the environment, I have named these factors "the hygiene" factors in a poor analogy with the way the term is used in preventive medicine. The factors on the right I call the "motivators" because other results indicate they are necessary for improvement in performance beyond that pseudo improvement which in substance amounts to coming up to a "fair day's work."

In these terms we can recapitulate the major findings of the original study by stating that it is the hygiene factors that affect job dissatisfaction and the motivator factors that affect job satisfaction; with the further understanding that there are two parallel continua of satisfactions. I have only reported on the first study because of the required brevity of this paper. Corroboration can be found in the studies with the following references, (1), (2), (4), (13), (14), (15), (16).

FIGURE 1

Comparison of Satisfiers and Dissatisfiers

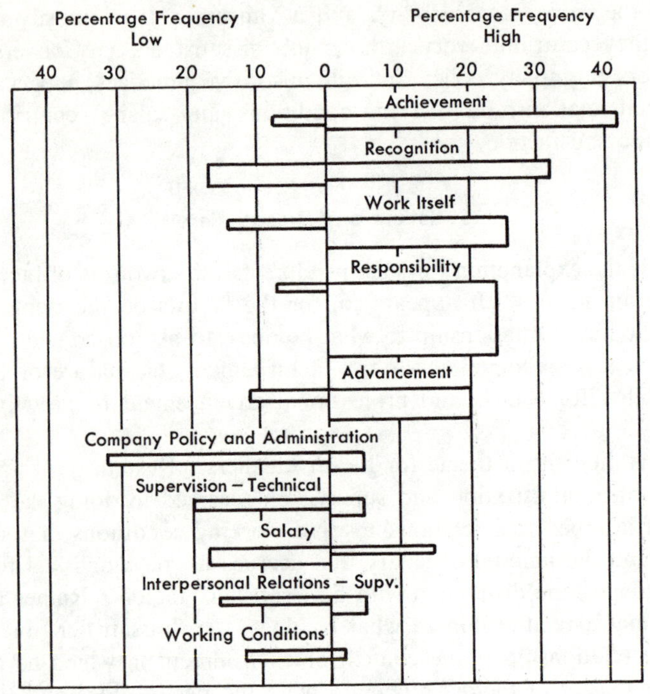

The wider the box the longer the duration of the attitude. Reproduced from *The Motivation to Work*, Frederick Herzberg, et al. John Wiley and Sons, New York, 1959.

Significance of Hygiene Factors

Why? We next explore the reasons given by our respondents for the differential effects that the two sets of factors have on job attitudes. In brief, the hygiene factors meet man's need to avoid unpleasantness. "I don't like to be treated this way; I don't want to suffer the deprivation of low salary; bad interpersonal relationships make me uncomfortable." In other words they want their lives to be hygienically clean. The motivator factors on the other hand make people happy with their jobs because they serve man's basic and human need for psychological growth; a need to become more competent. A fuller commentary on these two separate needs of man are contained in the following publications, (5), (6), (7), (8), (10), (11), (12).

This theory opens wide the door for reinterpretations of industrial relations phenomena. To begin with, job attitudes must be viewed twice; what does the employee seek — what makes him happy; and then a separate question not deducible from the first, what does he wish to avoid — what makes him unhappy? Industrial relations that stress sanitation as their modus operandi can only serve to prevent dissatisfactions and the resultant personnel problems. Of course such attention to hygienic needs is important, for without it any organization, as we well know, will reap the consequences of unhappy personnel. The error of course lies in assuming that prevention will unleash positive health and the returns of increased productivity, lowered absenteeism, turnover, and all the other indices of manpower efficiency. One additional deduction from the theory which is supported by empirical findings should be added. The effect of improved hygiene lasts for only a short time. In fact man's avoidance needs are recurrent and of an infinite variety, and as such we will find that demands for improved salary, working conditions, interpersonal relations and so on will continue to occupy the personnel administrator without any hope of escaping the "what have you done for me lately."

There is nothing wrong with providing the maximum of hygienic benefits to the employee, as much as the society can afford (which appears to be more than the historic cries of anguish which have always accompanied the amelioration of work hygiene would indicate). What is wrong is the summation of human needs in totally hygienic terms. The consequences of this onesided view of man's nature has led to untoward consequences of much greater import than the direct monetary costs of these programs to our organizations. The more pertinent effect has been on the psychological premises of industrial relations and its effect in turn on the self concepts of the employees.

Since hygiene is the apparent key to industrial success, the motivators are given but lip service, and attention to the challenge and meaningfulness of jobs is satisfied via the pious espousal of cultural noises. We are today familiar with the industrial engineering principle of leveling jobs down to the lowest common talent as it applies to the rank and file assembly operation. The same denigration of human talent at the managerial and professional level, the sacrificing of human performance and potentiality to insure that no one will fail or make for unpleasantness, is obscured by referring to the rank and file when acknowledging the lack of meaning in work. At these higher levels, the effects of the assembly line are accomplished by the overuse of rules and regulations, rational organizational principles and the insidious use of interpersonal *skills*. We find that more and more training and education is required to do less and less; more and more effort on surround and less and less substance on accomplishment. Pride in work, in successful accomplishment, in maximizing one's talent is becoming socially gauche or more tragically a victim of progress. We cry for nurturance of human talent and find that we have no place for most of it; human talent on the job has become as much of a surplus commodity as our wheat. And where are our personnel managers? Their problem is hygiene, not the creative function of maximizing human resources.

Significance of Motivators

The Protestant Ethic is being replaced by an Avoidance Ethic in our world of work, and those in charge of personnel utilization have almost totally directed their efforts to maintenance procedures. This is seen from the very beginning of employment in the practice of college recruitment on the campus, where each company sets up its own enticing tent, and selection is transformed into public relations, luring of candidates, and in fact the incredible situation of the candidate interviewing the interviewer.

Job attitude data suggest that after the glow of the initial year on the job, job satisfaction plummets to its lowest level in the work life of individuals (9). From a life time of diverse learning, successive accomplishment through the various academic stages, and periodic reinforcement of efforts, the entrant to our modern companies finds, that rather than work providing an expanding psychological existence, the opposite occurs; and successive amputations of his self-conceptions, aspirations, learning, and talent are the consequence of earning a living. Of course as the needs and values of our industrial enterprises have become the template for all aspects of our lives, the university is preparing many young people by performing the amputations early, and they enter already primed for work as only a means of hygienic improvement; or for those still capable of enjoying the exercise of their human talents, as means of affording off the job satisfactions. If the number of management development programs is a valid sign, the educational system has done its job too well.

A reaction to retirement policies is beginning to set in as the personal consequences of organizational definitions of human obsolescence are being told. Prior to retirement, however, are 30 to 40 years of partial retirement and partial commitment to work for the too many who have not "succeeded" in terms of organizational advancement. From the first orientation to the farewell party, the history of work careers is a history of human waste. What a paradox we face! There is a shortage of talent in the country at a time when our problems are defined in planetary dimensions and to meet these circumstances we have evolved a system and a philosophy to use and motivate our talent that serves to decrease further this precious resource.

What alternatives are there? A spate of new research and literature is becoming available that is reacting to personnel and managerial psychology that has too long tried to emulate the vast and short term goals of the military. The new literature while encompassing diverse problems, exhortations, solutions, and conceptions, seems to have the common theme of emphasizing the motivator needs of man and the necessity for the personnel function of industry to pause in its search for the Holy Grail of instruments, to become creative in finding ways to meet the motivator needs. Man is distinguished from all other animals in that he alone is a determiner. How strange that when it comes to the satisfactions of his special psychological growth needs he finds himself a victim of outside determinisms and helpless in affecting the way he is utilized in work. The short term economic "necessities" cannot justify the larger economic loss and the denial of human satisfaction that the restriction of human talent inevitably costs. I might add that many of the barriers to fuller utilization of manpower that are "justified" by economic reasons, are in reality, devices of fearful and inadequate managers who are not prepared to meet the challenge of managing adults. The philosophy of management which prizes such men is changeable. We need a goal of industry which includes the expansion of manpower utilization in addition to the expansion of productivity and profit. The acceptance of such a goal as basic will lead to the means for its implementation. Personnel cannot remain the one management function that only establishes objectives for which techniques and procedures are available.

References

1. Fantz, R. "Motivation factors in rehabilitation." Unpublished doctoral dissertation. Western Reserve University Library, Cleveland, 1961.

2. Gibson, J. "Sources of job satisfaction and job dissatisfaction." Unpublished doctoral dissertation. Western Reserve University Library, Cleveland, 1961.

3. Guilford, J. P., P. R. Christensen, N. Bond, and M. Sutton. "A factor analysis study of human interests." *Res. Bull.* (1953), 53–11, Human Resources Research Center, San Antonio, 1953.

4. Hamlin, R. and R. Nemo. "Self-actualization in choice scores of improved schizophrenics." *J. clin. Psychol.*, 18 (1962).

5. Herzberg, F. "New approaches in management organization and job design." *Industrial Med. and Surgery* (November 1962).

6. Herzberg, F. "Basic needs and satisfactions of individuals." *Industrial Relations Monograph,* No. 21, Industrial Relations Counselors, Inc., New York, 1962.

7. Herzberg, F. "Comment on the Meaning of Work." Proceedings of symposium of the Worker in the New Industrial Environment. *Industrial Med. and Surgery* (June 1963).

8. Herzberg, F. "The meaning of work to the individual." In *Basic Psychology and Physiology of Work,* H. Hellerstein (ed.). Ft. Lauderdale: C. C. Thomas Press. In press.

9. Herzberg, F. et al. *Job Attitudes: Research, and Opinion.* Psychological Service of Pittsburgh, 1957.

10. Herzberg, F., B. Mausner, and B. Snyderman. *The Motivation to Work.* New York: John Wiley and Sons, 1959.

11. Herzberg, F., and R. Hamilton. "A motivation-hygiene concept of mental health." *Mental Hygiene* (July 1961).

12. Herzberg, F., and R. Hamilton. "Motivation-hygiene concept and psychotherapy." *Mental Hygiene* (July 1961).

13. Lodahl, T. *Patterns of job attitudes in two assembly technologies.* Ithaca: Graduate School of Business and Public Administration, Cornell University, 1963.

14. Saleh, S. "Attitude change and its effect on the pre-retirement period." Unpublished doctoral dissertation. Western Reserve University Library, Cleveland, 1962.

15. Schwarz, P. *Attitudes of Middle Management Personnel.* Pittsburgh: American Institute for Research, 1961.

16. Schwartz, M., E. Jenusaitis, and H. Stark. "Motivation factors among supervisors in the utility industry." *Personnel Psychology,* 16 (1963).

14

A Theory of Human Motivation

A. H. Maslow
Brooklyn College

Introduction

In a previous paper (4) various propositions were presented which would have to be included in any theory of human motivation that could lay claim to being definitive. These conclusions may be briefly summarized as follows:

1. The integrated wholeness of the organism must be one of the foundation stones of motivation theory.
2. The hunger drive (or any other physiological drive) was rejected as a centering point or model for a definitive theory of motivation. Any drive that is somatically based and localizable was shown to be atypical rather than typical in human motivation.
3. Such a theory should stress and center itself upon ultimate or basic goals rather than partial or superficial ones, upon ends rather than means to these ends. Such a stress would imply a more central place for unconscious than for conscious motivations.
4. There are usually available various cultural paths to the same goal. Therefore conscious, specific, local-cultural desires are not as fundamental in motivation theory as the more basic, unconscious goals.
5. Any motivated behavior, either preparatory or consummatory, must be understood to be a channel through which many basic needs may be simultaneously expressed or satisfied. Typically an act has *more* than one motivation.
6. Practically all organismic states are to be understood as motivated and as motivating.
7. Human needs arrange themselves in hierarchies of pre-potency. That is to say, the appearance of one need usually rests on the prior satisfaction of another, more pre-potent need. Man is a perpetually wanting animal. Also

A. H. Maslow, "A Theory of Human Motivation," *Psychological Review,* Vol. 50, No. 4, July 1943, pp. 370–371, 394–396.

no need or drive can be treated as if it were isolated or discrete; every drive is related to the state of satisfaction or dissatisfaction of other drives.

8. *Lists* of drives will get us nowhere for various theoretical and practical reasons. Furthermore any classification of motivations must deal with the problem of levels of specificity or generalization of the motives to be classified.

9. Classifications of motivations must be based upon goals rather than upon instigating drives or motivated behavior.

10. Motivation theory should be human-centered rather than animal-centered.

11. The situation or the field in which the organism reacts must be taken into account but the field alone can rarely serve as an exclusive explanation for behavior. Furthermore the field itself must be interpreted in terms of the organism. Field theory cannot be a substitute for motivation theory.

12. Not only the integration of the organism must be taken into account, but also the possibility of isolated, specific, partial or segmental reactions.

It has since become necessary to add to these another affirmation:

13. Motivation theory is not synonymous with behavior theory. The motivations are only one class of determinants of behavior. While behavior is almost always motivated, it is also almost always biologically, culturally and situationally determined as well.

The present paper is an attempt to formulate a positive theory of motivation which will satisfy these theoretical demands and at the same time conform to the known facts, clinical and observational as well as experimental. It derives most directly, however, from clinical experience. This theory is, I think, in the functionalist tradition of James and Dewey, and is fused with the holism of Wertheimer (5), Goldstein (3), and Gestalt Psychology, and with the dynamicism of Freud (2) and Adler (1). This fusion or synthesis may arbitrarily be called a "general-dynamic" theory.

It is far easier to perceive and to criticize the aspects in motivation theory than to remedy them. Mostly this is because of the very serious lack of sound data in this area. I conceive this lack of sound facts to be due primarily to the absence of a valid theory of motivation. The present theory then must be considered to be a suggested program or framework for future research and must stand or fall, not so much on facts available or evidence presented, as upon researches yet to be done, researches suggested perhaps, by the questions raised in this paper. . .

Summary

1. There are at least five sets of goals, which we may call basic needs. These are briefly physiological, safety, love, esteem, and self-actualization.

In addition, we are motivated by the desire to achieve or maintain the various conditions upon which these basic satisfactions rest and by certain more intellectual desires.

2. These basic goals are related to each other, being arranged in a hierarchy of prepotency. This means that the most prepotent goal will monopolize consciousness and will tend of itself to organize the recruitment of the various capacities of the organism. The less prepotent needs are minimized, even forgotten or denied. But when a need is fairly well satisfied, the next prepotent ("higher") need emerges, in turn to dominate the conscious life and to serve as the center of organization of behavior, since gratified needs are not active motivators.

Thus man is a perpetually wanting animal. Ordinarily the satisfaction of these wants is not altogether mutually exclusive, but only tends to be. The average member of our society is most often partially satisfied and partially unsatisfied in all of his wants. The hierarchy principle is usually empirically observed in terms of increasing percentages of non-satisfaction as we go up the hierarchy. Reversals of the average order of the hierarchy are sometimes observed. Also it has been observed that an individual may permanently lose the higher wants in the hierarchy under special conditions. There are not only ordinarily multiple motivations for usual behavior, but in addition many determinants other than motives.

3. Any thwarting or possibility of thwarting of these basic human goals, or danger to the defenses which protect them, or to the conditions upon which they rest, is considered to be a psychological threat. With a few exceptions, all psychopathology may be partially traced to such threats. A basically thwarted man may actually be defined as a "sick" man, if we wish.

4. It is such basic threats which bring about the general emergency reactions.

5. Certain other basic problems have not been dealt with because of limitations of space. Among these are (a) the problem of values in any definitive motivation theory, (b) the relation between appetites, desires, needs and what is "good" for the organism, (c) the etiology of the basic needs and their possible derivation in early childhood, (d) redefinition of motivational concepts, *i.e.,* drive, desire, wish, need, goal, (e) implication of our theory for hedonistic theory, (f) the nature of the uncompleted act, of success and failure, and of aspiration-level, (g) the role of association, habit and conditioning, (h) relation to the theory of inter-personal relations, (i) implications for psychotherapy, (j) implication for theory of society, (k) the theory of selfishness, (l) the relation between needs and cultural patterns, (m) the relation between this theory and Allport's theory of functional autonomy. These as well as certain other less important questions must be considered as motivation theory attempts to become definitive.

References

1. Adler, A. *Social Interest.* London: Faber & Faber, 1938.

2. Freud, S. *New Introductory Lectures on Psychoanalysis.* New York: Norton, 1933.

3. Goldstein, K. *The Organism.* New York: American Book Co., 1939.

4. Maslow, A. H. "A preface to motivation theory." *Psychosomatic Med.* 5 (1943), 85–92.

5. Wertheimer, M. Unpublished lectures at the New School for Social Research.

PART SIX

Personnel Systems

Part Six focuses on the major subsystems of personnel management. These subsystems are viewed as crossing organizational lines and as areas of concern to all managers. Each subsystem also represents an important interface between the personnel unit and the other units in the organization — necessitating a high degree of interaction and collaboration for optimal effectiveness.

One major subsystem, collective bargaining, is treated only indirectly — in Scott's "Employee Appeal Systems." Yet *Personnel Management and Organization Development: Fields in Transition* has implications, throughout, for bargaining and quasi-bargaining relationships. For instance, Part Seven suggests that, as an alternative to "win-lose" bargaining relationships, there may be models useful in complementing traditional forms of group interaction.

A. PLANNING AND ANALYSIS

Cox (Selection 15) presents an integrated system for personnel planning and analysis that emphasizes techniques applicable to most organizations. The purpose of the planning model is to show how a greater degree of integration between personnel administration and the other organizational activities might be attained.

Likert and Bowers (Selection 16) do two other important things. First, they develop a research plan for measuring what they identify as causal, intervening, and end-result variables. Second, they outline a system of human resource accounting. This system should improve ability to incorporate such data in personnel planning and analysis models that, heretofore, could be considered only qualitatively or in an ad hoc manner. Through the development of a human resource accounting system, it may become possible to estimate, in dollars and cents, the present and changing value of the human organization. Further, the dollar impact of alternative human resource decisions can be approximated, thus enhancing the ability of managers to make decisions which maximize the probability of integrating individual and organizational goals for greatest total effectiveness.

15

Personnel Planning, Objectives and Methods: Presentation of an Integrated System

ARNE COX
Swedish Council for Personnel Administration

The *reason* for beginning to work with personnel planning may be completely different in different companies depending on the nature of the company, its stage of development and many other factors. The techniques of personnel planning may apply just as much to management as to workers or any limited group of company employees.

Although there may be great differences, we consider that there are also considerable *similarities* in the techniques for different companies:

The *aim* of personnel planning may be studied from the viewpoint both of the company and the individual: *From the company viewpoint* the function of personnel planning is to assure the company both quantitatively and qualitatively of sufficient manpower to satisfy its future development. *From the individual viewpoint* the object of personnel planning is to give the individual support in his development and to see that his personal capacities as a human being and an individual are made use of in the best way. In our attempts to work with these matters we have attempted to combine these two aims into a common plan of action aiming at an interplay between the company's requirements and supply of manpower and the personal opportunities for the employee to find his niche. It is in general easier for the company to satisfy individual wishes if personnel matters are handled with the aid of long term planning.

Personnel planning has been conducted in many companies for several years but as a rule the personnel planning has had limited objectives and can be said to have been passive, consisting of the personnel department dealing in a rational way with the requisitions received from line manage-

Taken and adapted from *Management International Review,* Vol. 8, No. 4–5, 1968, pp. 104–114. Used by permission.

ment. Nowadays it appears more justified to attempt to achieve a greater degree of integration between personnel administration and other company activities. This should be done more actively, foresightedly and systematically than has hitherto been the case.

What is then the *object of personnel planning?* A practical way of looking at this is to say that it is a question of planning company personnel resources or manpower resources. If we then make a further analysis of the components which together constitute company manpower resources, we find that there are components of completely different types (Figure 2, p. 171).

There is the *number of employees* and the personnel structure, which is changed through mobility, i.e. hirings and departures, transfers and promotion. Furthermore there are *working hours:* each employee works for a given time. Working hours for the individual worker are as a rule regulated by law or collective agreement but can vary within that framework through his absence, which can be very considerable, through over-time or through other types of distribution of these working hours: vacations, shift work and on-call duty.

These two types of factors contributing to determine the size of company manpower resources are easy to measure and control. This is not, however, the case for the third type of factor, namely *individual contributions.* An employee works for a given time with a certain individual contribution. This individual contribution is difficult to measure and our knowledge of the factors influencing it are insufficient. It is, however, obvious that aptitude or suitability for a job is one factor, as is skill or know-how attained by means of education or training. In addition we have the will to work or motivation. A fourth sub-factor which might be included in the individual contribution is state of health.

It appears to be the interplay between the three groups of factors which determines the magnitude of manpower resources within a company or department. For instance, if there is a shortage of personnel it might be necessary to work considerable overtime, which in turn may result in lower motivation or a greater strain on the employees.

This description of components determining company manpower resources does not of course exhaust the factors which should be included in a coordinated company planning of employee conditions. Further examples which might be mentioned are wages and housing.

All planning means that measures should be taken with future consequences in mind. Let us devote a few words to the *time horizon* in personnel planning. What *can* be planned for different time horizons?

Short term	Long term	Very long term	time
Order stock	Total company long term plans		

Planning for the immediate future may be based on orders already placed with the department or company. We know fairly exactly which orders have been made and using this as a base we are able to adjust the number and quality of the employees. This might be called short term personnel planning and can be said to be concluded when the current order stock is exhausted. If we extend the planning perspective a little further, when there is no order stock to be used as a base, it is necessary to use other sources.

This long term personnel planning must be based on company plans for investment, products, marketing, etc., and on the plans for company organizational development based thereon.

If we wish to extend the planning horizon beyond the limit of the company's total planning of its activities, it is then necessary to base the personnel planning decisions on the same material as company management uses in its more general assessment of the company's future in a changing and confusing world. This will include observations on demographic changes, long term community planning, the planning of roads, schools, etc. I do not intend to treat this very long term personnel planning since it so seldom occurs in systematic form in the company of today.

It is important to realize that personnel planning will take different forms depending on the time horizon involved: In the short term it can take place at a low level in the company, in the long term it must take place in the management group which deals with company long term planning. In the short term the order stock can be used as a base and it is relatively simple to compute the personnel which is required for a given number of days, weeks or months. In the long term another more complicated planning technique is required, taking other alternatives into account. In the short term the necessity of documenting the planning is relatively slight; in the long term it is extremely important to establish in written form the planning decisions which have been made, partly as a reminder, partly in order to spread the information within the company, and partly in order to be able to follow up the plans and learn by mistakes and make the adjustments which changes in circumstances necessitate.

The Relationship Between Company Long Term Planning and Personnel Planning

A prerequisite of long term planning of company personnel resources is the long term planning of company activities as a whole. It may be said that company long term planning can be put into concrete form as a planning of changes in company organization structure. Long term planning should in any case give information about in which essential respects company organization will be changed in subsequent years. This type of relationship between long term planning and personnel planning is perhaps patently obvious. But there is also another type of relationship between personnel planning and long term planning to which attention has gradually been devoted in Sweden during the years when a manpower shortage has been particularly noticeable. Company after company has been forced to realize that long term planning also depends on data concerning labour market developments and the company's opportunities of recruiting, retaining and training suitable personnel.

A Planning System

On the bases of these ideas we have attempted to develop a planning system which takes into account both collective conditions, i.e. the personnel structure as a whole and individual conditions, i.e. planning directed towards the personal development of the individual employee.

The *analysis* which we have made is in the first instance an analysis of the important planning decisions. Which decisions are they? Who makes them? What is the result of these decisions? What material is required in order for the decisions to be made?

After identifying these important decisions and defining their output and input, we have been able to arrange them in a yearly cycle where each decision is based on previous ones.

The *system* is based on the one hand on manpower planning, which is the collective planning of the personnel structure and on the other hand the individual planning for individual employees, which is connected with work planning.

As secondary plans intended to achieve the intended manning and individual development, we have primarily a planning of personnel mobility into, out of and within the company together with planning of training.

These main components in the personnel planning system are as has been suggested based on a determination of the organizational situation in force during the planning period. This can be seen in the figure (Figure 1, p. 170).

But the personnel planning is not only based on decisions recurring with a given regularity during a yearly cycle. A form of *basic service* is necessary, consisting of co-ordination, a personnel inventory, and personnel statistics. Analysis of training requirements for different types of jobs, the development of company personnel policy and the development of the day-to-day personnel administrative routines as well as a continuous follow-up of changes in the company's labour market. Notably, this basic service requires that the company has sufficient capacity within, for instance, the personnel and training department.

A personnel statistical program is necessary if the personnel planning system is to function properly. Company opportunities for data processing will thereby be of considerable importance in this connection. The most important part of such a personnel statistical program is an inventory of the available personnel resources in each unit, occupation, level, training or education, age, sex and period of employment. Many decisions about the future can be made merely on the basis of this descriptive material. Of special importance here are forecasts or assessments of the departures from the company which can be expected in the coming years.

Let us now examine more closely the *components in a personnel planning system.*

The planning components whose function is to determine the personnel structure which the company should aim at for different time periods is called *manpower planning.* One of the most important problems when determining the personnel requirements for the company as a whole and for given units is that the quantitative requirements must initially be divided up into occupational, training or other qualitative categories. It is impossible to overestimate the importance of a correct division into categories.

Manpower planning for the coming year is usually expressed in a personnel budget. For longer periods we speak of a *manpower forecast.* On the basis of what has been said above, manpower planning takes place as a form of gliding planning which each year involves the whole of the planning period as can be seen in the figure (Figure 3, p. 171).

The *personnel budget* has come to be used in a large number of companies in recent years and has become an important instrument for guiding company short term manning.

We propose that the personnel budget consists of a table showing the number of positions of various types or requiring different qualifications, which company management has set up as a directive for different units. We thus distinguish between *personnel budgets* which gives the number of positions as opposed to the reformulation of this personnel budget in terms of money, which we call a *wages budget* and which might be expanded into a *personnel cost budget.*

The personnel budget is specified for different company units or cost centers in order to act as an aid towards guidance and control. The positions are then grouped in accordance with the factors which management wishes to guide in a first instance. Common groupings are for type of employment, e.g. regular or temporary employees, for educational or training categories, for sex or for occupation. A division into age groups would also be justified in many companies.

The most common method of *constructing the personnel budget* has been to send out lists of employees to heads of departments who have been asked to make budget proposals. We have found in this situation that it is important for departmental heads to be aware of the organizational objectives for their own department and for them to have a base for the assessment of changes in work loads, opportunities for rationalization, etc. Then only can department heads present realistic budget proposals.

We believe for psychological reasons that it is important for departmental heads to present budget proposals but we believe it is also important for the budget proposals to be collected and compiled centrally within the company and discussed in co-operation with the planning department, organization department, personnel department, finance department, etc. By doing so it is possible to obtain a personnel budget proposal which is acceptable to the whole company and which can with costs specified then be put before company management for a decision.

The value of the personnel budget as an administrative aid is in the first instance that deviations between the actual manpower and the personnel budget are regularly reported, usually every month to company management and departmental heads.

Long term manpower planning, the *manpower forecast,* is to be sure in principle based on the same type of material as the personnel budget, but we have found it unrealistic to expect that departmental managers will be in a position to provide a suitable base for more long term manpower planning. We thus recommend as a rule that this work is performed centrally in the company, primarily in co-operation between the organization, planning and personnel functions.

It is suitable to report the manpower forecasts in two ways: The first is in the form of a quantitative plan, showing the personnel distribution in units, levels and occupational categories. In addition a more detailed qualitative analysis of changes in certain positions or types of positions is often strongly motivated.

I should like to sum up by means of a little diagram the main features of manpower planning as we see it (Figure 4, p. 172).

The diagram also illustrates the way in which we work when analysing key decisions in the company's planning of its personnel resources.

The second basic aspect of personnel planning is *planning based on the individual employee.*

Certain information required for personnel planning can only be obtained from the supervisor in question. Thus the planning which a manager arrives at for a given employee with the latter's participation is of central importance in our personnel planning system. Work planning for the individual employee may take place in many different forms. Among the essential elements is, however, an assessment of the nature and extent of the work and work requirements on the one hand and an assessement of the employee on the other.

It is these ingredients which are weighed up when discussing difficulties, time taken and job results. Since the data which are required for personnel planning purposes deal with the work and the individual and the relation between them, work planning is the natural link for individual planning from the view-point of the employee. It is for this reason we consider it suitable to link the concepts of individual work planning and individual personnel planning.

We thus stress that the central personnel and training department periodically requires decisions or suggestions from supervisors concerning measures dealing with individual employees: Measures such as transfer, special duties, training, social or medical care. In its simplest form this may be done by every manager sending lists of his subordinates to the personnel department with notes on measures planned for the future.

Various systematic forms may be used in order that decisions concerning these measures might be made in the best possible way. One form of systematization is regular planning meetings in which superior and subordinate take part, where both should be in possession of the necessary background information. The most important part of the meeting is producing a list of future duties including changes in the quantity and type of work. A simple but essential form of guidance is then a discussion on the priorities of different duties. Perhaps also the performance standards which are regarded as a criterion of a good performance. On the basis of this discussion it is possible to formulate the requirements which coming duties may be expected to place upon the superior and subordinate and the resources which are required in order to fulfill work schedules. It is this type of discussion which in a natural manner can lead on the measures which must be taken.

Intentionally, I have still not used the expression *personnel appraisal.* This is for two reasons. The first is that in my opinion a personnel planning system is able to function without including systematic personnel appraisal. The second reason is that personnel appraisal is one of the most difficult fields a personnel department may be asked to deal with and that many companies who have attempted to apply personnel appraisal have been disappointed that the system has quickly crumbled away to nothing.

This does not of course mean that we underestimate the advantages of a systematic system of personnel appraisal. But we believe that such a system should be the result of the wishes of management and not of the ambitions of the personnel department.

From the manpower forecast, management thus obtains information about the composition of company personnel structure which is necessary for the next few years in order to be in accordance with the company's other objectives.

By means of the personnel budget the company personnel structure for the coming year is guided in order to correspond with company requirements.

By combining the individual plans it is possible to obtain an overview of the measures which are required with regard to the employees' adjustment to the duties in question.

These planning instruments are the most important ones and together they are the starting point for the more detailed program which is required to attain the objectives intended.

I am referring to the programs which are required for the planning of internal and external personnel changes, i.e. hirings, departures, transfers and promotions together with those required for training planning.

The basic aids to *planning,* at least in the short term, of *personnel mobility* are lists of vacant positions which can be expected to arise, and lists of employees who may be considered in connection with reduction, transfer and/or promotion. These lists should be present in one form or another in all personnel departments.

A third type of aid to mobility planning which has been used increasingly in recent years are *replacement tables* or *replacement lists.* They are of special interest for promotion but have shown themselves to be very useful for transfers at one given level as well. Promotion planning consists of three tasks. In the first place to determine the vacancies which might be expected to arise with various degrees of certainty. Secondly to list the promotable material available within the company. And thirdly to determine the training requirements of replacements and the period of development required in order to make them promotable.

In the long term the planning of personnel changes takes on the character of *project programs:* A long term recruitment program may for example be supported with the aid of project programs for improving working methods and employment routines or for the obtaining of houses or for adaptable remuneration structures.

I shall not devote much time to the types of supervision and the types of mobility which are particularly valuable for development purposes. A few words on the *planning of the formal training* are, however, necessary.

Experience shows that there are three types of training plans which companies apply. The first type aims, for a given time period of say a year, at working out a plan for the year's activities and computing the costs involved, access to premises, teaching staff, etc. *A yearly plan* for training should be based partly on training connected with personnel mobility and partly on training connected with changes in job requirements.

For this reason two further types of training planning are required, firstly a planning of training for different personnel categories. *These category plans* involve an investigation of the recruitment material on which the training is to be based for different personnel categories and a determination of the promotion channels existing in the company. This also involves a description of the various training stages which should take place for the personnel category and the relationship between these stages and different positions or levels. The category plans also include the training content, the organization of training and the period of training judged suitable by the company.

The category plans notably involve a coordination of company recruitment, promotion and training policy. These plans will of course be long term ones. It is suitable for the category plans to be worked out and revised successively and decisions about them should be made by company management. One type of material for the yearly plan is thus obtained with the aid of the category plans for training and the concrete program for mobility through recruitment, promotion and transfer.

The other type of training plans is connected with changes in requirements placed on job incumbents. We have called them *further training plans*. They may in principle have two different bases. The first alternative is that they are a summary of the courses included in the individual planning. The second alternative is that a training administrator or consultant analyses the further training requirements for certain personnel groups and by doing so aids the company's decisions concerning training.

Concerning the *introduction* of a complicated system of this type we have as a rule found that the introduction of one routine at a time is better than attempting to introduce everything at once. It is also usually the case that some of the necessary routines already exist in more or less systematic form within the company and that what is required for the system to function more satisfactorily is in the first instance the addition of some routine or perhaps an adjustment of the time-table.

Certain companies are sometimes interested in attempting to start with a given sector or company department. Our experience has been that the advantages of the introduction of the system can scarcely be achieved by doing so. The system is obviously intended for the company as a whole. In those cases where a limitation of the personnel involved is suitable we should therefore like to advise as a rule that steps be taken one level at a time, i.e., that a start is made with company management and that successive expansion takes place downwards in the company hierarchy.

The various components of a personnel planning system are interrelated and must be co-ordinated. Furthermore, these components do not merely concern the personnel department or certain other specialist departments but also management and supervision at all levels.

In conclusion it is perhaps worth stressing in this connection something experienced by many: Active and integrated personnel planning is not a matter for the personnel department alone but for company management as a whole.

FIGURE 1

The Major Features of an Annual Personnel Planning Cycle

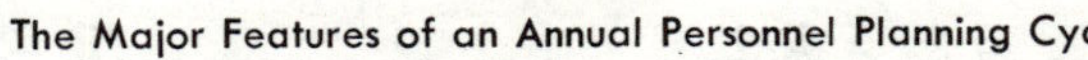

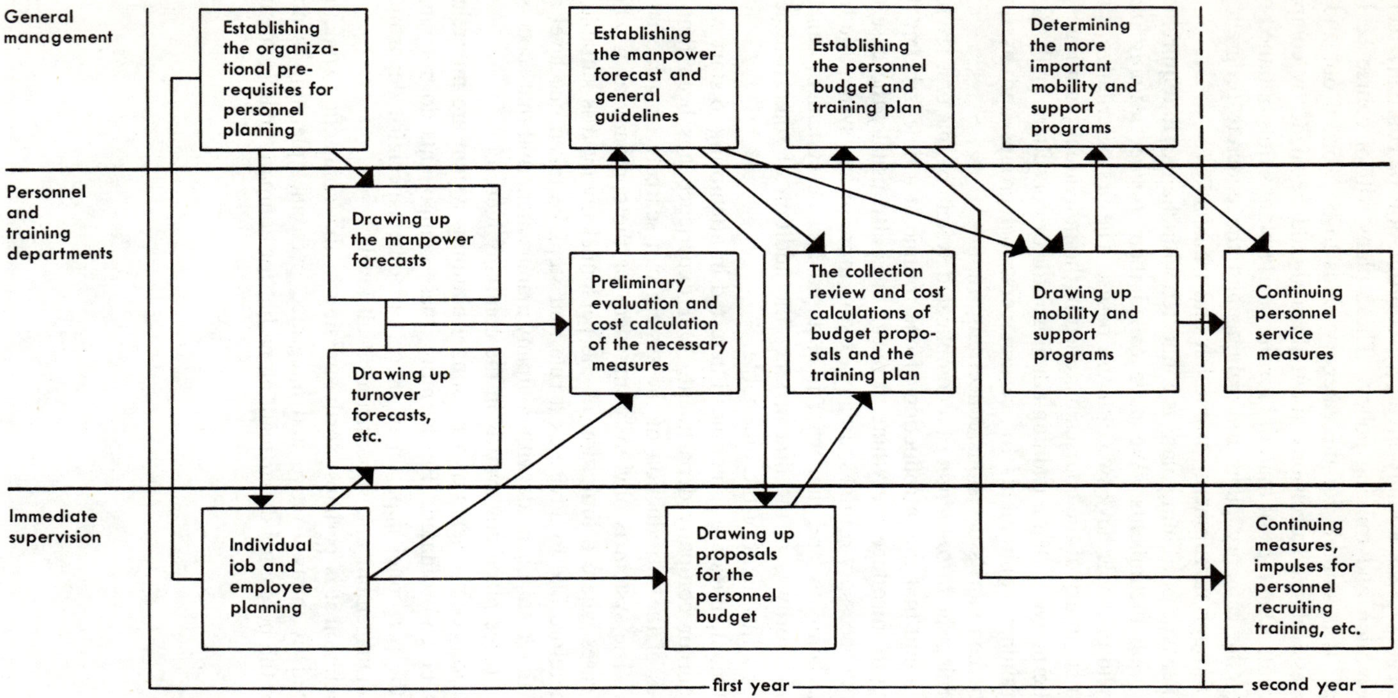

The arrows indicate how various measures and decisions constitute the prerequisites for later duties. Information and consultation, modifications of plans, etc. are obviously not included in this simplified chart. The timing of the different decisions and measures must be adjusted to the planning rhythm of the company, its desired distribution of the work load, etc.

FIGURES 2 and 3

The Manpower Resources of the Enterprise

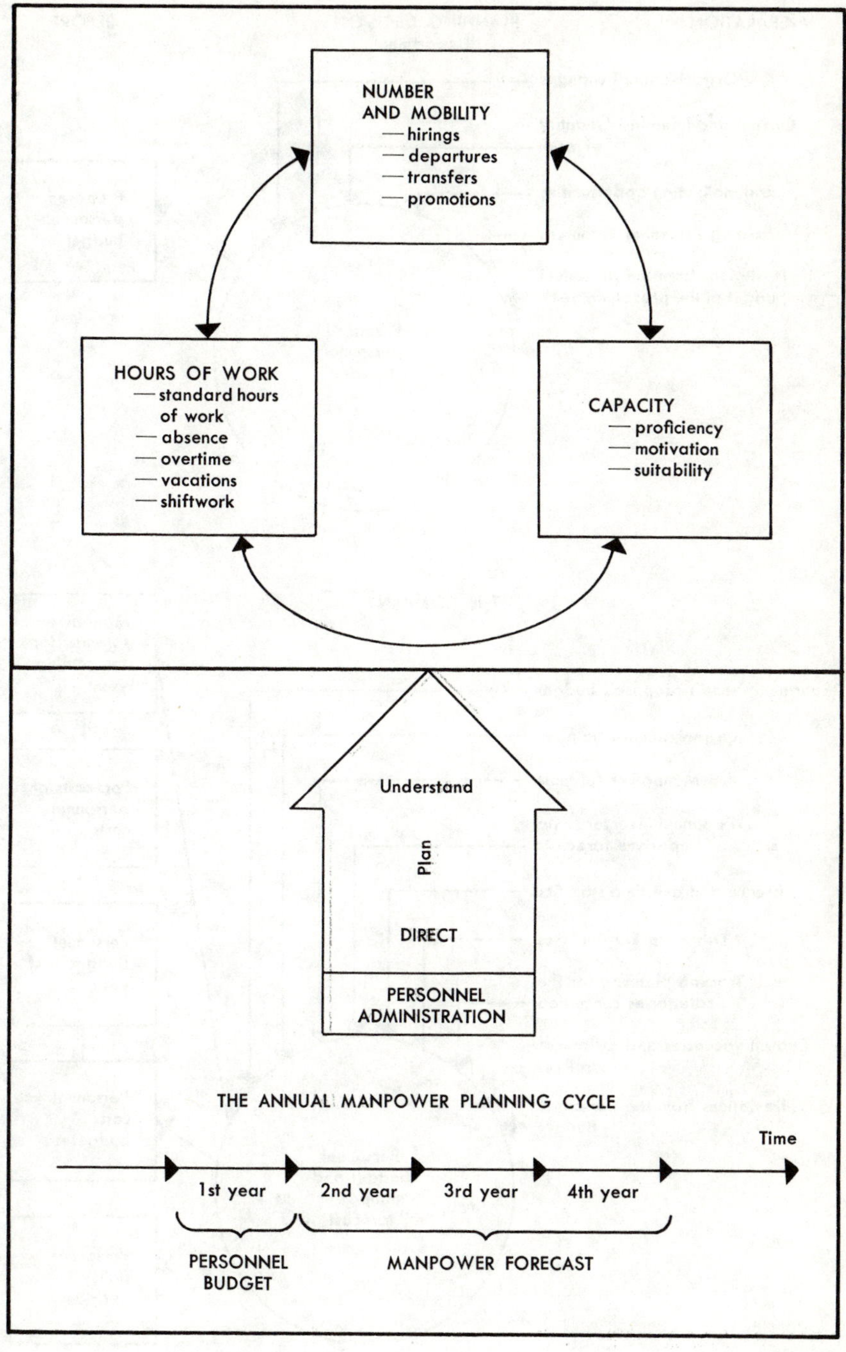

FIGURE 4
Manpower Planning

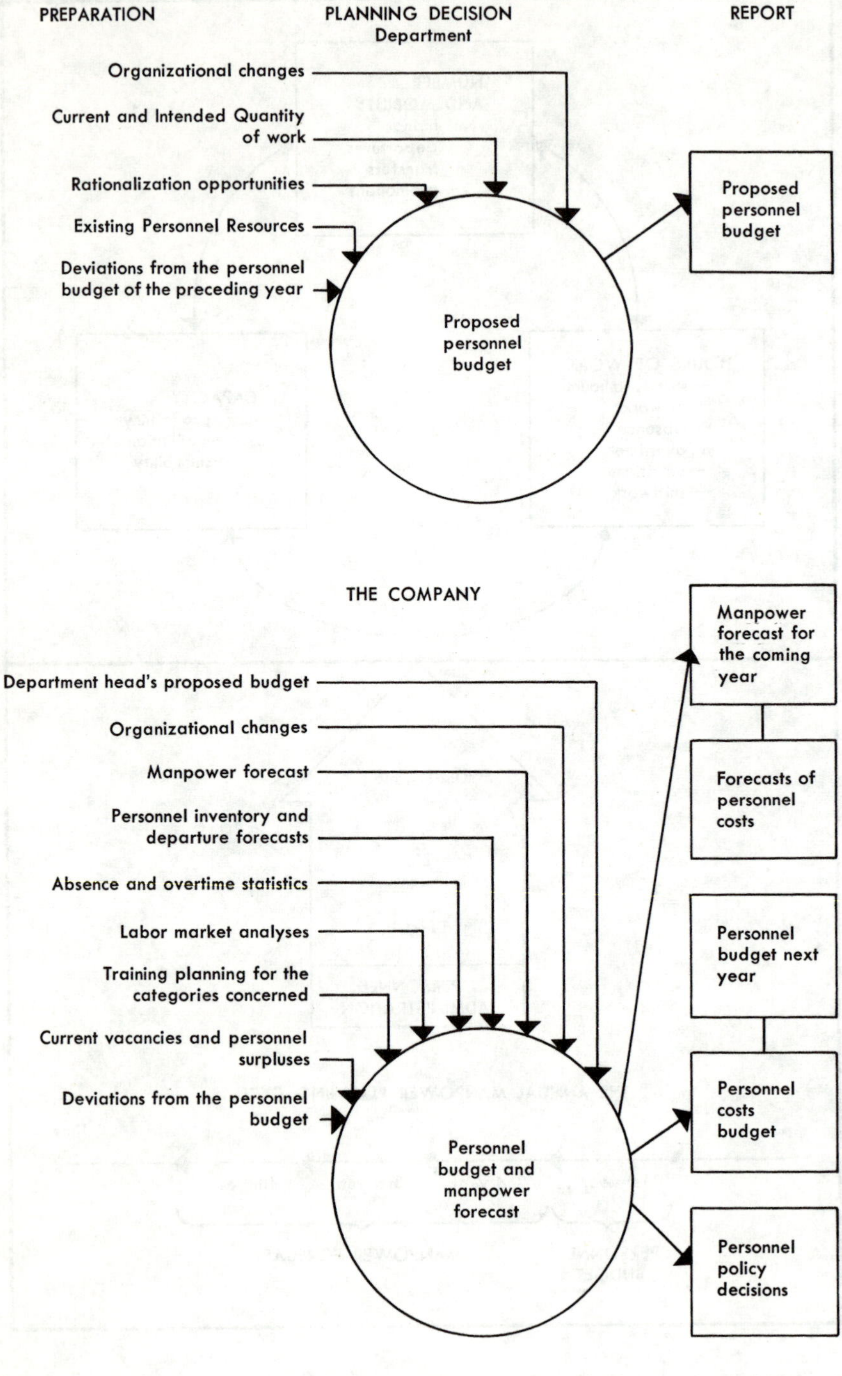

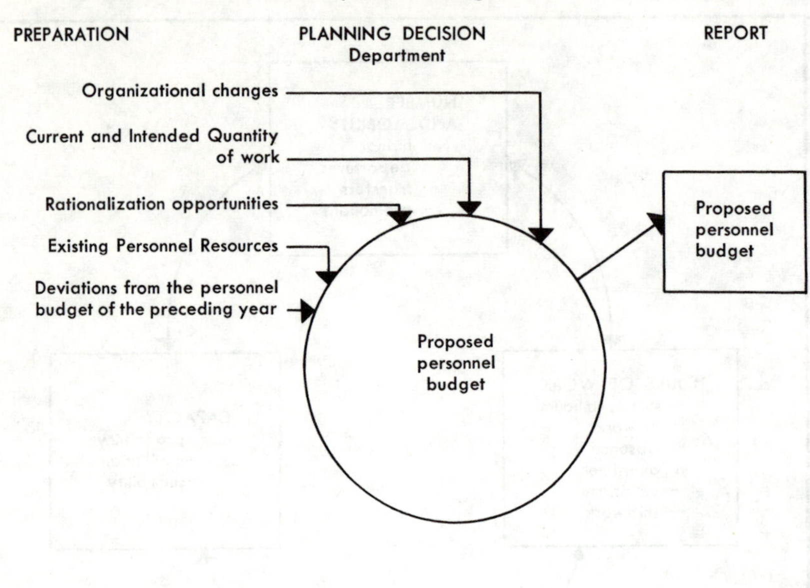

PREPARATION
PLANNING DECISION
Department
REPORT
Organizational changes
Current and Intended Quantity of work
Rationalization opportunities
Existing Personnel Resources
Deviations from the personnel budget of the preceding year
Proposed personnel budget
Proposed personnel budget
THE COMPANY
Department head's proposed budget
Organizational changes
Manpower forecast
Personnel inventory and departure forecasts
Absence and overtime statistics
Labor market analyses
Training planning for the categories concerned
Current vacancies and personnel surpluses
Deviations from the personnel budget
Personnel budget and manpower forecast
Manpower forecast for the coming year
Forecasts of personnel costs
Personnel budget next year
Personnel costs budget
Personnel policy decisions

16

Organizational Theory and Human Resource Accounting

RENSIS LIKERT
University of Michigan

DAVID G. BOWERS
University of Michigan

Organizational research in business companies has the potential for making major and often unique theoretical contributions to the social sciences as well as helping to solve some of the most serious problems of present day society. To make these theoretical and practical contributions, however, more rapid progress must be made in organizational research and theory development than has occurred in the past two decades. The present researchers believe that we are on the verge of accelerating such progress, and in this article the reasons for this opinion will be indicated. Finally, examples of the unique and valuable contributions that organizational theory is likely to make in the next decade toward the solution of some of the grave social problems will be given.

Social scientists engaged in research on management and organizational performance initially expected to find a marked and consistent relationship between the management system of a leader, the attitudes and loyalties of his subordinates, and the productivity of his organization. A number of studies undertaken in the decade following World War II, including studies made at the Institute for Social Research, University of Michigan, have wielded many different relationships among these variables. In summarizing the relationships between the attitudes of employees and their productivity, various reviewers (e.g., Brayfield & Crockett, 1955; Dubin, Homans, Mann, & Miller, 1965; Herzberg, Mausner, Peterson, & Capwell, 1957; Miller & Form, 1964) have concluded generally that the studies taken altogether show no simple, consistent, dependable relationship among the variables.

These generally unexpected research findings raise an important question.

Rensis Likert and David G. Bowers, "Organizational Theory and Human Resource Accounting," *American Psychologist*, Vol. 24, No. 6, June 1969, pp. 585–592.

What accounts for the failure to find consistent relationships among these variables?

The answer appears to be that the relations among these variables are so complex that taking measurements of these variables at one point in time in an organization or group of organizations and computing correlations among the variables is much too simple a research design to yield accurate knowledge and insights. This design ignores the influence of (a) many powerful conditioning or moderating variables and (b) the serious inaccuracies in the time-bound performance data. It yields, as surveys of the literature show, a confused and contradictory body of results.

Progressively, the nature of the variables causing these contradictory results is being discovered as well as their influence on the interrelationships among the leadership, motivational, and performance dimensions. The variables causing the contradictory results include: (a) the discrepancy between the leader's report of his behavior and his actual behavior; (b) the values, expectations, and skills of subordinates; (c) the manager's capacity to exercise influence upward; (d) the size of the unit or firm; (e) the kind of work being done; (f) time and changes over time; and (g) inaccurate or inadequate measurements of the criterion variables, such as productivity and earnings.

Data are available which indicate that, when one takes into consideration all of these variables that cause contradictory conclusions, especially the trends over time, the results are likely to show that there are consistent, dependable relationships among leadership, motivational, and performance variables (Likert, 1967, Ch. 5).

To test further this assumption, a series of related studies, referred to generally as the Inter-Company Longitudinal Studies, are being undertaken. A related program of research is being instituted for the development of human resource accounting, to provide far more accurate financial criteria. This involves developing the methodology to enable a firm (a) to estimate dollar investments made in building its human organization, and (b) to estimate the present discounted productive value of that human organization.

Research Plan for the Longitudinal Studies

In this article, three broad classes of variables will be referred to, labeled, respectively, causal, intervening, and end-result. They can be defined briefly as follows:

1. The *causal* variables are independent variables that can be directly or purposely altered or changed by the organization and its management and that, in turn, determine the course of developments within an organization and the results achieved by that organization. "General business conditions," for example, although comprising independent variables, are *not*

viewed as causal since the management of a particular enterprise ordinarily can do little about them. Causal variables include the structure of the organization and management's policies, decisions, business and leadership strategies, skills, and behavior.

2. The *intervening* variables reflect the internal state, health, and performance capabilities of the organization; for example, the loyalties, attitudes, motivations, performance goals, and perceptions of all members and their collective capacity for effective action, interaction, communication, and decision making.

3. The *end-result* variables are the dependent variables that reflect the results achieved by that organization, such as its productivity, costs, scrap loss, growth, share of the market, and earnings.

Collection of periodic measurements from a set of business firms over about a five-year period will be required to obtain sufficient data for testing hypotheses concerning the nature and magnitude of the interrelationships among the causal, intervening, and end-result variables. Present indications are that data over approximately the same span of time will be needed for the computations required to develop that phase of human resource accounting devoted to estimating the present and changing value of the human organization.

Planning for this project has been under way for more than two years. Pilot studies were started over a year ago. The activities to date have involved 20 organizational sites, including over 11,000 persons in eight different companies. Since February 1966, a machine-scored core questionnaire has been developed, computer programs have been created that are adequate to process the data in the form required for the major venture, and pilot efforts have been conducted in applying existing knowledge and current data to improve organizational capabilities and performance.

The following considerations illustrate the approach used in selecting research sites:

1. To study time lag effectively requires some variation in that lag. Enormous differences, on the other hand, would confound the analysis. Some variation, therefore, will be sought, but within reasonable limits. Factors that affect the time lag will be taken into account. Available evidence shows, for example, that the time lag between changes in the causal variables and performance differ with regard to: (*a*) *Size* — Lag time appears to be longer in larger organizations; (*b*) *Type of work* — Lag time may well be longer in repetitive, tightly engineered assembly manufacturing plants and probably is shorter in sales, research and development, and service industries; (*c*) *Organizational complexity* — Complexity of organizational structure, as well as size, probably affects lag time. The cycle time is likely to be longer where events must cross many layers of hierarchy (tall organiza-

tions) and where operations are functionally different, yet interdependent in the long run.

2. Sites must be sufficiently autonomous in their operations to permit organizational improvement programs to succeed. It would not be desirable to include one section of a large installation that is highly dependent in its operation upon related components when these components are not also a part of the project.

3. Sites for which accurate, reliable performance records exist should be sought. The problems created by ambiguous and unreliable end-result performance criteria should be avoided. (This problem is discussed in greater detail in a subsequent section of this article.)

4. Sites with a history of unstable operation should be avoided, as, for example, those sites that experience recurring technical or market upheaval and those that are subject to rapid and frequent product and technological changes.

Data To Be Collected

Four distinct bodies of data are to be collected:

Questionnaire Data

Questionnaires will be administered at least once a year, initially by Institute of Social Research personnel. In addition, questionnaires will be administered in most firms on a sample basis more often than once a year. This additional query will obtain evidence concerning changes in relationships among the variables not adequately reflected in the annual measurements.

The instrument that will be employed contains a core of organizational measures covering both causal and intervening variables. This core consists of 18 indexes based on 48 multiple-choice items and reflects the theory of organization structure and functioning presented in *New Patterns of Management* (Likert, 1961) and *The Human Organization* (Likert, 1967). A much-simplified version of the concepts is shown as Figure 1.

The questionnaire includes, also, a supplement of approximately 70 additional items for diagnostic and research purposes, plus provision for optional specific items desired by each firm.

Performance Data

A major problem in this study is that of establishing criteria of performance comparable from one organization to another. Within any one firm, or perhaps among firms from the same industry, these measures may be more or less comparable. For comparisons across all firms and units, however, some broad conceptualization and data transformation of the performance variables of the kinds commonly encountered in organizational studies are clearly necessary.

Performance is viewed in terms of an overall criterion of long-term profitability influenced by results in six subordinate areas: volume, efficiency, quality, development, attendance, and human costs (Figure 2).

A major problem results from the fact that in any one of the six subordinate areas, there will be available in a particular firm only a partial representation of the total content. Measures in each area may be vastly

FIGURE 1

Schematic Relationships among Causal, Intervening, and End-result Variables

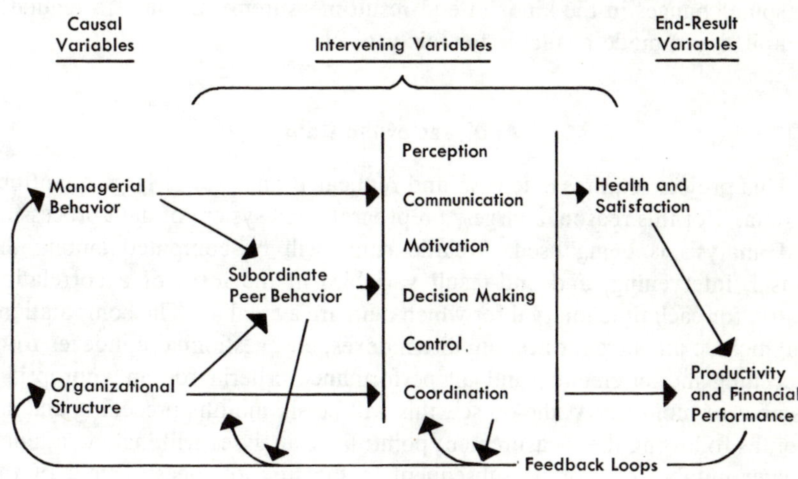

FIGURE 2

Categories of Subordinate Criteria Contributing to an Overall Criterion of Long-Term Profitability

Volume of work	Efficiency	Quality	Attendance	Development	Human costs
Volume of output Market penetration	Production costs Waste Scrap Down time Performance versus Schedule Performance versus Standard Rate of earnings	Quality output Rework ratio Accuracy Customer returns Customer complaints Repeat business Rejection rate	Absence Hours worked per week Turnover	Growth in volume Manpower development Innovation	Accidents Physical health Psychological health Tension Stress Conflict Grievances Disciplinary actions

different from one firm to another. It may be necessary, therefore, to transform all measures in some fashion to obtain criteria that are at least conceptually comparable from firm to firm. These analyses of the available end-result data will employ sophisticated methods and concepts of accounting and financial analysis. They also will make full use of recent research on performance criteria and organizational effectiveness carried out by Seashore and his colleagues (Seashore, 1965; Yuchtman & Seashore, 1967). The work employing accounting concepts will be directed by R. Lee Brummet, Professor of Accounting, Graduate School of Business Administration, The University of Michigan. It is probable that these analyses will increase the accuracy of the end-result data, making them more useful not only for research but also for operating purposes. As this occurs, there are likely to be some changes in the kinds of end-result measurements that are regularly compiled and made available for this project.

Analyses of the Data

This project requires extensive and replicated analyses of large quantities of data. For this reason, a largely preprogrammed system of data processing and analysis is being used. Relationships will be computed among the causal, intervening, and end-result variables in the form of a correlation matrix for each time interval for which data are available. The computations will include all current questionnaire indexes, all questionnaire indexes from preceding measurements, and all performance criteria for an appropriate number of months. At the outset, this will be six months preceding and six months following the measurement point; later analyses will include a much greater number of months subsequent to the time of measurement of the causal and intervening variables. Correlations will be plotted as curves over time. By inspection, peaks can be located and the time intervals and the levels of maximum relationships observed.

Human Resource Accounting

The financial performance records of any firm and especially trends in the financial data will contain serious inadequacies and errors as long as human resources are ignored. These resources include the value of all such assets as a firm's human organization, its customer loyalty, shareholder loyalty, supplier loyalty, its reputation among the financial community, and its reputation in the community in which it has plants and offices.

The magnitude of these investments is revealed by the substantial sums paid for acquisitions and mergers in excess of the value of the physical assets. It also is revealed, as far as the value of the human organization is concerned, by the answers of company officers to the following question:

> Assume that tomorrow morning every position in your firm is vacant, that all of the present jobs are there, all of the present plants, offices, equipment, patents, and all financial resources but no people. How long would it take and how much would it cost to hire personnel to fill all of the present jobs, to train them to their present level of competence, and to build them into the well-knit organization which now exists?

In response to this question the top management of several companies have estimated that it would take from two to ten times their annual payroll to cover the cost of rebuilding their human organization to the performance capabilities of their present staff. The most frequent estimates are from three to five times.

By using this procedure to obtain an estimate of the value of a firm's human organization, one can readily relate this estimate to earnings since payrolls usually exceed earnings by two- to ten-fold. Computing an estimate for a typical firm by using conservative estimates, such as that the human organization is worth three times payroll and the payroll is about five times earnings, then the human organization of such a firm is worth about 15 times earnings (3×5). With this ratio of the value of the human organization to earnings, relatively minor fluctuations, for example, 10%, in the value of a firm's human organization can be equal to a substantial proportion of its annual earnings.

When the value of the other human resource assets are included, such as customer loyalty, supplier loyalty, shareholder loyalty, and financial reputation, even smaller fluctuations than 10% in all of the human resource assets can be equal to or exceed a typical year's earnings of a firm. When all forms of human resources are ignored in a firm's accounting reports, as at present, the stated earnings can show a favorable picture for several years when the actual assets and true value are steadily *decreasing* by a substantial fraction.

The development of human resource accounting is necessary to provide a firm with accurate financial reports to guide its decision. It also is needed to increase the validity of criteria measurements used in organizational research.

The methodology for all forms of human resource accounting will be developed. Initial efforts, however, are focused on developing accounting procedures for dealing with a firm's investment in its human organization. Presently the investigators are engaged in developing procedures for estimating the actual costs incurred in recruiting, selecting, training employees and familiarizing them with all aspects of their work, and in establishing effective working relations with others in the organization. This work will enable a firm to estimate its investment in individuals and groups of individuals in the organization. Appropriate amortization assumptions have been developed to permit these investments to be written off over appropriate time spans.

Procedures for computing personnel replacement costs are being developed also. These procedures can provide another set of estimates that have relevance in personnel planning accounting as well as providing the usual check on incurred cost estimates.

Firms already are deriving valuable insights into operating problems from these outlay and replacement cost measurements. Turnover figures, for example, often take on completely different meaning when expressed in these terms. The loss of a manager or engineer shortly after he has been given extensive training is quite different from the loss of a manager or engineer who is near retirement.

It is essential, however, for a firm to know not only its investment in human resources but to know as well the present productive capability of that human organization, that is, its present value to the firm. These value estimates cannot be made until reasonably accurate estimates of the relationships over a span of years among the causal, intervening, and end-result variables have been compiled. Data to permit these estimates are being obtained. Experimental calculations indicate that useful estimates can be derived from this approach.

Within 5 to 10 years, procedures will be available for making reasonably accurate estimates of the trends in all of these various forms of a firm's human assets. The financial reports will then reflect, with reasonable accuracy, the financial state and changes of financial condition through time and not ignore, as at present, serious fluctuations in one-third to one-half of its assets. When these more accurate financial reports become available, the correlations between such causal variables as leadership style and such end-result variables as financial performance, even when measured at one point in time, will be much more likely to show consistent, dependable relationships than at present. Moreover, these more accurate and valid reports will encourage a company in its own self-interest to shift much more rapidly than now to the application of more complex and more effective management systems emerging from organizational research. These systems will provide more accurate data to a manager, enabling him to evaluate correctly any new development he undertakes.

Some Preliminary Results from Longitudinal Research

From the pilot studies started a couple of years ago, the second year of measurements are becoming available. The early data are confirming our expectations that measurements, over at least a few years time, are necessary to obtain correct estimates of the relationships that actually exist among the causal, intervening, and end-result variables. Some initial results will show the findings beginning to emerge.

In one continuous process plant, employing over 500 persons, measurements of the causal and intervening variables obtained in 1966 were related by work groups ($N = 40$ groups) to performance data for the same period of time. Three indexes of managerial behavior were used. The first index reflects the extent to which the manager is seen as being supportive and applying the principle of supportive relationships. This index is called "managerial support." The second refers to his efforts to use group problem solving in dealing with work problems and to build his work group into a cohesive effective team; this is called "managerial interaction facilitation." The third reflects the manager's attempts to aid his subordinates on job problems and to provide the knowledge and technical resources they need for their work, and is labeled "managerial work facilitation."

These three measures of managerial behavior were related to monthly performance measurements for these 40 work groups for the four successive months just prior to and subsequent to the period when the causal variables were measured. The performance measurements were actual incurred costs, expressed as a percentage of the standard; the lower this ratio of costs, the better the performance. None of the 12 possible coefficients of correlation (three managerial variables related to performance for four separate months, or 3×4) was large enough to be statistically significant (for .05 level, $r = .31$).

When these measurements of managerial behavior, obtained in 1966, were related to monthly performance measured one year later, all 12 of the correlation coefficients were statistically significant. They varied from −.48 to −.58. These correlations should be negative, of course, since the better the managerial behavior is, the lower the costs should be. Clearly, in this case, managerial behavior is related to cost performance one year later but *not* at the time of the behavior assessment.

Similar results were obtained when the analysis was based on peer leadership within the work group. The same three leadership variables were used, but this time they dealt with the extent to which work-group members saw their own colleagues providing peer leadership in the form of support, interaction facilitation, and work facilitation. Using 1966 measurements of peer leadership, and again using performance data for four consecutive months in 1966, only 1 of the 12 possible correlations was significant. Peer support yielded −.31 correlation with performance in one of the four months.

The results again were quite different when the 1966 measures of peer leadership behavior, namely, peer support, peer work facilitation, and peer interaction facilitation, were related to performance results for four consecutive months one year later. All of the 12 possible correlations between the 1966 measurements of peer leadership and the 1967 measurements of performance are statistically significant. They range in magnitude from −.41 to −.59.

Comparable findings were obtained for five different indexes measuring intervening variables. These variables reflect the level of (a) work motivation; (b) communication, upward, downward, and lateral; (c) control, including managements' capacity to control work-group behavior; (d) interdepartmental coordination; and (e) decision making. The 1966 measurements of these variables when correlated with 1966 performance data for four consecutive months yielded only 2 statistically significant correlations out of a possible 20 (i.e., 5 × 4). When the 1966 measurements of the five intervening variables were related to 1967 performance data, that is, one year later, all 20 of the correlation coefficients were significant and varied from −.37 to −.68. For the communication index, the correlations with the four monthly performance indexes were −.57, −.58, −.67, and −.68.

When measurements of the causal and intervening variables made in 1967 are related to performance data for four consecutive months in 1967, more of the correlations are statistically significant than for the 1966 data for both sets of measurements. Eight of 12 correlations relating managerial behavior to monthly measurements of performance, 4 of 12 peer correlations, and 17 of 20 correlations relating intervening variables to performance measurements are large enough to be statistically significant at the .05 level.

Nevertheless, the correlations between the 1966 measurements of causal and intervening variables and the performance data for one year later are quite consistently higher than the correlations between measurements of performance data and causal and intervening variables made at or near the same time in 1967. Thus, 12 of 12 correlations between the three measures of managerial behavior (support, work facilitation, and interaction facilitation) and four monthly measurements of performance are higher for the 1966–67 comparison than for the correlations based entirely on 1967 data. The same is true for 12 of 12 correlations dealing with peer leadership, and for 17 of 20 correlations relating intervening variables to performance data.

The results just reported are for a continuous process manufacturing plant. Yuchtman (1966) found similar results in data from sales organizations. For example, he found that causal variables related to performance data measured at the same time yielded 10 significant correlations. When these same causal variables were related to performance data measured one year after the measurement of the causal variables, he obtained higher correlations generally and 14 instead of 10 significant correlations.

These results of the relationships over time among the causal, intervening, and end-result variables are, of course, consistent with theoretical expectations. Data from other research sites involving other kinds of work and industries and for longer time periods soon will be available. The pattern that these results display will be extremely interesting.

Although the current findings correspond, in general, with expectations, it is important to add that often the relationships are appreciably more complex than expected and require the development and use of more elaborate analytical models than originally had been anticipated.

An example of these complex interrelationships involves the relationship between the capacity to exercise influence on decisions affecting a man's work and his productivity. Among scientists and engineers, the capacity to influence decisions concerning one's own work is associated with greater productivity (Pelz & Andrews, 1966). But, as Farris has shown, for engineering personnel, these relationships can be circular. Outstanding past performance increases the likelihood that a man can exert influence on decisions affecting his technical goals (Farris, 1966). This relationship, which Farris found to be more marked than the converse, shows the pervasive influence of excellent performance. The high-performing engineer saw himself as being able to exert more influence on establishing the goals designated for him. He was more absorbed in his work, had more competent subordinates, and a better salary. These results make a great deal of sense. One would expect that individuals who have demonstrated greater capacity would have more influence on decisions and related activities both within their work group and in the organization generally. Effective group decision making enables every person to be heard, but the weight of each in the decision-making process is influenced appreciably by his demonstrated competence. This effect of a person's performance upon his capacity to exert influence is shown diagrammatically in Figure 1 by the feedback loops.

Applications of Organizational Theory and Principles of Organizational Change

The available and growing evidence justifies the view that further research very probably will demonstrate strong and consistent relationships among the causal, intervening, and end-result variables; that certain leadership styles and management systems consistently will be found more highly motivating and yielding better organizational performance than others.

If this proves to be the case, the emergence of more valid effective organizational theory and improved management systems will have a widespread impact on all kinds of administration: education, hospital, business, and government. The application of improved management systems will lead to substantial improvement in organizational performance, accompanied by better physical and mental health and greater member satisfaction. The most important consequences, however, are likely to occur in fields other than administration.

To illustrate briefly, it is obvious that our society faces some extremely difficult and serious problems: deterioration of inner cities and urban riots; worldwide population explosion; student demonstrations and riots; social and economic development in the newer nations; conflicts among nations; and threats of nuclear and biological warfare.

In the past, nations have relied primarily on trial and error and "muddling through" to deal with these and other global problems. One can hope that the world's most enlightened leaders will turn soon to social science research for the solution of these problems.

If this were to occur tomorrow and if substantial funds were made available for the research, the progress initially would be slow. The nature of these serious problems is such that researching them is a very difficult task. The causes of the problems are extremely complex, the frequencies of the cause and effect cycles tend to be low (e.g., urban riots or student demonstrations), and the cycles are of long duration. Another primary reason for the research being retarded and difficult is that the performance criteria available for evaluating any particular approach or solution to such major problems are usually inadequate or inaccurate. Studies designed to discover cause and effect relationships make progress more slowly and require vastly more data when the effects, that is, performance data, are inadequate, inaccurate, or "rare event" phenomena. Urban riots, for example, are rare events phenomena since they occur in any one city rather infrequently. When the performance criteria are inadequate or inaccurate, attempts to evaluate the effectiveness of any solution or strategy for dealing with the problem often yield unclear or contradictory relationships because of the "noise" or errors of measurement present. Under these conditions, starting *de novo* in research on a problem and gradually establishing cause and effect relationships is a slow process requiring a large number of observations to compensate for the errors in the performance criteria. On these kinds of problems, much faster progress can be made in the discovery and testing of new, more workable solutions if a relevant general theory or model can be applied and tested. All available fragmentary and relatively unreliable data can be used to evaluate such an overall theory and the strategies based on it. An effective valid theory can then be confirmed even though the performance criteria are spotty and at times contain errors.

Organizational research in business firms can provide the relevant general theory needed to accelerate the progress of research on these serious societal problems. There are two reasons for this being possible. First, the *fundamental* variables dealt with in business organizational research are essentially the same as those involved in these societal problems, namely, such variables as leadership, motivation, communication, interaction and the structure through which interactions occur, and conflict management. Second, organizational research in business establishments frequently can be undertaken in situations where there are (a) relatively accurate measurements of performance and (b) large populations of cause and effect cycles. Organizational research of this type, therefore, can provide the general theory and models for research and successful experimentation in seeking sound solutions to societal problems. In addition, the theory presently emerging from business organizational research can be used to derive potentially promising steps and strategies for dealing with these problems on an interim basis.

The theories from research in business companies can be used, for example, to suggest more effective organizational structure through which more constructive interactions can occur than is now the case. They can suggest programs for aiding leaders and other relevant persons to develop greater skill in establishing cooperative interaction and problem solving among conflicting parties. Another contribution would be the use of these theories to guide the building of appreciably more effective interaction-influence systems than presently exist. Effective multiple, overlapping, group interaction-influence systems (Likert, 1961, Ch. 12; 1967, Ch. 10) are required to cope successfully with the kinds of problems suggested above. These examples illustrate the immediate contributions that organizational research can be expected to make toward the solutions of serious societal problems.

If expectations are realized, or even partially realized, with regard to finding consistent dependable relationships among the causal, intervening, and end-result variables, one can expect, in the next decade, great progress in the development of appreciably more complex and powerful theories of organization and organizational change. These theories and related principles and procedures can contribute greatly toward the solution of any problems that involve conflict, interaction, or social organization. Business organizational research will then become, much more than at present, a source of general knowledge with wide applicability.

References

Brayfield, A. H., and W. H. Crockett. "Employee attitudes and employee performance." *Psychological Bulletin,* 52 (1955), 396–424.

Dubin, R., G. C. Homans, F. C. Mann, and D. C. Miller. *Leadership and Productivity: Some Facts of Industrial Life.* San Francisco: Chandler, 1965.

Farris, G. F. "A causal analysis of scientific performance." Unpublished doctoral dissertation. University of Michigan, 1966.

Herzberg, F., B. Mausner, R. O. Peterson, and D. F. Capwell. *Job Attitudes: Review of Research and Opinion.* Pittsburgh: Psychological Services of Pittsburgh, 1957.

Likert, R. *New Patterns of Management.* New York: McGraw-Hill, 1961.

———. *The Human Organization: Its Management and Value.* New York: McGraw-Hill, 1967.

Miller, D. C., and W. H. Form. *Industrial Society: The Sociology of Work Organizations.* (2nd ed.) New York: Harper & Row, 1964.

Pelz, D. C., and F. M. Andrews. *Scientists in Organizations: Productive Climates for Research and Development.* New York: Wiley, 1966.

Seashore, S. E. "Criteria of organizational effectiveness." Unpublished doctoral dissertation. University of Michigan, 1966.

Yuchtman, E., and S. E. Seashore. "A system resource approach to organizational effectiveness." *American Sociological Review,* 32 (1967), 891–903.

B. JOB DESIGN AND ENRICHMENT

The gap between our knowledge of good job design and common practices is unnecessarily great, according to Davis (Selection 17) and others. The motivation to apply job design knowledge should be substantial: the organization stands to gain through improved productivity and quality with lower costs of performance; the workers, through increased personal satisfactions. The possibilities of realizing such goals are documented in the case studies reviewed and evaluated by Davis. (Since we have reprinted only a few of the studies, the reader with a specialized interest may want to refer to Davis's original article.) We find Davis's analysis to be one of the more significant treatments of job design in that he demonstrates some of the ways for obtaining compatibility among technological, organizational, and personal requirements. He notes:

> *This suggests that here, as elsewhere, the systems approach leads to more effective designs of organizations and jobs. The component or piecemeal approach (so prevalent at present), which concentrates on job designs exclusively tailored to one component of the system, namely technology, tends to result in less than optimal total performance.*

The theme developed by Davis is presented by Myers (Selection 18) in the form of a theoretical model. The model defines the characteristics of meaningful work and some techniques for analyzing and enriching work. It offers guidance for managers coping with the problem of job design in different circumstances and institutional settings. The utility of the model is richly illustrated with some of the job design experiments which have been undertaken at Texas Instruments.

17

The Design of Jobs

Louis E. Davis
University of California, Los Angeles

On the side of organizational, social, and personal requirements, what is the state of job design today? There is a large discrepancy between available knowledge and practice, although — paradoxically, perhaps — there is much evidence that management faithfully keeps abreast of developments in job and organization design research. The thinking of many a management today appears to be not unlike that of an old farmer who went to a lecture delivered by a county agent to a group of small farmers in a remote rural area about a new development in farming that would increase crop yield. When asked by the county agent whether he would use the new development, the old-timer said, "I won't — I already know how to farm better than I am doing."

Managements are well aware that there now exists a considerable body of evidence which challenges accepted organizational and job design practices. Experimental and empirical findings, for instance, indicate that imposed pacing of work is detrimental to output and to quality, yet paced work is common and is considered to be desirable.[1] There is extensive evidence concerning the positive effects of group reward systems in achieving an organization's primary objectives. There is also considerable evidence of the effects of variety of job content and of task assignments that permit social relationships and communication patterns to develop, all of which enhance performance and personal satisfaction on the job.[2] Yet in a very few instances do we find application of such findings to job designs.

The incentive to apply job design knowledge must be presumed to be strong, for the very simple reason that there are gains to be made all round — for the organization in productivity, quality, and costs of performance, and for workers in personal satisfactions. On the other hand, inhibitions against application are formidable. The status quo bristles with institutional barriers in the form of established personnel policies, job evaluation plans, union relationships and contracts, supervisory practices at all levels, and, not least, managerial practices. All of these barriers are perpetually present, prompting the manager to choose the path of least resistance and to do as

Taken and adapted from *Industrial Relations; A Journal of Economy and Society,* Vol. 6, No. 2, Feb. 1967, pp. 21–45. Used by permission.

little as the situation compels, that is, to satisfy the obvious needs of technology. At a deeper level, the status quo is reinforced by more basic and pervasive inhibitions which again and again lead the manager to fall back on time-honored, but inappropriate and unrealistic models which are based on unsupported dogma or on popular cliches regarding human behavior in productive organizations.

The practical consequences are inconsistent and incompatible job designs, as well as ad hoc use of piecemeal research results. With minor modifications, there is still a strong commitment to the proposition that meeting the requirements of the technology (process, equipment) will yield superior job performance, measured by organizationally relevant criteria, and a deep-seated conviction that the same performance will *not* be achieved if technological requirements are not given exclusive consideration. Requirements such as communication, group formation, personality development, decision-making, and control are seen as marginal at best, and at worst as opposed to the satisfaction of technological requirements. This fictitious conflict reveals the poverty of present conceptualization of human behavior in productive organizations and helps to maintain the dominance of technological requirements as exclusive determinants of job contents and relationships. . . .

Recent Job Design Studies

Job design research is relatively new, having originated only in the last decade. More recently, a few industrial firms have begun to manipulate some job contents and configurations. The first such experiment that was reported took place in the late forties in a large U.S. electronics firm which undertook a series of job changes in the form of job enlargement.[3] The changes were instituted as a part of management industrial relations policy.

What characterizes the difference between job design research and personnel, industrial psychological, and sociological studies? Job design studies take technology as an operant variable and, as a consequence, are concerned with the interaction between personal, social, and organization needs and technology as manifested in jobs. The other studies take technology as given and therefore do not consider it as a variable to be examined. Job design studies can be classified into two groups, both based on field experiments: those carried out in the United States under the name of job design and those carried out in England, where they are known as socio-technical systems studies. The former studies have sought to manipulate the configuration of technology, as interpreted in task designs and assignments making up jobs, and to determine what variations are possible and what the effects of these are on personal, social, and organization variables. The latter studies have approached jobs and organization configurations from the direction of social psychology, modifying technological configurations of tasks to permit the development of social structure in support of functions and objectives of work groups. Both types of studies are concerned with jobs and organizations as socio-technical systems. . . .

Operator, Assembly Line: Home Appliance Manufacture[4]

Enlargement of assembly-line jobs was undertaken recently by a midwestern home laundry manufacturing firm which sought to improve workers' attitudes toward work and to increase output and quality. The company felt it might have gone beyond the "optimum" division of labor on its assembly lines, so that increased costs of nonproductive work and line-balance delay might have exceeded the savings of fractionation. To the company job enlargement meant providing jobs that involved an increased number and variety of tasks, self-determination of pacing, increased responsibility for quality, increased discretion for work methods, and completion of a part- or sub-assembly. For a number of years the company had been pursuing a deliberate program of transferring work from progressive assembly lines to single-operator work stations; this transfer permitted study of the effects of enlarged jobs on workers' performance and attitudes.

Over a five-year period, 14 bench assembly jobs had been established. Thirteen of these were from elements previously performed on assembly lines. One of the jobs was pump assembly, in which six operators each doing six work elements on an assembly line had required 1.77 minutes to complete a unit. This was transformed into one job having 35 elements requiring 1.49 minutes per assembly, including inspection. Costs for pump assembly were reduced $2,000 annually. The other 13 jobs were similarly enlarged, with their average allowed time changed from 0.78 to 3.15 minutes and average number of work elements from 9 to 33. They showed an average decrease in rejects from 2.9 to 1.4 per cent and a slight average decrease in output efficiency from 138 to 126 per cent.

Social interaction opportunities and actual work interaction showed sharp reductions in bench work. This may have resulted largely from the creation of independent jobs. The indications were that conditions were not very favorable for developing stable informal groups among the workers on enlarged jobs.

The attitudes and preferences of workers having experience on both line and bench work were examined by questionnaire. Enlarged bench jobs were preferred 2 to 1 over assembly-line jobs. There were no preferences associated with personal characteristics. All of the attributes of the enlarged jobs were liked; except for social interaction and short learning time, all of the attributes of the line jobs were disliked. Preference for self-pacing was the reason given in half of the cases for liking bench jobs. Where line work was preferred, no single reason was given; rather it was less disliked than bench work.

This study demonstrates that there may be an "optimum" division of labor on assembly lines. The authors make a case for job enlargement based on reduction of costs of nonproductive work and line-balance delays. It is unfortunate that these reductions were permitted to mask worker contributions to output flowing from enlarged job design. The results indicate strong contributions in the form of greatly improved quality of output and increased worker satisfaction with their jobs. These are gains for the company, perhaps otherwise unobtainable, along with savings in labor costs and greater production flexibility.

Operator, Machine Tender: Textile Weaving[5]

The third operator study indicates the impact of the organizational component of job design on the productivity of work groups. A socio-technical systems study in an Indian textile mill revealed the poor consequences of job designs which center only about worker-machine allocations and lead to inhibition of interaction of workers. The field study took place in a mill which had recently been intensively studied by engineers for the purpose of laying out equipment and assigning work loads based on careful time measurements of all of the job components. After installation of the layout and work assignments, the mill still failed to produce at satisfactory productivity and quality levels. The job designs required 12 specialist activities to operate the equipment assigned to a weaving room containing 240 looms.

1. A weaver tended approximately 30 looms.
2. A battery filler served about 50 looms.
3. A smash-hand tended about 70 looms.
4. A gater, cloth carrier, jobber, and assistant jobber were each assigned to 112 looms.
5. A bobbin carrier, feller-motion fitter, oiler, sweeper, and humidification-fitter were each assigned to 224 looms.

The occupational tasks were all highly interdependent, and the utmost coordination was required to maintain continuity of production. However, the worker-machine assignments and consequent organizational grouping produced an interaction pattern which militated against continuity of production. The interaction resulting from work assignment brought each weaver into contact with five-eighths of a battery filler, three-eighths of a smash-hand, one-quarter of a gater, and one-eighth of a bobbin carrier.

After study of travel and communication patterns, the jobs were redesigned so that all of the workers who were interdependent were made part of the same work group. Work groups were organized so that a single group was responsible for the operation and maintenance of a specific bank of looms. Geographic division rather than functional division of the weaving room produced interaction patterns which made for regularity of relationships among individuals whose jobs were interrelated, and they could be held responsible for their production. As a result of these changes efficiency rose from an average of 80 per cent to 95 per cent, and damage dropped from a mean of 32 per cent to 20 per cent after 60 working days. In the adjacent part of the weaving shed, where job design changes were not made, efficiency dropped to 70 per cent and finally rose to 80 per cent, while damage continued at an average of 31 per cent. . . .

Supervisor: Aircraft Instruments Repair and Manufacture[6]

The design of supervisory jobs is also plagued by poor models of individual-organization relationships and of human behavior in productive organizations. It is further complicated by the supervisor's conflicting objectives vis-à-vis workers and management, by the conflict between the supervisor's management objectives and his superior's, by his uncertainty over behavior required for effective leadership, by the implied threat to his status and effectiveness inherent in the authoritarian-participation conflict, and by the ambiguity that exists over the discharge of his responsibility. For purposes of design of supervisory jobs there is a general lack of information and data apart from some generalities concerning leadership behavior.

The management of the industrial facility of a large West Coast military installation introduced modifications in organization and in duties, responsibilities, and authority of some first-line supervisors, as part of a planned experimental field study directed by a University of California research team. The primary function of the facility was to overhaul, repair, and test military aircraft and their components. With the exception of the senior executives, all of its 5,900 employees were civilians, of whom 3,800 were in line functions. The study was confined to 11 shops, the basic (first level) organization units, in which the sensing, power, and control accessories of aircraft systems were overhauled, repaired, and tested. The shops, each under a supervisor, employed from 12 to 30 craftsmen and processed many subtypes of relatively homogeneous types of equipment, such as flight instruments.

The study was intended to test the primary hypothesis that higher economic productivity (lower total cost) and greater need satisfaction for all members of a work group will result when the supervisor's authority and responsibility is increased by giving him direct control over all operational and inspection functions required to complete and determine final acceptance of the products or services assigned to his work group. A response mechanism model was developed which postulated that changes in a supervisor's performance result from intervening sequential changes in his perceptions, attitudes, motivations, and consequent behavior toward tasks and toward other members of the organization. Intervening criteria reflecting perceptions, attitudes, and behavior toward others were developed; questionnaires and interviews were used as measuring instruments. Changes in supervisors' task behaviors were assessed by random activity sampling and job content inventory.

Two modifications in supervisors' jobs were introduced separately into a number of experimental shops. Control shops matched to these as to type of work, style of supervision, worker skills, and past performance were used. The treatments were as follows:

1. Product Responsibility treatment provided supervision of all functions required to complete the products processed in a shop. It was introduced into two experimental shops with two control shops.
2. Quality Responsibility treatment added inspection to the functions required to complete a product, including authority for final quality acceptance of products. It was introduced into four experimental shops with three control shops.

The Product Responsibility treatment moved two experimental shops from their initial or functional organizational state to the second or product organizational state. In the initial state, the functions of overhaul and repair, calibrate and test, and quality acceptance were each performed by different groups. In the second state, all functions required to complete its products, with external quality acceptance, were performed by one work group. The differences in functions between the first and second states were technically complex, requiring the acquisition of additional knowledge and skills by supervisors and workers.

The Quality Responsibility treatment moved four experimental shops from the second to the third organizational state of full responsibility for product completion, including quality acceptance. The tasks added in the third state were largely replicative and only trivially different from those performed by the shops in their initial (second) state. The major differences were in the explicit delegation of responsibility for quality and authority to perform quality acceptance. For this purpose quality control inspectors were withdrawn from the experimental shops and their authority for product acceptance was transferred to the shop supervisors, who, not long afterward, transferred the authority to key workers.

Proper evaluation of the treatment responses required that the pre-existing organizational environment be completely delineated, particularly since the expected effects were generated through supervisors of units which tended to become more autonomous as a result of the treatments. This environment was one of known overall demand for products and services, varying in the short run and requiring a highly skilled work force. Such skilled workers were in limited supply in the area, making it difficult, if not impossible, to rely on hiring as a means of adding workers to a unit to suit immediate needs. This situation generated manpower-maintenance goals directed at conserving manpower in preparation for meeting overall known demand requirements under "emergency" (short-run) conditions. Goal conflicts could and did arise between this real goal of supervisors and such usual and stated goals of top management as efficiency and cost reduction.

In implementing its goals, management reviewed each supervisor's performance every three months by comparing the productivity, quality, and costs of his shop against a standard. Based on this review and planned quarterly work load, a supervisor would expect to have workers added or removed from his shop for the next calendar quarter. When unplanned increases in work load occurred, a supervisor could request, and receive, additional workers transferred from other shops. Whether these were the workers he wanted, or may even previously have lost, can be left to conjecture.

If supervisors responded positively to the treatments, they were expected to achieve changes in the objective criteria of cost reduction and quality improvement, satisfying management's stated goals without violating their own real goal of manpower-maintenance. Achievement of improvement in productivity was not expected since this might have resulted in a loss of manpower, constituting a negative incentive to the supervisor in maintaining the capability of his shop to meet anticipated fluctuating work load.

The study lasted for 24 months. During the first 9 months data were collected on all of the criterion variables for operation of the 11 shops in their initial states. After the experimental treatments were introduced into 6 shops, data on objective criteria were collected for 6 months and data on intervening criteria were collected for 15 months. The results of the study can be summarized as follows.

Personnel costs in the form of absenteeism, grievances, transfers, injuries, etc., were not significantly affected by the treatments. It is difficult to evaluate whether the nonsensitivity was specific to the treatments or to the short duration of the study. Historically personnel costs were markedly low and unchanging in the organization and this pattern continued into the post-change period.

The treatment which enlarged the responsibility and authority of the supervisors and the operational functions of their organizational units resulted in the following changes in objective criteria:

Criteria	*Product Responsibility* (Technically complex change)	*Quality Responsibility* (Technically trivial change)
1. Compatible with supervisors' goal:		
a. Quality	Significant improvement	No significant change, but indications of improvement
b. Costs	No change	Significant improvement
2. Incompatible with supervisors' goal:		
a. Productivity	No change	No change

As can be seen, those objective performances improved that were compatible with the supervisors' goal of manpower maintenance.

Supervisor behavior became more autonomous and more oriented to the technical problems of producing the product and to worker training. The treatments shortened the quality and process information feedback loops to workers and concentrated dispersed functional authority. In moving toward technological aspects of management, giving more time to planning, inspection, control, etc., supervisors did so at the expense of management of men. This change in managment style appeared to be salutary as judged by positive worker attitudes.

Positive attitudes of workers and supervisors were enhanced, indicating satisfaction of personal needs in the direction of developing individuals who were contributing to the organization's viability or health. The major response perceptions and attitudes were:

Treatment	*Favorable*	*Unfavorable*
Product Responsibility (Technically complex change: new tasks and skills required)	1. Greater autonomy	1. Loss of man-orientation
	2. Less limiting internal structure	2. Loss of concern for worker
	3. Greater skill for workers in long run	3. Low rate of transfer of treatment tasks and responsibilities
	4. Greater product control	4. Low delegation
	5. Increased information flow to workers	
Quality Responsibility (Technically trivial change: addition of inspection and authority for product acceptance)	1. Greater authority	1. Loss of man-orientation
	2. Greater autonomy	2. Greater internal structure
	3. Greater concern for worker	3. Low delegation
	4. Higher rate of transfer of treatment tasks and responsibilities to workers	
	5. Reduced conflict with staff group	
	6. Increased information flow to workers	

Conclusions

The studies reviewed here lend support to the general model of responsible autonomous job behavior as a key facet of individual-organizational-technological relationships in productive organizations. Responsible behavior as defined here implies (1) acceptance of responsibility by the individual or group for the cycle of activities required to complete the product or service, (2) acceptance of responsibility for rate, quantity, and quality of output, and (3) recognition of interdependence of the individual or group on others for effective progress of a cycle of activities. Similarly, autonomous behavior encompasses (1) self-regulation of work content and structure within the job, where the job is an assignment having inputs, facilities, and outputs, (2) self-evaluation of performance, (3) self-adjustment to changes required by technological variability, and (4) participation in setting up of goals or objectives for job outputs.

Furthermore, the studies provide a partial demonstration of the positive effects on total performance of job and organization designs which lead to responsible autonomous job behavior, i.e., positive effects on objective organization performance, as well as on the attitudes, perceptions, and satisfactions of members of the organization. Such designs also tend to maintain a production system in an on-going stage of relative equilibrium. For example, in many of the studies total performance was found to have been enhanced substantially by job designs which provided compatibility among technological, organizational, and personal requirements. This suggests that here, as elsewhere, the system approach leads to more effective designs of organizations and jobs. The component or piecemeal approach (so prevalent at present), which concentrates on job designs exclusively tailored to one component of the system, namely technology, tends to result in less than optimal total performance. While failing to achieve the output and quality levels possible, it imposes higher direct costs on management and workers alike, reflected in increased inspection, supervision, and absenteeism, coupled with reduced satisfactions, negative attitudes, and hostility.

That some processes or activities may be automated does not alter the fact that for the organization as a whole people are the prime agents for the utilization of technology in the interests of achievement of an organization's objectives. The model of responsible autonomous job behavior makes it both permissible and imperative to view personal requirements in the focus of job design activity. But if the model is to be used as a basis for job (and organization) design, then these nonmodifiable personal requirements and the characteristics of their interactions with technology and the organization will have to be specified as design criteria aimed at achieving compatibility. Variations in design may result from interpretations of nonmodifiable criteria and from the introduction of others.

Some of the job characteristics of importance to job and organization design have asserted their dominance in the studies reviewed. They can be classified into two types: (1) job content and structure characteristics, which reflect the interaction between personal and technological requirements, and (2) job environment characteristics, which reflect the interaction between personal and organizational requirements. Job content characteristics are concerned with the number and kinds of tasks and their interrelationships. Many of these are specific illustrations of the need for the development of a work role which provides comprehensiveness, i.e., the opportunity to perform all tasks required for product or process completion and at the same time imposes the responsibility and confers the authority for self-direction and self-regulation.

Improvement in total performance was thus frequently obtained when the scope of jobs included all tasks required to complete a part product, or service; when the job content included all four types of tasks inherent in productive work: auxiliary or service (supply, tooling), preparatory (set-up), processing or transformation, and control (inspection); when the tasks included in the job content permitted closure of the activity, if not product completion, permitting development of identity with product or process. Tangible gains in performance were also obtained by the introduction of task variety in the form of larger numbers and kinds of tasks and skills as well as more complex tasks. The characteristics of processing tasks which led to improved performance were self-regulation of speed of work and self-determination of work methods and sequence. Total performance also improved when control tasks were included in jobs, permitting outputs to be evaluated by self-inspection, and when product quality acceptance was within the authority of the jobholder.

The job environment characteristics that contributed to improvement in total performance were again those that supported the development of responsible autonomous job behavior. They indicate a job structure that permits social interaction among jobholders and communication with peers and supervisors, particularly when the maintenance of continuity of operation is required. A reward system that supports responsible autonomy was shown to provide gains beyond those of simple increases in task output.

Appropriate management behavior is, of course, required for jobs having these characteristics. The behaviors called for are supportive in providing service, general planning of activities, and evaluation of results on the basis of organizationally meaningful objectives. They stand in contrast to present overly specific task planning and work measurement, obtrusive supervision, coercive external control, imposed external integration of specialized tasks, and external coordination of fractionated activities.

Certain important aspects of organizational design were also brought to light by the studies. Where small organizational units, or work groups, are required, group structures having the following features appeared to lead to improved performance: (1) group composition that permits self-regulation of the group's functioning, (2) group composition that deliberately provides for the full range of skills required to carry out all the tasks in an activity cycle, (3) delegation of authority, formal or informal, to the group for self-assignment of tasks and roles to group members, (4) group structure that permits internal communication, and (5) a group reward system for joint output. As regards the design requirements for larger organizational units with more complex interactions, it would be hazardous to draw any conclusions from the studies reviewed. Whether or not present extensive research will make a contribution to our understanding of the design requirements of large organizations is not yet clear.

Overall it is obvious that we are only beginning to identify relationships among technology, organization, and the individual which are capable of being translated into organization and job design recommendations. Nevertheless, it requires no very great powers of foresight to suggest that we are rapidly approaching the time when re-evaluation of management precepts and practices will have to take place. Many currently fashionable management programs are mere palliatives, addressed to patching up essentially inappropriate organization and job structures. Among these, the so-called worker communications programs, participation techniques directed at providing workers with "feelings of importance," and human relations programs dealing with personal relationships and supervision (often in the abstract, outside the industrial or business context) do not stand up under objective scrutiny. Almost without exception their achievements fall short even of their own stated objectives.

In summary, changes in organization and job design similar to those reviewed are indicated, as are associated changes in management behavior. Whether and when they will take place cannot be forecast. Industrial and business history is replete with examples of the continuation of superannuated institutions and procedures.

Notes

1. R. Conrad, "Comparison of Paced and Unpaced Performance at a Packing Task," *Occupational Psychology,* XXIX (1955), 15–28; and L. E. Davis, "Pacing Effects on Manned Assembly Lines," *International Journal of Production Research,* IV (1966), 171.
2. L. E. Davis and R. Werling, "Job Design Factors," *Occupational Psychology,* XXXIV (1960), 109; L. E. Davis, "Toward a Theory of Job Design," *Journal of Industrial Engineering,* VIII (1957), 305; L. E. Davis, R. R. Canter, and J. F. Hoffman, "Current Job Design Criteria," *Journal of Industrial Engineering,* VI (1955), 5; and F. L. W. Richardson and C. R. Walker, *Human Relations in an Expanding Company* (New Haven: Labor and Management Center, Yale University, 1948).
3. Richardson and Wallace, *op. cit.*

4. E. H. Conant and M. D. Kilbridge, "An Interdisciplinary Analysis of Job Enlargement: Technology, Costs and Behavioral Implications," *Industrial and Labor Relations Review,* XVIII (October, 1965), 377.

5. A. K. Rice, "Productivity and Social Organization in an Indian Weaving Shed," *Human Relations,* VI (November, 1953), 297.

6. L. E. Davis and E. S. Valfer, "Supervisor Job Design," Proceedings of the Second International Congress on Ergonomics, *Ergonomics,* VIII (1965), 1; and "Intervening Responses to Changes in Supervisor Job Designs," *Occupational Psychology,* XXXIX (1965), 171.

18

Every Employee a Manager

M. Scott Myers
Texas Instruments

This article is an extension of earlier studies in motivation made at Texas Instruments and published in the *Harvard Business Review.*[1] These and similar studies done elsewhere provide corrobative evidence of the wastefulness of bureaucracy and the advantages of democracy. Terms made familiar through these publications include participative management, consultative supervision, theory Y leadership, self-direction and self-control, 9 to 9 supervision, goal-setting, work simplification, team effort, personal commitment, and self-actualization. All have in common the fuller and more voluntary utilization of human talent and, as such, represent some form of job enlargement or enrichment of the job holder's life at work.

Unquestionable Benefits

The informed manager no longer needs to be convinced of the merits of job enrichment. Experiments at Texas Instruments and elsewhere have shown tangible improvements in terms of such diverse criteria as reduced costs, higher yields, less scrap, accelerated learning time, fewer complaints and trips to the health center, reduced anxiety, improved attitudes and team efforts, and increased profits. Hence, the desirability of job enrichment is no longer in question, but, rather, the quest now is for definitions and implementation procedures. Most reports on job enrichment are situational descriptions which offer little guidance for supervisors in dissimilar circumstances, and slavish emulation of inappropriate models usually leads to failure.

The primary purpose of this article is to present a theoretical model for defining the characteristics of meaningful work and some techniques for analyzing work and enriching it. But, first, I will define and give some examples of job enrichment and analyze the traditional barriers to its implementation, then define the emerging role of the supervisor.

Taken and adapted from *California Management Review,* Vol. 10, No. 3, Spring 1968, pp. 9–20. Used by permission.

A Better Use of Talent

Job enrichment. Though job enrichment is the new shibboleth of today's managers, few have had first-hand experience with it. But, McGregor's[2] message is getting through, and testimonials of the efficacy of theory Y are commonplace — people are responsible and creative when given the opportunity! Unfortunately, many managers still see job enlargement as a form of benevolent autocracy, and their unguided attempts to enlarge jobs fall more within the realm of manipulation than job enrichment. Job enrichment may result from horizontal or vertical job enlargement, or a combination of both, as illustrated in Figure 2. Horizontal job enlargement is characterized by adding a variety of similar functions, and, though it usually ameliorates the boredom of a simple job, it seldom offers the enrichment opportunity provided through vertical job enlargement. Vertically enlarged jobs enable employees to have a hand in doing some of the planning and control work previously restricted to persons in supervisory and staff functions.

Job enrichment sometimes results naturally from the intuitive practices of goal-oriented, emotionally mature managers who evoke commitment through a "language of action" which grants freedom and reflects respect, confidence, and high expectations. When job enrichment is attempted by reductive, authority-oriented managers by duplicating job designs evolved by goal-oriented managers, they may fail to inspire involvement and commitment, because their motives are suspect and their "language of action" comes through as manipulation and exploitation rather than as acts of trust, confidence, and respect.

Hence, job enrichment depends on style of supervision as well as job requirements and is not simply a matter of duplicating patterns of work and relationships found to be successful elsewhere.

Management functions. The role of the manager is explicitly defined in business administration textbooks in terms of functions generally labeled as planning, organizing, leading, and controlling, as illustrated in Figure 1. Despite the uniformity and universality of these management functions,

FIGURE 1

The Functions of Management

1 / Planning: objectives, goals, strategies, programs, policies, forecasts.

2 / Organizing: manpower, money, machines, materials, methods.

3 / Leading: directing, motivating, instructing, delegating, coaching, recognizing.

4 / Controlling: auditing, measuring, evaluating, correcting.

FIGURE 2

Examples of Horizontal and Vertical Job Enlargement

Horizontal

Assemblers on a transformer assembly line each performed a single operation as the assembly moved by on the conveyor belt. Jobs were enlarged horizontally by setting up work stations to permit each operator to assemble the entire unit. Operations now performed by each operator include cabling, upending, winding, soldering, laminating, and symbolizing.

A similar transformer assembly line provides horizontal job enlargement when assemblers are taught how to perform all operations and are rotated to a different operation each day.

Vertical

Assemblers on a radar assembly line are given information on customer contract commitments in terms of price, quality specifications, delivery schedules, and company data on material and personnel costs, breakeven performance, and potential profit margins. Assemblers and engineers work together in methods and design improvements. Assemblers inspect, adjust, and repair their own work, help test completed units, and receive copies of customer inspection reports.

Female electronic assemblers involved in intricate assembling, bonding, soldering, and welding operations are given training in methods improvement and were encouraged to make suggestions for improving manufacturing processes. Natural work groups of five to 25 assemblers each elect a "team captain" for a term of six months. In addition to performing her regular operations, the team captain collects work improvement ideas from members of her team, describes them on a standard form, credits the suggestors, presents the recommendations to their supervisor and superintendent at the end of the week, and gives the team feedback on idea utilization. Though most job operations remain the same, vertical job enlargement is achieved by providing increased opportunity for planning, reorganizing and controlling their work, and earning recognition.

Horizontal Plus Vertical

Jobs are enlarged horizontally in a clad metal rolling mill by qualifying operators to work interchangeably on breakdown rolling, finishing rolling, slitter, pickler, and abrader operations. After giving the operators training in methods improvement and basic metallurgy, jobs are enlarged vertically by involving them with engineering and supervisory personnel in problem-solving, goal-setting sessions for increasing production yields.

Jobs in a large employee insurance section are enlarged horizontally by qualifying insurance clerks to work interchangeably in filing claims, mailing checks, enrolling and orienting new employees, checking premium and enrollment reports, adjusting payroll deductions, and interpreting policies to employees. Vertical enlargement involves clerks in insurance program planning meetings with personnel directors and carrier representatives, authorizes them to sign disbursement requests, permits them to attend a paperwork systems conference, and enables them to recommend equipment replacements and to rearrange their work layout.

their application mirrors a wide variety of practices and management styles. In the eyes of the typical manager, management functions pertain to the job of a "manager," but not to the job of the "worker." For example, a manager in an automotive factory, if asked to describe his job, might say, "I am building automobiles, and my job includes planning, organizing, leading, and controlling. I have about 50 foremen who are leading and controlling." And, almost as an afterthought, he might add, "Oh yes, I also have 2,000 workers on the assembly line turning wrenches and screw drivers." This concept is reflected in Figure 3.

FIGURE 3
The Manager's Traditional Perception of his job

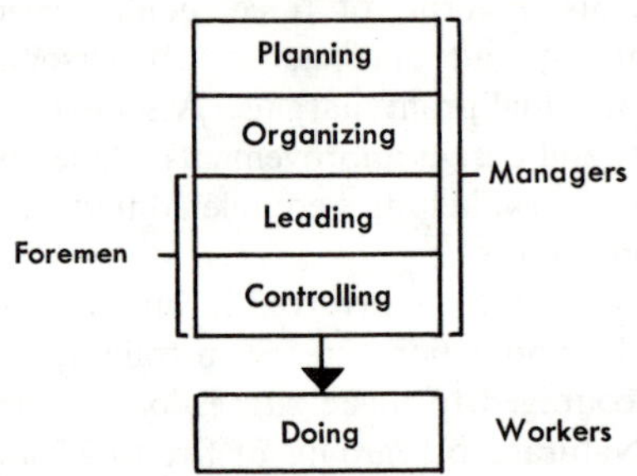

The management-labor dichotomy. This typical point of view excludes employees from the realm of management and creates, subconsciously if not deliberately, a dichotomy of people at work — unintelligent, uninformed, uncreative, irresponsible, and immature workers who need the direction and control of intelligent, informed, creative, responsible, and mature managers.

The consequences of this point of view are widely evident in industry and are reflected in Figure 4, which shows the cleavage between management and labor in terms of social distance and alienation.

Though the gap between the employer and the employed has a long heritage and, in some respects, seems inescapably inherent to the relationship, it has become more formalized and widened through the efforts of labor unions whose charters depend on their success in convincing labor that management is their natural enemy. The union, while pressuring management to share its affluence and prerogatives, has at the same time clearly defined the laboring man's charter as being separate from, and indeed in conflict with, that of management. Managers typically and naturally align themselves with the goals of the company, but workers divide their allegiance between the union and the company, often with a feeling of closer identification with the union than with the company.

FIGURE 4

The Management–Labor Dichotomy

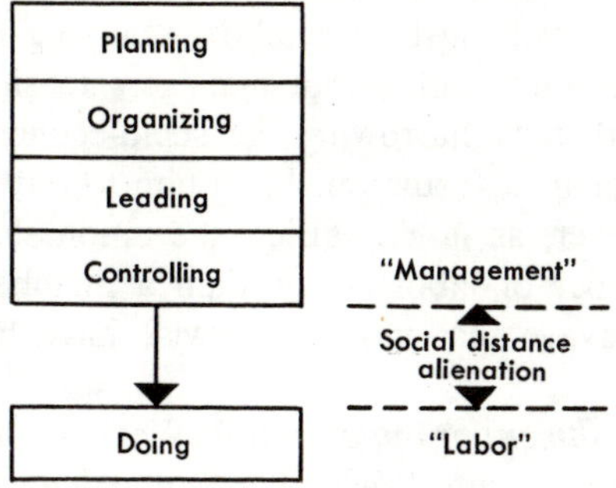

Two forces in America have the potential for rendering this labor-management dichotomy obsolete. One is the improving socio-economic status and the consequent value changes of the previously less-privileged, accelerated by legislated equality and increasing enlightenment in a democratic and increasingly affluent society.

The second force is a growing awareness on the part of managers of the inevitability of democracy as the pattern for a healthful entrepreneurial society and the importance of their role in supporting it. This article is devoted more to this second force — defining a concept of meaningful work to guide tomorrow's managers in redefining their roles.

The changing needs of man. Maslow's[3] hierarchy of needs theory is useful in understanding the consequences of the increasing affluence of man. Primeval man's efforts were directed primarily toward survival needs — safety, food, and shelter — leaving little time or energy for preoccupation with his latent high-order needs. However, as his survival needs were satisfied, he became sensitized to social and status needs. Finally, in the affluence of recent decades, these lower-order or maintenance needs have been satisfied to the point that he is ready to realize his potential, to experience self-actualization in terms of intellectual, emotional, and esthetic growth, or to satisfy his motivation[4] needs.

Management and the union have both contributed to the worker's readiness for self-actualization. Efficiency engineers of the Industrial Revolution, under the label of "scientific management," simplified tasks and created the mass production technology. Jobs were fractionated for efficiency in training (also to escape management's dependency on prima donna journeymen) and to satisfy the implicit assumption that workers would be happy and efficient doing easy work for high pay. And though mass-production technology made man an appendage of tools and destroyed his journeyman's pride and autonomy, it did price automobiles, washing machines, refrigerators, etc., within his reach. These and other effects of the mass production economy accelerated the satisfaction of man's lower-order needs and readied him to become aware of his dormant and unfulfilled self-actualization needs.

The union's role was just as vital in readying the worker for self-actualization, for it forced industrial managers to share company success with the worker, thereby narrowing the socio-economic gap between the worker and the manager, further enabling him to buy the products of mass production. However, as noted earlier, the union sharpened the worker's identity as a member of labor rather than a member of management — preserving the cleavage that might otherwise have been reduced through economic trends.

Work — punishment or opportunity? Work, in the eyes of many workers, is a form of punishment. It is uninteresting, demeaning, oppressive, and generally unrelated to, or in conflict with, their personal goals. But, it is an unpleasantness they are willing to endure to get the money needed to buy goods and services which are related to personal goals.[5] In contrast, the manager's job is often experienced as meaningful, satisfying, and at least partially aligned with his personal goals. This difference in job attitude between manager and worker is usually ascribed to immaturity of the worker rather than to the real causes: fundamental differences in the content of the worker's job and his opportunity to manage it. Workers are frequently only appendages of tools or links between them — doing what is necessary to satisfy the requirements of inflexible, inanimate monsters. Work itself, to be meaningful, must make tools the appendage of man and place man in a role not restricted to obedient doing. It must include planning and controlling, as well as doing, as illustrated in Figure 5.

Meaningful work. The plan phase includes the planning and organizing functions of work management and consists of problem solving, goal setting, and planning the use of manpower, materiel, and systems. The do phase is the implementation of the plan, ideally involving the coordinated expenditure of physical and mental effort, utilizing aptitudes and special skills. Control is the feedback and correction process for measuring achievements against planned goals. Feedback gives work its meaning, and its absence is a common cause of job dissatisfaction. The measurement, evaluation, and correction functions of the control phase is the basis for recycling planning, doing, and controlling. People who work for themselves generally have meaningful work in terms of a complete cycle of plan, do, and control.

The farmer, for example, plans and organizes in terms of crop selection, utilization of land, purchase of equipment, and the employment of manpower. He typically has a major role in implementing his plan, and, of course, he is the person most involved in measuring, evaluating, and correcting his program as the basis for future success. An analogy may be drawn for others in the entrepreneurial situation of working for themselves.

FIGURE 5
Meaningful Work

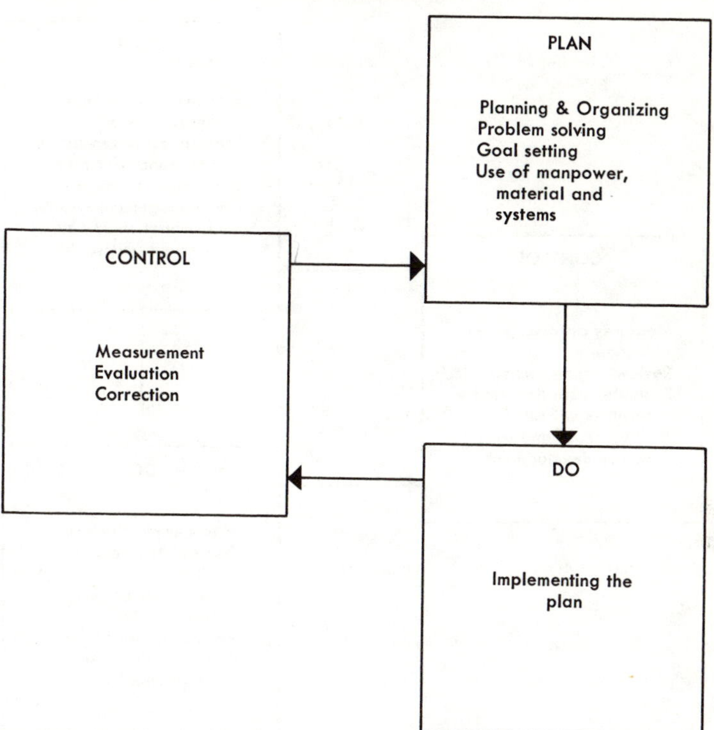

Managers in industry, though seldom having the autonomy of the entrepreneur, typically have jobs rich in plan, do, and control phases, particularly at the higher levels. Let's look at three levels of management jobs in Texas Instruments — operating vice-president, manufacturing manager, and foreman — terms of planning, doing, and controlling. Organizational levels are as follows:

- President
- Operating Vice-President
- Department Manager
- Manufacturing Manager
- Superintendent
- Foreman
- Operator

Note, first, the operating vice-president's job in Figure 6. As division manager he plans in the realm of economic and technological trends, facili-

FIGURE 6

Meaningful Work – Operating Vice-president

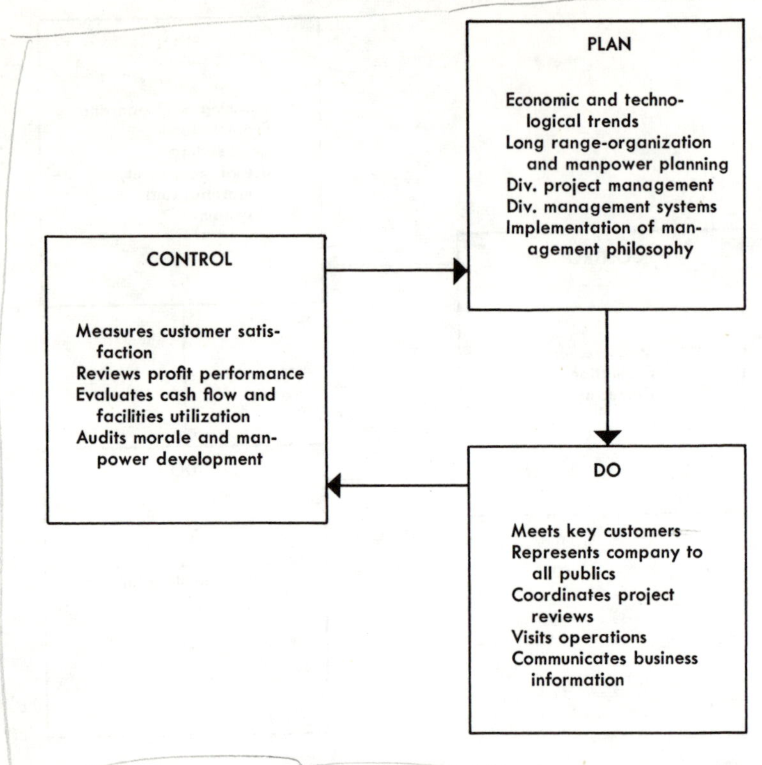

ties expansion, manpower and management systems, and has a hand in shaping policy. The doing aspect of his job involves him with key customers, in public relations roles, visits to various operating sites, and in the exchange of business information. His control functions include the measurement, evaluation, and correction of factors associated with customer satisfaction, profits, cash flow, facilities utilization, morale, and manpower development. Hence, the division director's job is rich in plan, do, and control, much like the self-employed individual.

Similarly, Figure 7 shows the middle-management job of a manufacturing manager to be relatively rich in the meaningful aspects of work. Though two levels below the division manager's position and narrower in scope, it is nonetheless rich in plan, do, and control. A company is rarely plagued with a lack of commitment of a manufacturing manager.

Even the foreman's job, two levels below the manufacturing manager, may be rich in terms of meaningful work concepts.

For example, we see in Figure 8 that the foreman's job, though narrower in scope than the superintendent's, offers him considerable latitude in man-

FIGURE 7
Meaningful Work – Manufacturing Manager

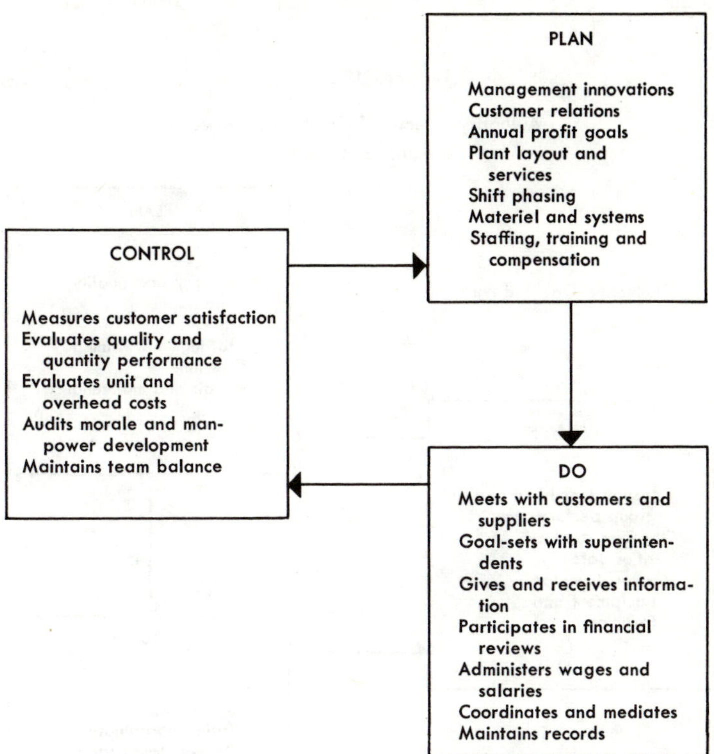

aging his work. This example purposely portrays a traditional authority-oriented supervisor who will be contrasted later with a goal-oriented supervisor in Figure 12.

The foreman's job portrays a complete plan-do-control cycle, which, because it is authority-oriented, creates frustrations that do not plague the goal-oriented supervisor, who will be discussed later. Furthermore, the structuring of the do phase in accordance with this authority-orientation prevents the delegation of a complete plan-do-control cycle of responsibility to the operator. The operator lives in a world circumscribed by conformity pressures to follow instructions, work harder, obey rules, get along with people, and be loyal to the supervisor and the company, quashing any pleasure that work itself might otherwise offer. His role puts him in a category with material and other nonhuman resources to be manipulated by managers exercising their "management prerogatives" (as kings once exercised their "divine rights") in pursuit of "their" organizational goals.

Conformity-oriented workers tend to behave like adolescent children responding to the punishments and rewards of authoritarian parents, and their prerogatives, which are generally expressed in terms of privileges wrested from management, are only in a very incidental fashion aligned with company goals.

FIGURE 8

Authority-oriented Relationship between Foreman and Operator

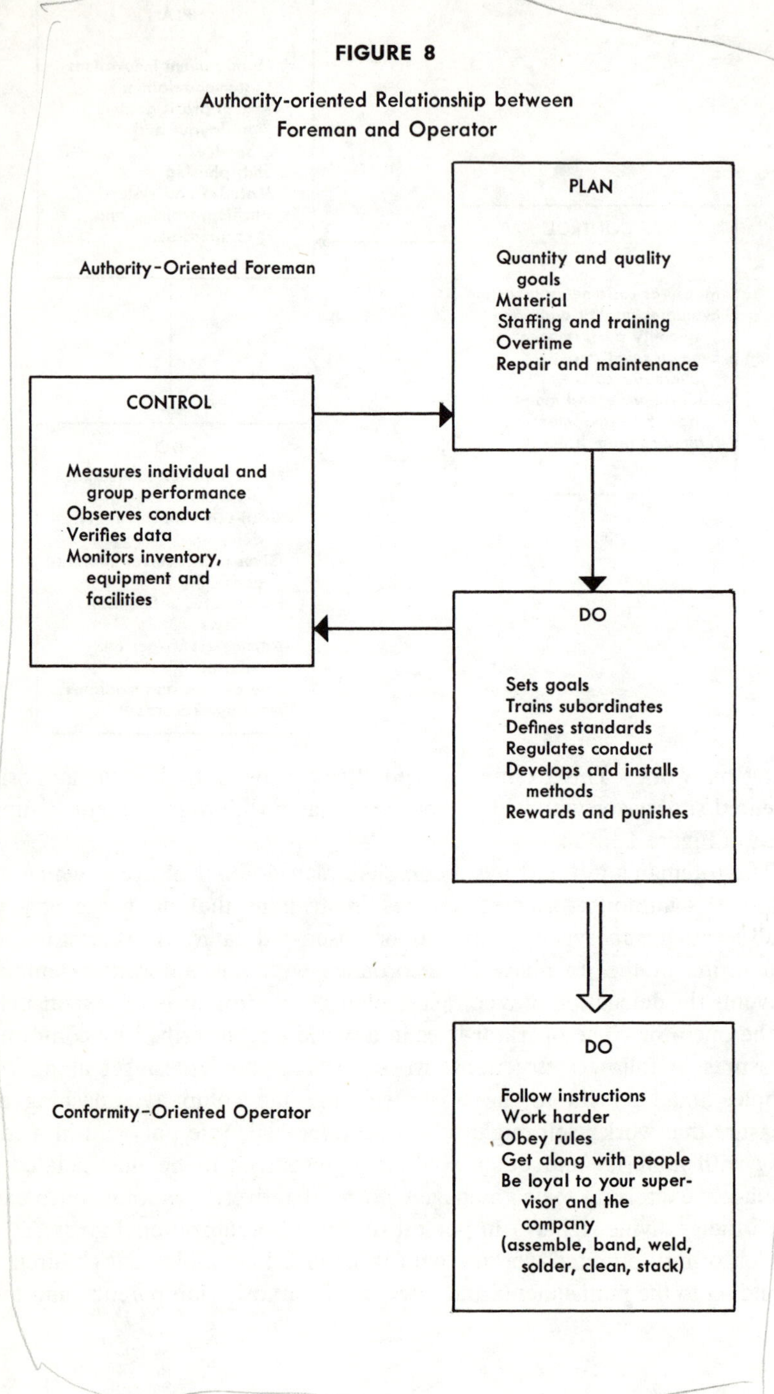

Analyzing work. The foregoing examples show that meaningful work includes planning and controlling, as well as doing, and that the conformity pressures of the authority-oriented supervisor defined in Figure 8 prevent the expression of the full plan-do-control cycle of work for the operator. The meaningfulness of a job can be determined by answering questions related to each of the three phases of work. This is illustrated below — in Figure 9.

FIGURE 9

Sample Items from Supervisor Worksheet for Analyzing Meaningfulness of Work

Planning. Can the individual or group —

- Name customers and state delivery dates for products or services?
- State the product quality and quantity commitments?
- Organize their work layout and influence personnel assignments?
- Set goals and standards based on customer needs and fix priorities?
- State the sources of their materials and problems in obtaining them?
- List direct and overhead costs, selling price and other profit and loss information?

Doing. Does the job —

- Utilize people's talents and require their attention?
- Enable people to see the relationship of their work to other operations?
- Provide access to all the information they need to do their work?
- Have a satisfactory work cycle — neither too long nor too short?
- Give people feedback on how well they are doing?
- Enable them to see how they contribute to the usefulness of the product for the customer?

Controlling. Can the individual or group —

- State customer quality requirements and reasons for these standards?
- Keep their own records of quality and quantity?
- Check quality and quantity of work and revise procedures?
- Evaluate and modify work layout on their own initiative?
- Identify and correct unsafe working conditions?
- Obtain information from people outside the group as a means of evaluating performance?

The supervisor's involvement in answering this type of question may give him his first insight into the scope of meaningful work. The planning and control items may at first appear unrealistic to him in terms of his perception of his people's competence, but they can be made more realistic by having him analyze a similar job managed by a person who works for himself.

For example, analysis of a company oil driller's job in the field may show it to be largely devoid of planning and control phases when compared to his entrepreneurial counterpart's job of managing his own drilling rig. The self-employed driller, who must manage the total plan-do-control cycle of his work to succeed in business, thus serves as a model for planning the enrichment of the company driller's job.

Jobs may be analyzed with the help of job incumbents themselves by involving them in answering the questions in the Supervisor Worksheet, or they may assess their own work by completing checklist items illustrated in Figure 10. This checklist asks the incumbent whether his job permits him to perform various plan, do, and control phases of his job, whether performance of each is essential to good job performance and whether he wants more of this type of opportunity. This type of checklist provides a basis for assessing individual jobs, making inter-group comparisons, and for measuring time trends in the development of meaningful work opportunities. In Texas Instruments, items of this type have been added to the annual attitude survey to measure progress in the institutionalization of meaningful work.

The supervisor's self-evaluation. During the early applications of job enrichment, Texas Instrument supervisors found their traditional roles becoming incompatible with the increasing problem-solving, goal-setting responsibilities of the operators. For example, operators would often work directly with the engineers, taking the initiative in rearranging their workplace, and the problem-solving process did not always of necessity involve the supervisors. One supervisor, in joining his work group for a "problem-solving, goal-setting" session was told, "Look, Bill, we don't need to take up your valuable time in this meeting; we'll go ahead with it and keep you posted on what we come up with." Needless to say, this was a threatening experience, and a less secure person would have insisted on staying. Supervisors encouraged these new work roles of the operators, primarily because they resulted in improved performance, but they were understandably uncomfortable with the ambiguity of their own roles induced by this process. Consequently, a group of supervisors, with the assistance of the division training director, undertook the task of defining their new role.

The results of this group's efforts are reflected in Figure 11. Initial efforts of the group produced the traditional authority-oriented role outlined in the left-column — not because they were committed to this role, but, rather, because their anxiety and haste regressed them temporarily to the typical

FIGURE 10

Sample Items from Job Incumbent Checklist for Describing Meaningfulness of Work

	No	Some-times	Yes
Planning			
• Does my job allow me to set my own performance goals?	( )	( )	( )
• Is setting my own goals essential to good job performance?	( )	( )	( )
• Do I want more opportunity to set my own performance goals?	( )	( )	( )
Doing			
• Does my job provide variety?	( )	( )	( )
• Is variety in my job essential to good job performance?	( )	( )	( )
• Do I want more variety in my work?	( )	( )	( )
Controlling			
• Does my job allow me to measure my work performance?	( )	( )	( )
• Is opportunity to evaluate my own work essential?	( )	( )	( )
• Do I want more opportunity to measure my own job performance?	( )	( )	( )

textbook definition of the role of supervisor. After evaluating and rejecting this traditional role as an inaccurate description of their actual emerging role, they finally developed the items listed in the goal-oriented column.

Though most of the items in the left column are acceptable in the light of tradition, their collective effect tends to reinforce the authority-oriented relationship, depicted in the diagram at the foot of the column, in which people conform to the plan-lead-control directions received from their supervisors. Items in the goal-oriented column do not differ completely with the authority-oriented column, but their net effect provides opportunity for people to manage the full plan-do-control phases of their work, involving supervisors as resources.

During the discussion of the emerging role of the supervisor, the group concluded that an effective supervisor is one who provides a climate in which people have a sense of working for themselves. In terms of their day-to-day relationships, they further defined the supervisor's role as:

- Giving visibility to company (customer) goals.
- Providing budgets and facilities.
- Mediating conflict.
- But primarily, staying out of the way to let people manage their work.

FIGURE 11

The Role of Supervision

Authority-Oriented	Goal-Oriented
Set goals for subordinates, define standards and results expected.	Participate with people in problem solving and goal solving.
Train subordinates how to do the job.	Create situation for learning to occur naturally.
Check subordinates' performance to make sure they are doing things right.	Enable people to check their own performance.
Discipline to keep people in line and set examples.	Mediate conflict and help people see the need for rules and consequences of violations.
Stimulate subordinates by forceful leadership and persuasion.	Allow people to set challenging goals.
Develop and install new methods.	Provide opportunity for methods improvement by job incumbents.
Develop and free subordinates for promotion.	Provide opportunity for people to pursue and move into growth opportunities.
Recognize achievements and point out failures	Recognize achievements and help people learn from failures.

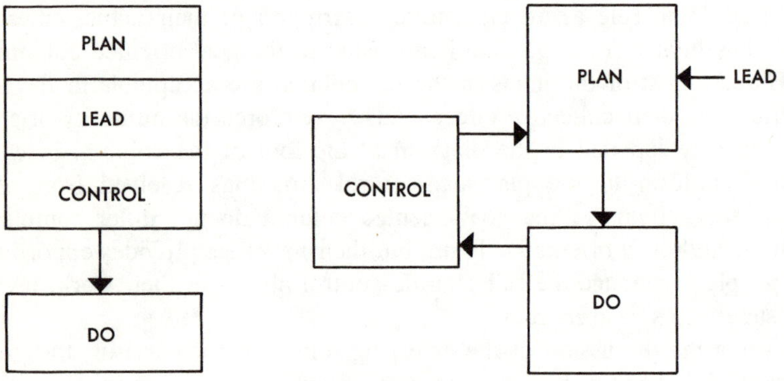

This redefinition of the supervisor's role to provide opportunity for people to manage their own work is portrayed in Figure 12. In contrast to the authority-conformity-oriented roles of the supervisor and operator shown in Figure 8, each now has a goal-oriented role in which the revised do phase of the supervisor and plan phase of the operator comprise the realm of interface between them. Figures 11 and 12 both show the goal-oriented supervisor to be a resource person whose involvement is invoked primarily at the initiative of the operator.

Experience is showing that this relationship, illustrated in this article with the foreman and operator, is a model representing ideal supervisory relationships at any level. Furthermore, enriching the operator's job has changed higher-level jobs. Two levels of jobs (assistant foreman and assistant superintendent) were eliminated, thereby reducing the division hierarchy level from eight to six. The foreman, now freed of many detailed maintenance and control functions, has more time to devote to higher-level planning functions and is also more available to meet his responsibility as a mediator and resource person when he is needed in those capacities — important ones — by the operators.

FIGURE 12
Goal-oriented Relationship between
Foreman and Operator

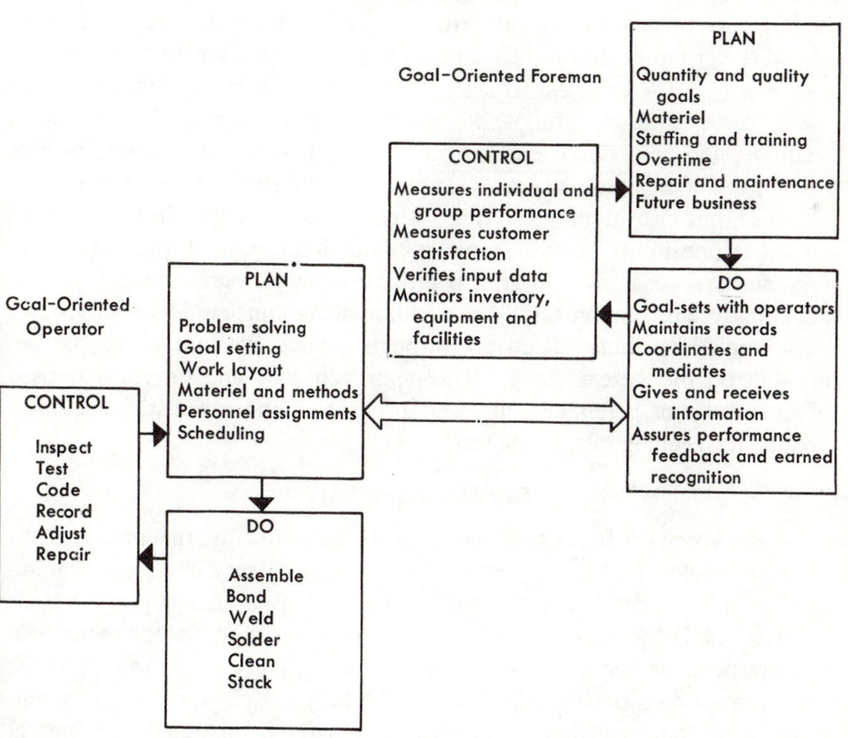

The new role of the supervisor is not always accepted easily. One manager in a multi-company seminar, in hearing a testimonial from another who solved a production problem by involving his operators, said, "You're a fool — you have just cut your own jugular vein! Now that your subordinates have solved your problem for you, they'll have no respect for you as their leader." Initial reactions of this type are not uncommon, as authority-oriented relationships fostered in many homes and schools find natural expression in most job situations. An authority-oriented supervisor does not switch roles by edict or as an immediate consequence of reading a book or hearing an inspiring speech. An intellectual message may sensitize him to his problem, but he must work through the process of self-evaluation, self-acceptance, adjusted values, and changed behavior at his own pace, in his own way, and in an atmosphere of approval. The pressure of an edict to "be democratic" will only regress him to familiar old authority-oriented patterns, from which stance he will obediently recite the intellectual message.

Gone are management prerogatives. The divine rights of "King Supervisor" are being relinquished by the self-imposed pressures of enlightenment. Their price in terms of quashed initiative and alienation is much too high for all but those with pathological needs for adulation. Prerogatives have given way to responsibility — to customers, shareholders, employees, and the community. Influence is still needed to satisfy this new role, but it is not the influence of supervisory authority, but, rather, the influence of all members of the group based on their competence and commitment to goals.

A way of life at work. It is important that people, particularly supervisors, perceive meaningful work, not as another program (which has a beginning and an end) or current fad, but, rather, as a continuing way of life at work which finds expression not only through the pursuit of regular job goals, but also in administering systems which are outside the realm of normal responsibility. For example, methods improvement, job evaluation, wage surveys, insurance programs, attitude surveys, performance reviews, and employee recreation activities, traditionally adminstered by staff groups, are administered more effectively through the involvement of people being affected by these systems. This approach taps and develops unused talent, results in better systems, and provides a more sensitive feedback medium for keeping systems on track.

Self-Managed Jobs

Conclusion. A framework has been presented to erase the management-labor dichotomy and give substance to a slogan "every employee a manager" — a manager being defined as one who manages a job. A self-managed job is one which provides a realistic opportunity for the incumbent to be responsible for the total plan-do-control phases of his job. Though many jobs in their present forms cannot be fully enriched, most can be improved and some can be eliminated. Whether the mission be to enrich, improve, or eliminate the job, it is achieved best by utilizing the talents of the incumbents themselves, provided, of course, this involvement will lead to equivalent or better opportunity. Job enrichment is an iterative process. Though it finds most dramatic expression at the lower levels, it depends on supportive climate and action at the top. When achieved at the lower levels, its impact in terms of both organizational and human criteria reinforces its suppport from the top.

The application of meaningful work offers substantial short-range incentive for managers to support it. Judged as they are, year-to-year, in terms of profit, cost reduction, cash flow, and return-on-assets criteria, job enrichment is seen as a significant resource for achieving success. But it offers even greater rewards on a long-term basis, particularly if criteria of success are broadened to include aspects of human effectiveness, such as self-actualization of employees, responsible civic and home relationships, and the profitable and self-renewing growth of the organization. The role of business and industry in an entrepreneurial society such as the United States has a profound influence on the health of that society. Approximately eighty per cent of people at work are in traditional conformity-oriented, nonexempt job categories. Hence, the implementation of job-enrichment principles in industry has great potential for developing a pattern of responsible behavior learned through a way of life at work which can influence people's behavior in their multiple roles in the community and family.

Therapeutic Value

William Glasser's[6] new approach to psychotherapy points up the therapeutic value of enriched work. Rejecting a classical concept of mental illness and style of therapy, Dr. Glasser defines a process to help the individual face reality and accept responsibility for satisfying his needs in a way that does not deprive others of the ability to fulfill their needs. He shows that opportunity to love and be loved and to feel worthwhile to themselves and others is essential for responsible behavior — that is based largely on the here-and-now and need not probe the subconscious past. Enriched work offers such an opportunity for healthful interpersonal relationships by enabling people to act responsibly in the pursuit of meaningful goals.

Most people have the potential for maladjustment or mental health, and the quality of their vocational roles and relationships is a critical determinant. Hence, organizations applying these principles represent unequaled resources for character building and developing a nation's mental health.

Job enrichment can do much to conserve the competitive agility of the organization by avoiding the usual encumbering consequences of growth, such as excessive layers of supervision, proliferating control processes and conformity pressures, obscure charters, and inflexible systems. It provides a model of applied democracy to stem socialistic trends and represents a rich resource for influencing secondary schools and universities which are shaping candidates for tomorrow's work forces and managerial positions.

A Common Meeting Ground

Management development results from job enrichment as a circular phenomenon. In the first instance, job enrichment requires action (or discontinuation of previous action) on the part of the supervisor to supply conditions of human effectiveness. The results of this action in turn reinforce it and encourage its application by others. Its application brings about subtle changes in the perceptions, values, and, finally, the habits of the supervisors, so that in a gradual branching and multiplying process a new way of life at work is put into motion which simultaneously changes and effects changes through the supervisor. Hence, the supervisor is the originator of, and medium for, change — providing conditions for the development of others and thereby bringing about his own self-development.

The business organization exists to serve society and survives only to the extent that it does so. Society's needs are served best in the long run by sustaining the health of the organization and its members. The health of a business organization is measured in terms of profitable growth, the health of its members in terms of realized potential. Hence, job enrichment is the common meeting ground of the hard-headed businessman and the altruist.

Notes

I am indebted to division training directors and line managers in Texas Instruments for their applications which have resulted in and are validating concepts presented in this paper. I am particularly indebted to Earl D. Weed, Corporate Manager of Training and Development, who helped formulate some of these concepts and plan the application of job enrichment at Texas Instruments.

1. "Who Are Your Motivated Workers?" *Harvard Business Review,* Jan.-Feb. 1964; "Conditions for Manager Motivation," *ibid.,* Jan.-Feb. 1966; "Breakthrough in On-the-Job Training," *ibid.,* July-August 1966.

2. Douglas McGregor, *The Human Side of Enterprise* (New York: McGraw-Hill Book Company, Inc., 1960).

3. A. H. Maslow, *Motivation and Personality* (New York: Harper & Brothers, 1954).

4. Maintenance and motivation needs are defined on page 86 of "Who Are Your Motivated Workers?" *Harvard Business Review,* Jan.-Feb. 1964.

5. Furthermore, work (even uninteresting menial tasks) serves several other roles, such as removing role ambiguity, offering socializing opportunity, increasing solidarity through shared ritual, winning approval of authority figures, providing escape mechanisms for sublimating and channeling energy and thwarted intellectual capability, avoiding unpleasant home environments, and the prevention of guilt and anxiety feelings evoked by idleness in an achieving society. However, most of these roles tend to increase dependency and discourage self-actualization.

6. William Glasser, *Reality Therapy* (New York: Harper & Row, 1965).

C. STAFFING

Typically, the staffing process is conceived of as finding the "right" man for each position. Implicit in this approach are the assumptions that the position is a "constant" and that abilities, attitudes, and motivations of applicants are relatively fixed. Clearly, this is an oversimplification: job design is a function of many variables; people can and do adapt and change. While we want to emphasize that the staffing process leads to the interface between position and person, we do want to caution the reader to keep in mind a dynamic model of organizations and people as he reads the following selections.

Odiorne and Miller (Selection 19) develop a model of selection by objectives — a model which reduces the traditional emphasis placed upon personality tests, aptitude tests, or academic degrees. While we do not doubt the usefulness of these traditional tools, we need to consider them in their proper perspective. We suspect that many organizations are biased toward an acceptance of test scores as valid measures and predictors of certain types of behavior rather than as partial indicators which need to be used with other data in reaching selection decisions. In many cases, of course, the failures of tests can be attributed to misapplication. The energy expended on the development of revised or new tests may seem disproportionate to the energy expended on their proper application. For instance, tests may not be inherently discriminatory against minority groups but their application may be. Studies have indicated that certain tests are good predictors of performance for white middle-class individuals, but not for blacks or *whites from lower socio-economic backgrounds.*

Odiorne and Miller review and evaluate four of the more common selection methods in use today and advance a fifth approach which they label the "objectives-results approach." They suggest that this "approach doesn't presume to displace all of the presently-used methods. It merely subsumes them to other criteria and shapes the plan for selection in somewhat different terms." Although their analysis focuses upon the selection of management personnel, essentially it is applicable to most occupational groups.

Campbell and Bray (Selection 20) provide empirical evidence that our "batting average" in the selection of managerial personnel from among craftsmen can be improved. The means for improvement is the Assessment Center Program. Several features make this program worthy of our attention. One feature is that multiple factors and techniques are used in an attempt to capture the contributions of each while minimizing weaknesses. The Assessment Center concept can be used to facilitate integration between a specialized unit, as illustrated by the Assessment Center, and line management. An unanswered question is whether or not the results of such assessments can be used in a developmental way with those candidates who are not recommended for promotion.

19

Selection by Objectives: A New Approach to Managerial Selection

GEORGE S. ODIORNE
University of Michigan

EDWIN L. MILLER
University of Michigan

The foreman of a gang of lumberjacks was being solicited for a job by a rather spindly looking little man. The giant gang-boss scoffed: "Why, this work would kill you. Just to show you what I mean, why don't you take this ax and go chop down that giant fir?"

Despite the grins of the regular crew, the little man approached the tree and with a quick flurry of blows had the giant conifer on the ground. The grins turned to whistles of awe, and the foreman's voice took on a tone of respect.

"Holy Mackeral, fella, that's great! Where did you learn to chop down trees like that?"

"I worked on the Sahara forest job."

"Forest? I thought the Sahara was a desert."

"*Now* it is."

This tale might be an illustration of how selection by objectives would look in the lumbering business. No personality tests, no aptitude tests, little

Taken and adapted from *Management of Personnel Quarterly,* Vol. 5, No. 3, Fall 1966. Used by permission.

concern about degrees held. Just a good record of having achieved good results in the past and an on-the-spot demonstration of some of the key behavior which might be required on the job ahead.

The entire matter of employment methods is under serious fire from a number of quarters, and perhaps a new approach to the selection of persons for employment, or for promotion — which is really internal selection — is indicated.

What's Wrong With Present Selection Methods

The major shortcomings of present day selection methods seem to fall into these major categories:

• *Techniques are mainly for low-level workers.* Since Hugo Munsterberg and others about sixty years ago seriously undertook the study of employment testing, the major emphasis has been upon the selection of workers.[1] The problems of early identification of high talent manpower and the techniques for hiring and promoting managers, engineers and staff persons are different and at this stage very problematical.[2]

• *Psychological testing has come under serious fire.* From within the profession and from outside, numerous attacks have been leveled at psychological tests.[3] They comprise an invasion of privacy, some hold. They have logical improprieties, say others. They breed conformity, say still others. Whatever the merits of these charges, the effect nonetheless has been to cast a cloud over their use in selection. A small fringe of charlatans promising psychological miracles in a manner akin to the snake-oil peddlers of old have not done much to clarify the issues.

• *The civil rights laws have shaken many long-accepted practices.* The civil rights law of 1964 has shaken traditional employment practices seriously.[4] Not only are racial guidelines to hiring barred, but women are protected from discrimination in hiring and promotion because of sex.

• *The mad rush is to college graduates.* Despite a rapidly rising curve of enrollments in the colleges, the rush at the exit door of the institutes of higher learning is greater.[5] Surely one of the most bizarre and absurd fads ever to sweep industry, the clamor to collect degree holders for every white collar position shows no sign of abatement. There is apparently little inkling of manpower planning to identify which job requires a degree and which one doesn't.

While all of these shortcomings could be expanded at length, and the list itself lengthened, they comprise typical evidence of the illness that presently besets the hiring and promotion process.

This article outlines a *new approach* to the selection process. It makes a quick tour of the four major methods now being used in selection, then turns to a more detailed explanation of a new — or fifth — approach to selection. The purpose isn't to deny the value of the four, but to place them in a new perspective and improve the effectiveness with which they are used.

The paper is based on experiments done in industrial and governmental organizations in applying the system of management by objectives to the selection process. The method described here thus becomes *Selection by Objectives.*

The article presumes that the first step in management is to establish objectives and to obtain commitments in advance to seek them.[6] It also presumes that the person who has achieved objectives consistently in the past is more likely to achieve them in new situations. It is further proposed that these selection criteria have primacy over testing, hunch, behavioral inventories, or background. Thus, the major purpose of selection procedures should be to uncover evidences of achievements against objectives in the past.

Personnel staffing decisions are gambles in much the same way that a decision to bet on a particular horse is a gamble. Both decisions are based on predictions of performance among alternative choices. Predictions of the future are estimates or expectations based upon observations of past and present achievements and the known or assumed relationships between these observations and future wants.[7] For the horseplayer, prediction of the outcome of a race might be based on such variables as ancestry of the horse, performance in previous outings, current times, and physical condition of the horse and the jockey. For the manager involved in personnel staffing decisions, the prediction of a candidate's performance will be based upon observations of variables believed to be associated with or determinative of the desired level of future performance. In either case, the horseplayer or the manager is seeking to identify the winner. Needless to say, there are many poor choices and many disappointed people.

Employment managers and supervisors have always concerned themselves with trying to identify the best man for the job. Typically the supervisor makes his decision based upon his ability to size up a man. In far too many instances, this method has led to failure and unsatisfactory performance. Errors in personnel staffing decisions can be costly mistakes. For the individual poorly placed, his inability to perform his work competently, and the consequent prospect of reprimand or dismissal can lead to his frustration and possible personal bodily harm. For the company, mistakes in personnel staffing decisions frequently lead to increased expense to the business in terms of recruiting, selection, training, and production. Although major stages in the development of a scientific approach to selection are well known, the objectives-result approach — tried experimentally by the authors (and on a tentative and sometimes unconscious basis in many places) — has not to their knowledge been consciously described. Such a description of the Fifth Approach is the purpose of this article.

The Four Approaches to Selection Now in Use

The systems of selection used to date have fallen into four major categories, described here in summary form. These selection techniques are based upon the major presumptions of the person applying them.

1. The personal preference method. This is still the most commonly-used method, even when disguised by the apparatus of science; the hunch of the manager, his biases, or his likes and dislikes determine the selection of employees.
2. The occupational characteristics approach. Earliest of the scientifically based methods, this method applied aptitude measurements to applicants, and allowed one to attempt to predict success on the job.
3. The behavioral approach. Another scientific approach to selection of employees was that of identifying behavior patterns out of the past, and predicting that such behavior (as demonstrated in tests or verified through resumé and reference checks) would continue into the future. With these results matched against job requirements, success could be predicted.
4. The background approach. The fourth method is evidenced most strongly in the career pattern studies of Warner and Abblegen, and evidenced by the search for college graduates in campus recruiting. It presumes that successful managers and professionals can best be selected by studying the careers of the already successful, and hiring those who best seem to duplicate them.

The Fifth Approach

What is suggested here is that a new approach is now possible, synthesizing the useful features of the others plus an important new addition, a new point of origin for selection. Because it proposes to supplant the others, and in fact has proven more successful where applied, a brief review of each of the former four methods is in order.

The Personal Preference Method

The proprietary right of an owner to make the decisions about who shall be hired or who shall not be hired to work in his business grows out of the property rights of ownership. If the small merchant or manufacturer decides to hire only members of his own lodge, church, or family, there are few constraints upon his doing so. Title VII of the Civil Rights Act of 1964, if applicable to him, theoretically limits his exercise of this right in the public interest. Clearly he cannot flout the law openly, but his preferences may lead him to the creation of standards which make the law ineffective while serving his preferential biases. The administration of the law in future years may corner him in these subterfuges, although at present the strong voluntary compliance aspects of the law can leave him relatively untouched. Since many of his biases are unconscious — and hotly denied if pointed out — they are difficult to eradicate from outside the firm. Kahn's studies of the employment of Jews,[8] and the open challenging of tests in the Motorola decision on the basis of their "culture biased" aspects illustrate the tacit application of how bias might be used or alleged.

These personal preferences originate in the emotions and sentiments of the employer and extend from hiring alumni to Zulus simply because the employer feels the way he does about the people he wants around.

The Internal Characteristics Approach

Since psychologists are usually the only professionals qualified to devise and validate tests of psychological characteristics it is not surprising that testing of various kinds has all of the strengths and limitations of psychology itself as a science. In recent years, this approach has come under fire for a variety of reasons. Writers of a moralist type have written with great fervor about the invasion of privacy which attends testing. By selecting questions out of the body of extensive test batteries congressional committees and critical writers have generated righteous wrath. "Did you ever want to kill your father," for example, reads poorly when it becomes a headline in a Washington newspaper. Martin Gross, Vance Packard, and others have attacked the indignities which occur when psychlogists pry.[9] Other criticisms have come from within the profession itself. Logical improprieties in testing are often discussed in professional journals. Still other critics have been behavioral scientists who have queried the scientific propriety of some testing methods.[10] As a result, it is now forbidden in government agencies to use personality tests upon job applicants, and this ban has recently been extended to government contractors by letters sent to all such contractors. Not totally banned, the list of limits placed upon their use has been sufficiently complicated that the actual effect will be a falling-off of this kind of testing.

Two Families of Tests. The purpose here isn't to outline the varieties of tests and their advantages and disadvantages; the aim is to outline only the objectives of tests which comprise the "inward characteristics" approach to selection. Achievement tests would not fall into this approach, since they measure demonstrable behavior being observed, but two others do: aptitude and personality tests.

Aptitude Tests. Because of the magnitude of the wastes and losses in selection there has arisen a more and more insistent demand to reduce errors in staffing decisions. It is this necessity that has given rise to aptitude prediction by means of testing. At the present, various kinds of psychological tests are the chief means for making aptitude prognosis.

Testing in all applied sciences is performed on the basis of samples, and human aptitude testing is not essentially different from the application of tests in other sciences. The thing sampled in aptitude tests is, in most cases, human behavior. Specifically, a psychological test is the measurement of some phase of a carefully chosen sample of an individual's behavior from which extrapolations and inferences are made. Measuring differences among people through the use of psychological tests has made a signal advance to understanding and predicting human behavior.

In its simplest terms, aptitude testing rests on a correlation relationship between a normally distributed predictor variable (which may or may not be related to the skills and abilities required on the job) on the one hand, and another normally distributed measure of satisfactory performance on the other hand.[11] The simple matching task is to eliminate, on the basis of the relatively inexpensive predictor variable, those individuals with little likelihood of success on the job — obviously an easy task in theory but beset by complexities in practice.

The conception of specialized aptitudes and the desirability of having tests of behavior which will indicate in advance latent capacity has its roots in ancient history. Over twenty-three hundred years ago, Plato proposed a series of tests for the guardians of his ideal republic. His proposal was realized in the United States Army mental tests of World War I.

The use of tests to measure aptitudes didn't receive much interest until the late nineteenth century when a number of psychologists became interested in mental testing and the psychology of individual differences.[12] The tests of the early aptitude psychologists were largely individual tests. This approach changed with the advent of World War I. Based on the pioneering work of A. S. Otis, a set of tests which not only could be administered to a large number of subjects at the same time but could be scored by semimechanical means appeared on the scene.[13] Nearly two million army recruits were tested, and aptitude testing on a group basis was born.

Following rapidly upon the heels of the spectacular accomplishment of psychological testing in the army, industry picked up the cue that tests could be effectively used in employment and personnel work. The individual worker came to be considered a conglomerate of traits that could be measured by tests. It did not matter whether these traits were regarded as innate or acquired. What mattered from the employer's viewpoint was that tests could be utilized in the selection and job placement of workers. The result of this hasty and ill-advised exploitation of an approach really useful in its own field was temporary failure and disillusionment. Quite naturally, a distinct reaction against aptitude testing set in.

The road back from almost complete denial of aptitude testing in industry has been paved with both successes and failures. Today, aptitude testing is finding ever-increasing use in American industry. Aptitude testing has proven to be helpful in staffing decisions involving clerical personnel, salesmen, and certain other industrial occupations; however, in that area where effective prediction is most desperately needed — in managerial selection — aptitude testing has met with only limited success.[14]

One of the most telling criticisms of aptitude testing is that made by Hull in 1928.[15] He suggested that something in the neighborhood of .50 might be a practical limit for validities of tests. Nothing in the history of selection testing has radically revised this figure after almost 40 years. Nevertheless the quest goes on — to develop tests which can efficiently estimate or forecast aptitudes and success on the job from test scores.

Personality Tests. Success on the job is not solely determined by ability; it is also attributable in part to the personality and interest of the worker. Aptitude tests are not tests of motivation and interest; consequently something else is needed to measure these dimensions of the worker. Not only is the supervisor interested in finding out whether the worker *can do* the job, he is also interested in determining whether he *will do* the job. It is to this question that personality and interest inventories in the industrial setting are addressed.

The instruments used to assess the "will do" side in prediction come in all shapes and sizes. Some of these devices are simple inventories, others are based on specific personality or motivational theories. Some seek to measure those aspects of the personality called temperament traits. Still others are projective in design and are intended for "global assessments" of personality.[16]

These instruments are impressive in their diversity and approach. However, notwithstanding their multiplicity of technique and design, the history of personality and interest measurements in industrial selection has been something less than spectacular. Much of the variety in approaches to the measurement of personality stems from the desire to overcome the deficiencies in existing tests and the fact that the relationship between the predictor variable and the criteria are infinitely complex and dynamic.

Many of the tests presently used in assessment, particularly in the selection of managers, are general personality tests which have not been validated for managerial performance but rather for the identification of particular personality traits. The relevance of these traits or characteristics to successful performance on the job frequently comes about because of some intuitive judgment as to the type of man one would like to have. Relatively few attempts have been made to forecast accurately the demands placed on the applicant once he is in the organization. Thus, it seems that we may be playing Russian Roulette with the future of the enterprise by attempting to select managers through screening devices which in effect merely assure us that all those admitted to managerial ranks are alike. Fortunately, this is not the problem for the organization today as it might be in the future. At present, the validities of personality tests are low enough so that the consistent use of any of the personality tests will allow enough people to slip by that the organization will be protected against poor judgment about the qualities it thinks it is selecting.

What is needed by management with regard to its personnel staffing is apparently a heterogeneous supply of human resources from which individuals can be selected to fill a variety of specific but unpredictable needs. Thus the problem with personality tests is much more than that of overcoming distortion due to faking, presenting an idealized concept of oneself rather than a realistic self-appraisal, and a lack of self-insight. The basic issue is ability to predict the future with an extremely high level of probability. This clairvoyance will be a long time in coming.[17]

The Behavioral or Skills Approach

A third approach to selection has been through tests which are less concerned with inner qualities, or inferences about such qualities. Behavior — activity which can be seen or measured — has been the subject of measurement and observation in this cluster of selection devices. In its simplest form, it was the test applied to the itinerant craftsman who wandered from town to town in the early part of the century. The boss of the machine shop would simply give him a piece of metal and a drawing and tell him to "make this." If he made the piece to precise specifications, did it quickly, with few errors, he was hired. The achievement test of typing skill was to place the applicant in front of a typewriter and have her type. Her work was timed, checked for errors, and if she performed well she was hired.

Such tests — which certainly aren't any more psychological than the height and weight of the applicant are psychological — are still used, and are extremely useful screening devices. There has been an attempt to extend such testing to selection of managerial applicants, or candidates for sales, professional, or technical positions. Perhaps the most comprehensive plan for this approach is that of Robert N. McMurry, whose pattern interview program,[18] coupled with tests and full dress exploration of behavior histories, is widely used by many firms.

Actually a combination of personality, aptitude, and behavior history approaches, McMurry's system hypothesizes that the prediction of what a man will do in future assignments is already written in the record of his past behavior. Determinism is the underlying assumption here. If a man has been a job hopper in the past (has held five jobs in the past five years) he will probably be a job hopper in the future. The goal of the pattern interview then is to probe intensively into the resumé, filling in each gap to uncover "patterns" of behavior. It is presumed that these patterns will persist into the future.

The McMurry system, which has been widely adopted and copied by firms and by a corps of consultants who have developed similar plans, delves into attitudes by eliciting verbal reactions to the conditions of past employment. An applicant who states that most of his past employers have been incompetent, unpleasant, or otherwise deficient may be predicted to adopt similar verbal responses about the new employer after the initial period of adjustment is over. Further, one may predict such things as leadership, creativity, and maturity by asking questions which get at past behavior from which reasonable inferences can be made. Figure 1 shows how such questions might be devised in this behavioral approach to managerial selection.

FIGURE 1

Using verbal responses to obtain predictors of future attitudes or capacities.

Trait	*Question which will highlight the trait*
Creativity	Has the applicant ever created anything?
Leadership	Has he ever led anything?
Loyalty	Does he speak well for former employers, school, parents, and associates?
Maturity	Has he been dependent upon others? Has he destroyed things which were his responsibility?
	Has his behavior been excessively oriented toward pleasurable activities?

The assumptions in this line of questioning are that people's behavior doesn't change, or that it may be costly to change it. Such being true, the time to find the undesirable behavior patterns in applicants is when they are still applicants. One might even hire persons with less than desirable behavior patterns, knowing what the defects are and allowing for them.

Clearly more scientific than some of the more esoteric methods of personality and aptitude testing, McMurry's system nonetheless shares the limitation that it is deterministic, and is more apt to achieve conformity in hiring than any other outcome.

The distinctive feature of this approach is that it presumes that a *pattern of behavior* is the key ingredient in hiring. Reference checks, intensive attention to past behavior, and the reports of past observers about the behavior of individuals, are coupled with the hardest possible probing into every aspect of the applicant's past results in order to create an extensive dossier which gives the interviewer the equivalent of many years of personal acquaintanceship with the applicant. The interview which is vital in this approach may be non-directive when it will manipulate the individual into revealing things he might not otherwise divulge. Telephone checks of former employers are larded with probing questions to strip aside the amenities which former employers customarily drape over people they've fired.

The method's most important shortcoming, although it comes closer than many other approaches, is that it deals mainly with behavior and not with the effects of that behavior in results.

The Background Approach to Selection

One of the fastest rising in popularity, the background approach has resulted in a dramatic rise in campus recruiting in recent years. In fact, much of the pressure upon the campus recruiting process has grown out of an unstated and sometimes unconscious assumption that a college degree is needed for most managerial and staff positions. There are some interesting assumptions here.

1. It is assumed that the person who has a degree learned something in college. It is further assumed that this learning is something which he will carry to his first and subsequent positions. It is further assumed that the learning will convert into behavior on the job, and the behavior in turn will produce results that could not be produced by the non-college graduate.
2. Much of the drive to garner diploma-holders was caused by studies which show that 75% of the present crop of chief executives of the largest firms are college graduates. The studies of Warner, Abblegan and others, it is held, comprise predictors of the promotability of college graduates.[19] To some extent, this has become describable by the favorite cliché of the psychologists — "a self-fulfilling prophecy." Companies which presume that only college graduates can do managerial work enact policies which permit only college graduates to become managers. As a result, over time their ranks become filled with college graduate managers. As example, one utility company for many years recruited at colleges, limiting interviews to those in the upper brackets of their class in grades. Later they found that only high mark students succeeded.[20]

Where are the soft spots?

- There are many studies which show that the most successful automobile dealers, real estate men, and successful small business operators are not college men.[21]
- The two largest firms in the country in sales and profit have diametrically opposed policies with respect to the promotion of college men into managerial positions. In AT&T the college man enjoys a distinct edge. In General Motors, where results are primary guides to internal selection, a vast majority of managers are not college graduates, including at this writing the president. GM *has* an extensive college recruiting program; however, its assumptions are different from some of its corporate counterparts. GM assumes when it hires a college graduate that he will demonstrate what he has learned once he is on the job, and that this learning will be verified by the results he achieves rather than by the degree he acquired before joining

the firm. (Ford, number two in manufacturing industries, shares GM's pattern of selecting managers.)

• The background approach has the limitations of all the single-cause approaches to selection. It examines a single variable (academic degree) and generalizes this as a predictor. In fact, some combinations of degrees are automatic guarantees of rapid rise in the large corporation. The man with a BS degree from Massachusetts Institute of Technology and an MBA from Harvard, for example, may never have to really work again. His rise to the general management post is assured. Admittedly, he has already, as a youth, gone through several screens that many fail to survive, but his subsequent progress will not be measured by his results-achieved until he reaches a crucial position in the firm. Who would dare to give him a bad appraisal? He might remember it when he gets on top. His salary progress will be swift in order that the jump need not be too great when he arrives at the top.

The suggestion here isn't that background is not useful information, but rather that as a single predictor it has the limitations of all single-cause explanations for multiple-cause outcomes. Meanwhile, this approach to selection gains momentum. The average cost of recruiting an MBA at Michigan in 1966 was $2100. This doesn't include any of the cost of education, merely the cost of moving the inexperienced graduate from classroom to his first office. After he arrived he received an average monthly pay of $750, with a range running up to $2000 for certain rare types in the upper reaches of academic grade achievement.[22] What this is doing to salary administration inside these firms staggers the imagination. The average monthly salary in 1966 was some 30% above that offered three years ago.

The Fifth Approach

An objectives-result approach doesn't presume to displace all of the presently-used methods. It merely subsumes them to other criteria and shapes the plan for selection in somewhat different terms.

It starts with statements of job objectives for the job being filled, rather than with job descriptions which have been oriented toward skills, experience, and man-requirements. The method turns secondly to a measurement of the candidates' results on past jobs.

The approach breaks these objectives down into three major categories of objectives, and uses the selection process to uncover predictors in the individual's history which would point up probabilities of his operating at each of the three levels. The presumption in this selection of managers is that routine duties are a *must* requirement and that movement into the higher levels is demonstrated by problem solving results and, most especially, by innovative or change-making abilities. (A special and somewhat temporary kind of objective will be learning-objectives, in which the candidate must complete a learning or training program in order to bring himself up to the minimum (regular) requirements of the position for which he is applying.)

These duties comprise an ascending scale of excellence in management achievement, and the tools of selection should be designed to identify these objectives in the job and to uncover, in the candidate's results on past jobs, predictors of these kinds of results for the future.

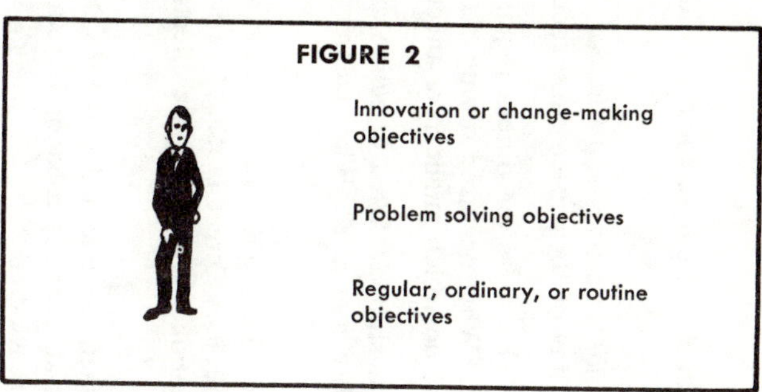

Defining the Objectives

This fifth approach to selection starts with a clarification of the objectives of regular or routine duties, of the problems to be solved, and of the innovations sought. The first step in the fifth approach calls for a change in the job requisitioning procedures. For a typical position in which a job applicant might be considered, the employment manager or recruiter — or the manager himself if he is to do his own hiring — constructs a roster of job objectives, broken into the major categories. A sample description of the objectives for a general foreman (manufacturing) is shown in Figure 3. From this guide it is seen that this position has more regular duties than it has problem-solving or innovative duties. These could be broken out as selection criteria. Other positions might emphasize the requirements of problem solving.

Figure 4 shows the objectives for a systems engineer. This list of objectives, constructed by a group of 100 managers in systems engineering laboratories, could inspire an entirely different approach to selection from the traditional method. Here is an example of a different approach to selection, based on this set of objectives. Acme System Company is recruiting people for engineering posts to fulfill a long-run contract. It also hopes that out of this group will emerge some managers for the future. Some tangible effects might alter the selection procedure:

1. Despite the common nature of many of the activities, this work will be primarily innovative or problem solving. All job information sought in in-

FIGURE 3

Sample Job Objectives for General Foreman—Manufacturing

Objectives	*Indicative past achievements*
1. To aid in selection of foreman for production	Has he ever picked a foreman, or does he have some firm ideas on what a foreman's functions should be?
2. Train foremen on the plant floor	Does he know the foreman's major objectives and functions? Has he ever broken in a new one? How many? Have any of them been subsequently released? Promoted?
3. Production quantity	What departments has he led? What were the output requirements? Did the department meet them? Exceed them? What occurred during his tenure in office in terms of levels of output? What did he do which might have affected output?
4. Quality	What was the reject rate when he started? What direction did it go? How did he get along with the inspectors? quality manager? What techniques for improvement did he use?
5. Cost Control	What cost results did he achieve? How did his prime costs vary? His indirect labor? Indirect materials? Direct materials? Direct labor? Did he use any cost reduction methods such as work simplification? What were the effects? Has he submitted any improvement ideas in cost?
6. Employee relations	What was the turnover rate when he assumed charge? Did it change? Grievance rates? Absenteeism? Any special methods used or introduced? Were any attitude surveys done in his area, and with what effect?

FIGURE 4

List of Typical Functions and Results Criteria for a Systems Engineer

Function	*Result criteria*
1. Interprets organization objectives when laying out project	Upon receiving tasks, projects, or assignments must develop working plans and approaches to achieve them which requires interpretation of sponsor's objectives.
2. Checking progress for compliance	Must check with superior or customer to determine whether direction and rate of progress are satisfactory. Has few if any complaints that he is checking back too often (being too dependent) or too infrequently, thus getting off the track too far.
3. Making stop-or-proceed decisions	Makes decisions on work whether to proceed a course of study or action or to drop that course and try another. Generally gets concurrence of customer or superior. Should run into occasional blank wall if he is really experimenting.
4. System engineering skill	Applies law and principles of systems to the solution of specific problems in the project. Has well stocked memory for principles, has access to many more, and learns new ones quickly. Manipulates memories into new and original mixes.
5. Visual display of concepts	Devises, plans and executes visual displays (drawings, sketches, working models, breadboards, etc.) of the underlying concepts.
6. Communicating ideas	Clarifies ideas, converts them into the language of the receiver, transmits them effectively, gets feedback to assure understanding: includes report writing and technical manuals.
7. Adherence to policy	Stays customarily within accepted and promulgated guides to technical action in that firm, the industry, the lab unless overriding reasons dictate otherwise.

Others rated highly important included Self-Development activity, and introduction of new ideas.

terview should aim at reaching a conclusion about such results achieved by the candidate in the past.

2. Certain kinds of objectives cannot be expected from new hires directly from college. In the objectives shown in Figure 4, those which could be expected of the beginner are handled apart from those which would be required of the experienced professional who might be expected to start in immediately and achieve most of his objectives.

3. The inquiry about the candidate should aim at uncovering how his past results in each of these areas indicate probable achievements of similar results in the future. Such questions as the following might be used.

Objective	*Line of questioning*
To apply laws and principles of systems engineering to specific problems in a project.	• Courses taken? • Grades? • Do they apply here? • Special research done? • List of past projects? • Key issues in technical field? • Does he see any interdisciplinary approaches? • Is he mathematically sound?
To interpret objectives for technical projects.	• What projects has he designed experiments for? • How has he decided on working plans and approaches?

It is apparent that the one conducting the interview and making umpire-like judgments as to past achievements in terms of results must be conversant with the objective of the man's job. The specifics of the question aren't of major concern here, but rather that the interviewer be seeking evidence of results in both kind and amount. The short illustration presented above demonstrates that the end product of selection by objectives comes from a different look at the work the man is expected to do when he is hired.

When Objectives are Set for the First Time

Before a company can select by objectives, it must establish what the objectives for the position being filled actually are. The statements of the systems engineer's functions had to be constructed for this study since they did not exist in the firm at the time of the study. The statements of responsibilities were hammered out in small conference groups with the managers of these engineers. Only those statements which over 90% of the managers felt were of above average significance for the jobs of the systems engineers in that lab were included. Others were specifically reflected by the majority. (Community and civic activities, training technicians, and delegation to technicians were rated as of little or no significance.) While one may deplore the standards set by the managers in some areas, it must be realised that this is the climate into which the new engineers are going to be hired.

The same step can be taken elsewhere, partially by asking the present encumbents what they think their objectives are, but more importantly, by asking the manager of the position to clarify the objectives for that position. It is he who will administer salaries, appraise for the annual performance report, coach, and recommend promotions.

Predicting Success on the Basis of Results

Once job objectives are in hand, all selection methods should focus on uncovering result-getting activity in the history of the applicant. If the accustomed way of thinking about hiring suggests "Why, we're doing that right now," please read on. Most application forms or proposed resumé forms do not demand specific statements of results achieved. Take the case of the government agency which was stymied by its selection problem because it found so many people at the higher levels had resumés including such information as the following:

> 1956–59 Director of Underground Utilization of Overhead Manpower, Department of Midair Coordination and Development. GS-15
>
> Had full responsibility for coordination and implementation of all liaison missions of this service base. Reported directly to the deputy chief of staff-Coordination. Base operated with 6000 military and civilian personnel, and annual budget of $32 million.

Such nonsense implies that the applicant is the sole leader of 6000 men, spending thirty million dollars yearly, and it surrounds him with an aura of responsibility. The agency required that resumés be written to include answers to the question:

> What did you actually achieve during that period; give year by year summaries. Who could we talk with to verify these achievements? How many of them were attributable to your efforts, how many were jointly performed with others?

The replies were matched with some intensive looks at the vacant positions to see what the objectives and criteria were for the persons being hired. The result was a drastic change in the way selections were made, and while it is still early to be certain, preliminary reports indicate a sharpening of performance in the newly-placed persons.

Another example occurred in a firm which was seeking a college grad trainee for a marketing management position. One of the prime candidates was labelled as having "leadership" because he was president of the student council in college. At the urging of the writers, the firm probed a little deeper along these lines:

> During your year as president what did the council do? What condition was the treasury in when you took over? When you left? Did you finish any projects which would make a lasting effect on student life? Who could we talk to that would know best what the achievements of the council were under your leadership?

This intensive line of questioning elicited from the young man himself the fact that the year had been marked with constant trouble growing out of his inability to handle the officers and get programs going. He had been selected "on my good looks, I guess, and the coeds make up a big part of the vote." The very king-pin criterion of the selection decision proved to be the weakest link.

Job applicants have increasingly recognized the values of listing accomplishments on their resumés rather than claiming attributes or positions which emit golden glows. Some personnel men have shied away from the use of such information, because "Most people will dress it up, and you can't really tell whether the interviewee was responsible, or just went along for the ride."

The same cautious skepticism is needed in evaluating accomplishments and results as is needed in statements of responsibilities, personality, or background. How can one overcome the tendency of applicants to paint an over-rosy picture?

1. Ask specifically how much of the achievements listed are genuinely attributable to their own efforts and how much were shared with others. For example the following question has produced some candid responses in interviews observed and reported:

   "Your record shows some fine achievements in this past job. Now many of us do things jointly with others. What *percentage* of this achievement would you say is directly attributable to you or your subordinates?"

   "Now, you note that these achievements are partially shared with Mr. A, the controller. You estimate that . . . . % of this is rightly attributable to you and your organization. Do you think that Mr. A would agree with your estimate of that percentage?"

The only reason, generally, a candid and honestly-held estimate may be withheld is that the applicant doesn't know, is deluding himself, or is lying. Verification procedures, reference checks and telephone reference chats substantiate the information. Rather than checking such matters as initiative, drive, personality, and the like, the interviewer restates the achievements the applicant has claimed and simply asks the informant, "Would you agree that the achievements he has stated for his performance in your company are accurate? If not, how did they differ?"

Private Good and Public Weal — a Conclusion

Hiring and promotion policy and practice badly need an overhaul. The perpetuation of our firms, and the observance of public interest through equitable selection are at stake. We have learned from all of our past experiences. Selection by objectives won't guarantee success, but may help us improve our averages. It may also stem the onrushing trend toward hiring overqualified people and ease the job opportunities for the present unemployables. It is a method of rewarding excellence rather than conformity or social class of origin.

Notes

1. Hugo Munsterberg, *Psychology of Industrial Efficiency,* Boston, Houghton Mifflin, 1913.

2. M. Joseph Dooher and Elizabeth Mauting, *Selection of Management Personnel,* Vol. 1, New York, American Management Association, 1957.

Thomas A. Mahoney, Thomas H. Jerdee, and Allen N. Nash, *The Identification of Management Potential,* Dubuque, Wm. C. Brown Co., 1961.

3. William H. Whyte, Jr., *The Organization Man,* New York, Simon and Schuster, 1956.

4. Howard C. Lockwood, "Critical Problems in Achieving Equal Employment Opportunity," *Personnel Psychology,* XIX, Spring, 1966, pp. 3–10.

A. G. Bayroff, "Test Technology and Equal Employment Opportunity," *Personnel Psychology,* XIX, Spring, 1966, pp. 35–39.

5. John S. Fielden, "The Right Young People for Business," *Harvard Business Review,* XLIV, March–April, 1966, pp. 76–83.

6. George S. Odiorne, *Management by Objectives,* New York, Pitman Publishing Corp., 1965.

Edward C. Schleh, *Management by Results,* New York, McGraw-Hill Book Co., 1961.

7. Marvin D. Dunnette and Wayne K. Kirchner, *Psychology Applied to Industry,* New York, Appleton-Century-Crofts, 1965.

8. Robert Kahn *et al., Discrimination Without Prejudice,* Institute for Social Research, Survey Research Center, University of Michigan, 1964.

9. Vance Packard, *The Pyramid Climbers,* New York, McGraw-Hill Book Co., 1962, pp. 279–285.

Martin Gross, *The Brain Watchers,* New York, Random House, 1962.

10. Harry Levinson, "The Psychologist in Industry," *Harvard Business Review,* XXXVII, September–October, 1959, pp. 93–99.

11. Mason Haire, "Psychological Problems Relevant to Business and Industry," *Psychological Bulletin,* LVI, May, 1959, pp. 174–175.

12. Anne Anastasi, *Psychological Testing,* New York, Macmillan Co., 1954, pp. 8–18.

13. Clark Hull, *Aptitude Testing,* New York, World Book Co., 1928, pp. 16–19.

14. Robert M. Guion, *Personnel Testing,* New York, McGraw-Hill Book Co., 1965, pp. 469–471.

15. Hull, *op. cit.*

16. Five widely used inventories are:
    1. California Psychology Inventory
    2. Gordon Personal Profile
    3. Guilford-Zimmerman Temperament Survey
    4. Minnesota Multiphasic Personality Inventory
    5. Thurston Temperament Schedule

17. As Guion has commented concerning personality measurement: "The available measures have generally been developed for clinical and counseling purposes rather than for selection, they are too subjective, and the evidence of their value is too weak."

18. Robert N. McMurry, "Validating the Patterned Interview," *Personnel,* XXIII, January, 1947, pp. 263–272.

19. W. Lloyd Warner and James C. Abegglen, *Occupational Mobility in American Business and Industry,* Minneapolis, University of Minnesota Press, 1955, pp. 95–97.

20. Frederick R. Kappel, "From the World of College to the World of Work," *Bell Telephone Magazine,* Spring, 1962.

21. Warner and Abegglen, *loc.cit.*

22. Arthur S. Hann, *Salary Summary of Job Offers and Acceptances to Date, Spring, 1966,* Graduate School of Business Administration, Ann Arbor, University of Michigan, June, 1966.

20

Assessment Centers: An Aid in Management Selection

RICHARD J. CAMPBELL
AT&T

DOUGLAS W. BRAY
AT&T

The Bell System Assessment Center Program

The first Bell System assessment center procedure was developed as a research tool by D. W. Bray, with the assistance of others, for the assessment of men participating in a long-range study of management development (Bray, 1946). The information gathered about these men was for use in the study, and all information about specific individuals was kept confidential. It was not long before this assessment center procedure was recognized as a potentially valuable technique that could be used as an aid in the selection process. One of the associated companies, Michigan Bell Telephone, wanted to improve its selection of new managers from the craft ranks, and the research assessment center procedure was modified for use by a local staff.

The assessment center designed for Michigan Bell, similar to those now used in other Bell Companies, processes 12 candidates per week. The candidates spend two and a half to three days at the center, with the remainder of the week being used by the staff for report writing, rating, and evaluation conferences. While at the center the candidate is given a comprehensive interview, completes several paper and pencil tests of mental ability and knowledge, and participates in individual and group simulations. The individual simulation is a lengthy administrative exercise known as the In-Basket. The candidate is required to handle a number of items actually taken from the in-baskets of Bell System managers.

Each candidate also participates in two group problems. One is a miniature business game involving a group of six men; the other is a leaderless

Reprinted by permission from the March–April 1967 issue of *Personnel Administration*.

group discussion preceded by more formal presentations by each member of a six-man group. Another technique involves both individual work and group interaction concerning a problem in labor-management relations. The performance of each candidate in each of the various techniques is described and analyzed in a detailed written report prepared independently for each exercise.

Rating the Candidate

The final step is the staff evaluation conference, in which each candidate is considered in turn. The main objective of the evaluation session is to rate the candidate's potential for promotion, assigning him to one of three categories: "acceptable for promotion now," "questionable," and "not acceptable now and unlikely to become acceptable." The evaluation begins with a presentation of the reports prepared by the various staff members on the candidate's performance in each exercise so that all members of the assessment center staff gain a complete picture of the man's behavior during his time at the assessment center. The candidate is then rated on approximately 20 variables relevant to success in management, such as skill in planning and organizing, decision-making ability, and leadership skills. The staff members then make independent ratings of the man's potential for management, and the evaluation concludes with a discussion of any differences that may appear. The director later prepares a descriptive report on the candidate outlining and documenting his strengths and weaknesses as seen at the center.

The assessment results are then fed back to management. The line organization integrates the assessment center data with appraisal information (based on the man's job performance) to make a decision on the candidate's promotion. Local management is expected to make a careful comparison of the description of the man provided by the assessment center process and the man's performance on his present job. The assessment center information can be over-ridden, but it cannot be lightly ignored. More extensive discussions of the Bell System assessment center procedures are given by Bray (1964a) and Jaffee (1965).

The use of this assessment center process to aid in the selection of first line managers has won wide acceptance, and the program has grown rapidly in size and scope since its introduction. Fourteen associated companies now have an assessment program, and about 12,000 non-management men and 6,000 non-management women have been assessed.

Another point must be made in any attempt to delineate the impact of the assessment center program. Only about one-third of the candidates seen at the assessment center are rated as ready for promotion by the assessment staff. In other words, more than half of those nominated for promotion by the line organization using traditional procedures are rejected at the assessment center. Since assessment center judgments are considered in decisions about promotions, it becomes obvious that the program has a substantial impact upon the selection of managers.

Evaluations of the Program

The objective of the assessment center program is to identify craftsmen who will perform well at the first level of management *and* have the potential to advance to higher levels of management. Bell System manpower projections dictate that the program must do more than help to select passable performers at the first level. It must provide a pool of men with the potential to advance to higher levels.

One indication of the effectiveness of the program has been its acceptance by management. The rapid growth of the program is largely attributable to line managers who have seen the program and its results and are convinced that it has made a valuable contribution to the selection of managers.

More definitive information on the validity of the assessment center process, or its ability to identify those with management potential, is available in the early results of the Management Progress Study (Bray, 1964b). This is a long-term, intensive study of the development of over 400 young college and non-college managers. The results of the study to date consistently show that assessment center ratings are good predictors of a man's eventual success as a manager (Bray & Grant, 1966). The combined results for college and non-college hires in the five companies in the study show that 51 per cent of those who were predicted to make middle management have, in fact, made it. Only 14 per cent of those predicted *not* to make middle management have actually achieved that level.

While this research study demonstrates that assessment center ratings do predict success in management, it does not follow that all applications of the procedure will prove equally successful. A number of factors could influence the effectiveness of the process in any given location — for example, the competence of the staff, training of the staff, and adequacy of feedback. Even though the process may be basically sound, good administration of the program is necessary if it is to be effective.

Follow-up studies of operational programs are one way of checking on their administration and effectiveness. Unfortunately, these studies contain a number of methodological problems that cannot be completely overcome. One is that in an operational program in most cases only those who do well at the assessment center are promoted. As a result, it is difficult to find a group that can be legitimately compared with those who have done well at the assessment center and are now in management. A second problem is the difficulty of obtaining good ratings of a man's performance in management. A third problem is that the results of assessment are fed back to the line organization. In a tight research study this would not be done because the assessment rating influences the job placement of the man and the opinions others have of his ability and his performance.

There are at least two earlier follow-up studies that have made good efforts to overcome these problems and have provided some information on the effectiveness of the assessment center program. One study, conducted by Michigan Bell Telephone, compared the first 40 men assessed and promoted with the last 40 men promoted before the assessment center program began. The findings show that approximately two-thirds of the assessed group were rated "better than satisfactory" in job performance as compared to only one-third of the group not assessed. The findings for potential for higher levels of management were equally positive.

The other study, conducted in the New England company, compared men rated "acceptable" at the assessment center with men rated "not acceptable." It included not only craftsmen who were assessed and promoted, but also first level managers who were assessed and promoted to second level. A comparison of the ratings and rankings of the performance and potential of the two groups of men following promotion showed the "acceptable" group was definitely superior to the "not acceptable" group.

The writers have made a further study of the program in four other associated companies that have had such a program for several years. As part of the follow-up on the over-all effectiveness of the program, an analysis was made of the relative success of the line organization in promoting men who were never assessed versus those who did not achieve an acceptable rating at the assessment center.

Design of the Current Follow-up Study

In all, five groups of men were studied. Three of the groups consisted of men who were assessed as "acceptable," "questionable," or "not acceptable" and subsequently promoted to management. A fourth group was composed of men who were never assessed but who were promoted *after* the assessment program began. The last group was made up of men promoted before the program began.

Several measures of performance at the first level and potential for further advancement were obtained for each man. The performance measures were the man's last formal appraisal rating and a rating and ranking made by his middle management level supervisor in a special interview. No objective index of performance was available that could be used, nor was it practical to develop such measures for the study. The measures of potential obtained were the rating of potential from the last formal appraisal and a potential ranking, again made by the middle management level supervisor. Actual promotion beyond the first level was, of course, also included as a measure of potential.

Assessment ratings and criterion measures were obtained for over 500 men in the four companies studied. The "average man" in the sample was 35 years old and had 13 years of service. The total sample averaged more than three years of service in management, and the comparison groups varied considerably in this respect despite attempts to control for this variable. The main difference was that the group promoted prior to the start of the assessment program averaged two years more service in management than the other comparison groups.*

Results of Current Follow-up Study

Of the total sample of 506 men, 471 were at the first level at the time of the follow-up study. Seven men (1%) had been returned to craft, and 28 men (6%) had been promoted to second level. At least 85 per cent of the men were still at the first level in each of the companies studied.

Performance

According to the formal appraisals, none of the 471 men was considered unsatisfactory. Over 90 per cent were rated completely satisfactory or outstanding. On the basis of performance ratings made by the supervisors in the interview, over 80 per cent of the men were seen as outstanding or completely satisfactory. On the basis of rankings given by the supervisors, which clearly provided the best differentiation between the men, approximately one-third of the men were ranked in the bottom half of their work group.

The performance measure used for comparison of the groups is a combination of the three performance measures described above. The men were split into two groups designated "above average performer" and "below average performer." In order to be included in the above average performer group the man had to be ranked in the top half of his work group and had to be rated completely satisfactory or outstanding on his last performance appraisal *and* by the middle management level supervisor in the interview. If a man failed to meet all of these requirements he was classified as a "below average performer." The 28 second-level men were classified as above average performers and the 7 craftsmen were placed in the below average group.

The percentage of above average performers in each of the five groups of men studied is presented in Figure 1. The percentage of above average performers in the group promoted before the assessment program began is 55 per cent as compared to 68 per cent of the group rated "acceptable" at the assessment center. This is a statistically significant finding, and it represents fairly substantial improvement. It indicates that the assessment pro-

* Further details relating to the design of the study are omitted because of limitations of space but are available from the writers on request.

FIGURE 1
Percentage of Men in Each Group Who Were "Above Average" in Performance at the First Level of Management

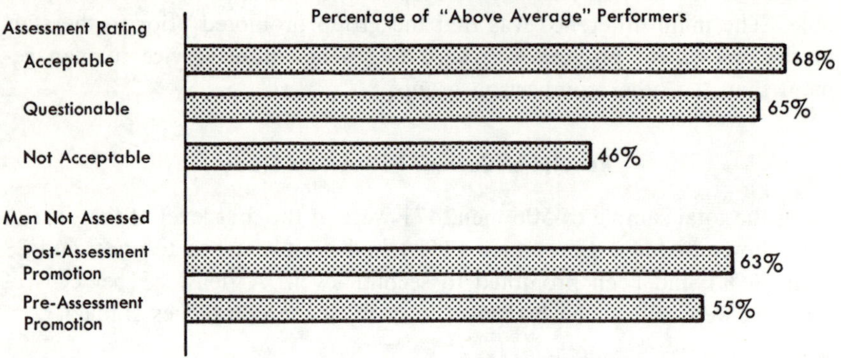

gram has been a definite aid in the selection of better performers at the first level of management.

The results further show that the line organization has been fairly successful in promoting some men who were not assessed (post-assessment group) and some who were assessed as "questionable." Both of these groups compared well with the "acceptable" group in terms of their performance at the first level. The results for the "not acceptable" group are not as favorable. More than half of these men were below average performers. Even with careful selection of only a very small percentage of the large pool of "not acceptable" men, the line organization did not find it at all possible to select a group that performed as well as the "acceptable" men.

Potential

Three measures of potential were obtained for each man in the study. One was the present level of the man — one of the best indications of a man's potential is his promotion to second level. The other two measures obtained were the rating on potential given the man in his last formal appraisal and the ranking by his middle management level supervisor of his potential for advancement in the business as compared with the others in his work group.

Analysis of the data on potential indicated that the man's length of time in management definitely affected his potential rating. The group of men who were in management less than two years were given a substantially lower percentage of high potential ratings than those who had been in management more than two years. This occurred mainly in the formal appraisal ratings of the men. This effect of time in management on appraisals of potential was not found in the appraisal of job performance. Apparently it takes a longer period of time for supervision to evaluate or be convinced of a man's potential than it does to evaluate his performance. Because of the relationship between time in management and the potential ratings, it was necessary to drop those men with less than two years in management from the analysis of the data on potential. This still left a large sample of men (425) for the analyses of differences in potential between the five groups.

The first information to be examined on potential is promotion to second level. Only 7 per cent of the 425 men have been promoted, but the trends show that a greater percentage of the "acceptable" men have reached second level. Eleven per cent of the men assessed as "acceptable" have been promoted as compared to 5 per cent of the "questionable" group and none of the "not acceptable" group. In the two groups of nonassessed men, only 5 per cent have been promoted.

While these figures indicate the "acceptable" men have greater potential, it is also important to look at the other two potential measures. No doubt many of those still at first level will eventually be promoted. The formal appraisal and the ranking by the supervisor provide information on the potential of those still at first level.

According to the appraisal data, 40 per cent of the men had potential for at least second level. The supervisors' rankings of the men placed 61 per cent of them in the top half of their work group in terms of potential. These two measures, appraisals and the supervisor's rankings, were combined to get the best over-all estimate of the man's potential. The men were split into a "high potential" group and a "low potential" group. In order to be placed in the high potential group, the man had to be appraised as having potential to advance to at least second level and be ranked in the top half of his work group. Those men presently at second level were placed in the high potential group and those returned to craft were placed in the low potential group. The results are presented in Figure 2 for all five groups of men studied.

The "acceptable" group is substantially better than all of the comparison groups except the "questionable" men. Half of the "acceptable" men were in the high potential group, whereas only 28 per cent of the main comparison group (pre-assessment promotions) was considered to have high potential.

The difference in potential between men assessed "acceptable" and those assessed "questionable" is only moderate. As is the case with the performance results, the "not acceptable" men do not compare well with the "acceptable" men. Less than a third of the "not acceptable" men are considered to have high potential. The poorest group in terms of potential is the men promoted after the assessment program began but without the benefit of assessment. Only 19 per cent of these men were in the high potential group.

FIGURE 2

Percentage of High Potential Men in Each Group

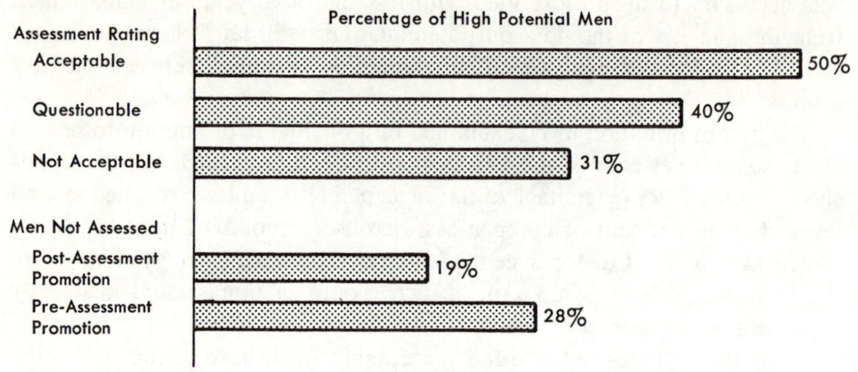

Conclusions

1. The assessment center method is a valuable technique for the identification of management potential. Promotion of those who achieved a good rating at the assessment center led to an improvement in the quality of management at the first level of supervision, particularly in building a pool of men at the first level who have the potential to advance to higher levels. In comparison with men promoted before the assessment program began, almost twice as many men rated highly at the assessment center have demonstrated potential to advance beyond the first level of management.
2. The assessment center produced a modest, but significant, improvement in performance at the first level. The difference in the results for performance and potential suggest that the management skills measured at the assessment center are more important in higher levels of supervision.
3. Promotion of a small percentage of the total group of men assessed as neither fully acceptable nor clearly unacceptable, after careful review by the line organization, resulted in generally good selections for management.
4. Promotion of a small, select percentage of the men assessed as clearly unacceptable did not lead to a favorable outcome.
5. Promotion of men who had never been assessed led to satisfactory results in terms of performance at the first level, but only a small percentage of these men had potential to advance to higher levels of management.
6. Any selection program, impressive research results notwithstanding, has limited chance for success if it is unacceptable to the line organization. One of the chief factors in the rapid growth of the Bell System Assessment Center Program has been the very positive reaction of line managers. The face

validity of the program for line managers is only one factor in their endorsement of it. They have been encouraged to attend evaluation sessions, and many have served as staff observers. The feedbacks they receive on their candidates contain an over-all rating, but they also include a summary report of the strengths and weaknesses of the candidate. This is not a set of abstract scores and cut-off points that the manager may or may not understand, but statements about the candidate's management skills, such as decision-making and leadership. These are skills that the supervisor is expected to observe in evaluating the man's performance and potential.

With this type of feedback, the supervisor is not forced to simply accept or reject a summary judgment of "promote" or "don't promote." He is given an opportunity to evaluate the diagnostic information, written in terms he can understand, against the performance he has seen. This permits greater involvement of the line organization in the selection process and maintains line management's authority for promotions.

Finally, the line manager has an opportunity to follow up on the promoted men and to examine the reliability of the assessment information he has received and the quality of his own judgments. This has been a key factor in the success of the Assessment Center Program, and it is one that seems all too frequently overlooked.

References

Bray, D. W., "The Assessment Center Method of Appraising Management Potential." In J. W. Blood (ed.). *The Personnel Job in a Changing World.* New York: American Management Association, 1964(a).

Bray, D. W., "The Management Progress Study." *American Psychologist,* 19 (1964)(b), 419–420.

Bray, D. W. and Grant, D. L., "The Assesment Center in the Measurement of Potential for Business Management." *Psychological Monographs,* 80 (1966).

Cronbach, L. J., *Essential of Psychological Testing.* (2nd ed.) New York: Harper, 1960.

Jaffee, C. L., "Assessment Centers Help Find Management Potential." *Bell Telephone Magazine,* 3 (Autumn 1965), 18–25.

Taft, R., "Multiple Methods of Personality Assessment." *Psychological Bulletin,* 56 (1959), 333–352.

D. PERFORMANCE APPRAISAL AND COUNSELING

Through a question and answer format, Miner (Selection 21) synthesizes our present state of knowledge and theory with respect to the evaluation of managers. Although Miner focuses on managers, we believe that most of his findings and conclusions will be increasingly applicable to the bulk of the work force. This article overlaps to some extent with the previous ones on staffing, since Miner deals with selection as one of several purposes in appraisals.

The General Electric study reviewed by Miner is reported in detail by Meyer, Kay, and French (Selection 22). These authors review the characteristics of the Work Planning and Review program which has been substituted for the traditional performance appraisal discussions in some of the units at General Electric. This program has been implemented for both management and non-management personnel. Meyer, Kay, and French's analysis also deals with such fundamental questions as:

- What is the purpose of the appraisal interview?
- How much effect does performance evaluation have on job performance?
- Is the appraisal interview in conflict with salary action?
- Can the appraisal interview be designed to motivate workers to want to improve their performance?

21

Management Appraisal: A Capsule Review and Current References

John B. Miner
University of Maryland

Does a supervisor appraise your performance? Is this appraisal written, formal, and permanent? Does it affect your performance? Are you a manager who must appraise subordinates and write up these appraisals? Has the company recently instituted a system of appraisal and development by objectives? The chances are that you answered "yes" to many or all of these questions, for approximately 80 per cent of all U.S. companies have a formal management appraisal system (10); the shift is away from appraisal of the rank and file (42). (The numbers in parentheses apply to the current references listed on page 259.)

Many of these companies, and most of the managers being appraised, are unsatisfied with their formal appraisal system. This is a justifiable position, for the whole concept is in a state of flux — new approaches, new plans, and new methods. With this constant change, where is a manager to turn for guidance?

For most of us, management appraisal is extraordinarily difficult. It is hard to pass judgment on a fellow man, especially if that judgment will become a permanent part of his company record, affecting his future. The procedure is further complicated by the absence of needed facts and of widely accepted theories. Yet the attainment of any organization's goals requires that the performance of our managers be measured, compared, and recorded. Growth requires that potential be evaluated. These requirements can best be met by a thoughtfully adopted formal appraisal system, one that best conforms to current knowledge and theory.

The purposes of this article are to provide this knowledge and theory in capsule form, and to provide a reference to current work. I have done this by asking — and answering — questions, those most frequenty asked about the evaluation of executives.

Taken and adapted from *Business Horizons,* Vol. 11, No. 5, Oct. 1968. Used by permission.

What are the Relative Merits of Appraisals Made by Superiors, Peers, Subordinates, and the Man Himself?

Appraisals made by superiors, peers, subordinates, or the man himself all have merit, but for different qualities. About 98 per cent of all evaluation forms are designed to be completed by the immediate superior. This approach appears to have widespread acceptance, and subordinates usually prefer it (21).

There is ample evidence that ratings made by peers differ considerably from those made by superiors. The results of a study conducted at North American Aviation (39) indicate that two levels of supervision agree reasonably well; superiors and co-workers do not. Co-workers apparently consider somewhat different factors and, on the average, give higher ratings.

Similar discrepancies occur when self-ratings are compared with those of superiors. While various levels of supervision tend to agree, superior and self-ratings rarely do (34). Self-ratings emphasize getting along with others as important for success, while superiors stress initiative and work knowledge (21). Furthermore, self-ratings are usually inflated (32).

There is reason to believe that self-interest can influence peer, subordinate, and self-ratings to the point where the evaluations may lack organizational relevance. Where favorable results have been reported with these techniques, it has been almost exclusively in an artificial research setting. It seems likely that their use as the *primary* element of a regular on-going appraisal system would produce somewhat different results, and that mutual and/or self-protection could well become a more important consideration than the profitability of the company (2).

Although these findings seem to argue strongly for appraisal by superiors, certain additional facts contradict this conclusion. For one, many companies use a management-by-objective approach, which has a strong participative component. Managers have a say in setting their own objectives and in determining whether these objectives have been met. This is really self-rating. Experimental evidence from studies at General Electric indicates that such participation in the appraisal situation can contribute to more effective performance (12). Thus, at least for purposes of management development, self-rating of a kind has some value.

Peer rating has also received significant support from recent research. A study utilizing middle-level managers at IBM indicates quite clearly that those men rated high by other managers at the same level were more likely to be promoted (36). It seems entirely possible that at the middle and upper levels of management, where organizational commitment is often high, objective peer evaluations that are relatively free of protective bias can be obtained. Such evaluations may well prove particularly valuable in the identification of leadership potential, just as self-evaluations appear to be most useful for developmental purposes. The Air Force is currently experimenting rather extensively with peer ratings, working on the theory that they are particularly significant in the measurement of potential.

A recent proposal favors a combination appraisal process utilizing superior, peer, and self-ratings (19). The advantages are considerable. The knowledge that ratings by superiors are also being obtained reduces bias in the two; these can capitalize on their unique observational opportunities. The match, or correlation, between the different types of ratings provides a measure of integrated perception among different people in the company, and thus of the capacity to concentrate effort behind goals (29). To the extent that peer and self-ratings support superior ratings, acceptance is likely, and personnel actions, such as promotion and firing, can be carried out without resistance. To the extent they do not, resistance is likely to develop. Furthermore, self-ratings and peer ratings are available for purposes of development and the identification of potential. Finally, special attention can be focused on those individuals whose ratings differ sharply. An appraisal involving high superior and self-ratings combined with very low peer ratings is clearly not the same as one with high ratings from all three sources. Yet, if superior evaluations only are obtained, significant aspects of the situation may go undetected.

The major advantage for the three-rating approach is that it provides a wealth of information about the individual and the organization, and pulls together a number of schools of thought on appraisals. All in all, it appears to be *the* approach to management appraisal of the future. Development of such complex programs and effective utilization of the information made available will, however, require expertise beyond that currently available in many companies.

Are There Advantages in Using More Than One Rater?

Research shows consistently that using more than one rater is advantageous. The best evidence comes from studies conducted by the U.S. Army (4), which indicate a clear superiority for the average of ratings made by several individuals over those made by only one person.

The rationale behind averaging ratings from the same type of source — superiors, peers, or subordinates — is that an average tends to reduce the impact of any single biased rating. For example, in one study, managers who were found to be particularly considerate and kind to their subordinates also gave them high ratings (17). When averaged with the evaluations of more production-oriented managers, such lenient ratings have less impact on the final appraisal.

However, the availability of raters with access to a sufficiently large sample of work behaviors can limit the number of raters who should be used. Increasing the size of the rating group by adding people who are not really qualified to evaluate and who, therefore, will give erroneous data defeats the value of the averaging process. One of the potential values of peer and subordinate appraisals is the availability of a large number of individuals who can qualify as raters because of their particularly good opportunities for observation.

What Is the Value of Rating Reviews by a Hierarchical Superior of the Rater?

Various provisions for reviews by the direct-line superior of a rater are a common feature of appraisal systems (21). In the U.S. Army procedure, there are in essence two reviews — one by the indorser, who also makes his own rating, and one by the reviewer, who merely indicates that a review has been made. Thus, the original rater has his evaluations scrutinized twice, the indorser once (7).

A review procedure may operate in a number of ways. One approach requires the rater to present his evaluations orally to a review board of superiors (37). In other cases, as with the military, only the written forms are reviewed at higher levels. A reviewer may have the authority to change evaluations directly without any consultation, to personally require the rater to make changes, to advise on changes, or merely to indicate disagreement. Under appropriate circumstances, such a review does appear to contribute to evaluation quality (2). Ideally, adequate knowledge of a manager's performance exists at several hierarchical levels above him. In this case, the best approach is to pass the appraisals upward so that each manager can make his evaluation either independently, as in the case of the immediate superior, or with knowledge only of what those below him think. This chain of evaluation should stop when it reaches a level in the hierarchy where adequate knowledge of performance does not exist; there is little point in including a reviewer who does not also rate. If such an individual has no basis for evaluating a man, nothing is gained by adding his signature to a form. If he does have a basis, his ratings should be averaged with the others.

This rater-indorser chain approach has an advantage in that each manager, except the one at the top, knows that his evaluations will be scrutinized. The approach also provides for multiple ratings under conditions that protect against undue influence from a superior who may have the least adequate basis for appraisal. The information flow is upward from what can be presumed to be the most knowledgeable individual to the least, rather than the reverse. The use of such an approach assumes that a superior will not change or influence his subordinates' ratings in any way. Evidence indicates that, when actual changes at higher levels are permitted, they do nothing to improve the evaluation process. The superior can, however, disagree in his own ratings and thus mitigate the effects of what he feels is an error.

Should Management Appraisals Be Made at the Same Time as Salary Recommendations?

The real problem here is not whether management appraisals and salary recommendations should be made together, although traditionally this is the way it is done. Rather, the problem is to find some method of avoiding the common tendency to decide on salary first and then adjust the performance ratings to fit. Because salary is in practice influenced by many factors other than merit, the ratings are frequently distorted.

I cannot locate any research that bears directly on the question. Nonetheless, studies at General Electric clearly indicate that feeding back information on salary actions along with management appraisal data is not desirable insofar as motivational and developmental goals are concerned (24). Criticism tied directly to pay action produces so much defensiveness that there is little prospect of learning. Energies focus primarily on self-protection rather than self-improvement (33).

Separating appraisals and salary actions in time is one way of reducing distortion, but many managers unquestionably do prefer to couple them. An approach that would overcome bias and still allow both decisions to be made simultaneously would clearly be helpful. A means of changing perceptions — of the process of salary administration and of the appraisal process — seems called for. Although evidence is lacking, I believe this change could be achieved through a training program, provided the content of the program truly represented top management philosophies. The training would consider merit as well as various factors that inevitably influence salary actions — the labor market, previous salary history, budgetary limitations, equity considerations, and rate ranges. The training would also consider sources of bias in appraisal. Possibly, with such an approach, pay and performance could be separated in the manager's mind at least as effectively as with elapsed time.

What are the Pros and Cons of Feedback from the Rater to the Man Being Rated?

Usually, the results of appraisals are given to the man who has been evaluated; this may be done in a number of different ways and with varying amounts of detail (21). But the question is whether it should be done at all. An adequate answer requires two kinds of information: the effect of the feedback on the ratings and the effect of the feedback on the man who has been rated.

Feedback and Ratings

A Lockheed Aircraft study (40) provides the best example of how the feedback requirement may influence ratings. The regular evaluations, which were not revealed to subordinates, were followed in two weeks by a second appraisal, which included discussions of the ratings with the men. The mean score for the 485 men involved rose dramatically — from an initial 60 to 84 out of a possible 100. Apparently, when faced with the prospect of making face-to-face negative comments, many managers avoided the problem by inflating their ratings.

This problem has plagued the Armed Forces for years (7). Although direct feedback by the superior is not required by law, the legal structure does indicate that an officer may inspect the evaluations in his file and that under certain conditions he may appeal. Anticipating that efficiency reports may be inspected, raters tend to make favorable statements. A variety of techniques including forced choice, forced distribution, and critical incidents have been introduced with little success over the years to deal with the inflation of ratings.

Thus, where valid ratings are necessary for salary administration, promotion, transfer, discharge, and evaluation of selection procedures, feedback is not desirable. It is particularly important to avoid optional feedback, in which a manager does as he pleases. Under such circumstances, managers who plan to discuss their evaluations with subordinates will inflate them; those who do not plan to discuss their evaluations will not inflate them. As a result, the two types of ratings will actually be on different scales. Assuming the existence of a single scale under these circumstances will not only result in injustice to the individual, but will produce decisions detrimental to the organization as well.

Feedback and the Man Rated

The major source of information on the motivational or developmental effects of feedback is a series of studies conducted at General Electric (12, 16, 24). The findings of this research on the dynamics of the feedback interview are summarized as follows:

Criticism tends to have a negative impact on achievement of goals.

Praise has little effect, either positive or negative.

Performance tends to improve when specific objectives are established.

Defensiveness as a consequence of criticism results in inferior performance.

Coaching is best done on a day-to-day basis and in direct association with specific acts, not once a year.

Mutual goal setting by superior and subordinate yields positive results.

Interviews intended primarily to improve performance should not at the same time deal with salary and promotion.

Participation by the subordinate in establishing his own performance goals yields favorable results.

Separate performance evaluations are required for different purposes.

Generally, the results of the General Electric research seem to provide appropriate guides for action. Nonetheless, subsequent research has raised some doubts about the value of goal setting as it is actually done within the context of the management-by-objectives approach (22).

Feedback can be an effective motivational and developmental tool, but often it is not. Whether systematic appraisal interviews should be attempted depends on the approach taken and the skill of the interviewer. Clearly, feedback can do more harm than good. Ideally, a feedback interview should be goal oriented and should take a problem-solving approach, but this is not easy to do. Getting a manager to agree on a set of objectives and standards is one thing; getting him to recognize where and why he has fallen short in his performance is quite another (25). However, the requisite skill can be developed in managers through training (23, 31).

Based on the evidence currently available, the appropriate conclusion seems to be that only those ratings made specifically for motivational or developmental purposes should ever be fed back, and then only by a fully trained and skilled interviewer. Feedback has tremendous potential for harm as well as good. It *can* be a major source of managerial turnover.

On What Types of Characteristics Should Managers be Rated?

In selecting the types of characteristics on which to rate a manager, it is most important to include only those that manifest themselves in the work situation. The rating factors should be firmly anchored in behavior that characteristically occurs on the job and that influences performance (10). There is a tendency to include a variety of traits that do not meet these requirements. Often rating scales deal with aspects of "good" and "bad" people that cannot be adequately judged from job contact alone, or that matter little, if at all, in effective performance. In this connection, it is well to note that it is not always the "good" people who do well. One study found that an intense sense of honesty and ethics almost guaranteed failure in a particular type of sales job (26).

Ratings should also deal with characteristics that can be described clearly so all raters will have the same kinds of behavior in mind (2). Considerable evidence indicates that certain personality traits, such as "character" and "aggressiveness," are viewed so nebulously that agreement is almost impossible on whether people possess them. Generally, the closer the factors are to job behavior and results, the more raters will agree in their evaluations.

How Can Ratings be Spread Out Along a Scale Most Successfully?

One approach to spreading out ratings is the forced distribution technique, which is a variant of ranking. However, rather than having as many categories as there are managers to be rated, the number of categories is predetermined, as is the percentage of the man to be placed in each category. In theory, the technique, like ranking, has considerable appeal. In practice, however, it presents so many difficulties that, at least for *management* appraisal, it cannot be recommended. One problem is that the percentages are meaningless unless a large group is to be rated by a single manager. Where spans of control are limited, this condition is not met. Furthermore, there is the difficulty of combining groups. Is the lower 10 per cent of one group likely to be at the same performance level as the lower 10 per cent of another? This problem also occurs with ranking, of course.

Furthermore, raters tend to resist forced distribution (42). The result is a continuing conflict between those responsible for administering the appraisal system and the managers doing the rating. In the end, either the ratings are adjusted to fit the required percentage distribution, with great potential for error (17), or the forced distribution technique is abandoned entirely.

Given the conclusion that forced distribution techniques are not satisfactory for management appraisal, what other procedures are available to produce a meaningful spread of ratings along a scale? The armed services have faced this problem continually over the years. As indicated previously, since the man rated has ready access to the armed service efficiency reports, scores tend to pile up at the high end of the scales. In the late 1940's and early 1950's, two rather complex procedures were developed to deal with this problem. The forced choice approach was introduced by the Army and then adopted by the Air Force, which subsequently developed the critical incident technique to replace it. Neither approach proved successful (9). Forced choice failed because rating officers resisted a procedure that made it difficult, if not impossible, for them to determine how they had actually rated a man. In addition, leniency was not entirely overcome. The critical incident approach proved too complicated, too time consuming, resulted in too much concern with the final score, and did not really solve the leniency problem. In both cases, resistance from rating officers in the field was sufficient to terminate use of the technique. Research evidence indicates that graphic rating scales are actually just as valid as these more complex procedures (4).

All this does not mean that steps cannot be taken to produce a satisfactory spread of ratings. The following procedures used in business organizations have proved successful in extending this range:

Maintain security so evaluations are not available to the men rated or fed back to them (40).

Avoid ambiguous descriptions of the characteristics to be rated and of steps on the scale; the rater must have a clear understanding of exactly what job behaviors he is to consider (3).

Carry out training aimed at providing an understanding of the desirability of a wide range of scores (20). Particular stress should be placed on getting overly considerate managers, who want more than anything else to help their men, to spread their ratings out. These are the raters who typically have the smallest ranges (17).

If these three conditions are met, and an adequate number of steps or levels exist in the scale, the usual graphic rating scales should yield a satisfactory spread of scores and should prove the most generally useful (2).

Does a Tendency to Stress Recent Events Serve to Bias Ratings?

Studies indicate, as many have hypothesized, that specific instances of effective or ineffective behavior occurring shortly before evaluations unduly affect the ratings (10). Apparently, raters remember recent events more vividly and, therefore, weigh them more heavily.

This situation suggests the need for relatively frequent ratings — at least every three to six months. Averaging such evaluations to yield a running appraisal score will minimize the effects of any recent events. Another antidote involves keeping managers aware of this problem; some managers might be induced to keep notes on performance throughout the rating period and then to review these at appraisal time. All of this, of course, represents another training area.

Is There any Method of Communicating Information Regarding an Appraisal System that Will Ensure Consistency of Application?

Evidence on the value of introducing an educational process as an integral part of a total appraisal system is consistently positive. Normally, this process is based on the spoken word, but, on occasion, it may utilize written materials as well. Some uses of these procedures have already been noted, but additional features of the communication problem should be mentioned.

Studies indicate that training can serve to increase the agreement between different raters, reduce bias (40), increase accuracy generally, prevent inflation of scores (5), and spread out the rating distribution (20). In general, training sessions should be conducted by a person qualified as an expert on management appraisal and familiar with the details of the particular system in use. There should be an opportunity for considerable discussion and some practice with the rating forms. Various sources of error and bias, as well as factors that will make the ratings most useful, need primary attention (41).

Despite the consistently favorable evidence, a great many companies do not build training procedures into their appraisal systems. In fact, a lack of adequate training is the major problem of most programs (21). In addition, there is reason to believe that many programs that have succumbed to widespread managerial resistance could have survived had they been introduced with adequate training. Group sessions, which are usually used, may be supplemented with some individual assistance at the time the ratings are made. Also, manuals containing information similar to the training program have proved useful (5).

What Can be Done to Overcome the Resistance to Appraisal Systems?

Many people have a negative view of the whole process of evaluating performance. This feeling appears related to fear of low ratings, if an appraisal system is instituted and survives, and also to a strong belief in the seniority principle (30). Evidence shows that less effective managers tend to be the ones most opposed to performance appraisal (14). Furthermore, many managers, in addition to rank-and-file employees, strongly believe seniority is the best guide for making personnel decisions.

As a result of these factors, and perhaps others, any management appraisal system will encounter some resistance. This resistance may block the initiation of a program, but it is particularly likely to manifest itself once a program is instituted and there is something to shoot at. Resistance will vary, depending on the values predominant in the company, and it may relate rather specifically to certain kinds of approaches.

Obviously, the greater the resistance the more those who are instituting the program will have to move toward those who will do the rating and the more the management group as a whole will have to be involved in developing the system. These approaches demonstrate the willingness of those who will be using the data to do part of the work to ensure a successful program. The alternative procedure involves inducing the raters to come to the users of the data. This procedure is entirely satisfactory where acceptance is high, but, where it is not, merely mailing out forms along with directives and follow-up memoranda will only increase negative feeling. Another successful approach is to have large numbers of managers participate in the construction of the system itself (2). This can be done if managers are used both as a source for developing items and as judges of proposals (38).

The need for special procedures to help overcome resistance will vary, depending on the nature of the program. Many managers tend to resist feeding back appraisal results, for instance. Thus, acceptance problems may be anticipated when this is required. Many managers strongly dislike peer and subordinate ratings (2). Thus, the use of a three-rating system along the lines noted previously may require special attention. Forced choice and forced distribution procedures are known to be sources of resistance and, accordingly, require more than the usual efforts to develop favorable attitudes.

How Can Potential be Evaluated and What Factors Predict Potential?

To determine a method for evaluating potential and the characteristics that indicate potential, research must show that some measure did in fact predict success in management over a considerable period of time after the original measurement. The following discussion is restricted entirely to studies of this kind. Predictions made by managers are considered first, then predictions by psychologists.

Managerial Prediction

The difficulty with using ratings of potential for advancement is that they are available and known, and quite obviously can influence a man's career entirely apart from his actual competence. Even with this bias included, results with these potential ratings by superiors are not impressive. Clearly, a great many individuals identified in this manner as having high potential do not advance very far (11). In one study, departments within a single company varied considerably in the extent to which potential ratings predicted even the first promotion after appraisal (29). Results like these have led some writers to conclude that the evaluation of potential is beyond the scope of the usual management appraisal system and that the matter should be left to specialists (35). Many ratings of potential are believed to be merely the inverse of the manager's age and thus convey little new information.

The armed forces have carried out most of the research on the predictive value of ratings by superiors, usually with relatively short intervals between the initial predictions and the subsequent measurement of success (18). The correlations obtained are not impressive. These findings contrast sharply with those for peer ratings, which offer much better predictions of potential. Why this difference exists between superior and peer predictions is a matter of conjecture at the present time.

Psychological Prediction

A considerable amount of predictive research has used psychological techniques. Some studies utilize separate measures like psychological tests or biographical inventories; others use the over-all evaluations of psychologists derived from a combination of sources, including interviews, observation of behavior, and tests. In general, tests of intelligence and mental abilities do seem to predict success. However, in many highly selected managerial groups, intelligence tests are not very helpful in identifying potential, because all the managers score at such a high level. At the foreman level, intelligence tests are more effective as indicators of subsequent performance (18).

Psychological tests in the personality area have produced uneven results when used individually. In a number of cases, they have not proved useful (18), yet exceptions do exist. In general, measures of such characteristics as dominance, self-confidence, and persuasiveness are most useful (10).

Consistently positive results have been obtained with the Miner Sentence Completion Scale in a series of predictive studies (27). This measure was designed specifically for predicting success in management. Although the test discriminates most effectively at the graduate level, it can identify individuals with managerial potential as early as the third year of college (28).

A considerable amount of research has used biographical inventories containing questions similar to those found in application blanks. This research has produced sufficiently positive results to recommend the approach (10, 18). However, companies tend to keep the specific results of these studies secret, so that managerial candidates do not learn the "right" answers. Thus, studies aimed at establishing those factors that are predictive in a given company must be carried out individually. Nonetheless, published research does show that a prior pattern of success is likely to be predictive of subsequent success.

Results with comprehensive evaluations by psychologists using a variety of source data are also encouraging, despite significant failures. Studies using this approach have predicted success over a period as long as seven years (1, 8).

A related approach, even more comprehensive in that managers are studied over a period of days with a whole host of techniques, is the assessment center. AT&T has conducted much of the research with this technique under the title of "The Management Progress Study." Staff assessments of potential for advancement derived from these assessment situations have consistently proved predictive of promotion and salary progress over periods up to eight years (6). These assessments were not made available to those making promotion and compensation decisions. Research indicates that those who have moved up most rapidly are more intelligent and more active, control their feelings more, are more nonconforming, exhibit a greater work orientation (6), are more independent, desire more leadership, and have stronger achievement motivation (13). Although this type of approach is extremely expensive relative to the usual psychological evaluation (15), it appears to yield even higher correlations with later success in management jobs.

There is reason to believe that any psychological approach is likely to be effective only to the extent it is attuned to the value and reward structures of the particular organization (29). Thus, the development of psychological predictors to identify potential within a given company must involve a complex interaction between analysis of the individual and analysis of the organization. Such an interaction involving both individual assessment and social psychological research seems to provide the best guide for management appraisal systems of the future.

References

1. Albrecht, P. A., E. M. Glaser, and J. Marks. "Validation of a Multiple-Assessment Procedure for Managerial Personnel." *Journal of Applied Psychology,* XLVIII (1964), 351–60.

2. Barrett, R. S. *Performance Rating.* Chicago: Science Research Associates, 1966.

3. ———, E. K. Taylor, J. W. Parker, and L. Martens. "Rating Scale Content, I: Scale Information and Supervisory Ratings." *Personnel Psychology,* XI (1958), 333–46.

4. Bayroff, A. C., H. R. Haggerty, and E. A. Rundquist. "Validity of Ratings as Related to Rating Techniques and Conditions." *Personnel Psychology,* VII (1954), 93–113.

5. Bittner, R. "Developing an Industrial Merit Rating Procedure." *Personnel Psychology,* I (1948), 403–32.

6. Bray, D. W., and D. L. Grant. "The Assessment Center in the Measurement of Potential for Business Management." *Psychological Monographs,* LXXX (1966), 1–27.

7. Brooks, W. W. "An Analysis and Evaluation of the Officer Performance Appraisal System in the United States Army." M. S. thesis. George Washington University, 1966.

8. Dicken, C. F., and J. D. Black. "Predictive Validity of Psychometric Evaluations of Supervisors." *Journal of Applied Psychology,* XLIX (1965), 34–47.

9. Druit, C. A. "An Analysis of Military Officer Evaluation Systems Using Principles Presently Advanced by Authorities in This Field." M.A. thesis. The Ohio State University, 1964.

10. Dunnette, M. D., E. E. Lawler, J. P. Campbell, and K. E. Weick. "Identification and Enhancement of Managerial Effectiveness." Richardson Foundation Survey Report, 1966.

11. Ferguson, L. L. "Better Management of Managers' Careers." *Harvard Business Review,* XLIV (1966), 139–52.

12. French, J. R. P., E. Kay, and H. H. Meyer. "Participation and the Appraisal System." *Human Relations,* XIX (1966), 3–20.

13. Grant, D. L., W. Katovsky, and D. W Bray. "Contributions of Projective

Techniques to Assessment of Managerial Potential." *Journal of Applied Psychology,* XLI (1967), 226–32.

14. Gruenfeld, L. W., and P. Weissenberg. "Supervisory Characteristics and Attitudes Toward Performance Appraisals." *Personnel Psychology,* XIX (1966), 143–51.

15. Hardesty, D. L., and W. S. Jones. "Characteristics of Judged High-Potential Management Personnel — the Operations of an Industrial Assessment Center." *Personnel Psychology,* XXI (1968), 85–98.

16. Kay E., H. H. Meyer, and J. R. P. French. "Effects of Threat in a Performance Appraisal Interview." *Journal of Applied Psychology,* XLIX (1965), 311–17.

17. Klores, M. S. Rater Bias in Forced-Distribution Performance Ratings." *Personnel Psychology,* XIX (1966), 411–21.

18. Korman, A. K. "The Prediction of Managerial Performance: a Review." *Personnel Psychology.* In press.

19. Lawler, E. E. "The Multitrait-Multitrater Approach to Measuring Managerial Job Performance." *Journal of Applied Psychology,* LI (1967), 369–81.

20. Levine, J. and J. Butler. "Lecture vs. Group Decision in Changing Behavior." *Journal of Applied Psychology,* XXXVI (1952), 29–33.

21. Lopez, F. M. *Evaluating Employee Performance.* Chicago: Public Personnel Association. In press.

22. Mendelson, J. L. "Manager Goal Setting: an Exploration Into Its Meaning and Measurement." D.B.A. thesis. Michigan State University, 1967.

23. Meyer, H. H., and W. B. Walker. "A Study of Factors Relating to the Effectiveness of a Performance Appraisal Program." *Personnel Psychology,* XIV (1961), 291–98.

24. ———, E. Kay, and J. R. P. French. "Split Roles in Performance Appraisal." *Harvard Business Review,* XLIII (1965), 123–29.

25. Michael, J. M. "Problem Situations in Performance Counselling." *Personnel,* XLII (1965), 16–22.

26. Miner, J. B. "Personality and Ability Factors in Sales Performance." *Journal of Applied Psychology,* XLVI (1962), 6–13.

27. ———. *Studies in Management Education.* New York: Springer Publishing Co., Inc., 1965.

28. ———. "The Early Identification of Managerial Talent." *The Personnel and Guidance Journal,* XLVI (1968), 586–91.

29. ———. "Bridging the Gulf in Organizational Performance." *Harvard Business Review,* XLVI (1968), 102–10.

30. ———. *Personnel and Industrial Relations — a Managerial Approach.* New York: The Macmillan Company, 1969.

31. Moon, C. G., and T. Hariton. "Evaluating an Appraisal and Feedback Training Program." *Personnel,* XXXV (1958), 36–41.

32. Parker, J. W., E. K. Taylor, R. S. Barrett, and L. Martens. "Rating Scale Content: III. Relationships Between Supervisory and Self-Ratings." *Personnel Psychology,* XII (1959), 49–63.

33. Patton, A. "Executive Motivation: How It Is Changing." *Management Review,* LVII (1968), 4–20.

34. Prien, E. P., and R. E. Liske. "Assessments of Higher Level Personnel:

III. Rating Criteria: a Comparative Analysis of Supervisor Ratings and Incumbent Self-Ratings of Job Performance." *Personnel Psychology,* XV (1962), 187–94.

35. Richards, K. E. "A New Concept of Performance Appraisal." *Journal of Business,* XXXII (1959), 229–43.

36. Roadman, H. E. "An Industrial Use of Peer Ratings." *Journal of Applied Psychology,* XLVIII (1964), 211–14.

37. Rowland, V. K. "Management Inventory and Development." *Personnel,* XXVIII (1951), 12–22.

38. Smith, P. C., and L. M. Kendall. "Retranslation of Expectations: an Approach to the Construction of Unambiguous Anchors for Rating Scales." *Journal of Applied Psychology,* XLVII (1963), 149–55.

39. Springer, D. "Ratings of Candidates for Promotion by Co-Workers and Supervisors." *Journal of Applied Psychology,* XXXVII (1953), 347–51.

40. Stockford, L., and H. W. Bissell. "Factors Involved in Establishing a Merit-Rating Scale." *Personnel,* XXVI (1949), 94–116.

41. Tiffin, J., and E. J. McCormick. *Industrial Psychology.* (5th ed.) Englewood Cliffs, N.J.: Prentice-Hall, Inc., 1965.

42. Whisler, T. L., and S. F. Harper. *Performance Appraisal.* New York: Holt, Rinehart & Winston, Inc., 1962.

22

Split Roles in Performance Appraisal

Herbert H. Meyer
General Electric Company

Emanuel Kay
General Electric Company

John R. P. French, Jr.
University of Michigan

In management circles, performance appraisal is a highly interesting and provocative topic. And in business literature, too, knowledgeable people write emphatically, pro and con, on the performance appraisal question.[1] In fact, one might almost say that everybody talks and writes about it, but nobody has done any real scientific testing of it.

At the General Electric Comany we felt it was important that a truly scientific study be done to test the effectiveness of our traditional performance appraisal program. Why? Simply because our own experience with performance appraisal programs had been both positive and negative. For example:

- Surveys generally show that most people think the idea of performance appraisal is good. They feel that a man should know where he stands and, therefore, the manager should discuss an appraisal of his performance with him periodically.

- In actual practice, however, it is the extremely rare operating manager who will employ such a program on his own initiative. Personnel specialists report that most managers carry out performance appraisal interviews only when strong control procedures are established to ensure that they do so. This is surprising because the managers have been told repeatedly that the system is intended to help them obtain improved performance from their subordinates.

Herbert H. Meyer, Emanuel Kay, and John R. P. French, Jr., "Split Roles in Performance Appraisal," *Harvard Business Review,* Vol. 43, No. 1, Jan.–Feb. 1965, pp. 123–129.

We also found from interviews with employees who have had a good deal of experience with traditional performance appraisal programs that few indeed can cite examples of constructive action taken — or significant improvement achieved — which stem from suggestions received in a performance appraisal interview with their boss.

Traditional Program

Faced with such contradictory evidence, we undertook a study several years ago to determine the effectiveness of our comprehensive performance appraisal process. Special attention was focused on the interview between the subordinate and his manager, because this is the discussion which is supposed to motivate the man to improve his performance. And we found out some very interesting things — among them the following:

- Criticism has a negative effect on achievement of goals.
- Praise has little effect one way or the other.
- Performance improves most when specific goals are established.
- Defensiveness resulting from critical appraisal produces inferior performance.
- Coaching should be a day-to-day, not a once-a-year, activity.
- Mutual goal setting, not criticism, improves performance.
- Interviews designed primarily to improve a man's performance should not at the same time weigh his salary or promotion in the balance.
- Participation by the employee in the goal-setting procedure helps produce favorable results.

As you can see, the results of this original study indicated that a detailed and comprehensive annual appraisal of a subordinate's performance by his manager is decidedly of questionable value. Furthermore, as is certainly the case when the major objective of such a discussion is to motivate the subordinate to improve his performance, the traditional appraisal interview does not do the job.

In the first part of this article, we will offer readers more than this bird's-eye view of our research into performance appraisal. (We will not, however, burden managers with details of methodology.) We will also describe the one-year follow-up experiment General Electric conducted to validate the conclusions derived from our original study. Here the traditional annual performance appraisal method was tested against a new method we developed, which we called Work Planning and Review (WP&R). As you will see, this approach produced, under actual plant conditions, results which were decidedly superior to those afforded by the traditional performance appraisal method. Finally, we will offer evidence to support our contention that some form of WP&R might well be incorporated into other industrial personnel programs to achieve improvement in work performance.

Appraising Appraisal

In order to assure a fair test of the effectiveness of the traditional performance appraisal method, which had been widely used throughout General Electric, we conducted an intensive study of the process at a large GE plant where the performance appraisal program was judged to be good; that is, in this plant —

. . . appraisals had been based on job responsibilities, rather than on personal characteristics of the individuals involved;

. . . an intensive training program had been carried out for managers in the use of the traditional appraisal method and techniques for conducting interviews;

. . . the program had been given strong backing by the plant manager and had been policed diligently by the personnel staff so that over 90% of the exempt employees had been appraised and interviewed annually.

This comprehensive annual performance appraisal program, as is typical, was designed to serve two major purposes. The first was to justify recommended salary action. The second, which was motivational in character, was intended to present an opportunity for the manager to review a subordinate's performance and promote discussion on needed improvements. For the latter purpose, the manager was required to draw up a specific program of plans and goals for the subordinate which would help him to improve his job performance and to qualify, hopefully, for future promotion.

Interview Modifications

Preliminary interviews with key managers and subordinates revealed the salary action issue had so dominated the annual comprehensive performance appraisal interview that neither party had been in the right frame of mind to discuss plans for improved performance. To straighten this out, we asked managers to split the traditional appraisal interview into two sessions — discussing appraisal of performance and salary action in one interview and performance improvement plans in another to be held about two weeks later. This split provided us with a better opportunity to conduct our experiment on the effects of participation in goal planning.

To enable us to test the effects of participation, we instructed half the managers to use a *high participation* approach and the other half to use a *low participation* technique. Thus:

• Each of the "high" managers was instructed to ask his appraisee to prepare a set of goals for achieving improved job performance and to submit them for the manager's review and approval. The manager also was encouraged to permit the subordinate to exert as much influence as possible on the formulation of the final list of job goals agreed on in the performance improvement discussion.

The "low" managers operated in much the same way they had in our traditional appraisal program. They formulated a set of goals for the subordinate, and these goals were then reviewed in the performance improvement session. The manager was instructed to conduct this interview in such a way that his influence in the forming of the final list of job goals would be greater than the subordinate's.

Conducting the Research

There were 92 appraisees in the experimental group, representing a cross section of the exempt salaried employees in the plant. This group included engineers; engineering support technicians; foremen; and specialists in manufacturing, customer service, marketing, finance, and purchasing functions. None of the exempt men who participated as appraisees in the experiment had other exempt persons reporting to them; thus they did not serve in conflicting manager-subordinate roles.

The entire group was interviewed and asked to complete questionnaires (a) before and after the salary action interview, and (b) after the delayed second discussion with their managers about performance improvement. These interviews and questionnaires were designed to achieve three objectives:

1. Assess changes in the attitudes of individuals toward their managers and toward the appraisal system after each of the discussions.
2. Get an estimate from the appraisee of the degree to which he usually participated in decisions that affected him. (This was done in order to determine whether or not previous lack of participation affected his response to participation in the experiment.)
3. Obtain a self-appraisal from each subordinate before and after he met with his manager. (This was done in order to determine how discrepancies in these self-appraisals might affect his reaction to the appraisal interview.)

Moreover, each salary action and performance improvement discussion was observed by outsiders trained to record essentially what transpired. (Managers preferred to use neither tape recorders nor unseen observers, feeling that observers unaffiliated with the company — in this case, graduate students in applied psychological disciplines — afforded the best way of obtaining a reasonably close approximation of the normal discussions.) In the appraisal for salary action interviews, for example, the observers recorded the amount of criticism and praise employed by the manager, as well as the reactions of the appraisee to the manager's comments. In the performance improvement discussions, the observers recorded the participation of the subordinate, as well as the amount of influence he seemed to exert in establishing his future success goals.

Criticism and Defensiveness

In general, the managers completed the performance appraisal forms in a thorough and conscientious manner. Their appraisals were discussed with subordinates in interviews ranging from approximately 30 to 90 minutes in length. On the average, managers covered 32 specific performance items which, when broken down, showed positive (praise) appraisals on 19 items, and negative (criticism) on 13. Typically, praise was more often related to *general* performance characteristics, while criticism was usually focused on *specific* performance items.

The average subordinate reacted defensively to seven of the manager's criticisms during the appraisal interview (that is, he reacted defensively about 54% of the time when criticized). Denial of shortcomings cited by the manager, blaming others, and various other forms of excuses were recorded by the observers as defensive reactions.

Constructive responses to criticism were *rarely* observed. In fact, the average was less than one per interview. Not too surprising, along with this, was the finding that the more criticism a man received in the performance appraisal discussion, the more defensively he reacted. Men who received an above-average number of criticisms showed more than five times as much defensive behavior as those who received a below-average number of criticisms. Subordinates who received a below-average number of criticisms, for example, reacted defensively only about one time out of three. But those who received an above-average number reacted defensively almost two times out of three.

One explanation for this defensiveness is that it seems to stem from the overrating each man tended to give to his own performance. The average employee's self-estimate of performance *before* appraisal placed him at the 77 percentile. (Only 2 of the 92 participants estimated their performance to be below the average point on the scale.) But when the same men were asked *after* their performance appraisal discussions how they thought their bosses had rated them, the average figure given was at the 65 percentile. The great majority (75 out of 92) saw their manager's evaluation as being less favorable than their self-estimates. Obviously, to these men, the performance appraisal discussion with the manager was a deflating experience. Thus, it was not surprising that the subordinates reacted defensively in their interviews.

Criticism and Goal Achievement

Even more important is the fact that men who received an above-average number of criticisms in their performance appraisal discussions generally showed *less* goal achievement 10 to 12 weeks later than those who had received fewer criticisms. At first, we thought that this difference might be accounted for by the fact that the subordinates who received more criticisms were probably poorer performers in general. But there was little factual evidence found to support this suspicion.

It was true that those who received an above-average number of criticisms in their appraisal discussions did receive slightly lower summary ratings on over-all performance from their managers. But they did not receive proportionally lower salary increases. And the salary increases granted were *supposed* to reflect differences in job performance, according to the salary plan traditionally used in this plant. This argument, admittedly, is something less than perfect.

But it does appear clear that frequent criticism constitutes so strong a threat to self-esteem that it disrupts rather than improves subsequent performance. We expected such a disruptive threat to operate more strongly on those individuals who were already low on self-esteem, just as we expected a man who had confidence in his ability to do his job to react more constructively to criticism. Our group experiment proved these expectations to be correct.

Still further evidence that criticism has a negative effect on performance was found when we investigated areas which had been given special emphasis by the manager in his criticism. Following the appraisal discussion with the manager, each employee was asked to indicate which one aspect of his performance had been most criticized by the manager. Then, when we conducted our follow-up investigation 10 to 12 weeks later, it revealed that improvement in the most-criticized aspects of performance cited was considerably *less* than improvement realized in other areas!

Participation Effects

As our original research study had indicated, the effects of a high participation level were also favorable in our group experiment. In general, here is what we found:

- Subordinates who received a high participation level in the performance interview reacted more favorably than did those who received a low participation level. The "highs" also, in most cases, achieved a greater percentage of their improvement goals than did their "low" counterparts. For the former, the high participation level was associated with greater mutual understanding between them and their managers, greater acceptance of job goals, a more favorable attitude toward the appraisal system, and a feeling of greater self-realization on the job.
- But employees who had traditionally been accustomed to low participation in their daily relationships with the manager did not necessarily perform better under the high participation treatment. In fact, those men who had received a high level of criticism in their appraisal interviews actually performed better when their managers set goals for them than they did when they set their own goals, as permitted under the high participation treatment.

In general, our experiment showed that the men who usually worked under high participation levels performed best on goals they set for themselves. Those who indicated that they usually worked under low levels performed best on goals that the managers set for them. Evidently, the man who usually does not participate in work-planning decisions considers job goals set by the manager to be more important than goals he sets for himself. The man accustomed to a high participation level, on the other hand, may have stronger motivation to achieve goals he sets for himself than to achieve those set by his manager.

Goal-Setting Importance

While subordinate participation in the goal-setting process had some effect on improved performance, a much more powerful influence was whether goals were set at all. Many times in appraisal discussions, managers mentioned areas of performance where improvement was needed. Quite often these were translated into specific work plans and goals. But this was not always the case. In fact, when we looked at the one performance area which each manager had emphasized in the appraisal interview as most in need of improvement, we found that these items actually were translated into specific work plans and goals for only about 60% of our experiment participants.

When performance was being measured 10 to 12 weeks after the goal-planning sessions, managers were asked to describe what results they hoped for in the way of subordinate on-the-job improvement. They did this for those important performance items that had been mentioned in the interview. Each manager was then asked to estimate on a percentage scale the degree to which his hoped-for changes had actually been observed. The average per cent accomplishment estimate for those performance items that *did* get translated into goals was 65, while the per cent estimate for those items that *did not* get translated into goals was about 27! Establishing specific plans and goals seemed to ensure that attention would be given to that aspect of job performance.

Summation of Findings

At the end of this experiment, we were able to draw certain tentative conclusions. These conclusions were the basis of a future research study which we will describe later. In general, we learned that:

• *Comprehensive annual performance appraisals are of questionable value.* Certainly a major objective of the manager in traditional appraisal discussions is motivating the subordinate to improve his performance. But the evidence we gathered indicated clearly that praise tended to have no effect, perhaps because it was regarded as the sandwich which surrounded the raw meat of criticism.[2] And criticism itself brought on defensive reactions that were essentially denials of responsibility for a poor performance.

• *Coaching should be a day-to-day, not a once-a-year, activity.* There are two main reasons for this:

1. Employees seem to accept suggestions for improved performance if they are given in a less concentrated form than is the case in comprehensive annual appraisals. As our experiment showed, employees become clearly more prone to reject criticisms as the number of criticisms mount. This indicates that an "overload phenomenon" may be operating. In other words, each individual seems to have a tolerance level for the amount of criticism he can take. And, as this level is approached or passed, it becomes increasingly difficult for him to accept responsibility for the shortcomings pointed out.
2. Some managers reported that the traditional performance appraisal program tended to cause them to save up items where improvement was needed in order to have enough material to conduct a comprehensive discussion of performance in the annual review. This short-circuited one of the primary purposes of the appraisal program — that of giving feedback to the subordinates as to their performance. Studies of the learning process point out that feedback is less effective if much time is allowed to elapse between the performance and the feedback. This fact alone argues for more frequent discussions between the manager and the subordinate.

• *Goal setting, not criticism, should be used to improve performance.* One of the most significant findings in our experiment was the fact that far superior results were observed when the manager and the man *together* set specific goals to be achieved, rather than merely discussed needed improvement. Frequent reviews of progress provide natural opportunities for discussing means of improving performance *as needs occur,* and these reviews are far less threatening than the annual appraisal and salary review discussions.

• *Separate appraisals should be held for different purposes.* Our work demonstrated that it was unrealistic to expect a single performance appraisal program to achieve every conceivable need. It seems foolish to have a manager serving in the self-conflicting role as a counselor (helping a man to improve his performance) when, at the same time, he is presiding as a judge over the same employee's salary action case.

New WP&R Method

This intensive year-long test of the performance appraisal program indicated clearly that work-planning-and-review discussions between a man and his manager appeared to be a far more effective approach in improving job performance than was the concentrated annual performance appraisal program.

For this reason, after the findings had been announced, many GE managers adopted some form of the new WP&R program to motivate performance improvement in employees, especially those at the professional and administrative levels. Briefly described, the WP&R approach calls for periodic meetings between the manager and his subordinate. During these meetings, progress on past goals is reviewed, solutions are sought for job-related problems, and new goals are established. The intent of the method is to create a situation in which manager and subordinate can discuss job performance and needed improvements in detail without the subordinate becoming defensive.

Basic Features

This WP&R approach differs from the traditional performance appraisal program in that:

- There are more frequent discussions of performance.
- There are no summary judgments or ratings made.
- Salary action discussions are held separately.
- The emphasis is on mutual goal planning and problem solving.

As far as frequency is concerned, these WP&R discussions are held more often than traditional performance appraisal interviews, but are not scheduled at rigidly fixed intervals. Usually at the conclusion of one work planning session the man and manager set an approximate date for the next review. Frequency depends both on the nature of the job and on the manager's style of operating. Sometimes these WP&R discussions are held as often as once a month, whereas for other jobs and/or individuals, once every six months is more appropriate.

In these WP&R discussions, the manager and his subordinate do not deal in generalities. They consider specific, objectively defined work goals and establish the yardstick for measuring performance. These goals stem, of course, from broader departmental objectives and are defined in relation to the individual's position in the department.

Comparison Setting

After the findings of our experiment were communicated by means of reports and group meetings in the plant where the research was carried out, about half the key managers decided they would abandon the comprehensive annual performance appraisal method and adopt the new WP&R program instead. The other half were hesitant to make such a major change at the time. They decided, consequently, to continue with the traditional performance appraisal program and to try to make it more effective. This provided a natural setting for us to compare the effectiveness of the two approaches. We decided that the comparison should be made in the light of the objectives usually stated for the comprehensive annual performance appraisal program. These objectives were (1) to provide knowledge of results to employees, (2) to justify reasons for salary action, and (3) to motivate and help employees do a better job.

The study design was simple. Before any changes were made, the exempt employees who would be affected by these programs were surveyed to provide base-line data. The WP&R program was then implemented in about half of the exempt group, with the other half continuing to use a modified version of the traditional performance appraisal program. One year later, the identical survey questionnaire was again administered in order to compare the changes that had occurred.

Attitudes and Actions

The results of this research study were quite convincing. The group that continued on the traditional performance appraisal showed no change in *any* of the areas measured. The WP&R group, by contrast, expressed significantly more favorable attitudes on almost all questionnaire items. Specifically, their attitudes changed in a favorable direction over the year that they participated in the new WP&R program with regard to the —

. . . amount of help the manager was giving them in improving performance on the job;

. . . degree to which the manager was receptive to new ideas and suggestions;

. . . ability of the manager to plan;

. . . extent to which the manager made use of their abilities and experience;

. . . degree to which they felt the goals they were shooting for were what they *should* be;

. . . extent to which they received help from the manager in planning for *future* job opportunities;

. . . value of the performance discussions they had with their managers.

In addition to these changes in attitudes, evidence was also found which showed clearly that the members of the WP&R group were much more likely to have taken specific actions to improve performance than were those who continued with the traditional performance appraisal approach.

Current Observations

Recently we undertook still another intensive study of the WP&R program in order to learn more about the nature of these discussions and how they can be made most effective. While these observations have not been completed, some interesting findings have already come to light — especially in relation to differences between WP&R and traditional performance appraisal discussions.

Perceived Differences

For one thing, WP&R interviews are strictly man-to-man in character, rather than having a father-and-son flavor, as did so many of the traditional performance appraisals. This seems to be due to the fact that it is much more natural under the WP&R program for the subordinate to take the initiative when his performance on past goals is being reviewed. Thus, in listening to the subordinate's review of performance, problems, and failings, the manager is automatically cast in the role of *counselor*. This role for the manager, in turn, results naturally in a problem-solving discussion.

In the traditional performance appraisal interview, on the other hand, the manager is automatically cast in the role of *judge*. The subordinate's natural reaction is to assume a defensive posture, and thus all the necessary ingredients for an argument are present.

Since the WP&R approach focuses mainly on immediate short-term goals, some managers are concerned that longer range, broader plans and goals might be neglected. Our data show that this concern is unfounded. In almost every case, the discussion of specific work plans and goals seems to lead naturally into a consideration of broader, longer range plans. In fact, in a substantial percentage of these sessions, even the career plans of the subordinates are reviewed.

In general, the WP&R approach appears to be a better way of defining what is expected of an individual and how he is doing on the job. Whereas the traditional performance appraisal often results in resistance to the manager's attempts to help the subordinate, the WP&R approach brings about acceptance of such attempts.

Conclusion

Multiple studies conducted by the Behavioral Research Service at GE reveal that the traditional performance appraisal method contains a number of problems:

1. Appraisal interviews attempt to accomplish the two objectives of—
. . . providing a written justification for salary action;
. . . motivating the employee to improve his work performance.
2. The two purposes are in conflict, with the result that the traditional appraisal system essentially becomes a salary discussion in which the manager justifies the action taken.
3. The appraisal discussion has little influence on future job performance.
4. Appreciable improvement is realized only when specified goals and deadlines are mutually established and agreed on by the subordinate and his manager in an interview split away from the appraisal interview.

This evidence, coupled with other principles relating to employee motivation, gave rise to the new WP&R program, which is proving to be far more effective in improving job performance than the traditional performance appraisal method. Thus, it appears likely that companies which are currently relying on the comprehensive annual performance appraisal process to achieve improvement in work performance might well consider the advisability of switching to some form of work-planning-and-review in their industrial personnel programs.

Notes

1. Douglas McGregor, "An Uneasy Look at Performance Appraisal," HBR May–June 1957, p. 89; Harold Mayfield, "In Defense of Performance Appraisal," HBR March–April 1960, p. 81; and Alva F. Kindall and James Gatza, "Positive Program for Performance Appraisal," HBR November–December 1963, p. 153.
2. See Richard E. Farson, "Praise Reappraised," HBR September–October 1963, p. 61.

E. COMPENSATION

We firmly believe that no scheme is good or bad in itself, but only in particular circumstances, and when judged on particular criteria. Our aim is therefore firstly to get methods of wage payment into focus by an objective analysis of their principal characteristics; and secondly to propose a systematic approach to selection of the method most appropriate to the situation obtaining in the individual firm.

This is how Grinyer and Kessler (Selection 23) introduce their cognitive map for an analysis of incentive compensation systems. We feel their greatest contribution has been to present an analytical model for evaluating alternative compensation programs. However, they also incorporate in their article a valuable summary of the major types of incentive programs presently used.

Lawler (Selection 24), on the other hand, probes the psychological meaning of money and how it motivates people. His article is especially useful in that it presents the commonly accepted assumptions about pay and attempts to determine their validity. While dealing generally with the role of money, the author focuses primarily on the psychological aspects of compensation practices as they relate to managerial personnel.

23

The Systematic Evaluation of Methods of Wage Payment

PETER H. GRINYER
The City University, London

SIDNEY KESSLER
Manchester School of Business

The use of financial incentive schemes has aroused considerable controversy in recent years. They seem to be falling into disfavour in the United States, and a number of major companies in the U.K., e.g. Glacier Metal, Vauxhall Motors, F. Perkins, and Philips Electrical, have expressed their dissatisfaction by abandoning them in favour of day-work. The N.C.B. has virtually abandoned piecework and, indeed, the Prices and Incomes Board, in its report on coal prices, recommended that it should do so.

On the other hand, many have expressed satisfaction with output-based financial incentives. According to a recent survey conducted by the Institution of Works Managers, five-sixths of the 229 firms that returned questionnaires operated incentive schemes. Theses firms ranged in size from 24 to over 10,000 employees, and it claimed that they account for 1 per cent of the working population. In 95 per cent of the firms that operated financial incentive schemes, more than 50 per cent of the employees were covered by them. Sixty-one per cent of the firms operating incentive schemes stated that they "were satisfied," 8 per cent were dissatisfied due to the high cost of operating them, and the rest thought that they had "lost their edge" or should be replaced by something else. Although its sampling method is suspect,[1] this study provides evidence that in a considerable number of firms output-based incentive schemes are considered by management to be adequate. The actual national coverage of payment-by-results is also significant — the latest Ministry of Labour figures[2] showing that 33 per cent of workers, overall, were paid on this basis, and 42 per cent in manufacturing industry alone. Within manufacturing industry, percentage coverage varied from 65 per cent in shipbuilding and marine engineering to 19 per cent in paper and printing.

Taken and adapted from *The Journal of Management Studies,* Vol. 14, No. 3, Oct. 1967. Used by permission.

Controversy has been increased by the clamour of proponents of alternative payment schemes. At Glacier Metal, the abandonment of piecework was loudly proclaimed by W. Brown,[3] and time-span was conceived by E. Jacques.[4] In addition interest in the Rucker and Scanlon type schemes[5] has revived in recent years, measured daywork[6] has its advocates, and the advantages of productivity bargaining[7] have been widely discussed. Yet financial incentive schemes have been stoutly defended by R. M. Currie[8] and others.[9] Throughout the debate over the last decade the protagonists have implicitly claimed their findings or views to be of general significance. However, they have often generalized from experience in particular work situations, and furthermore applied different criteria when evaluating the alternatives. This, we think, has not been helpful. We firmly believe that no scheme is good or bad in itself, but only in particular circumstances, and when judged on particular criteria. Our aim is therefore *firstly* to get methods of wage payment into focus by an objective analysis of their principal characteristics; and *secondly* to propose a systematic approach to selection of the method most appropriate to the situation obtaining in the individual firm.

An Analysis of Methods of Wage Payment

Before we can approach the systematic appraisal of systems of wage payment in specific circumstances, it is clearly necessary that we should define our terms and examine the broad range of alternative schemes. The term "financial incentive scheme" may be most simply defined by examination of each of the three words separately. "Financial" predicates that the scheme involves money. A "scheme" is, according to the Oxford Dictionary, a "systematic arrangement." "Incentive" means "urging, stirring up to action or to do." Thus, a financial incentive scheme is a systematic arrangement involving money intended to urge to action.

This exercise in semantics may appear to be trivial. It does, however, lead on to the question "to act or do what?" In other words, we need to establish precisely what we want to urge people to achieve by the offer of financial reward. Perhaps the most obvious objective is to induce greater effort to increase output per man-hour. Output-based schemes such as piecework or premium-bonus schemes are clearly devised to contribute to this end. But there are other possible objectives. For instance, a scheme might be planned to encourage learning, the willingness to bear responsibility, acceptance of change, or co-operation in cost reduction. Other objectives could be added.

The definition also provides a spring-board for exploration of the nature of the "systematic arrangement" implied by it. This arrangement may be examined under five heads:

(i) the basis for reward calculations, e.g. output, cost reduction,
(ii) the procedure for calcualting rewards from (i),
(iii) the manner of establishing the norms entering such calculations,

(iv) the frequency of such payments,
(v) the size of the group to which payment is made.

Methods of Wage Payment may be analysed under each of these heads and this is done in Figure 1. In Figures 2 and 3 the major stated advantages and disadvantages of the various methods are listed. Individual schemes under each of the main types could be analysed in a similar way.

It will be noticed that productivity bargaining has been included. One might, with some justice, object that this is not valid. It is certainly not similar in its mode of operation to, say, traditional piecework systems. On the other hand, there is a relationship between the *expected* achievement of objectives sought and the monetary payments made, and such payments are certainly intended by management to be the incentive to the operative to change his traditional work practices (i.e. to co-operate by accepting change). There is a good practical reason, too, for its inclusion. It makes the range of alternatives more comprehensive.

The Systematic Evaluation of Alternative Schemes

When faced with the problem of selecting an appropriate scheme for its own work situation, management is principally concerned with making a reasonable selection from among the broad types set out in Figure 1, then devising the detailed procedures and methods of operation and finally implementing the decision. The drawbacks and advantages found repeatedly in certain particular kinds of situation need to be recognized as such and borne in mind when evaluating alternative schemes for any given firm.

To aid such an evaluation, we propose that the familiar problem-solving model[12] should be followed. This involves:

(A) Definition of the problem.
(B) Recording of relevant data.
(C) Setting out of the alternatives and their evaluation.
(D) Selection of a "preferred" alternative. Evaluation of this in terms of the criteria laid down in stage (A).
(E) Implementation of the proposed alternative.

These stages are considered below.

(A) Definition of the Problem

. . . comprises a statement (a) of the objectives of management and the relative priority of each, (b) of the boundaries to the problem, and (c) of the constraints limiting alternatives that might be adopted and also the amount of time or resources that should be devoted to the solution of the problem.

Possible objectives have already been mentioned in both the text and in Figure 1. Most members of management would probably pay lip service to

FIGURE 1

Analysis of Methods of Wage Payment

Characteristic	I Output Incentives	II Cost reduction	III Productivity bargaining	IV Profit sharing	V Measured daywork	VI Merit rating
(1) EXAMPLES	(a) Piecework (b) Standard hour plans, e.g. Halsey-Weir, Bedaux Point.	Scanlon	Esso Refinery at Fawley	I.C.I.	Philips Electrical Ford Vauxhall	Ford
(2) OBJECTIVES	(a) Greater effort to increase output. (b) Encourage learning. (c) Remove need to discipline.	(a) Co-operation to reduce costs, e.g. to reduce material wastage, to improve methods. (b) Acceptance of change. (c) Greater effort to increase output. (d) Greater general co-operation between operatives and management.	Acceptance of change (may be once-and-for-all) e.g. in manning and methods.	(a) Increase co-operation generally. (b) Co-operation to reduce costs. (c) Acceptance of change. (d) Encourage effort to increase output. (e) By above to increase profits.	(a) To provide stable earnings. (b) To encourage effort to achieve standard norms. (c) To promote climate permitting sound management labour relations. (d) To remove impediments to exercising of full supervisory authority and to change.	(a) To encourage co-operation generally. (b) To encourage willingness to bear responsibility.
(3) BASIS FOR WAGE CALCULATIONS	Output.	Reduction in labour and sometimes material costs.	Expected increase in productivity based on changes in work rules.	Increase in profit.	Meeting production standards.	Subjectively assessed performance.

Characteristic	I Output incentives	II Cost reduction	III Productivity bargaining	IV Profit sharing	V Measured daywork	VI Merit rating
(4) PROCEDURE FOR CALCULATING REWARDS FROM (3)	Set formulae.	Payment of agreed percentage of saving in labour costs.	Negotiation between management and workers' representatives.		Reward set.[10] Disciplinary action may follow failure to achieve norm.	Subjective assessment by supervisor and his immediate superiors at pre-set intervals.
(5) MANNER OF DETERMINING NORMS ENTERING (4)	(a) Management initiative with right of union challenge. (b) Rate fixer negotiating with individual or group. Appeal to union and higher management. (c) Time study may or may not be used in (a) and (b).	Joint determination.	As for 4.	Management initiative.	(a) Management initiative with union right of challenge. (b) Management initiative with labour representatives participating in setting rewards and production standards.	As for 4.
(6) FREQUENCY OF REWARDS	Hourly, daily, or weekly.	Monthly.	Increase in daily, hourly, or weekly wage rates and/or other benefits.	Yearly.	Daily or weekly.	Hourly, daily, or weekly (increased wage rate).
(7) NORMAL SIZE OF GROUP TO WHICH REWARD IS PAID	Individual or small group.	Entire plant.	Usually plant-wide (may be restricted to specific trade).	Company wide.	Individual or small group.	Individual.

FIGURE 2

Stated Advantages of Different Methods of Wage Payment[11]

I Output incentives	II Cost reduction	III Productivity bargaining	IV Profit sharing	V Measured daywork	VI Merit rating
(1) Higher output per man hour. (2) Consequently lower manufacturing costs per unit, certainly in overheads and probably in labour costs, dependent on actual scheme. (3) Higher earnings for operatives. (4) Less supervision by foremen required. (5) Greater freedom for operatives.	(1) Are plant-wide schemes and therefore integrate the whole plant, encouraging teamwork and co-operation. (2) Reward not just higher output, but cost saving, e.g. use of materials. (3) A permanent incentive to increase efficiency and accept change, because workers know they will share fairly in any improvements.	(1) A direct means of securing acceptance of change. (2) A means of altering deep-rooted work practices and attitudes. (3) The process is said to result in improved management *per se* and certainly improved management control. (4) Improved Industrial Relations. (5) Substantial gains for workers, e.g. higher pay, greater security of pay and increased leisure.	(1) Increases co-operation generally, e.g. encourages efficiency, higher output, reduced costs, and acceptability of change. (2) Gives the worker a sense of "belonging" and, in some cases, of participating with management. (3) Only pays rewards when they can be afforded.	(1) Provides stable earnings. (2) Reduces opposition to mobility within plant, which exists under output incentive schemes. (3) Reduces opposition to introduction of new methods of production. (4) Avoids wage drift and other defects, said to be inherent in most output incentive schemes. (5) Lower cost of wage administration than under output incentive schemes.	(1) Can reward and hence encourage co-operation generally and a wide range of individual factors and qualities. (2) Can be used for indirect as well as direct workers and not related to measurability of output.

FIGURE 3

Stated Disadvantages of Different Methods of Wage Payment

I Output incentives	II Cost reduction	III Productivity bargaining	IV Profit sharing	V Measured daywork	VI Merit rating
(1) Inherent tendency to wage drift-"ratchet" and "dexterity" effects.	(1) Because they are plant-wide, the incentive effect on the individual worker or small group may be very remote.	(1) May be rewarding the inefficient and the restrictive.	(1) The annual reward is too remote in time and uncertain in amount to markedly influence behaviour.	(1) Productivity may be less than under an output incentive scheme.	(1) Based largely on subjective assessments.
(2) Problems of indirect workers and of integrating the labour force.	(2) Bonuses may be affected by factors outside the workers' control.	(2) May encourage the growth of new restrictive practices.	(2) Profits are determined by a wide variety of factors unrelated to workers' efforts and outside their control.	(2) More and better supervision required — more disciplinary action may be required with detrimental effects on industrial relations.	(2) Suspicion of workers because of (1) and hence jealousy, fear of abuse and favouritism.
(3) Problems of rate-fixing — loose and tight times — inequities created — resultant strains on supervisors and on labour relations.	(3) Lag between effort and bonus may be such as to reduce incentive effect.	(3) May create a sense of disturbance within (and without), the enterprise among those not affected by the Agreement, and consequently inflationary pressure.	(3) Because related to entire company, effect on behaviour of individual or group likely to be very small.	(3) Problems inherent in setting work norms and subsequently changing them as required.	(3) Suspicion of Unions because of (1) and (2) and because counter to basic concept of "rate for the job."
(4) Reduced mobility of labour within plant.	(4) Involve establishing an historic norm. If norm is fixed, as in Rucker, then it will not reflect changing circumstances: if it is variable, as in Scanlon, may lead to a loss of confidence in entire concept.	(4) A very time consuming process.			(4) Disliked by supervisors because of (1) and (2).
(5) Fluctuations of earnings or devices by workers to reduce fluctuations.					
(6) Tendency for quality to decline unless a stringent system of inspection.					
(7) Cost of administration.					
(8) May lead to resistance to improvements in method.					

all of them. Unfortunately, the attainment of all by any one scheme is extremely unlikely, and the intensity of the incentive to achieve specific objectives will vary between schemes. Consequently, it is imperative that management should rank objectives in order of their priority, and even attempt to estimate an approximate weight for each. Only once objectives have been determined may criteria for evaluation of alternative schemes be established. A criterion such as the percentage reduction in unit labour costs is clearly derived directly from the objective "to encourage co-operation in the reduction of labour costs." Criteria are measurable, or at least recognizable, indications of attainment of objectives.

If the problem is to be systematically and effectively studied, it must be delimited; boundaries must be set. For instance, the problem might relate to an individual, group, department, plant or entire company, and it might be confined to one trade or all trades employed in the group, department, plant or company.

Constraints upon solution may be of two kinds. Firstly, the constraint may relate to the alternatives that might reasonably be considered, some being excluded on the grounds of company policy or known union views. This kind of constraint might, of course, be sometimes removed by means of persuasion and negotiation. Secondly, there may be a constraint placed upon the resources that might be devoted to the study, and the time within which it should be completed. Such limits may be imposed, or set as targets, for purposes of control. Nonetheless, they will affect the manner in which the exercise is planned and executed.

The reader will, no doubt, recognize that these three aspects of problem definition are interrelated. Objectives will be influenced by the boundaries set to the problem, these boundaries will themselves depend to some extent upon the objectives of the company, and both may be conditioned by constraints of the first kind.

(B) Recording Relevant Data

Before alternatives can be set out and evaluated, it is necessary to conduct research into the types of scheme available, experience of firms with similar circumstances with these, the existing method of wage payment and indications of its success or failure.[13] Information about the management structure, level of supervisory ability, labour relations, rates of pay, average earnings, fluctuations in weekly earnings, and the nature of the production processes and skills involved is also necessary. Views of the workers' representatives and all levels of management on alternatives available need to be sought, too.

(C) Evaluation of the Alternatives

Stages (A) and (B) should reveal the alternatives, provide information about each, and also yield criteria for their evaluation. Such evaluation may be difficult. It is, in essence, a matter of asking critical questions of each of the alternatives and attempting in the answers obtained to assess realistically the extent to which each would meet the criteria and so contribute to the objectives. A number of such questions, framed with the reported performance of the different types of scheme and the possible objectives in mind, are tentatively suggested below. It should be stressed, however, that these are intended only to provoke thought, and are in no way comprehensive or indeed relevant to all situations.

Is Individual or Group Contribution to the Objectives Quantifiable? If so, how accurate may the index of contribution be? For example, how variable are material quality, the elements involved in the job and the amount of dexterity that might reasonably be expected at different stages of a production run, and how consistent is rating by time study officers, in the case of an output-based index? If the level of accuracy is adequate, how might effort be systematically related to reward under each alternative scheme, and would such a relationship be understood and accepted as fair by both management and men? If contribution to the objectives is not quantifiable, how can wage or salary payment be related to the achievement of objectives, for example, by fostering sound management–labour relations, and which alternatives, for example, output-based schemes, must be excluded as inoperable?

Is Financial Gain an Adequate Motivation in the Given Situation? How strong are group work norms in the departments, plant, company, area and industry? Are these likely to restrict the incentive effect of any of the alternatives? Are any of the alternatives under consideration likely to generate self-defeating pressures in the work climate or might they alternatively improve this climate and indirectly provide a non-financial incentive to contribute to achievement of the objectives? Which of the alternatives will be accepted as equitable, or rejected as unfair, by the employees given the existing management–employee relationship? Are employees likely, under each of the alternatives, to see clearly the relationship between their own efforts or contribution and their financial reward? Will the financial reward under each scheme be immediate enough to act as a spur? Are there any general social factors that might diminish or increase the motivational power of money and, if so, might these affect the way in which bonuses should be paid?[14] If financial gain does not appear to be an adequate motivation, what alternative forms of motivation, for example, salary status, security of employment, are available in wage payment systems other than financial incentive schemes? How powerful would such incentives be, and what would be the cost?

Is Improved Operative Motivation Likely to Achieve the Objectives? For example, can the operative control the rate or quality of output, the amount of waste material, or the machine down time? If not, there is little point in providing an inducement to greater effort, which would suggest that this particular objective was misguided.

Are the Side-effects of Each of the Alternatives Likely to be Favourable or Adverse? For instance, will industrial relations deteriorate because of piece-rate haggles, and in what circumstances is this likely? Is the quality of supervision likely to be increased or reduced by each alternative in terms of authority and control over work, time available to undertake supervisory as opposed to purely clerical duties, willingness and ability to initiate changes in methods and layout, and the willingness of able men to accept promotion to supervisory positions? Is any of the alternatives likely to restrict the optimal allocation of jobs to men or of men to departments? For example, could disparities in piece-rates between either jobs or departments, which might have these effects, be avoided? Might any of the schemes under consideration lead to a resistance to change for fear of upsetting the effort/wage balance?

Is the Management Structure and Staffing Adequate? Are the procedural systems, and the general administrative arrangements adequate, or could they be readily reorganized to make them adequate, to ensure the successful operation of each of the alternatives? For instance, can management shortcomings that will frustrate greater effort on the part of the operatives, such as poor material quality or flow, excessive machine breakdowns, poor production planning, be avoided? Likewise, can loose and tight times, that give rise to discontent among operatives on standard hour systems, be reduced to reasonable levels? Can effective arrangements be made to adjudicate, in conjunction with workers' representatives, in the event of complaints of unreasonable norms? Will it be possible to ensure the regular review of norms to ensure that they are both fair and under control and how will this affect the operation of each of the possible schemes? What steps would be necessary, and could be taken, in each case to both maintain quality standards and to keep records of workers' contributions to the attainment of the objectives?

Finally, what would be the probable labour and clerical costs attendant upon the operation of each of the alternative schemes?

(D) Selection of the "Preferred" Alternatives

Answers to the kind of critical questions set out under (C) will probably vary not only between possible financial incentive schemes but also between different work situations for any one scheme. Selection will be influenced by the extent to which each scheme is found to satisfy the criteria, perhaps loosely weighted according to the relative importance of the objectives from which they are derived, established during the initial definition of the problem. Such selection would probably proceed by a process of elimination during the stage of evaluation. Final choice will therefore be between those alternatives remaining after this and consequently simpler than would otherwise have been the case. The financial incentive scheme, or any other system of wage payment, finally selected as most attractive should nonetheless be separately evaluated in terms of the criteria developed during the initial definition of the problem to check on its suitability. In most circumstances it would also be essential to consult fully with workers' representatives before committing oneself to a specific alternative. Such consultation would normally have occurred, to some extent, during the process of recording information.

Conclusions

The main burden of this paper is that, rather than advocacy of one or another system of wage payment, a systematic approach to evaluation of alternatives with regard to unique work situations is required. An outline of such an approach has been given. This has five stages. Firstly, the objectives of management are defined and ranked, the boundaries of the work situation with which the study is concerned are stated, and any constraints on possible solutions are made clear. Secondly, information is collected about alternative systems available, experience with operating them and the work situation for which the new system is to be devised. Thirdly, each alternative is examined critically to determine the extent to which it is likely to contribute to the declared objectives within the given work situation. Fourthly, one alternative is selected as the best. Fifthly, implementation of the selected scheme is planned and executed.

Evaluation of the alternatives on these lines is, of course, not a sufficient condition of success. Nonetheless, by requiring statement of the relative importance of the objectives sought and systematic analysis of the likely contribution of each alternative to their achievement, it should greatly promote better selection of systems of wage payment. Wage payments have normally a number of purposes to fulfill. The importance of each of these purposes varies between work situations. Yet no one system is likely to achieve all of the ends sought by management. Hence ultimate selection between alternatives hinges largely upon the relative weights attached to objectives. Thus clarity of objectives is a *sine qua non* of a rational approach to this, as to any other, problem.

However, we would stress, above all, the need for acceptability of the adopted scheme to both workers and supervisory line managers. Any system of wage payment involves, whether explicitly or implicitly, a bargain between workers and managements.[15] Should its terms be rejected by the workers, the incentive to contribute toward achievement of the objectives of management will be at best low, and may be negative due to worsening human and industrial relations. Clearly, to ignore the objectives of workers is to ask for trouble. Likewise, if foremen dislike the scheme adopted, they are scarcely likely to promote its success, and their morale and efficiency may well suffer. Moreover, such disenchantment is likely to infect those who work for them too. Thus wide consultation at all stages of the systematic procedure with both workers' representatives and those in line management likely to be affected is imperative.

Notes

1. Questionnaires were distributed through the I.W.M.'s branches. This in itself would reduce the random nature of the sample. Also only 229 of the 660 questionnaires issued were returned. This self-selection of the group of 229 probably introduced a bias toward firms interested in financial incentive schemes.

2. Ministry of Labour Gazette, September 1961.

3. W. Brown, *Piecework Abandoned,* London: Heinemann, 1962.

4. E. Jaques, *Equitable Payment,* London: Heinemann, 1961; and *Time-Span Handbook,* London: Heinemann, 1964.

5. F. R. Bentley, *People, Productivity & Progress,* London: Business Publications Ltd., 1964; F. G. Lesieur (ed.), *The Scanlon Plan,* Massachusetts Institute of Technology Press, 1958; B.I.M. *Notes on some Company-wide Incentive Schemes: Scanlon, Rucker & Kaiser Steel,* B.I.M., 1964.

6. A. Shaw, "One step towards a salaried work force," *The Manager,* January 1964.

7. A. Flanders, *The Fawley Productivity Agreements,* London: Faber & Faber, 1964; Royal Commission on Trade Unions & Employers' Associations. Research Paper No. 4, *Productivity Bargaining,* London: H.M.S.O., 1967; F. E. Oldfield, *New Look Industrial Relations,* London: Mason Reed, 1966; and "Symposium on Productivity Bargaining," *British Journal of Industrial Relations,* March, 1967.

8. R. M. Currie, *Financial Incentives based on Work Measurement,* B.I.M., London: 1963.

9. J. Davison, Florence P. Sargant, B. Gray, and N. S. Ross, *Productivity & Economic Incentives,* London: Allen & Unwin, 1958.

10. Reward and norm setting will normally involve:

(i) job evaluation,

(ii) setting grades of pay for jobs,

(iii) setting production norms for jobs.

11. See references 3–8 and also R. Marriott, *Incentive Payment Schemes,* London: Staples, 1961, which describes and considers in detail the advantages and disadvantages of a wide range of methods of wage payments. Other publications covering a variety of schemes include The Institute of Cost and Works Accountants' *Employee Remuneration and Incentives,* I.C.W.A., 1954; International Labour Office *Payment by Results* (I.L.O. 1951), and N. C. Hunt, *Methods of Wage Payment in British Industry,* London: Pitman, 1951. More critical assessments include T. Lupton, *Money for Effort,* H.M.S.O., 1961, R. B. McKersie, "Wage Payment Methods of the Future," *British Journal of Industrial Relations,* June 1963; D. Pym, "Is there a Future for Wage Incentive

Schemes," *British Journal of Industrial Relations,* July, 1964.

12. The reader will no doubt see the parallel between this and the stages involved in Method Study, e.g. see Barnes, "*Motion and Time Study,*" Wiley, 1963.

13. Inter firm comparison is useful for this purpose. Indices of labour cost per unit of output and of output per man hour may be used. Views may be elicited from both management and men. Analysis of reports on "exit" interviews and on wage grievances taken to the supervisor or above him are often revealing too.

14. For example, some Irish workers customarily take their unopened pay packets to their wives or mothers who then give them beer money. Because of this the financial incentive to increase effort was found in one weaving plant to be virtually inoperative.

15. See H. Behrend, "The Effort Bargain," *Industrial and Labour Relations Review,* July, 1959.

24

The Mythology of Management Compensation

EDWARD E. LAWLER III
Yale University

A host of decisions have to be made every day concerning compensation practices, decisions that are of critical importance in determining the success of any business organization. Unfortunately, relatively little is known about the psychological meaning of money and how it motivates people. Unanswered are such critical questions as:

- How often should a raise be given?
- What are the effects of secrecy about pay?
- How should benefit programs be packaged?

In the absence of systematic knowledge, executives have had to answer these kinds of questions for themselves. Many have drawn primarily from their own and others' experience in arriving at their answers. Unfortunately, common sense derived from experience can be loaded with implicit assumptions which may not be as valid as they seem. It is my purpose here to examine a number of commonly accepted assumptions about pay and to attempt to determine if they are valid.

What are the currently accepted principles and assumptions about how pay should be administered? In order to answer this question, a study was conducted among 500 managers from all levels of management and from a wide variety of organizations. The managers were asked to indicate whether they agreed or disagreed with five statements that contained assumptions about the psychological aspects of management compensation — assumptions which have important implications for the administration of pay. The following are the five assumptions and the percentage of managers agreeing with each:

- At the higher-paid levels of management, pay is not one of the two or three most important job factors (61 per cent).
- Money is an ineffective motivator of outstanding job performance at the management level (55 per cent).

• Managers are likely to be dissatisfied with their pay even if they are highly paid (54 per cent).

• Information about management pay rates is best kept secret (77 per cent).

• Managers are not concerned with how their salary is divided between cash and fringe benefits; the important thing is the amount of salary they receive (45 per cent).

As can be seen, better than 50 per cent of managers participating in the study agreed with the first four assumptions and 45 per cent agreed with the last assumption.

Recently, research results have begun to accumulate which suggest that some of the assumptions may be partially invalid and some completely invalid. Let us, therefore, look at each of these assumptions and examine the evidence relevant to it.

What Is the Role of Pay?

The history of the study of pay shows that we have progressed from a model of man that viewed him as being primarily economically motivated to a view that stresses social needs and the need for self-actualization. Unfortunately, in trying to establish the legitimacy of social and self-actualization needs, the proponents of this view of motivation tended to overlook the importance of pay. In some cases, they failed to mention the role of pay in their systems at all, and in other cases they implied that, because workers and managers are better off financially than they used to be, pay is less important than it was previously.

Because of this failure to deal with the role of pay, many managers have come to the erroneous conclusion that the experts in "human relations" have shown that pay is a relatively unimportant incentive and, as a result, have accepted the view that pay is a relatively unimportant job factor.[1] This is illustrated in the results of my study mentioned above. When the managers were asked to indicate how they thought the typical expert in human relations would respond to the statement that for higher-paid managers pay is not one of the most important job factors, 71 per cent of the managers thought that the majority of the experts would agree with it, while 61 per cent said they agreed with it themselves.

Undeniably, those writers who have stressed social and self-actualization needs have performed an important service by emphasizing the significance of nonfinancial incentives. It is now clear that people are motivated by needs for recognition and self-actualization as well as by security and physiological needs. But does this mean that pay must be dismissed as unimportant? I do not think the evidence justifies such a conclusion.

The belief that pay becomes unimportant as an individual accumulates more money has its roots in an inadequate interpretation of Maslow's theory of a hierarchy of needs. Briefly, Maslow's theory says that the needs which individuals seek to satisfy are arranged in a hierarchy. At the bottom of the hierarchy are needs for physical comfort. These lower-order needs are followed by such higher-order needs as social needs, esteem needs, and finally, needs for autonomy and self-actualization.

According to Maslow's theory, once the lower-order needs are relatively well satisfied, they become unimportant as motivators, and an individual tries to satisfy the higher-order needs. If it is then assumed, as it is by many, that pay satisfies only lower-level needs, then it becomes obvious that once a person's physical comforts are taken care of, his pay will be unimportant to him.[2] But this view is based upon the assumption that pay satisfies primarily lower-level needs, an assumption which I question.

Pay as Recognition

I would like to emphasize the neglected viewpoint that pay is a unique incentive — unique because it is able to satisfy both the lower-order physiological and security needs and the higher-order needs, such as esteem and recognition. Recent studies show that managers frequently think of their pay as a form of recognition for a job well done and as a mark of achievement.[3] The president of a large corporation has clearly pointed out why pay has become an important mark in the progress toward achievement and recognition for managers.

> Achievement in the managerial field is much less spectacular than comparable success in many of the professions . . . the scientist, for example, who wins the Nobel prize. . . . In fact, the more effective an executive, the more his own identity and personality blend into the background of his organization, and the greater is his relative anonymity outside his immediate circle.

There is, however, one form of recognition that managers do receive that is visible outside their immediate circle, and that is their pay. Pay has become an indicator of the value of a person to an organization and as such is an important form of recognition. Thus, it is not surprising to find that one newly elected company president whose "other" income from securities approximated $125,000 demanded a salary of $100,000 from his company. When asked why he did not take a $50,000 salary and defer the other half of his salary until after retirement at a sizable tax saving, he replied, "I want my salary to be six figures when it appears in the proxy statement."[4]

It is precisely because pay satisfies higher-order needs as well as lower-order needs that it may remain important to managers, regardless of the amount of compensation they receive. For example, one recent study clearly showed (Figure 1) that although pay is slightly less important to upper-level managers (president and vice-president) than it is to lower-level managers,

FIGURE 1

Importance Attached to Six Needs by Managers at Three Levels

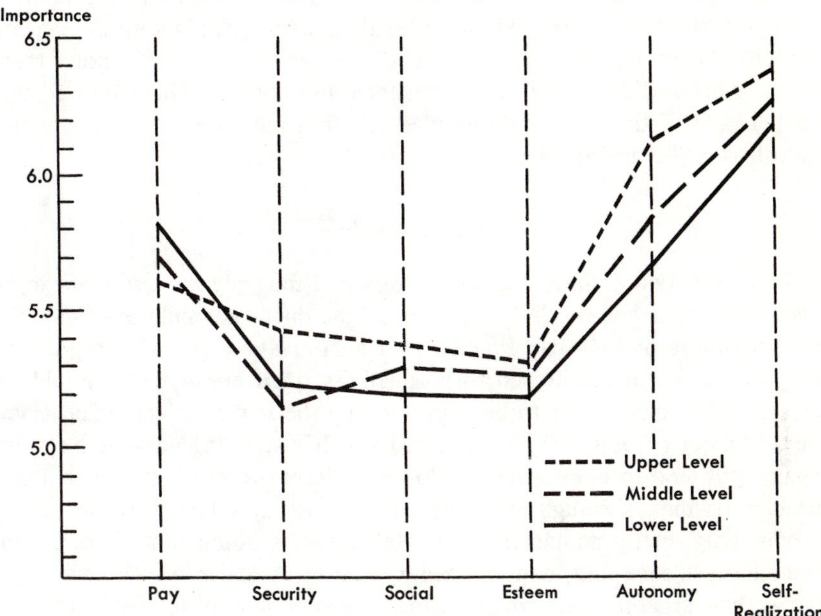

it is still more important than security, social, and esteem needs for upper-level managers.[5] At the lower management level, pay was rated as more important than all but self-actualization needs.

We can turn to motivation theory to help explain further why pay is important to many managers. Goals that are initially desired only as a means to an end can in time become goals in themselves. Because of this process, money may cease to be only a path to the satisfaction of needs and may become a goal in itself. Thus, for many managers, money and money making have become ends that are powerful incentives. As one manager put it when asked why his salary was important to him, "It is just like bridge — it isn't any fun unless you keep score." In summary, the evidence shows that, although pay may be important to managers for different reasons as the amount of pay they receive increases, pay remains important to all levels of management.

The evidence that is usually given to support the belief that pay is ineffective as an incentive is the finding that a number of incentive plans have failed to produce expected increases in productivity. This view is expressed well by the following statement of a company president: "Wage systems are not, in themselves, an important determinant of pace of work, application to work, or output."[6] That this view is being more widely accepted by managers in industry is reflected in the decline of the use of incentive systems at the worker level. In 1935, 75 per cent of a sample of companies replied that they used wage incentive programs. By 1939 the number had fallen to 52 per cent and by 1958 to 27 per cent. The fact that managers have tended to stop using incentive plans for their workers points up the general disillusionment with the effectiveness of pay as an incentive among managers. This disillusionment is also reflected in my study which showed that 55 per cent of the managers sampled felt that pay is not a very effective incentive at the management level.

Managers' Pay

What experiences have these managers had that might cause them to be disillusioned? I believe that one cause of the disillusionment is in the misunderstanding of how pay functions as a motivator. In current practice, the logic is that if pay is tied to productivity, then productivity should increase. This logic seems to be supported by the law of effect which states that behavior (productivity in our case) which is seen as leading to a reward (pay) will tend to be repeated.[7] However, recent research shows that one problem is that, although incentive schemes are designed to relate pay to productivity, many managers do not see them as doing this. I have considerable evidence that many managers who work under systems which, as far as their organizations are concerned, tie productivity to pay, simply do not feel that better job performance will lead to higher pay.

I recently distributed a questionnaire to over 600 middle- and lower-level managers in a variety of organizations. These managers were asked what factors determined their pay. The consensus of these managers was that the most important factor in determining their pay was their training and experience, and not how well they performed their jobs. A look at the relationship between how well they were performing their jobs as rated by their superiors and their pay showed that they were correct. There was virtually no relationship between their pay and their rated job performance. Under these conditions, there is no reason to believe that pay will function as an incentive for higher job performance, even though these organizations claimed to have incentive pay systems.

Some other data that I collected from the same managers show one condition under which pay can be an effective incentive for high job performance. Of the managers studied, those who were most highly motivated to perform their jobs effectively were characterized by two attitudes:

- They said that their pay was important to them.
- They felt that god job performance would lead to higher pay for them.

To return to the law of effect, for these highly motivated managers, pay was a significant reward and they saw this reward as contingent upon their job performance. Thus, it would seem that one of the major limits of the effectiveness of pay as an incentive is the ability of management to design compensation programs that create the perception that pay is based upon performance.

It is not enough to have a pay plan that is called an incentive system. Not only the people who design the plan but the people who are subject to the plan must feel that it is an incentive plan. At the management level, one step in the direction of typing pay more closely to performance might be the elimination of some of the stock option and other deferred payment plans that exist now. Many of these pay plans are so designed that they destroy rather than encourage the perception that pay is based upon performance. They pay off years after the behavior that is supposed to be rewarded has taken place, and in many cases the size of the reward that is given is independent of the quality of the manager's job performance.

There are two other factors which suggest that cash payments may be particularly appropriate at this time. A recent study found that managers preferred cash payments to other forms of compensation.[8] Further, the new tax laws now make it possible to get almost as much money into the hands of the manager through salary as through stock option plans and other forms of deferred compensation.

In addition to failing to create the perception that pay is based upon performance, there are two other reasons why incentive plans may fail. Many pay plans fail to recognize the importance of other needs to individuals, and, as a result, plans are set up in such a way that earning more money must necessarily be done at the cost of satisfying other needs. This situation frequently occurs when managers are paid solely on the basis of the performance of their subordinate groups. Conflicts appear between their desire for more production in their own groups, no matter what the organizational costs, and their desire to cooperate with other managers in order to make the total organization more successful.

A second reason why incentive plans fail is that they are frequently introduced as a substitute for good leadership practices and trust between employees and the organization. As one manager so aptly put this fallacious view: "If you have poor managers you have to use wage incentives." Wage incentives must be a supplement to, and not a substitute for, good management practices.

The results of Herzberg's study of motivation have been frequently cited as evidence that pay cannot be an effective motivator of good job performance.[9] According to this view, pay operates only as a maintenance factor and, as such, has no power to motivate job performance beyond some neutral point. However, this interpretation is not in accord with the results of the study. The study, in fact, found that pay may or may not be a motivator, depending upon how it is administered. A careful reading of Herzberg shows that where pay was geared to achievement and seen as a form of recognition by the managers, it was a potent motivator of good job performance. It was only where organizations had abandoned pay as an incentive and were unsuccessful in fairly relating pay and performance that pay ceased to be a motivator and became a maintenance factor.

Incentive for Performance

In summary, I think the significant question about pay as an incentive is not whether it is effective or ineffective, but under what conditions is it an effective incentive. It appears that pay can be an effective incentive for good job performance under certain conditions:

When pay is seen by individuals as being tied to effective job performance in such a way that it becomes a reward or form of recognition for effective job performance.

When other needs are also satisfied by effective job performance.

The statement is frequently made that, no matter how much money an individual earns, he will want more. And indeed, as was pointed out earlier, the evidence does indicate that pay remains important, regardless of how much money an individual earns. But the assumption, accepted by 54 per cent of the managers in my study, that managers are likely to be dissatisfied with their pay even if they are highly paid does not follow from this point. There is an important difference between how much pay an individual wants to earn and the amount he feels represents a fair salary for the job he is doing. Individuals evaluate their pay in terms of the balance between what they put into their jobs (effort, skill, education, etc.) and what they receive in return (money, status, etc.).[10]

Dissatisfaction with pay occurs when an individual feels that what he puts into his job exceeds what he receives in the form of pay for doing his job. Individuals evaluate the fairness of their inputs relative to their outcomes on the basis of the inputs and outcomes of other employees, usually their coworkers. Managers tend to compare their pay with that of managers who are at the same management level in their own and in other organizations. Thus, dissatisfaction with pay is likely to occur when an individual's pay is lower than the pay of someone whom he considers similar to himself in ability, job level, and job performance. But when an individual receives an amount of pay that compares favorably with the pay received by others who, he feels, have comparable inputs, he will be satisfied with his pay.

However, because an individual feels his pay is fair, it does not mean that an opportunity to make more money through a promotion or other change in inputs would be turned down, nor does it mean that more money is not desired. It simply means that at the moment the balance between inputs and outcomes is seen as equitable.

The results of a recent study of over 1,900 managers illustrates the point that managers can be, and in fact frequently are, satisfied with their pay.[11] The managers were first asked to rate on a 1 (low) to 7 (high) scale how much pay they received for their jobs. They were next asked to rate, on the same scale, how much pay should be associated with their jobs. As can be seen from Figure 2, which presents the results for the presidents who participated in the study, those executives who were paid highly, relative to other presidents, were satisfied with their pay. For this group[12] (earning $50,000 and over), there was no difference between how much pay they said they received and how much pay they thought they should receive. However, those presidents whose pay compared unfavorably with the pay of other presidents said there was a substantial difference between what their pay should be and what it was.

The same results were obtained at each level of management down to and including the foreman level. The highly paid managers at each level were quite satisfied with their pay; it was the low-paid managers at each level who were dissatisfied. In fact, highly paid foremen ($12,000 and above) were better satisfied with their pay than were company presidents who earned less than $50,000.

There is some evidence that managers can, and do, feel that they receive too much pay for their management positions. Of the 1,900 managers studied, about 5 per cent reported that they received too much pay for their management positions. These managers apparently felt that their outcomes

FIGURE 2

Attitudes of Corporation Presidents toward Their Pay

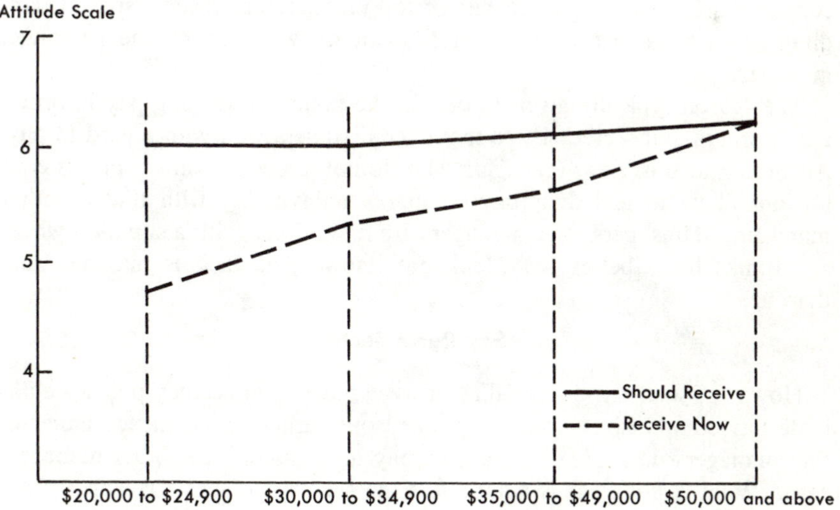

were too great in proportion to their inputs when compared with those of other managers. Although the number of managers who feel that their pay is too high is undoubtedly small, as indicated by the 5 per cent figure obtained in this study, the fact that this feeling exists at all is evidence that individuals do not always feel they deserve more and more pay.

The feeling of overcompensation by some managers is also evidence that some organizations are not doing the best possible job of distributing their compensation dollars. It may be wise for organizations to give more weight to the value that subordinates and peers place on a manager's job performance when they are considering pay raises for a manager. Giving a high salary to a manager who is considered to be a poor performer by other employees can have several negative effects.

First, it can cause dissatisfaction with pay among other managers: dissatisfaction that comes about because managers who are good performers may come to see their own pay as suddenly inadequate relative to the pay of someone whom they regard as a poor performer, but who has received a raise. If such practices are followed, it is undoubtedly true that good performers will never be satisfied with their pay.

Second, and more important, giving a raise to a poor performer is a signal to other managers that pay is not necessarily based upon merit: an attitude that can destroy any motivational impetus that might be created by an otherwise well-administered compensation program. As can be seen from the results of my study of manager's assumptions about pay administration, perhaps the most commonly accepted axiom of good personnel practice is that information about management compensation rates should be kept secret. Many organizations go to great lengths to maintain this secrecy. Information about management pay rates is frequently kept locked in the company safe and the pay checks of top management receive special handling so that the size of the check is not known even by the personnel manager.

The reason typically given to defend the policy of keeping pay information secret is that secrecy helps to reduce dissatisfaction with regard to pay. According to this view, managers who do not know how much others earn are not likely to feel their pay compares unfavorably with that of other managers. Thus, personnel managers are never faced with a situation where Joe thinks he is better than Jack but knows that Jack is making more than he.

Pay Rates Secret

However, such reasoning fallaciously assumes that secrecy policies eliminate pay comparisons. As was pointed out earlier, the evidence indicates that managers do evaluate their own pay in terms of what other managers earn. What is not clear is what effect the secrecy policies have on the accuracy with which managers estimate the pay of other managers and the effects of the secrecy on how satisfying and motivating these comparisons are.

In order to gather some evidence that might serve as a basis for evaluating the effects of secrecy, I recently conducted an attitude survey. Questionnaires were completed by 563 (response rate 88.7 per cent) middle and lower-level managers in seven organizations. Four of the organizations were private companies engaged in a wide variety of activities ranging from rocket manufacturing to supplying gas and electricity. The other three organizations were government agencies also engaged in a variety of activities. The four private companies all had strict secrecy policies with regard to management compensation rates, while the three government agencies did make some information public about their pay rates.

A two-part questionnaire was used. The managers were first asked to estimate the average yearly salary of managers in their organizations who were at their own level, one level above them, and one level below them. The organization provided actual average salaries in order that comparisons could be made. The managers were also asked to indicate how well satisfied they were with several aspects of their organizations' compensation systems. In addition to being asked to express their satisfaction with their own pay, they were asked to indicate whether there was too much or too little difference between their own pay and that of their superiors, and between their own pay and that of their subordinates.

The results of the study clearly showed that the managers did not have an accurate picture of what other managers in their organizations earned. Apparently, the secrecy policies were effective in keeping these managers from knowing what other managers earned. However, rather than committing random errors in estimating other managers' salaries, these managers consistently tended to overestimate and to underestimate. When the managers were asked to estimate the pay of their superiors, they consistently underestimated. When they viewed the pay of their subordinates, they consistently overestimated. One-third of the managers overestimated the pay of their subordinates by more than one thousand dollars. Similarly, they also tended to overestimate the pay of managers at their own level.

Interestingly, the managers in the government organizations were consistently more accurate in estimating the pay of other managers than were the managers in the private organizations. Because the government managers had more information about the compensation programs of their organizations, it was expected that they would be more accurate. However, this finding does serve to emphasize the point that the cause of the managers' misperceptions of other managers' pay was the secrecy policies of their organizations.

The question that now remains to be answered is what effects did these distorted pictures of what other managers earn have on the managers' job satisfaction and job performance. The effects on satisfaction with pay can be seen in the managers' answers to the three questions concerned with satisfaction with pay. They stated that there was too small a difference between their own pay and that of their superiors and also too small a difference between their own pay and that of their subordinates. These attitudes are not surprising since the managers tended to see these differences as smaller than they actually are.

Effects of Secrecy

Secrecy policies are causing some of this dissatisfaction by giving the managers inaccurate pictures of what others earn. Since managers evaluate their own pay in terms of what others earn, it is not surprising that the data show that those managers who feel their own pay is too close to that of their superiors and subordinates also feel that their own pay is too low. Undoubtedly, part of the managers' dissatisfaction with their own pay has its basis in unfavorable pay comparisons between what these managers know they make and what they think other managers make. On the basis of this evidence, it appears that one effect of secrecy policies is to increase dissatisfaction with pay.[13]

There is another way in which secrecy may contribute indirectly to both increased dissatisfaction with pay and lower motivation to perform a management job effectively. Secrecy allows a manager to avoid the responsibility of communicating to his subordinates his evaluation of their performance.

An example of what can and frequently does happen is that a manager who has to distribute raises capitalizes upon secrecy to avoid what he considers to be an unpleasant task. The manager does differentially distribute raises among his subordinates on the basis of their performance. So far, so good! However, when he explains the raises to his subordinates, if he does this at all, he tells all of them that he has given them as large a raise as he could and that he is satisfied with their performance. The manager may reason that he has done the right thing. "After all," he thinks, "I did reward good performance with higher pay and I didn't cause any unhappiness as I would have if I had told the poor performers how dissatisfied I was with them."

However, the differential raises have no positive effect since they do nothing to encourage the perception that pay is based upon performance. The good performer is not sure he is getting a larger raise than the poor performer, and the poor performer may feel he is being rewarded for the type of performance he has been demonstrating. Eventually, of course, the word begins to get around about how much other people got in raises (undoubtedly slightly inflated), and this information is bound to make a number of managers unhappy with their pay, as well as distrustful of their superiors.

The secrecy policies of organizations and the consequent tendency for managers to estimate incorrectly the pay of other managers may also affect the managers' motivation to perform their jobs effectively in other ways. Several studies have shown that accurate feedback about task performance is a strong stimulus to good job performance.[14] People perform better when they receive accurate information about how well they are performing relative to some meaningful standard. For managers, pay is one of the most significant and meaningful pieces of feedback information they receive. High pay is considered a sign that the manager's job performance is good. Low pay is a signal that the manager is not performing his job well and that new behavior is needed.

The results of this study indicate that, because managers have misperceptions about what other managers earn, they are unable to evaluate correctly their own pay. Because of the tendency managers have to overestimate the pay of their subordinates and peers, the majority of the managers see their pay as low and in effect are receiving negative feedback. Moreover, although this feedback suggests that they should change their job behavior, it does not tell them what type of change they should make in their behavior. In cases where managers are not doing their jobs well, this negative feedback is undoubtedly the type of information that should be communicated; in other instances, it gives a false signal to change to those managers who are performing their jobs effectively.

Reduced Motivation?

Increased pay is one of the most significant rewards that an individual receives in return for taking on the responsibilities and work associated with higher-level management jobs and, therefore, is one of the important incentives in motivating managers to work toward obtaining higher-level jobs. However, as pointed out earlier, our data indicate that managers tend to underestimate the pay of managers at higher levels. This has the effect of making the attainment of higher-level jobs less desirable because it causes managers to underestimate the rewards that are attached to the positions. Thus, the secrecy policies of organizations may be indirectly reducing the motivation of managers to gain higher-level jobs.

If, as the evidence indicates, secrecy policies have significant costs in terms of job satisfaction, motivation for effective job performance, and motivation for promotion, does it not seem logical that organizations should alter these policies? Perhaps organizations that now have secrecy policies could give out information on pay ranges and average salaries for all management levels. If they started by giving out only partial salary information, they could better prepare their employees for full disclosure, and eventually the salaries of all members of an organization should be made available to all other members of that organization. It may well be better to provide an individual with accurate information upon which to make pay comparisons than to have him make unfavorable comparisons based upon misinformation.

Role of Fringe Benefits

When any organization is asked to determine how much money it spends on compensation, it usually adds the money spent for salaries and fringe benefits. Similarly, an organization determines how much money an individual earns by adding his salary and the costs to them of his benefit package. Union contracts are typically spoken of as settlements involving an *x* cents per hour compensation package. Implicit in these measures of compensation cost is the assumption that a dollar spent on cash salary is equal to a dollar spent on life insurance or other fringe benefits. From an economic standpoint and in terms of costs to the organization, it seems reasonable that the value of a compensation package is equal to the simple sum of all its parts. It is probably the reason why 45 per cent of the managers sampled endorse the view that managers are not greatly concerned with how their pay is divided among various fringe benefits.

However, I would like to suggest that dollars spent on the different parts of the compensation package may not be equal in terms of what they earn in the recipient's perception of the value of his compensation package. Several studies have shown that individuals value some compensation benefits more than others, even though the cost to the company is the same.[15] For example, one study found that employees strongly preferred receiving hospital insurance to receiving additional pension money even though the insurance and the pension plan cost the organization the same amount. In effect a dollar spent on compensation can have a different value to the recipient, depending upon the type of benefit the organization chooses to buy with it.

The studies on compensation preferences among both workers and managers show that the preferences of individuals for different benefits vary greatly, depending upon such factors as their age, sex, number of children, and marital status. For example, older workers value pension plans much more highly than do younger workers, and unmarried men value a shorter work week more highly than do married men. These studies suggest that, at the very least, organizations may need different benefit packages in different locations, depending upon the personal characteristics of the workers in each installation.

A further step that organizations could take would be to design different packages for groups of individuals who have similar characteristics. Indeed, it may be that the optimum solution to this problem of different compensation preferences is for organizations to adopt a "cafeteria" compensation program. A "cafeteria" compensation plan would allow every employee to divide his compensation dollars among the benefits offered by his company. This would allow each employee to select the compensation options that he values most without adding to the compensation costs of the company. Previously, such a program would have been impractical because of the high costs that would be involved. However, with the advent of the computer, it is possible.

"Buffet" Benefits?

"Cafeteria" wage plans would appear to have a particularly bright future among managers where union negotiations and contracts are not likely to be a hindrance. "Cafeteria" wage plans have two additional benefits that strongly argue for their use.

First, they allow employees to participate in an important decision about their jobs. Even among managers, opportunities for actual participation as contrasted with pseudo-participation are rare enough so that in every situation where participation can be legitimately and reasonably employed, it should be.

Second, "cafeteria" wage plans help to make clear to the employees just how much money is involved in their total compensation package. There are many reports of situations where employees do not even know of the fringe benefits for which their organizations are paying. With "cafeteria" wage plans, this situation would be virtually eliminated.

Research Conclusions

What are the lessons to be learned from the recent research on the psychological aspects of compensation practices? I believe that the following conclusions are warranted.

- Even at the higher paid levels of management, pay is important enough to be a significant motivator of good job performance. However, it will be a motivator only when it is seen by the managers themselves to be tied to their job performance.

- Managers can be, and in fact frequently are, satisfied with their pay when it compares favorably with the pay of other managers holding similar positions.

- Secrecy policies have significant hidden costs attached to them. The evidence indicates that secrecy may lead to lower satisfaction with pay and to a decreased motivation for promotion.

- In order to get the maximum value for money spent on compensation, organizations may have to institute "cafeteria" wage payment systems. Such a system would allow each manager to select the benefits that have the greatest value to him.

What the Future Holds

Will organizations be willing to innovate in the area of salary administration and to implement such programs as "cafeteria" wage plans and openness about salary levels? This question can finally be answered only five or ten years from now when we will know what the wage program of the future looks like. However, there are at least two reasons for believing that organizations will be slow to consider these new programs.

First, as one critic has put it, most organizations seem intent on keeping their compensation programs up with, but never ahead of, the Joneses in a sort of "me too" behavior.[16] It is unfortunate that many organizations got so badly "burned" when they tried to install incentive wage schemes that ignored needs other than that of money. Undoubtedly, this experience has led to the current air of conservatism that exists where innovation with regard to salary administration is concerned.

Second, since none of the implications for practice that have been drawn from the results of this group of studies offers a miraculous cure for the present ills of any organizations' compensation program, slow movement may be desirable. These studies imply that there may be better ways to do things, but they also imply that there may be costs and risks involved in trying these new policies.

For example, the idea of eliminating secrecy, no matter how well handled, will probably cause problems for some employees. In particular, openness will be difficult for the relatively low-paid managers to handle. But I believe that the gains would outweigh the costs and that there would be an over-all gain in motivation as a result of openness with regard to pay. I am led to this belief because, by making pay information public, pay can become an effective satisfier of such needs as esteem and recognition and thereby become optimally effective as a stimulant of effective performance. The same general point is true about "cafeteria" wage plans or tying pay more clearly to performance. There are certain costs that are associated with this type of innovative behavior, but there are also large potential gains possible where practices are successfully installed.

I have found that the top management of organizations is always questioning and testing the value of their present compensation systems, and I hope that the ideas and research results presented here will be of aid in this process of inquiry and self-correction.

Notes

1. This is not to imply that the leading figures in the "human relations" movement do not understand the importance of pay. But, by emphasizing other rewards and by not dealing explicitly with the role of pay, they have opened the door for others to interpret their writings as implying that pay is unimportant.

2. It should be pointed out that neither Maslow nor any of the leading figures in the "human relations" movement has stated that pay satisfies only lower-order needs. Others make the interpretation that it satisfies only lower-order needs (e.g., Robert B. McKersie, "Wage Payment Methods of the Future," *British Journal of Industrial Relations,* I [March 1963], 191–212).

3. Edward E. Lawler and Lyman W. Porter, "Perceptions Regarding Management Compensation," *Industrial Relations,* III (Oct. 1963), 41–49; and M. Scott Myers, "Who Are Your Motivated Workers?" *Harvard Business Review,* XLII (Jan.–Feb., 1964), 72–88.

4. Arch Patton, *Men, Money, and Motivation* (New York: McGraw-Hill Book Co., Inc., 1961), p. 34.

5. Lyman W. Porter, "A Study of Perceived Need Satisfaction in Bottom and Middle Management Jobs," *Journal of Applied Psychology,* XLV (Feb. 1961), 1–10.

6. Wilfred Brown, *Piecework Abandoned* (London: Heineman and Co. Ltd., 1962), p. 15.

7. There is evidence that the law of effect can work where a clearly perceived relationship between the behavior and the reward does not exist. However, the important point is that rewards are maximally effective when they are seen as being clearly tied to the behavior that they are intended to reward. (See, e.g., John A. McGeoch and Arthur L. Irion, *The Psychology of Human Learning* [New York: Longmans, Green and Co., 1952].)

8. Thomas A. Mahoney, "Compensation Preferences of Managers," *Industrial Relations,* III (May 1964), 135–144.

9. Frederick Herzberg, Bernard Mausner, and Barbara Bloch Snyderman, *The Motivation to Work* (New York: John Wiley and Sons, 1959).

10. J. Stacy Adams, "Wage Inequities, Productivity and Work Quality," *Industrial Relations,* III (Oct. 1963), 9–16.

11. Edward E. Lawler and Lyman W. Porter, *op. cit.*

12. The presidents in this sample tended to come from smaller companies and, hence, the relatively low-level of their compensation.

13. Further support for this interpretation comes from the finding that there was a significant tendency for those managers who had an accurate picture of their subordinates' pay to be more satisfied with their own pay than were those managers who had an inaccurate picture of their subordinates' pay ($r = .35$, $p = .01$).

14. Victor H. Vroom, *Work and Motivation* (New York: John Wiley and Sons, 1964).

15. Stanley M. Nealey, "Pay and Benefit Preference," *Industrial Relations,* III (Oct. 1963), 17–28; Thomas A. Mahoney, *op. cit.;* and I. R. Andrews and Mildred M. Henry, "Management Attitudes Toward Pay," *Industrial Relations,* III (Oct. 1963), 29–39.

16. Marvin D. Dunnette and Bernard M. Bass, "Behavioral Scientists and Personnel Management," *Industrial Relations,* III (May 1963), 115–130.

F. TRAINING AND DEVELOPMENT

The readings in this section are concerned with the changing role of training and development and with some of the limitations of the techniques used to change management behavior. Part Seven will review change and development strategies or techniques.

Lippitt (Selection 25) outlines the forces of the 1970's which will affect training and development activities in organizations. Although he specifically develops the changes these forces will bring to training and development professionals, we feel his "look into the future" is meaningful for all managers. The reader may find it interesting to compare the similarities and differences with the earlier article by Myers (Selection 4) which discusses management decisions for the next decade.

House (Selection 26) presents an in-depth analysis of one type of training. He integrates theory and research to provide us with an understanding of why leadership training can have desirable or dysfunctional consequences with respect to its transfer into managerial performance.

25

Future Trends Affecting the Training and Development Profession

GORDON L. LIPPITT
ASTD

To project the future of the training and development profession and the American Society for Training and Development, it is necessary to examine the trends of the future that will be affecting such changes. Some of the larger trends that we will be confronting will be the greatly increased standard of living in our own country and throughout the world; an increasing gap between those who possess power and money and those that are unable to exert influence and are poor; a rapid increase in the world population; continued changes in our value systems; the increased influence of local, state and federal government; an increasing expression of desire for influence in power by minority groups by age, sex, and race; a continued increase in the influence of mass media; the extensive development of education as it applies to continued growth and development; a shift from the production to service economy; a continued increase in technology; the development of new avocations and vocations in society; increased international interdependence; continuation of the East-West conflict; an increased mobility of people with a lessening of commitment to an organization or community; an increased size of the social systems of mankind so that there will be a greater feeling of powerlessness on the part of members of such institutions.

In this, the 25th anniversary issue of the ASTD *Journal,* it is appropriate to explore the implications of the key changes confronting our United States as they impact on the role of training and development. I wish to examine some issues that have risen out of our technological revolution, civil rights revolution, student revolution, moral revolution, and the anti-establishment revolution that is so much in the center of our social economic forces in today's America. The issues that arise from these causes will create for those of us in the training and development field some major changes in the way we prepare ourselves for our jobs, the way we conduct our jobs and the criteria for determining our effectiveness.

What are the implications of these trends for the training profession? What are the implications for the American Society for Training and Development?

1. Organizations Will Require New Structures and New Processes to Cope with Change

Organizations of the future will become increasingly complex in terms of size, financial resources, manpower utilization and product diversification. Traditional structures will not be adequate. Organizations need to use "temporary systems." Task forces, project groups and other such operations will be required to help an organization adapt and react to its environment. To permit an organization to be proactive rather than reactive, matrix organization concepts will emerge. This will provide the flexibility to utilize resources wherever they can be found to effectively meet the needs of the organization. A greater emphasis will be placed on processes and systems within the organization that will permit self-renewing activities and innovation. The implications of this trend for education and development are:

a. Training and development professionals will have to understand and learn to apply the principle of matrix organizations. We will need to recognize that many early organization theories and assumptions are obsolete. Training and development will proceed from the assumption that people can and should be used anywhere in the organization that their talents are required. Focus will be on getting the job done. Systematic efforts will be made to present emphasis on working through organizational channels which tend to choke and prevent organizational growth and effectiveness.

b. Training professionals must learn to make organization analysis and to interpret the results for management.

c. Trainers must place greater emphasis on being communications linkers within the organization.

d. Training and development people must focus attention on helping people become comfortable in the presence of change and to work effectively within organizations characterized by continuous change.

2. Many Jobs and Skills Will Become Obsolete

The obsolescence rate of people in the organization of the future will make it necessary for individuals to cope with change in their own lives, careers, and organizations. We will need to confront the reality that people must have second and third careers in order to keep up with the rapid change required in the job and manpower market. The continued rapid growth of a service-oriented society will change the complexity and nature of many organizations and jobs. The implications for education and training are:

a. There must be a better balance between focus on individuals and focus on organization development, so that we may assist the organization to adapt more effectively in meeting its objectives and utilizing its human resources more creatively.

b. New methods of training and development will place greater emphasis on creativity and innovation. It will become increasingly futile to teach for jobs already in existence.

c. In assuming responsibility for organizational and individual diagnosis in the adaptive process, training professionals will need to use effectively both line and staff people.

d. Training and development people will place greater emphasis on their own development and the professionalism which will be required to face the needs of organizational change.

3. People Will Insist on a Greater Opportunity to be a Meaningful Part of the Organization

People will expect a chance to influence the position and role that they perform in the organization. They will want to be part of an organization that is relevant to the problems of the day and to the community. The old way of inducing people to be loyal to the organization will no longer be appropriate. Individuals will be increasingly concerned with their own self-actualization and will be loyal to themselves rather than to organizations. Organizations will need to capitalize on this motivation by structuring jobs to allow a greater sense of self-fulfillment and job enrichment. In addition, organizations will be able to secure individual commitment and loyalty only if they show relevance of the work and the company objectives to both individual aspirations and social objectives.

Many implications for training and development personnel derive from this trend:

a. They must find ways to appeal to individual motivations and their sense of achievement.

b. They must help people within the organization to establish targets and achieve them. This will involve helping people "to do their own thing."

c. They should begin to see the organization as a system designed to release human energy rather than to control human energy.

d. They must realize that organizations, like individuals, pass through levels of maturity, and that very often they get bogged down at the level of maintaining the status quo when they should be growing toward a mastery of change.

e. They must help the organization set targets and objectives, particularly in relation to the development of human resources.

4. Conflict, Confrontation, Coping, and Feedback Will Continue as a Way of Life

We must begin to recognize that confrontation is not a "bad" thing, but necessarily a way in which people "lay it on the line" and "tell it as it is." Millions of good productive ideas have been lost in organizations where the climate does not allow for honest differences in judgments and opinions. Many times pertinent points of view are "filtered out" before they get to top management. We must strive to avoid a win-lose concept in organizational and societal life and substitute wherever possible, the concept of win-win. Openness, candor, and frank feedback should not be equated with hostility or obstructionism. Quite the contrary: those who shut off the ideas and contributions of their subordinates are really the obstructionists. We will find an increasing need to use confrontation and conflict in a constructive way. People are no longer ready to blindly accept the judgment or actions of bosses, superiors or organizational leaders. The implications for education and training of this trend are:

a. Training and development personnel must help people learn how to handle conflict and to recognize that this is not simply a technique of "how to fight."

b. As professionals, we must avoid hang-ups in terms of expressing and implementing convictions solely because they meet our own "needs."

c. Training directors must be willing to confront managers with the insistence that clear-cut objectives be identified before any commitment is made to a specific training program.

d. Training professionals must learn to help others free themselves of hang-ups, as well as learning how to free themselves.

e. Training professionals should focus attention on changing the rewards systems in organizations as a means of rewarding new kinds of behavior and affecting organization change.

f. The training manager must help the organization determine when confrontation and conflict are appropriate and how they can be used constructively.

5. The Explosion of Knowledge and Technology Will Continue

The rapid increase of knowledge and the technological revolution makes it increasingly evident that education must be viewed as a continuing life-long process. We will need to avoid preoccupation with terminal degrees and place greater emphasis on continued education. We must find the means for involving the whole man on the job so that work and life become more meaningfully related. In this context, we must recognize that money alone is an insufficient motivator. Work itself must be viewed as a basic source of satisfaction. Organizational objectives, individual performance objectives and training objectives will need to be integrated; and in training, process and content must be integrated.

The implications of this trend are:

a. Training and development must help people learn how to learn. This will require focus on people being able to analyze the values inherent in their experiences.

b. People must have a greater control over their own development and learning processes.

c. Training professionals should take a searching look at their present program designs.

d. Training personnel should view themselves more as managers of training and development resources, and less as teachers.

6. There is a Need for Greater Interface Between Government, Education, and Industry

Increased interface between these three major segments of society will create problems. A better way will be needed to sense and identify the emerging problems before they become overwhelming. Opportunities for cross collaboration between education, industry and government will be required. Interchanging personnel among these organizational systems will increase.

The implication of this trend will be that training and development personnel will move in and out of specific training positions. They will widen their perspective by working in various types of organizational systems and develop collaborative skills with organizational systems other than their own. The trainer must learn where to turn to gain the benefits from this kind of interchange.

7. The Emergence of Under-utilized Groups Must be Recognized

Inadequate use of minority group members, such as blacks, Mexicans, Puerto Ricans, women, and older workers, will be a constant challenge in an evolving and changing society. There will be pressure to evolve manpower utilization opportunities for the use of the total manpower resources of the country. Under-utilized resources must be recognized at both individual and organizational levels. We must recognize that the middle-class puritan work ethic under which we probably were raised may be an inappropriate frame of reference for understanding the development problems of persons raised outside of this ethic.

The implications for education and training are obvious. We must learn to communicate with, and to develop ways for recognizing human potential in all persons in the various cultures of our society. The role of attitudes in the utilization of human potential must be recognized and techniques developed for minimizing prejudice in the work situation. New ways to interpret and train people for the world of work will be required. This will require an ever-continuing involvement in creating new designs for effectively developing the capabilities of human resources.

Looking Ahead

On this 25th Anniversary of ASTD, we confront many changes that will require effective search for meaningful response from our professional field. We may very well find that the word *training* may itself become obsolescent and that programs of individual and organization development emerge as the two foci of organization and personal change. We will see the need to examine the location within the organizational structure of the training and development function. We will see revisions and changes in job descriptions that are now obsolete in terms of their inability to be functional toward an organic system. These trends will have many challenges for us as professionals.

• There will be an increased need and emphasis on professional management of social systems throughout society. This will have direct implication for the increased development and training of people to serve as professional managers in all types of organizations, groups, communities and social systems.

• Those in the training profession will be required to increase their knowledge and skills about social systems and the process of change. Training people can be key persons in bringing about organizational change and renewal.

• Need for a greater emphasis in the training profession on helping persons cope with the various changes in their occupational and personal life.

• A greater emphasis on the need for organization development. Training people will need to develop their skills to take a look at the social system as a totality and change the organization in a "holistic" manner.

• The creation and use of innovational methods that will make training different in the future. Much of the training work will be oriented toward individual, group and organizational confrontation. Training directors of the future will do much of their work out of their own homes and through the media of various electronic communication methodology.

• Greater utilization of the multiple disciplines and resources throughout society in getting the goals of training and development achieved.

• A focus on the problem-solving process through confrontation, search and coping. The reality that time is at a premium and the modern problems are so tremendous that we cannot play "games" in achieving the solution of man's problems, and that training should focus more rapidly on helping an individual, group or organization confront their problems rather than be satisfied only with a gradualistic process of change.

These are but some of the predictions that seem indicated in the life of the training director of the future. The implications for the American Society for Training and Development are clear. We will need to revise much of our methodology, programs, and means of accomplishing our services. Our membership will increase threefold in the next ten years as the profession emerges as a fully recognized group interested in using the educational process in an action manner to help organizations, groups and individuals develop and grow. Regional centers and offices of ASTD with activities at a decentralized basis seem indicated. More services and creativity in innovations and education will be forthcoming from the ASTD organization of the future. We will need to confront these changes with all the wisdom, conviction and dedication that we can bring to bear.

Socrates once commented "The life unexamined is not worth living." It is also true that as we confront the next 25 years of ASTD that "The profession unexamined is not worthy of being one." Continued examination of the goals, procedures, and processes by which ASTD serves its members and its profession will be required by all of us. It is to be hoped that the words of that friendly philosopher, Pogo, will never apply to the training profession — "We have met the enemy, and they is us."

26

Leadership Training: Some Dysfunctional Consequences

ROBERT J. HOUSE
The City University of New York
The McKinsey Foundation for Management Research

In 1955, Philip Selznick stated that, "The whole program of leadership training and generally of forming and maintaining elites should receive a high priority in scientific studies of organization and policy."[1] The need for additional study of this problem training is revealed by some dysfunctional consequences of leadership training programs in large industrial and government organizations. Leadership-training programs have successfully increased the managerial motivations required in hierarchical organizations;[2] they have resulted in changing bureaucratic decision-making behavior of government officials;[3] and they have improved the social skills of leaders in relations with employees.[4] However, leadership training has also resulted in dysfunctional consequences for both the trainees and their organizations. Fleishman, Harris, and Burtt found that attempts to teach human relations principles resulted in both the intended change of opinions and in role

Taken and adapted from *Administrative Science Quarterly*, Vol. 12, No. 4, March 1968, pp. 556–571. Used by permission.

conflict for the trainees. The role conflict resulted from lack of congruence between the concepts taught in the training program and the behavior of their superiors.[5] A study by Sykes showed that although leadership training resulted in the intended change in role expectations of the trainees,[6] the newly formed expectations were so much in conflict with those of superiors that within one year after the course, nineteen of the 97 participating supervisors had left the company and twenty-five had applied for jobs outside the firm.

The purpose of this paper is to explain how the effects of leadership training depend on structural variables in complex organizations, to describe these structural variables, and to advance a proposition that explains and permits prediction of the consequences of leadership training in varying situations.

Complex organizations have structural properties and mechanisms that serve both to support and to hinder the effectiveness of leadership training. How the structure and mechanisms interact with the effect of leadership training, and the conditions under which leadership training can be expected to have functional or dysfunctional consequences can be interpreted in terms of psychological and sociological consequences.

Leadership-training programs may take any of several forms, but such training almost always implies the need for some change in the attitudes or behavior of the trainee. The programs are designed to bring about a change in the knowledge, attitudes, skills, or performance of trainees, and may also be used to change entire organizational units. For the trainee, the change is usually intended to: (1) improve his performance in his present position, (2) prepare him for the future requirements of his present position, or (3) prepare him to meet the requirements of promotion to a higher position.

Leadership training, as a method of change, differs from other methods in that it relies on learning and attitude formation as the major path toward behavior change. Other methods frequently rely on power, as for example, in bargaining; replacement of poor performers; realignment of responsibilities; or realignment of structural factors such as authority, policies, procedures, or controls. Change resulting from leadership training involves a commitment on the part of the trainee. Once attained, it is likely to be sustained over a longer period of time and without the use of organizational controls. When the trainee's commitment is in conflict with the prevailing value system of important reference groups, however, or when his commitment conflicts with the reward or punishment system of the organization, dysfunctional consequences result. Change based on power is likely to be sustained *only* as long as those exerting power maintain surveillance over the behavior of the subordinates. It also results in dysfunctions for the organization, but these are different from those resulting from leadership training, because the shifted subordinates are not committed to the values represented by the imposed change. When power is used, the shifted subordinates themselves become the source of resistance; when training is used, the trainees become the *object of resistance* from other parts of the organization.

Social Influences

In complex organizations, the social influences that serve to constrain or support leadership training arise from the formal authority system, the exercise of formal authority by the superiors of the trainee, and the primary work group of the trainee. Conflict between these influences and the attitudes or behavior taught in leadership training account for many of the dysfunctional consequences of training.

Formal Authority System

The formal authority system consists of the formal structural properties of the organization — the philosophy, practices, and precedents of policy-making executives. It is usually expressed in the legitimized practices and decision rules and the mechanisms by which formal authority is allocated — by policies, procedures, and position descriptions — and enforced — by performance appraisal and control systems. The formal practices of the organization influence organizational effectiveness and group cohesion,[7] and affect trainee attitudes[8] as well as the outcome of leadership training.[9]

The formal authority system represents the legitimate source of organizational rewards and punishments. For example, in an organization designed to decentralize authority, managers need to be able to delegate effectively. They are thus likely to be receptive to instruction about delegation practices, whereas managers in organizations with highly centralized authority are less likely to be motivated either to study or to accept delegation practices taught in leadership-training programs. In highly centralized organizations, trainees who have become predisposed toward delegating authority are likely to experience a conflict between their attitudes and the formal organization. They may try to modify the prevailing system, but attempts to change the formal authority system imply discontent and may be interpreted as disloyalty or as a threat to the prevailing hierarchy. When thus interpreted, negative sanctions may be applied to the trainee's superiors. This example illustrates how the formal authority system can be seen as a source of motivation to learn and to change behavior, as a potential constraint on behavioral change, and as a source of conflict or satisfaction for the trainee.

Exercise of Formal Authority by Superiors

Superiors influence trainees through their exercise of formal authority; i.e., through their right to administer rewards and punishments.[10] The most influential superior is usually the one in the hierarchical structure to whom the trainee reports directly. There is evidence that subordinates tend to: act as their superiors act,[11] have attitudes similar to those of their superiors,[12] and act in response to their perception of their superiors' desires.[13] For example, consider again the organization with a formal system designed to foster decentralization of authority. In such organizations, one occasionally finds top or middle managers who refuse to delegate substantial decision prerogatives to their subordinates. Trainees under such managers are less likely to attempt to apply delegation skills when they return to the job. The exercise of formal authority by superiors thus serves as an important social influence over the outcome of the training efforts and mediates the impact of the formal structural factors on the learner.

Kelman's theory of social influence[14] can be used to explain the mechanisms by which the superior exercises authority over his subordinates. First, the superior has the formal (legal) authority of his position, so that he can make crucial decisions about the career of his subordinates and thereby *extract compliance*. Second, the superior has an opportunity for frequent, if not constant, face-to-face contact with his subordinates; therefore, he has the advantage of proximity and personal relationship. If he can convince his subordinates that certain kinds of behavior are intrinsically rewarding in themselves, he can influence them to internalize his values. Finally, the subordinate tends to identify with the superior, to emulate his practices, and to look to him for example, coaching, guidance, and direction. Thus the superior may serve as a social-learning model for his subordinates.

Certain characteristics of the superior will influence the subordinate. The first is the level of knowledge of the superior. If he does not understand what is being taught to the trainee, it will be necessary for the trainee to train his own superior rather than vice versa, if knowledge or attitude change are to be translated into actual job performance. However, if the superior has a previous understanding of the program content, he will have a better basis for understanding any changed attitude or behavior of the trainee. Secondly, the attitudes of the superior condition the attitudes of the subordinates toward development and toward the acceptance of the principles taught in the program.

The overt management practices of the superior also influence the trainee. He cannot be expected to delegate to his subordinates any authority or responsibility that he himself does not have. Thus, the superior's practices of delegation establish a limit for the trainee's practices. If the superior does little long-range planning, it is not likely that the subordinate will be able to plan far ahead, even if he desires to do so. In order to arrive at a long-range plan with a time span in excess of the time span of his superior's plan, the trainee must necessarily ask questions about objectives and policies that will govern his long-range plan. If the superior has not developed such a plan, such questions might be embarrassing or be viewed as impertinent. Even if the superior encourages such questions, he would still not be likely to know the answers, since he has made no long-range plans of his own.

The coaching, counseling, and appraisal practices of superiors are especially pertinent to the development of the trainee. If the superior of a trainee coaches, counsels, and appraises the trainee to ensure adherence to principles taught in the training program, a change in the trainee's performance will be more likely.

Primary Work Group

The expectations of peers and the immediate subordinates of the trainee will also help to determine his attitudes toward the prescriptions taught in the training and his ability to transfer new knowledge and skills into job performance. Coch and French found that the introduction of participative leadership in an American factory resulted in increased productivity, employee cooperation, and satisfaction,[15] whereas in a Norwegian plant it had little effect on the performance or attitudes of work groups.[16] Post-experimental investigation suggested that the difference in the outcomes of the two experiments was due to different worker expectations. In the Norwegian factory, the employees did not view their participation in production decisions as legitimate and therefore were not influenced by the introduction of participative leadership. Similarly, Vroom found that people with high needs for independence and low tendencies toward authoritarianism were more motivated by participative leaders than their opposites.[17] These studies, as well as substantial small-group research, indicate that attempts to train managers in leadership practices that conflict with group norms or subordinate expectations will not only be ineffective, but will be likely to be met with resistance and frequently with open hostility.

A striking example of the effect of peer expectations on managerial attitudes toward training is reported by Burns,[18] based on his observations of informal behavior in a factory. The norm was promotion and the way to promotion lay not only in making the best of the tasks that were handed to one, but in perceiving and acquiring responsibility for new tasks, and, frequently, in encroaching on those of others. Within the factory there emerged a clique of those who resented the competition for promotion. The clique had a specific protective reassurance purpose, which expressed itself in a critical disassociation from the firm and from features of the formal organization such as the bonus system, rate fixing, progress meetings, and the formal communication system. The members of the clique described these practices of the formal organization as "the way the firm does things." A second clique of younger, highly ambitious men also emerged. The juniors attended evening training courses together, and their association was viewed as legitimate in terms of the factory organization, of the industry at large, and of society itself, since they were in common pursuit of technical proficiency.

This case illustrates that the informal group pressures to which the trainee is subjected will significantly influence his attitude toward the training. It further illustrates that when the development program represents values that are opposed to the values of the primary group, it will be viewed with suspicion, its worth will be depreciated, and application of the principles taught in the training program will be strongly resisted.

Dimensions of Social Influences

The three sources of social influence — the formal authority system, the exercise of formal authority, and the norms and expectations of the primary work group — may be evaluated in terms of three dimensions: congruence, clarity, and anxiety. The power of each of the social influences to modify the effect of leadership training is a function of these three dimensions.

Congruence

The congruence between the values represented by the social influences and the intent of the leadership training can be identified by determining the degree to which the social influences reward or punish the trainee for adopting the kinds of behavior or attitudes prescribed in training. The formal authority system in an organization determines the criteria used for performance appraisal, promotion, and compensation, as well as for the allocation of authority, status, and power. The trainee's superiors exercise authority by means of their personal contact with the participant, by allocation of job authority and benefits, and by appraisal. Finally, the primary group exercises reward and punishment pressures by means of norm enforcement. Thus, congruence between prescribed behavior and the formal authority system, the exercise of authority, and group norms is important for predicting trainee expectations and support or resistance offered by the social influences.

Clarity

When it is clear that the behavior taught in leadership training will be instrumental to the trainee in achieving rewards, he will be more motivated to apply it in job situations. The behavior taught in training is made instrumental to the trainee by making the rewards and punishments from the environment contingent upon the transfer of training to the job. This contingency is established and enforced by the three sources of social influence described above. The formal authority system determines the kind and amount of resources available for distribution to the members in the form of rewards. The policies of the formal system define the criteria for reward allocation and the procedures to be followed in making rewards. For example, merit rating and promotion procedures are frequently formalized to ensure some organizational control and some consistency in the allocation of rewards to members.

It is necessary that the contingent rewards be apparent to the trainee, because the more clear the contingent relationship between the trainee's performance and the rewards and punishments, the greater will be the force of the authority system and the exercise of authority by superiors.[19] Similarly, the clarity of group norms, goals, and procedures modifies the power of the primary group to influence the behavior of its members.[20] Clear, unambiguous norms are more easily enforced and followed.

Anxiety

When the trainee is in a state of anxiety as a result of threatening or punitive forces in the environment over which he has little control, his receptiveness to new information will be lower.[21] The abilities required for learning, such as his problem-solving abilities[22] and his ability to recall,[23] will be lower than if he were in a more secure environment. Anxiety has been shown to interfere with learning complex concepts and social skills,[24] both of which are usually taught as part of leadership-training programs.

The three social influences discussed are capable of inducing anxiety as a result of unpredictable and inconsistent policies, role ambiguity, punitive or threatening leadership, and organizational conflict. When the trainee views the policies or the exercise of such policies by his superiors as unfair and inconsistent, or when organizational conflict or uncertainty about the consequences of his acts is so great that anxiety is induced, learning efficiency, as well as the transfer of knowledge, attitudes, and skills into job behavior, will also be impaired.

Dysfunctional Consequences

The dysfunctional consequences of leadership training are psychological and sociological. If the training is administered to only a small number of individuals in the organization, and these individuals have little opportunity to interact with each other on the job, the effect of the training is likely to remain at the psychological level. Such individual training is frequently accomplished by sending a small number of managers to training programs conducted by other organizations, such as universities, professional organizations, or consulting firms. If the training is effective in bringing about changes in attitudes toward work behavior, and if the trainee finds that his newly formed attitudes conflict with the prevailing social influences in the environment, he may choose any of the following courses of action:

1. He may go back to his original methods and style of leadership and give up changing his behavior because the costs associated with such a change are too great and the rewards are too small; that is, he may adopt an attitude of indifference.
2. He may try to modify the environment, in which case his attempts to introduce such changes may be perceived as threatening by higher-status members of the organization, and he will run the risk of reprisal.

3. He may adopt an attitude of despair and seek employment elsewhere.
4. He may decide that the behavior taught in the training programs is desirable, but he will have to wait for a change in the organizational environment before it will be fruitful to practice such behavior; for example, until he changes his position or until his present superior is moved to another position.

Studies of the effects of leadership training have revealed that when the environment does not support the prescriptions taught in the training program, there may be increased role conflict for the trainee,[25] increased trainee grievances and turnover,[26] decreased job performance,[27] and increased stress between the trainee and the members of the organization with whom he must interact.[28]

When the trainee is confronted with some social influence that is contrary to an attitude he adopted as a result of participation in training, such as a rule of the formal authority system, a directive from a superior, or informal pressure from the primary group, he will experience conflict. Since such conflict is confined to the particular situations, he may find that one element of his environment conflicts with an attitude prescribed in the leadership training program, while another supports that attitude. Such conflict may be related both to specific attitudes and to localized situations, such as staff meetings, work-group setting, or personal contact with the superior.

The trainee is subjected to a general level of anxiety that results from the sum of the conflicting forces of the environmental elements, less the support he receives from the environment. This anxiety will affect his overall personal adjustment to his job.

There are, undoubtedly, amounts of conflict that are sufficient to disturb the equilibrium within an organization and thereby increase efforts toward or readiness for change. The same kind of conflict, in sufficiently large amounts, is likely to cause disruption and have deleterious effects on organizational performance and managerial health. The effects of conflict, and the conditions under which such conflict is likely to be beneficial or harmful to the trainee or the organization have not yet been explained by either theory or empirical research. Obviously such effects depend heavily on the emotional state of the trainee, his cognitive and managerial style, and the level of his knowledge and skill, as well as the human relationships within the organization.

In addition to these psychological effects, leadership training can have undesirable consequences for group cohesiveness, superior-subordinate relations, intergroup relations, and the formal authority system. If the newly adopted attitudes of the trainee are in conflict with the attitudes of his superior, there will be a need for redefinition of role expectations. Similarly, when the trainee's new attitudes are incongruent with the norms of his primary work group, attempts to change his behavior will result in informal resistance by others, will evoke norm enforcement upon him, and may lower the cohesiveness of the group.

Frequently, training efforts are designed specifically to meet the needs of the sponsoring organization and are administered within the organization to a large proportion of its leaders. Such training is more likely to bring about changes in group norms and significant pressures to change the formal structural arrangements for administering the organization. For example, Sykes[29] reports that as a result of participation in the supervisory training program mentioned, trainees changed their expectations of the foreman's role and found the existing communication and compensation practices of the organization incompatible with their newly formed role expectations. They then presented the top executives of the organization with a list of complaints about these practices and a list of suggestions for change. Failure on the part of the top executives to implement these suggestions resulted in increased foremen dissatisfaction, so that nineteen left the firm and twenty-five others sought other jobs. Twelve of those who left and fifteen of those seeking other jobs said that their action was precipitated by the program.

When the training is given to the managers of entire organizational units, not only can it influence the norms of the unit but it may also change its formal rules and practices. With such changes, there is again a need to redefine relationships with other units within the organization. Buchanan[30] reports a case in which leadership training resulted in changing the norms and the organizational practices of an entire organizational unit, only to result in increased stress between that unit and other groups within the firm. Since the top management of the organization did not support the new norms or practices, the head of the department was replaced and the trainees became highly dissatisfied.

Relative Weights of Social Influence Variables

This analysis suggests several questions relevant to a better understanding of leadership training in complex organizations. What are the relative weights of each of the three social influences? Under what conditions will the establishment of policies and the behavior of superiors result in cancelling each other out, or does the existence of merely one supportive social influence provide sufficient motivation and reinforcement to ensure desired change? What kinds of social influences are most effective for motivating and rewarding changed behavior?

Although there is little evidence on these questions, there is good theorectical basis for speculation. The behavior taught in leadership training may have implications for social and normative integration of the organization and for procurement and allocation of resources. Instruction about leadership styles, human-relations practices, and social skills will generally be viewed as having normative or social implications; whereas training concerned with administrative practices and skills, such as economic analysis, applications of mathematical techniques for decision making, and long-range planning, will be viewed as having implications for resource input and allocation. Some topics taught in leadership-training programs are likely to have both kinds of implications. For example, concepts concerned with management selection and development, delegation of authority, management compensation, design of organization structure, and administrative control are all likely to have implications for the allocation of symbolic rewards and power, as well as implications for the procurement and allocation of resources.

Etzioni[31] points out that since expressive behavior — behavior directed at normative and social integration — requires moral involvement, it is most effectively controlled by those who have the power to withhold or allocate symbolic rewards. And, since instrumental behavior — behavior directed at resource input and allocation — requires calculative involvement, it is most effectively controlled by those who have power to withhold or allocate financial and material rewards. Applying this rationale to leadership training, one can deduce that superiors will have influence over instrumental behavior only if the formal authority system makes it possible for the superior to allocate rewards to the trainee. Where the instrumental behavior taught in training is not congruent with the formal authority system, the superior must depend on the use of symbolic rewards, which are not likely to be effective for influencing instrumental behavior. Conversely, changes in expressive behavior depend primarily on the support of the members of the work group and of superiors who have informal influence as well as control of formal sanctions over the trainee. The formal authority system cannot control symbolic rewards such as coworker acceptance or recognition; consequently, it can be expected to have relatively little effect on changing expressive behavior. And superiors who are rejected by the work group cannot be expected to have influence over the expressive behavior of the learner.

Finally, one might speculate on the most effective combinations of social influence. For instrumental behavior, a congruent formal authority system appears to be a necessary, but not a sufficient condition, requiring in addition the congruent exercise of authority by superiors. For expressive behavior, the most effective combination seems to be supportive behavior by superiors accepted by the work group, plus congruent work-group norms. And, opposition of the work group would be expected to offset any influence by the superior.

Conclusion

Social influences in the work environment explain why leadership training produces both functional and dysfunctional consequences. A general proposition may be drawn from the empirical literature: *The consequences of leadership training depend on the degree to which the social influences in the trainee's work environment are viewed by the trainee as motivations to learn and the degree to which they reinforce the learned behavior during and after training.*

If trainee capabilities are taken as given, and if the prescriptions taught in the training have validity for improving job performance, the effects of leadership training can be predicted from structural factors within the organization. Specifically, the authority structure, the manner in which authority is exercised, and the norms of the trainee's primary work group can be analyzed into their motivational and reinforcement effects and assessed from: (1) their congruence with the prescriptions of the training, (2) the clarity of their relevance to trainee reward and punishment, and (3) their tendency to induce anxiety in the trainee.

Notes

1. P. Selznick, *Leadership in Administration: A Sociological Interpretation* (New York: Harper, 1957).
2. D. C. McClelland, "Achievement Motivation Can Be Developed," *Harvard Business Review,* 43 (November–December 1965), 6–16, 20–24, 178; J. B. Miner, *Studies in Management Education* (New York: Springer, 1965).
3. H. Guetzkow, G. A. Forehand, and B. J. James, "An Evaluation of Educational Influence on Administrative Judgment," *Administrative Science Quarterly,* 6 (1962), 483–500.
4. D. R. Bunker, "Individual Applications of Laboratory Training," *Journal of Applied Behavioral Science,* 1 (1965), 131–148; M. B. Miles, "Changes During and Following Laboratory Training: A Clinical Experimental Study," *Journal of Applied Behavioral Sciences,* 1 (1965), 215–242; W. J. Underwood, "Evaluation of Laboratory-Method Training," *Training Directors Journal,* 19 (1965), 34–40; H. Sherman, "Reducing Grievances Through Supervisory Training," in E. E. Jennings (ed.) *Wisconsin Commerce Reports, No. 3* (Madison: Bureau of Business Research, The University of Wisconsin, 1952).
5. E. A. Fleishman, E. Harris, and H. Burtt, "Leadership and Supervision in Industry" (Columbus, Ohio, 1955: Monograph No. 33, Bureau of Educational Research, Ohio State University).
6. A. J. Sykes, "The Effects of a Supervisory Training Course in Changing Supervisors' Perceptions and Expectations of the Role of Management," *Human Relations,* 15 (1962), 227–243.
7. A. L. Comrey, J. M. Pfiffner, and W. S. High, "Factors Influencing Organizational Effectiveness," mimeo. (Los Angeles: University of Southern California, 1954); P. M. Blau, and W. R. Scott, *Formal Organizations* (San Francisco: Chandler, 1962); S. J. Udy, Jr., "Bureaucratic Elements in Organizations: Some Research Findings," *American Sociological Review,* 23 (1958), 415–418.
8. S. Lieberman, "The Effects of Changes in Roles on the Attitudes of Role Occupants," *Human Relations,* 9 (1956), 385–402.

9. A. J. Sykes, *op. cit.;* T. Hariton, "Conditions Influencing the Effects of Training Foremen in New Human Relations Principles," unpublished Ph.D. dissertation (Ann Arbor: University of Michigan, 1951); F. C. Mann, "Studying and Creating Change: A Means to Understanding Social Organization," in *Research in Industrial Human Relations* (Madison, Wis.: Industrial Relations Research Association, 7 (1957); H. C. Triandis, "Attitude Change Through Training in Industry," *Human Organization,* 7 (1958), 27–30.

10. H. Meyer and W. Walker, "A Study of Factors Relating to the Effectiveness of a Performance Appraisal Program," *Personnel Psychology,* 14 (Autumn 1961); A. J. Sykes, *op. cit.;* T. Hariton, *op. cit.;* H. C. Triandis, *op. cit.;* E. A. Fleishman, E. Harris, and H. Burtt, *op. cit.*

11. D. Katz and R. L. Kahn, "Leadership Practices in Relation to Productivity and Morale," in D. Cartwright and A. Zander (eds.), *Group Dynamics: Research and Theory* (Evanston: Row, Peterson, 1953); D. Katz, N. M. Maccoby, and N. Morse, *Productivity, Supervision and Morale in an Office Situation* (Ann Arbor: Survey Research Center, University of Michigan, 1950).

12. E. A. Shils, and M. Janowitz, "Cohesion and Disintegration of the Wehrmacht in World War II," *Public Opinion Quarterly,* 12 (1948), 280–315; D. A. Trumbo, "Individual and Group Correlates of Attitude Toward Work-Related Change," *Journal of Applied Psychology,* 44 (1960), 338–344; A. J. Spector, R. A. Clark, and A. S. Glickman, "Supervisory Characteristics and Attitudes of Subordinates," *Personnel Psychology,* 13 (1960), 301–316.

13. H. Rosen, Managerial Role Interaction: "A Study of Three Managerial Levels," *Journal of Applied Psychology,* 45 (1961), 30–34.

14. H. C. Kelman, "Compliance, Identification, and Internalization: Three Processes of Attitude Change," *Journal of Conflict Resolution,* 2 (March 1958), 51–60.

15. L. Coch and J. R. P. French, "Overcoming Resistance to Change," *Human Relations,* 1 (1948), 512–532.

16. J. R. P. French, J. Israel, and D. As, "An Experiment on Participation in a Norwegian Factory," *Human Relations,* 13 (1960), 3–19.

17. Victor Vroom, *Work and Motivation* (New York: John Wiley, 1964).

18. T. Burns, "The Reference of Conduct in Small Groups; Cliques and Cabals in Occupational Milieu," *Human Relations,* 8 (1955), 467–486.

19. B. H. Raven and J. Rietsema, "The Effects of Varied Clarity of Group Goal and Group Path Upon the Individual and His Relation to His Group," *Human Relations,* 10 (1957), 29–45; Basil S. Georgopolous, G. M. Mahoney, and Nyle W. Jones, Jr., "A Path-Goal Approach to Productivity," *Journal of Applied Psychology,* 41 (1957), 345–353.

20. B. H. Raven and J. Rietsema, *op. cit.*

21. Paul R. Robbins, "Level of Anxiety, Interference Proneness, and Defensive Reactions to Fear-Arousing Information, *Journal of Personality,* 31 (1963), 163–178.

22. Probat K. Mukhopadhyay and Indira Malani, "A Comparative Study of Natural and Emotive Sets as Conditions for the Blinding Effects on the Process of Productive Thinking," *Psychological Study* (Mysore) 5 (1960), 90–96.

23. D. Wallen, "Ego-Involvement as a Determinant of Selective Forgetting," *Journal of Abnormal and Social Psychology,* 37 (1942), 20–39.

24. C. D. Spielberger, "The Effects of Anxiety on Complex Learning and Academic Achievement," in C. P. Spielberger (ed.), *Anxiety and Behavior* (New York: Academic, 1966).

25. E. A. Fleishman, E. Harris, and H. Burtt, *op. cit.*

26. A. J. Sykes, *op. cit.*

27. R. J. House, "An Experiment in the Use of Selected Methods for Improving the Effectiveness of Communication Training for Management," unpublished doctoral dissertation (Columbus: Ohio State University, 1960).

28. W. G. Bennis, "A New Role for Behavioral Sciences: Effecting Organizational Change," *Administrative Science Quarterly,* 8 (June 1963), 125–165; P. C. Buchanan, "Evaluating the Effectiveness of Laboratory Training in Industry," paper read at the American Management Association Seminar, New York, February 24–26, 1964; W. J. Underwood, *op. cit.;* E. H. Schein, and W. G. Bennis, *Personal and Organizational Change Through Group Methods: The Laboratory Approach* (New York: John Wiley, 1965).

29. A. J. Sykes, *op. cit.*

30. P. C. Buchanan, *op. cit.*

31. A. Etzioni, *Complex Organizations* (Glencoe, Ill.: Free Press, 1961).

G. EQUITY AND ORGANIZATIONAL JUSTICE

A general theory of inequity, based upon psychological concepts and processes, is presented by Adams (Selection 27). He identifies the conditions under which inequity may occur and the ways of reducing or eliminating it. And he summarizes field studies and laboratory experiments — several of which are based on wage inequities — which test and support certain aspects of his theory.

While Adams focuses on "distributive justice" in the Aristotelian sense, Scott (Selection 28) focuses on "corrective justice." Scott considers the institutional nature of appeal systems by analyzing the different types of appeal programs voluntarily established by top management. The emphasis here is on the formal or informal policies, procedures, and mechanisms for adjudicating grievances or perceived inequities. His discussion does not include grievance systems determined bilaterally between managements and unions.

In sum, Adams and Scott provide us with two of the ways of perceiving and coping with conflict in organizations.

27

Toward an Understanding[1] *of Inequity*

J. Stacy Adams
General Electric Company

Equity, or more precisely, inequity, is a pervasive concern of industry, labor, and government. Yet its psychological basis is probably not fully understood. Evidence suggests that equity is not merely a matter of getting

J. Stacy Adams, "Toward an Understanding of Inequity," *Journal of Abnormal and Social Psychology,* Vol. 67, No. 5, 1963, pp. 422–436.

"a fair day's pay for a fair day's work," nor is inequity simply a matter of being underpaid. The fairness of an exchange between employee and employer is not usually perceived by the former purely and simply as an economic matter. There is an element of relative justice involved that supervenes economics and underlies perceptions of equity or inequity (Homans, 1961; Jaques, 1956, 1961a, 1961b; Patchen, 1961; Stouffer, Suchman, DeVinney, Star, & Williams, 1949; Zaleznik, Christensen, & Roethlisberger, 1958).

The purpose of this paper is to present a theory of inequity, leading toward an understanding of the phenomenon and, hopefully, resulting in its control. Whether one wishes to promote social justice or merely to reduce economically disadvantageous industrial unrest, an understanding of inequity is important. In developing the theory of inequity, which is based upon Festinger's (1957) theory of cognitive dissonance and is, therefore, a special case of it, we shall describe major variables involved in an employee-employer exchange, before we proceed to define inequity formally. Having defined it, we shall analyze its effects. Finally, such evidence as is available will be presented in support of the theory. Throughout we shall emphasize some of the simpler aspects of inequity and try to refrain from speculating about many of the engaging, often complex, relationships between inequity and other phenomena, and about what might be termed "higher order" inequities. In the exposition that follows we shall also refer principally to wage inequities, in part because of their importance and in part because of the availability of methods to measure the marginal utility of wages (Adams, 1961; Jeffrey & Jones, 1961). It should be evident, however, that the theoretical notions advanced are relevant to any social situation in which an exchange takes place, whether the exchange be of the type taking place between man and wife, between football teammates, between teacher and student, or even, between Man and his God.

Whenever two individuals exchange anything, there is the possibility that one or both of them will feel that the exchange was inequitable. Such is frequently the case when a man exchanges his services for pay. On the man's side of the exchange are his education, intelligence, experience, training, skill, seniority, age, sex, ethnic background, social status, and, very importantly, the effort he expends on the job. Under special circumstances other attributes will be relevant: personal appearance or attractiveness, health, possession of an automobile, the characteristics of one's spouse, and so on. They are what he perceives are his contributions to the exchange, for which he expects a just return. Homans (1961) calls them "investments." These variables are brought by him to the job. Henceforth they will be referred to as his *inputs*. These inputs, let us emphasize, are *as perceived by their contributor* and are not necessarily isomorphic with those of the other party to the exchange. This suggests two conceptually distinct characteristics of inputs, *recognition* and *relevance*.

The possessor of an attribute, or the other party to the exchange, or both, may recognize the existence of the attribute in the possessor. If either the possessor or both members of the exchange recognize its existence, the attribute has the potentiality of being an input. If only the nonpossessor recognizes its existence it cannot be considered psychologically an input so far as the possessor is concerned. Whether or not an attribute having the potential of being an input is an input, is contingent upon the possessor's perception of its relevance to the exchange. If he perceives it to be relevant, if he expects a just return for it, it is an input. Problems of inequity arise if only the possessor of the attribute considers it relevant in the exchange. Crozier[2] relates an observation that is apropos. Paris-born bank clerks worked side by side with other clerks who did identical work and earned identical wages, but were born in the Provinces. The Parisians were dissatisfied with their wages, for they considered that Parisian breeding was an input deserving monetary compensation. The bank management, while recognizing that place of birth distinguished the two groups, did not, of course, consider birthplace relevant in the exchange of services for pay.

The principal inputs listed earlier vary in type and in their degree of relationship to one another. Some variables, such as age, are clearly continuous; others, such as sex and ethnicity, are not. Some are intercorrelated, seniority and age, for example; sex, on the other hand, is largely independent of the other variables, with the possible exception of education and some kinds of effort. Although these intercorrelations, or the lack of them, exist in a state of nature, it is probable that the individual cognitively treats all input variables as independent. Thus, for example, if he were assessing the sum of his inputs, he might well "score" age and seniority separately.

On the other side of the exchange are the rewards received by an individual for his services. These *outcomes,* as they will be termed, include pay, rewards intrinsic to the job, seniority benefits, fringe benefits, job status and status symbols, and a variety of formally and informally sanctioned perquisites. An example of the latter is the right of higher status persons to park their cars in privileged locations, or the right to have a walnut rather than a metal desk. Seniority, mentioned as an input variable, has associated with it a number of benefits such as job security, "bumping" privileges, greater fringe benefits, and so on. These benefits are outcomes and are distinguished from the temporal aspects of seniority (that is, longevity), which are properly inputs. As in the case of job inputs, job outcomes are often intercorrelated. For example, greater pay and higher job status are likely to go hand in hand.

In a manner analogous to inputs, outcomes are *as perceived,* and, again, we should characterize them in terms of recognition and relevance. If the recipient or both the recipient and giver of an outcome in an exchange recognize its existence, it has the potentiality of being an outcome psychologically. If the recipient considers it relevant to the exchange and it has some marginal utility for him, it *is* an outcome. Not infrequently the giver or "buyer," to use economic terms, may give or yield something which, perhaps at some cost to him, is either irrelevant or of no marginal utility to the recipient. An employer may give an employee a carpet for his office in lieu, say, of a salary increment and find that the employee is dissatisfied, perhaps because in the subculture of that office a rug has no meaning, no psychological utility. Conversely, a salary increment may be inadequate, if formalized status recognition was what was wanted and was what had greater utility.

In classifying some variables as inputs and others as outcomes, it is not implied that they are independent, except conceptually. Job inputs and outcomes are, in fact, intercorrelated, but imperfectly so. Indeed, it is because they are imperfectly correlated that we need at all be concerned with job inequity. There exist normative expectations of what constitute "fair" correlations between inputs and outcomes. The bases of the expectations are the correlations obtaining for a reference person or group — a co-worker or colleague, a relative or neighbor, a group of co-workers, a craft group, an industry-wide pattern. A bank clerk, for example, may determine whether her inputs and outcomes are fairly correlated — in balance, so to speak — by comparing them with the relationship between the inputs and outcomes of other female clerks in her section. The sole punch press operator in a manufacturing plant may base his judgment on what he believes are the inputs and outcomes of other operators in the community or region. For a particular physicist the relevant reference person may be an organic chemist of the same academic "vintage." While it is clearly important to be able to specify the appropriate reference person or group, it represents a distinct theoretical area in which work has begun (Merton & Kitt, 1950; Patchen, 1961; Stouffer et al., 1949) but which would take this paper too far afield. For the purposes of this paper, it will be assumed that the reference person or group will be one comparable to the comparer on one or more attributes, usually a co-worker.[3]

When the normative expectations of the person making social comparisons are violated — when he finds his inputs and outcomes are not in balance in relation to those of others — feelings of inequity result.

Inequity Defined

Although it has been suggested how inequity arises, a rigorous definition must be formulated. But we introduce first two references terms, Person and Other. Person is any individual for whom equity or inequity exists. Other is any individual or group used by Person as a referent when he makes social comparisons of his inputs and outcomes. Other is usually a different individual, but may be Person in another job, or even in another social role. Thus, for example, Other might be Person in the job he held 6 months earlier, in which case he might compare his present and past inputs and outcomes. Or, as Patchen (1961) has suggested, Other might be Person in a future job to which he aspires. In such an instance he would make a comparison of his present inputs and outcomes to his estimates of those in the future. The terms Person and Other may also refer to groups rather than to individuals, as for example when a class of jobs (for example, toolmakers) is out of line with another class (for example, maintenance men). In such cases, it is convenient to deal with the class as a whole rather than with individual members of the class. This is essentially what is done when the relative ranking of jobs is evaluated in the process of devising an equitable wage or salary structure.

Using the theoretical model introduced by Festinger (1957), inequity is defined as follows: Inequity exists for Person whenever his perceived job inputs and/or outcomes stand psychologically in an obverse relation to what he perceives are the inputs and/or outcomes of Other. The first point to note about the definition is that it is the perception by Person of his and Other's inputs and outcomes that must be dealt with, not necessarily the actual inputs and outcomes. The point is important, for, while perception and reality may be and often are in close accord, wage administrators are likely to assume an identity of the two. Second, if we let A designate Person's inputs and outcomes and let B designate Other's, by "obverse relation" we mean that not A follows from B. But we emphasize that the relation necessary for inequity to exist is psychological in character, not logical. Thus, there is no logical obversion in male Person's being subordinate to female Other, but, as Clark (1958) has observed, the inputs of Person and Other in such a situation may be dissonant, with the consequence that inequity is felt by Person.

As was previously suggested, the dissonant relation of an individual's inputs and outcomes in comparison to another's is historically and culturally determined. This is why we insist that the incongruity is primarily psychological, even though it might, in addition, have a logical character. Each individual has a different history of learning, but to the extent that he learns from people sharing similar values, social norms, and language, that is, the extent to which he shares the same culture, his psychological reactions will be similar to theirs. The larger the cultural group, the greater will be the number of individuals who perceive similarly and react similarly to a given set of relations between input and outcomes. In the United States there is a strong, but perhaps weakening, predilection for the belief that effort and reward must be positively correlated. Considering the population at large, this belief has the status of a cultural norm and partially explains rather uniform reactions toward certain kinds of inequity — toward "featherbedding," for example.

It is interesting to note that the American attitude toward work and reward is by no means universal. In highly industrialized Japan, for example, there is little relationship between the kind and amount of work an employee does and the monetary reward he receives. Pay is largely determined by age, education, length of service, and family size, and very little, if at all, by productivity. In his study of Japanese factories, Abegglen (1958) states:

> It is not at all difficult to find situations where workers doing identical work at an identical pace receive markedly different salaries, or where a skilled workman is paid at a rate below that of a sweeper or doorman. The position occupied and the amount produced do not determine the reward provided [p. 68].

This, of course, is not to suggest that inequity is nonexistent for Japanese workers. They and their employers enter into an exchange just as Americans, but the terms of the exchange are quite different. Hence, the basis for inequity is different.

In order to predict when an individual will experience inequity under given conditions of inputs and outcomes, it is necessary to know something of the values and norms to which he subscribes — with what culture or subculture he is associated. Granted this knowledge, it is then possible to specify what constitutes an obverse relation of inputs and outcomes for Person. In a given society, even ours, there is usually enough invariance in fundamental beliefs and attitudes to make reasonably accurate, general predictions.

It is shown in Figure 1 how inequity results whenever the inputs or outcomes, or both, of Person stand in an obverse relation to either the inputs or outcomes, or both, of Other. Though inputs and outcomes may in most cases be measured continuously (ethnicity and sex are obvious exceptions), we have dichotomized them into "high" and "low" for the purpose of simplicity. The entries in the table are relative rather than absolute quantities. Thus, 1 indicates more felt inequity than 0, and 2 indicates more felt inequity than 1. But before pursuing the implications of Figure 1 and of the definition

FIGURE 1

Amount of Inequity for Person as a Result of Different Inputs and Outcomes for Person and Other

	Inputs-Outcomes			
	Other			
Person	Low-High	High-Low	Low-Low	High-High
Low-High	0	2	1	1
High-Low	2	0	1	1
Low-Low	1	1	0	0
High-High	1	1	0	0

The first member of the pair indicates inputs and the second member, outcomes.

of inequity, let us agree to use amount of effort as an instance of inputs and pay as an instance of outcomes. Any other input and outcome would do as well; we wish merely to use constant instances for the illustrations that will follow.

The first important consequence to observe from the definition is that inequity results for Person not only when he is relatively underpaid, but also when he is relatively overpaid. Person will, for example, feel inequity exists not only when his effort is high and his pay low, while Other's effort and pay are high, but also when his effort is low and his pay high, while Other's effort and pay are low.

Although there is no direct, reliable evidence on this point, it is probable that the thresholds for inequity are different (in absolute terms from a base of equity) in cases of under- and overcompensation. The threshold would be greater presumably in cases of overcompensation, for a certain amount of incongruity in these cases can be acceptably rationalized as "good fortune." In his work on pay differentials Jaques (1961a) notes that in instances of undercompensation British workers paid 10% less than the equitable level show

> an active sense of grievance, complaints or the desire to complain, and, if no redress is given, an active desire to change jobs, or to take action . . . [p. 26].

In cases of overcompensation, he observes that at the 10–15% level above equity

> there is a strong sense of receiving preferential treatment, which may harden into bravado, with underlying feelings of unease . . . [p. 26].

He states further:

> The results suggest that it is not necessarily the case that each one is simply out to get as much as he can for his work. There appear to be equally strong desires that each one should earn the right amount—a fair and reasonable amount relative to others [p. 26].

While Jaques' conceptualization of inequity is quite different from that advanced in this paper, his observations lend credence to the hypothesis that overcompensation results in feelings of inequity and that the threshold for these feelings is higher than in the case of undercompensation.

From the definition and Figure 1, we may observe as a second consequence that when Person's and Other's inputs and outcomes are analogous, equity is assumed to exist, and that when their inputs and outcomes are discrepant in any way inequity will exist. We assume that it is not the absolute magnitude of perceived inputs and outcomes that results in inequity, but rather the relative magnitudes pertaining to Person and Other. For example, there will be no inequity if both Person and Other expend much effort in their jobs and both obtain low pay. The 0 entries in the main diagonal of Figure 1 reflect the fact that when the inputs and outcomes of Person and Other are matched, no inequity exists. It is further assumed, and shown in Figure 1, that no inequity will result if both the inputs and outcomes of Person are matched and those of Other are matched, but are different for Person and for Other. To illustrate: if Person expends low effort and receives low pay, while Other expends high effort and receives high pay, equity rather than inequity will result. The converse also holds true.

With regard to the amount of inequity that exists, we have assumed that greater inequity results when both inputs and outcomes are discrepant than when only inputs or outcomes are discrepant. This signifies, for example, that Person will experience more inequity when his effort is high and pay low, while Other's effort is low and pay high, than when Person's effort is high and pay low, while Other's effort and pay are both high. In Figure 1 only three relative magnitudes of inequity, ranging from 0 to 2, are shown. In reality, of course, many more degrees could be distinguished, especially with variables such as effort and pay which are theoretically continuous. The point to be emphasized is that equity-inequity is not an all-or-none phenomenon.

It will be noted that in the definition of inequity and in Figure 1, inputs have not been differentiated, nor have outcomes. There are two reasons for this. First, the processes that govern inequity are applicable irrespective of the specific inputs and outcomes obtaining in a particular situation. For example, inequity may result whether low inputs are in the form of low effort or of poor education, or whether high outcomes stem from high pay or from great rewards intrinsic to the job. Second, there is a degree of interchangeability between different inputs and between different outcomes; furthermore inputs are additive, as are outcomes. It is implied, therefore, that a given total of Person's inputs may be achieved by increasing or decreasing any one or more separate inputs; similarly, a given total of Person's outcomes may result from increasing or decreasing one or more separate outcomes. For example, if Person found it necessary to increase his inputs in order to reduce inequity, he could do so not only by increasing his effort, but also by acquiring additional training or education. If, on the other hand, greater outcomes were required to achieve equity, obtaining new status symbols might be equivalent to an increase in compensation, or a combination of improved job environment and increased discretionary content of the job might be.

The question of the interchangeability and additivity of different inputs on the one hand, and of different outcomes on the other is an important one. Does a man evaluating his job inputs give the same weight to formal education as he does to on-the-job experience? If he has completed high school and has held his job 2 years, and a co-worker, whom he uses as a comparison person, completed the ninth grade only and has been on the job 4 years, will he judge their inputs as equivalent or not? Is the frequently used practice of giving a man a prestigeful title an effective substitute for greater monetary outcomes? Definitive answers to such questions await research. However, this much may be hypothesized: Within certain limits of inequity there will be a tendency on the part of Person to manipulate and weight cognitively his own inputs and outcomes and those of Other in such a manner as to minimize the degree of felt inequity. Beyond these limits of inequity the tendency will be to manipulate and weight inputs and outcomes so as to maximize the inequity, because as will be discussed later, this will increase the motivation to adopt behavior that will eliminate the inequity entirely.[4] In both processes it is assumed that normal men are limited by reality in the amount of cognitive manipulation and weighting of inputs and outcomes they can perform. Except, perhaps, in the case of very small degrees of inequity such manipulation and weighting could not serve by themselves to achieve equity.

In discussing inequity, the focus has been exclusively on Person. In so doing, however, we have failed to consider that whenever inequity exists for Person, it will also exist for Other, provided their perceptions of inputs and outcomes are isomorphic or nearly so. A glance at Figure 1 will make this apparent, and we may predict from the table the inequity for Other as well as for Person. Only when the perceptions of Person and Other do not agree, would the inequity be different for each. In such a case, one would enter Figure 1 twice, once for Person and once for Other. It is sufficient at this point merely to note that inequity is bilateral or multilateral, and symmetric under some conditions. Later we shall consider the implications of this in greater detail.

Effects of Inequity

Having defined inequity and specified its antecedents, we may next attend to its effects. First, two general postulates, closely following dissonance theory (Festinger, 1957): (*a*) The presence of inequity in Person creates tension in him. The tension is proportional to the magnitude of inequity present. (*b*) The tension created in Person will drive him to reduce it. The strength of the drive is proportional to the tension created; *ergo,* it is proportional to the magnitude of inequity present. In short, the presence of inequity will motivate Person to achieve equity or reduce inequity, and the strength of motivation to do so will vary directly with the amount of inequity. The question, then, is *how* may Person reduce inequity? The following actions enumerate and illustrate the means available to Person when reducing inequity.

1. Person may increase his inputs if they are low relative to Other's inputs and to his own outcomes. If, for example, Person's effort were low compared to Other's and to his own pay, he could reduce inequity by increasing

his effort on the job. This might take the form of Person's increasing his productivity, as will be shown in experiments described later, or enhancing the quality of his work. If inputs other than effort were involved, he could increase his training or education. Some inputs cannot, of course, be altered easily — sex and ethnicity, for instance. When such inputs are involved, other means of reducing inequity must be adopted.

2. Person may decrease his inputs if they are high relative to Other's inputs and to his own outcomes. If Person's effort were high compared to Other's and to his own pay, he might reduce his effort and productivity, as is illustrated later in a study of grocery clerks. It is interesting to note that effort is the principal input susceptible to reduction; education, training, experience, intelligence, skill, seniority, age, sex, ethnicity, and so on are not readily decreased or devalued realistically, though they may be distorted psychologically within limits. They are givens; their acquisition is not reversible. The implication is that when inequity results from inputs being too high, decreases in productivity are especially likely to be observed. One may speculate that restrictive production practices often observed are in fact attempts at reducing inequity.

There exists in industry a tendency to select and hire personnel with education, intellect, and training which are often greater than that required by the job in which they are placed. Since it is likely that in many instances the comparison persons for these individuals will have lesser inputs and, perhaps, greater outcomes, it is evident that some of the newly hired will experience feelings of inequity. In consequence, education, intellect, and training not being readily modified, lowered productivity may be predicted.

3. Person may increase his outcomes if they are low relative to Other's outcomes and to his own inputs. When Person's pay is low compared to Other's and to his expended effort, he may reduce inequity by obtaining a wage increase. Evidence of this is given later in a study of clerical workers. He could also, if appropriate, acquire additional benefits, perquisites, or status. An increase in status, however, might create new problems, for the acquisition of higher status without higher pay would of itself create dissonance, particularly if the new status of Person placed him in a superordinate position vis-à-vis Other.

4. Person may decrease his outcomes if they are high relative to Other's outcomes and to his own inputs. This might take the form of Person's lowering his pay. Though an improbable mode of reducing inequity, it is nevertheless theoretically possible. Although it is usually assumed that persons with very high personal incomes are motivated by tax laws to donate much to charitable and educational institutions, it is not improbable that this behavior on the part of some is motivated as well by feelings of inequity.

5. Person may "leave the field" when he experiences inequity of any type. This may take the form of quitting his job or obtaining a transfer or reassignment, or of absenteeism. In a study by Patchen (1959) it was observed that

men who said their pay should be higher had more absences than men who said the pay for their jobs was fair. Although the author did not conceptualize "fair pay" as in the present paper, it is clear at least that "fair" was defined by respondents in relational terms, for he states:

> The data show also that the actual amount of a man's pay has, in itself, little effect on how often he is absent. The important question, regardless of how much he is getting, is whether he thinks the rate is fair [p. 12].

Leaving the field is perhaps a more radical means of coping with inequity, and its adoption will vary not only with the magnitude of inequity present, but also with Person's tolerance of inequity and his ability to cope with it flexibly. Though it has not been demonstrated, there are probably individual differences in tolerance and flexibility.

6. Person may psychologically distort his inputs and outcomes, increasing or decreasing them as required. Since most individuals are heavily influenced by reality, distortion is generally difficult. It is pretty difficult to distort to oneself that one has a BA degree, that one has been an accountant for 7 years, and that one's salary is $500 per month, for example. However, it is possible to alter the utility of these. For example, State College is a small, backwoods school with no reputation, or, conversely, State College has one of the best Business Schools in the state and the Dean is an adviser to the Bureau of the Budget. Or, one can consider the fact that $500 per month will buy all of the essential things of life and quite a few luxuries, or, conversely, that it will never permit one to purchase period furniture or a power cruiser.

7. Person may increase, decrease, or distort the inputs and outcomes of Others, or force Other to leave the field. Basically, these means are the same as discussed above, but applied to Other. The direction of change in inputs and outcomes would, however, be precisely opposite to changes effected in Person. Thus, for example, if Person's effort were too low compared to Other's and to his own pay, he might induce Other to decrease his effort instead of increasing his own effort. Or, if he were comparatively poorly qualified for his job, he might try to have his better qualified colleague fired or transferred.

8. Person may change his referent Other when inequity exists. If Person were a draftsman working harder, doing better quality work, and being paid less than Other at the next board, he might eschew further comparisons with Other and pick someone with more nearly the same capability and pay. The ease of doing this would vary considerably with the ubiquity of Other and with the availability of a substitute having some attributes in common with Person.

Not all means of reducing inequity that have been listed will be equally satisfactory, and the adoption of some may result in very unsteady states.

The nature of the input and outcome discrepancies and environmental circumstances may render some means more available than others, as may personality characteristics of Person and Other. To illustrate this we may consider a Person whose effort is high and whose pay is low, and an Other whose effort and pay are low. If Person acts to increase his pay and is successful, he will effectively reduce the inequity; but if he is unsuccessful, as well he might be, given rigid job and wage structures, inequity will continue. Person might, on the other hand, try to reduce his productivity. This, however, might be quite risky if minimal production standards were maintained and unsatisfactory productivity were penalized. There is the further consideration that if Person and Other are both on the same production line, a decrease in effort by Person might affect Other's production and pay, with the result that Other would object to Person's behavior. Another means for Person to reduce his inequity is to try to have Other increase his effort. If Other perceives his and Person's inputs and outcomes in the same way as Person, he might, indeed, accede to this influence and raise his effort. If, to the contrary, he perceives no discrepancy between his and Person's inputs, he may be expected to resist Person strongly. Alternatively, Person could resort to leaving the field, or to distortion, as discussed earlier. If distortion is unilateral on Person's part, it may resolve his inequity, though not Other's. This leads into another interesting aspect of inequity.

Person and Other may or may not constitute a social system, that is, Person may be to Other what Other is to Person, so that they are referents for one another. Or, Other's referent may be someone other than Person, say, an individual X, who is quite irrelevant to Person's social comparisons. When Person and Other do not form a social system, the way in which Person reduces his inequity will have no effect on Other and there will, therefore, be no feedback effects upon Person. When the two do constitute a social system, the interaction that may take place is of considerable interest. Considering only those instances when Person and Other have identical perceptions of their inputs and outcomes it is a truism that when inequity exists for Person it also exists for Other (though probably not in the same amount since one will be overpaid and the other underpaid). Hence, both will be motivated to reduce the inequity; but it does not follow that they will adopt compatible means. If compatible means are adopted, both will achieve equity. For example, if Person expended little effort and received high pay, while Other's effort and pay were both high, a state of equity could be achieved by Person's increasing his effort somewhat and by Other's reducing his a bit. Or, the two could agree that the easiest solution was for Other to reduce his effort to Person's level. However, this solution might prove inadequate, for other reasons; for example, this might endanger their jobs by reducing production to an economically unprofitable level.

Many possibilities of incompatible solutions exist for Person and Other. Continuing with the preceding example, Person could increase his effort and

Other could decrease his. From the point of view of each considered alone, these actions should reduce inequity. When considered simultaneously, however, it is apparent that now Person's effort and pay will be high, whereas Other will expend low effort and receive high pay. A new state of inequity has been created! As a further example, if Person's effort were high and his pay low, while Other's effort were low and his pay high, Person might reduce his own effort while Other was trying to induce the supervisor to increase Person's salary. If Other were unsuccessful in his attempt, a new, but reduced, state of inequity would result. If, on the other hand, Other were successful in obtaining a raise for Person, equity might be established, but a new situation, hardly more comfortable than inequity, would result: Person would have received a pay increment for a decrement in effort.

Private, psychological distortion of one's inputs and outcomes is especially likely to result in unsuccessful reduction of inequity, if done by only one party. For instance, if Person is overcompensated and manages to convince himself that he is not, it will be extremely difficult for Other to convince him, say, that he should work harder. Or, if Other were to convince himself that he was working just as hard as Person, Person could not effectively convince Other to increase his productivity or to take a cut in pay. The very fact that one of the parties is operating at a private, covert level makes it nearly impossible to communicate. The perceptions of the two parties being now different, the fundamental premises that must underlie joint action cannot be agreed upon. Distortion by one party in effect breaks the social system that had previously existed.

Supporting Evidence

The evidence in direct support of the theory of inequity will now be considered. The data that are available may be divided grossly into two types, observational and experimental. Directly supporting evidence is, on the whole, somewhat meager for the reason that little research has been focused on the specific question of job inequity. The work of Zaleznik et al. (1958), Homans (1953, 1961), and Patchen (1959, 1961) has dealt with significant aspects of the problem, but, with the exception of Homans' (1953) study of clerical employees, the data collected by these researchers are difficult to relate to the present theory.

A Case of Pay Inequity among Clerical Workers (Homans, 1953)

Rather than dealing with two individuals, we are here concerned with two groups of female clerical workers, cash posters and ledger clerks, in one division of a utilities company. Both groups worked in the same large room. Cash posting consisted of recording daily the amounts customers paid on their bills, and management insisted that posting be precisely up to date. It required that cash posters pull customer cards from the many files and make appropriate entries on them. The job, therefore, was highly repetitive and comparatively monotonous, and required little thought but a good deal of physical mobility. Ledger clerks, in contrast, performed a variety of tasks on customer accounts, such as recording address changes, making breakdowns of over- and underpayments, and supplying information on accounts to customers or company people on the telephone. In addition, toward the end of the day, they were required by their supervisor to assist with "cleaning up" cash posting in order that it be current. Compared to the cash posters, "ledger clerks had to do a number of nonrepetitive clerical jobs . . . requiring some thought but little physical mobility." They had a more responsible job.

Ledger clerks were considered to be of higher status than cash posters, since promotion took place from cash poster to ledger clerk. Their weekly pay, however, was identical. In comparison to cash posters, ledger clerks were older and had more seniority and experience.

These are the facts of the situation. In terms of the theory, the following may be stated:

1. The cash posters had lower inputs than the ledger clerks: They were younger, had less seniority and experience, and had less responsible jobs. Their outcomes were in some respects lower than the ledger clerks': Their job had less variety, was more monotonous, required greater physical effort, and had less intrinsic interest. Very importantly, however, their pay was equal to the ledger clerks'.
2. The ledger clerks had higher inputs than the cash posters: They were older, had more seniority and experience, and had more responsible positions. Their outcomes were higher on several counts: Their status was higher, their job had greater variety and interest, and physical effort required was low. Their pay, nonetheless, was the same as the cash posters'. The requirement that they help "clean up" (note the connotation) posting each day introduced ambiguity in their inputs and outcomes. On the one hand, this required greater inputs — that is, having to know two jobs — and, on the other hand, lowered their outcomes by having to do "dirty work" and deflating their self-esteem.

It is clear from the discrepancies between inputs and outcomes that inequities existed. In capsule form, the outcomes of ledger clerks were too low compared to their own inputs and to the inputs and outcomes of cash posters. The evidence is strong that the ledger clerks, at least, felt the inequity. They felt that they ought to get a few dollars more per week to show that their job was more important — in our terms, their greater inputs ought to be paralleled by greater outcomes. On the whole, these clerks did not do much to reduce inequity, though a few complained to their union representative, with, apparently, little effect. However, the workers in this division voted to abandon their independent union for the CIO, and Homans (1953) intimates that the reason may have been the independent union's inability to force a resolution of the inequity. He further implies that had management perceived and resolved the inequity, the representative function of a union would have been quite superfluous.

A Case of Status Inequity in Supermarkets (Clark, 1958)

We shall be concerned here with the checkout counters in a chain of supermarkets, which are manned by a "ringer" and a "bundler." Ringers are the cashiers who add on the register the sum due from the customer, take his payment, and make change. Bundlers take goods out of the cart and put them in bags to be taken out. Under normal conditions, ringing was a higher status, better paid job, handled by a permanent, full-time employee. Bundling was of lower status and lower pay, and was usually done by part-time employees, frequently youngsters. Furthermore, psychologically, bundlers were perceived as working *for* ringers.

Because customer flow in supermarkets varies markedly from day to day, a preponderance of employees were part-timers. This same fact required that many employees be assigned to checkout counters during rush hours. When this occurred, many ringer-bundler teams were formed, and it is this that resulted in the creation of status inequity, for employees differed considerably in a number of input variables, notably sex, age, and education. Not infrequently, then, a bundler would be directed to work for a ringer whose status (determined by sex, age, education, etc.) was lower. For example, a college male 21 years of age would be ordered to work for a high school girl ringer of 17. Or a college girl would be assigned as a bundler for an older woman with only a grade school education. The resulting status inequities may be described as follows in our theoretical terms: A bundler with higher inputs than a ringer had lower outcomes.

When interviewed by the investigator, the store employees were quite explicit about the inequities that existed. Furthermore, this was true of ringers, as well as bundlers, showing that inequities were felt bilaterally in these cooperative jobs. To restore equity it would have been necessary to form teams such that inputs and outcomes were matched. Clark (1958) has stated the principle in the following manner:

> A person's job status (which is determined by the amount of pay, responsibility, variety and absence from interference his job has) should be in line with his social status (which is determined by his sex, age, education, and seniority) [p. 128].

That store employees attempted to reduce existing inequities is evident from the data. The principal means of doing so appeared to be by the bundlers reducing their work speed — that is, by reducing their inputs, which would have effectively decreased inequity since some of their other inputs were too high relative to their own outcomes and to the inputs of the ringers. One girl explicitly stated to the investigator that when she was ordered to bundle for a ringer of lower social status than hers, she deliberately slowed up bundling.

Interestingly, this behavior is nicely reflected in the financial operation of the stores. A substantial part of the total labor cost of operating a supermarket is the cost of manning checkout counters. It follows, therefore, that one should be able to observe a correlation between the incidence of inequities among ringer-bundler teams and the cost of store operations, since the inequity reduction took the form of lowered productivity. This is indeed what was found. When the eight supermarkets were ranked on labor efficiency[5] and "social ease,"[6] the two measures correlated almost perfectly — that is, the greater the inequity, the greater the cost of operating the stores. To give an example, one of the two stores studied most intensively ranked high in inequity and had a cost of 3.85 man-hours per $100 of sales, whereas the other which ranked low in equity, had a cost of only 3.04 per $100 of sales. Thus, it cost approximately 27% more to operate the store in which inequities were higher.

A further finding of Clark's is worth reporting, for it gives one confidence that the relative inefficiency of the one store was indeed due to the presence of relatively more inequity. This store went through a period of considerable labor turnover (perhaps as a result of employees leaving the field to reduce inequity), and associated with this was an increase in labor efficiency and an increase in the social ease index. There is, therefore, quasi-experimental evidence that when inequities are reduced, individual productivity increases, with the result that operating costs decrease.

Experiment I (Adams and Rosenbaum, 1962)

One of the more interesting hypotheses derivable from the theory of inequity is that when Person is overpaid in relation to Other, he may reduce the inequity by increasing his inputs. Therefore, an experiment was designed in which one group of subjects was overcompensated and one was equitably compensated — that is, one group in which outcomes were too great and one in which outcomes were equitable, given certain inputs, relative to some generalized Other.

The task chosen was a one page controlled association public opinion interview (for example, "Which of these five automobiles do you associate with a rising young junior executive?"), which subjects were to administer in equal numbers to male and female members of the general public. The subjects were under the impression that they were being hired for a real task and that their employment would continue for several months. In actuality, however, they conducted interviews for 2.5 hours only, after which time they were told about the experiment and were paid for their participation.

Two groups of 11 male university students, hired through the college employment office, were used as subjects. Each was paid $3.50 per hour — an amount large enough so that a feeling of overcompensation could be induced, but not so large that it could not also be made to appear equitable. In one group (E), subjects were made to feel quite unqualified to earn $3.50 per hour, because of lack of interviewer training and experience. The other group of subjects (C) were made to feel fully qualified to earn $3.50 per hour, by being informed that they were far better educated than census takers and that education and intelligence were the prime requisites of interviewing. It may be noted that the referent Others for all subjects were trained interviewers at large, not a specific, known person. The complete instructions to the groups were, of course, much more elaborate, but details need not be given here. The critical point is that the E group felt overcompensated, whereas the C group felt fairly paid.

From the theory, it was predicted that the E group would attempt to increase their inputs so as to bring them in line with their outcomes and with the alleged inputs of trained interviewers. Since there was little they could do to increase their training and experience, this left productivity as the principal means of altering inputs. Theoretically, E group subjects could also have tried to reduce their outcomes; this, however, was impossible since the pay was fixed. In sum, then, it was predicted that the E group would obtain more interviews per unit time than the C group. This is what the results demonstrated. Whereas the C group obtained an average of only .1899 interviews per minute, the E group obtained a significantly greater average of .2694, or an average of 42% more ($\chi^2 = 4.55$, $df = 1$, $p < .05$).

Results comparable to these have been obtained by Day (1961) in a laboratory experiment with children who were given training trials in which they pushed a plunger mechanism to obtain M&M candies. The number of candies received varied between 1 and 6 and was directly dependent upon the magnitude of pressure exerted on the plunger. After responses had stabilized, 25 M&Ms were received by each subject on each of five trials regardless of the pressure exerted. Day's data show that a significant number of subjects respond to the increased reward by increased pressure on the overrewarded trials. In terms of our theoretical model, the children in Day's study are comparing their inputs (pressure) and outcomes (M&Ms) during the overrewarded trials with those during the training trials. The latter trials establish a base upon which to determine what constitutes "equity." The "overpayment" of 25 M&M candies results in inequity, which may be reduced by increasing pressure inputs.

Experiment II (Arrowood, 1961)

If it is reasonable to suppose that the results of the previously described experiment by Adams and Rosenbaum (1962) were a result of the E subjects' working harder to protect their jobs because they were insecure in the face of their "employer's" low regard for their qualifications, it is reasonable to suppose that the same results would not obtain if subjects were convinced that their "employer" would have no knowledge of their productivity. Conversely, if the theory we have offered is valid, overpaid subjects should produce more than controls, whether they thought the "employer" knew the results of their work or whether they thought he did not.

Following this reasoning, Arrowood (1961) designed a factorial experiment in which subjects from Minneapolis were either overpaid or equitably paid and performed their work under either public or private conditions. The first two conditions were similar to those in Experiment I: Subjects were hired at $3.50 per hour to conduct interviews and were made to feel unqualified or qualified for the job. The public-private distinction was achieved by having subjects either submit their work to the "employer" (the experimenter) or mail it in preaddressed envelopes to New York. In the latter case, subjects were under the impression that the experimenter would never see their work.

The results, shown in Figure 2, validate the hypothesis tested in Experiment I and permit one to reject the alternative hypothesis. In both the Public and Private conditions, overpaid subjects produced significantly more than equitably paid subjects. The fact that mean production in the Public conditions was significantly greater than in the Private conditions is irrelevant to the hypothesis since there was no significant interaction between the inequity-equity and public-private dimensions.

FIGURE 2

Production Scores of Subjects in Experiment II

	Public	Private
Overpaid	67.20	52.43
Equitably paid	59.33	41.50

Experiment III (Adams and Rosenbaum, 1962)

Since the results of the two previous experiments strongly corroborated a derivation from the theory, it was decided to test a further, but related, derivation. The hypothesis was that whereas subjects overpaid *by the hour* would produce more than equitably paid controls, subjects overpaid *on a piecework* basis would produce less than equitably paid controls. The rationale for the latter half of the hypothesis was that because inequity was associated with each *unit* produced, inequity would increase as work proceeded; hence, subjects would strive not so much to *reduce* inequity as to *avoid* increasing it. In other words, because inequity would mount as more units were produced, overpaid piecework subjects would tend to restrict production.

Nine subjects were assigned to each of the following groups: Overpaid \$3.50 per hour (H_e), equitably paid \$3.50 per hour (H_c), overpaid \$.30 per unit (P_e), equitably paid \$.30 per unit (P_c). In all major respects, the task and instructions were identical to those in Experiment I.

As may be seen in Figure 3, the hypothesis received unequivocal support. Overpaid hourly subjects produced more than their controls and overpaid piecework subjects produced less than their controls. The interaction between the inequity-equity and hourly-piecework dimensions is highly significant ($\chi^2 = 7.11$, $df = 1$, $p < .01$).

FIGURE 3

Mean Productivity and Median Distribution of Hourly and Piecework Experimental and Control Subjects in Experiment III

	Condition			
	H_e	H_c	P_e	P_c
Mean productivity	.2723	.2275	.1493	.1961
Cases above median	8	4	1	5
Cases below median	1	5	8	4

Experiment IV (Adams, 1963)

The prediction that piecework subjects experiencing wage inequity would have a lower productivity than subjects perceiving their wages as fair was supported by the previous experiment. The rationale for the prediction was that because dissonance is linked with units of production, dissonance would increase as more units were produced, and, consequently, subjects would attempt to avoid increasing dissonance by restricting production. There is, however, an alternative explanation that would account for the same manifest behavior. It is entirely possible for subjects to *reduce* dissonance by increasing their effort on the production of each unit, for example, by increasing the quality of their work, which would have the effect of increasing the production time per unit and, therefore, have the consequence of reducing productivity. In terms of the theoretical framework presented earlier, this explanation assumes that pieceworkers would reduce their dissonance by increasing their inputs, very much as the hourly workers. Only the mode of increasing inputs varies: Whereas hourly workers increase inputs on a *quantitative* dimension, pieceworkers increase them on a *qualitative* dimension.

Unfortunately, the task used in Experiment III did not lend itself to measuring quality of work. In the present experiment the work performed by subjects was so designed as to permit measurement of both amount of work and quality of work. The specific hypothesis tested is: Pieceworkers who perceive that they are inequitably overpaid will perform better quality work and have lower productivity than pieceworkers who are paid the same rate and perceive they are equitably paid.

The interviewing task used in the previous experiments was modified so as to permit the measurement of quality. The modification consisted of making the three principal questions open-end questions. As an example, one question was "Does a man who owns a shelter have the moral right to exclude others from it, if they have no shelter?" (Yes or No), which was followed by, "What are your reasons for feeling that way?" The subject's task was to obtain as much information as possible from a respondent on the latter part of the question. The measure of work quality thus was the amount of recorded information elicited from respondents. More specifically, the dependent measure of quality was the number of words per interview recorded in the blank spaces following the three open-end questions. As before, the measure of productivity was the number of interviews obtained per minute during a total period of approximately 2 hours.

Twenty-eight subjects were used, half randomly assigned to a condition in which they were made to feel overpaid, half to a condition in which the identical piecework rate was made to appear equitable. The results supported the hypotheses. First, as in the previous experiment, the productivity of subjects in whom feelings of inequitable overpayment were induced was significantly lower than that of control subjects. Productivity rates for these groups were .0976 and .1506, respectively ($t = 1.82$, $p < .05$, one-tailed test). Second, work quality was significantly higher among overpaid subjects than among controls (69.7 versus 45.3, $t = 2.48$, $p < .02$, two-tailed test).

These quality and productivity data support the hypothesis that under piecework conditions subjects who perceive that they are overpaid will tend to reduce dissonance by increasing their inputs on each *unit* so as to improve its quality and, as a result, will decrease their productivity. Thus, the alternative explanation for the results obtained with pieceworkers in Experiment III has some validity. This is not to say that the dissonance avoiding hypothesis originally offered is invalid, for if a job does not permit an increase of work input *per unit produced,* dissonance avoidance may well occur. This, however, remains to be demonstrated; the fact that we were unable to measure quality of work in Experiment III does not mean that subjects did not reduce dissonance by some means, including the improvement of quality, on each unit produced.

Conclusion

We have offered a general theory of inequity, reviewed its implications, and presented evidence in support of it. Although the support given the theory is gratifying, additional data are required to test particular aspects of it. In addition, research is needed to determine what variables guide the choice of comparison persons. While this is a theoretical and research endeavor in its own right, it would contribute much to the understanding of inequity.

The analysis of inequity in terms of discrepancies between a man's job inputs and job outcomes, and the behavior that may result from these discrepancies, should result in a better understanding of one aspect of social conflict and should increase the degree of control that may be exercised over it. In moving toward an understanding of inequity, we increase our knowledge of our most basic productive resource, the human organism.

Notes and References

1. This paper and some of the experimental work reported in it are part of a program of theory development and research on wages and productivity undertaken by the author at the Behavioral Research Service, General Electric Company. The author wishes to acknowledge his indebtedness to Leon Festinger for his work on cognitive dissonance and to George C. Homans for his ideas on distributive justice, which stimulated much of the present essay. He is also grateful to A. J. Arrowood, W. B. Rosenbaum, F. Tweed, and Patricia Jacobsen for assistance in conducting experiments.
2. M. Crozier, personal communication, 1960.
3. This assumption follows Festinger (1954), who states: "Given a range of possible persons for comparison, someone close to one's own ability or opinion will be chosen for comparison [p. 121]." Generally, co-workers will more nearly fit this criterion than will other persons.
4. This process is analogous to that postulated by Festinger (1957) when he discusses the relation of magnitude of cognitive dissonance to seeking information that will increase dissonance. He hypothesizes that at high levels of dissonance increasing information may be sought, with the result that the person will change his opinion and thus reduce dissonance.
5. As an index of labor efficiency, Clark (1958) used the number of man-hours per $100 of sales.
6. "Social ease" is a complex index, devised by Clark (1958), the value of which is basically the number of pairs of part-time employees, out of all possible pairs, whose inputs and outcomes were "in line," according to the definition given in the quotation from Clark.

Abegglen, J. G. *The Japanese Factory*. Glencoe, Ill.: Fress Press, 1958.

Adams, J. S. "The measurement of perceived equity in pay differentials." Unpublished manuscript. General Electric Company, Behavioral Research Service, 1961.

Adams, J. S. "Productivity and work quality as a function of wage inequities." *Industr. Relat., Berkeley,* 1963. In press.

Adams, J. S., and W. B. Rosenbaum. "The relationship of worker productivity to cognitive dissonance about wage inequities." *J. appl. Psychol.,* 46 (1962), 161–164.

Arrowood, A. J. "Some effects on productivity of justified and unjustified levels of reward under public and private conditions." Unpublished doctoral dissertation. University of Minnesota, Department of Psychology, 1961.

Clark, J. V. "A preliminary investigation of some unconscious assumptions affecting labor efficiency in eight supermarkets." Unpublished doctoral dissertation. Harvard Graduate School of Business Administration, 1958.

Day, C. R. "Some consequences of increased reward following establishment of output-reward expectation level." Unpublished master's thesis. Duke University, 1961.

Festinger, L. "A theory of social comparison processes." *Hum. Relat.*, 7 (1954), 117–140.

Festinger, L. *A Theory of Cognitive Dissonance*. Evanston, Ill.: Row, Peterson, 1957.

Homans, G. C. "Status among clerical workers." *Hum. Organiz.*, 12 (1953), 5–10.

Homans, G. C. *Social Behavior: Its Elementary Forms*. New York: Harcourt, Brace & World, 1961.

Jaques, E. *Measurement of Responsibility*. London: Tavistock, 1956.

Jaques, E. *Equitable Payment*. New York: Wiley, 1961 (a).

Jaques, E. "An objective approach to pay differentials." *Time motion Stud.*, 10 (1961) (b), 25–28.

Merton, R. K. and Alice S. Kitt. "Contributions to the theory of reference group behavior." In R. K. Merton and P. F. Lazarsfeld (eds.), *Studies in the Scope and Method of "The American Soldier."* Glencoe, Ill.: Free Press, 1950, pp. 40–105.

Patchen, M. *Study of Work and Life Satisfaction: Report II. Absences and Attitudes Toward Work Experiences*. Ann Arbor: Institute for Social Research, 1959.

28

Employee Appeal Systems

WILLIAM G. SCOTT
DePaul University

1. Introduction

Concrete information on management sponsored appeal programs for company employees is difficult to find. Descriptive articles occasionally appear in business publications, but otherwise, there is a shortage of statistical and analytical studies. To provide some data, we made a study of appeal rights and appeal procedures in a large number of firms. The nature, objectives, and findings of this study are discussed in this report.

2. Nature of the Study

This study was conducted by questionnaires which were mailed to personnel managers of 1,800 firms. Information was requested on three subjects:

A. whether or not the company had a formal (written) *policy* for handling employee appeals or complaints.
B. whether or not the company had a formal (written) *procedure* in addition to the policy for handling complaints.
C. If the company had neither of the above, the personnel manager was asked to explain any informal (unwritten) program for the handling of employee complaints.

We were *not* interested in any grievance procedures negotiated with a union. Our sole interest was in those programs granted to employees upon the initiative of management.

3. The Survey Response

The 1,800 firms sent questionnaires were classified by size and industry. The survey response according to these classifications is shown in Figure 1.

Taken and adapted from *Proceedings of the 24th Annual Meeting of the Academy of Management,* 1965. Used by permission.

It was gratifying to receive 793 completed questionnaires representing a 44 per cent response.

FIGURE 1

Survey Response by Industry by Size

Industry	Size			
	Small	Medium	Large	Total
Manufacturing	42	48	56	146
Finance	22	69	34	125
Retail	25	30	48	103
Transportation	29	52	46	127
Extractive	22	42	46	110
Public Utilities	82	74	26	182
Total	222	315	256	793

We separated those firms which had appeal programs from those which did not. 518 companies showed no type of appeal, formal or informal. Of the 275 firms with a program, 184 indicated that theirs were informal in nature. This left 91 companies with a formal appeal activity. We concentrated our study on these plans. Fortunately, many companies sent us their policy statement and procedure manuals on which we based the information which follows.

4. Formal Appeal Systems

The 91 respondents with formal appeal systems amount to about 11 per cent of the total returns. Figure 2 shows the formal appeal activities by industry by size of firm.

Two patterns are indicated in Figure 2. First of all, there is a division between industries with formal appeal programs. The manufacturing, transportation, and public utilities industries have much higher percentages of formal programs than the finance, retail, and extractive industries.

Secondly, a horizontal comparison of the statistical data in Figure 2 shows a distinct relationship between the size of the firm and its use of formal appeal activities. Clearly, the prevalency of such programs is directly related to firm size. The percentages of respondents using formal appeal programs range from 5.86 for all small firms, through 10.15 for medium size, to 17.97 for large ones.

5. The Content of the Formal Programs

The formal appeal programs found in 91 firms fell into two categories — "policy only" and "policy and procedure." Policy only refers to written

FIGURE 2

Formal Appeal Activities by Industry by Size of Firm

Industry	Small		Medium		Large		Totals By Industry		
	N	Total	N	Total	N	Total	N	Total	%
Manufacturing	3	42	7	48	14	56	24	146	16.43
Finance	2	22	2	69	6	34	10	125	8.00
Retail	0	25	1	30	7	48	8	103	7.76
Transportation	2	29	9	52	7	46	18	127	14.17
Extractive	6	22	3	42	6	46	9	110	8.18
Public Utilities	6	82	10	74	6	26	22	182	12.08
Totals	13	222	32	315	46	256	91	793	11.47

company statements indicating employees' right to appeal, but with no specific procedures for them to follow in carrying out the appeal. Policy and procedure covers firms with written methods or steps for employee use in registering complaints and carrying them through channels.

Thirty-six firms had policy only programs; 55, both policies and procedures. The following information is drawn from 25 policy only statements and 52 policy and procedure statements sent by responding companies.

A. Policy only Programs

In the twenty-five statements examined, the responding companies called this plan an "open door" policy. In general, this policy gives the employee the right to appeal or make a complaint to someone other than his immediate supervisor. Two variations of this policy were found.

The first variation, in 10 of 25 firms, gave the employee the right to take his complaint to members of *line* management above his immediate supervisor. These "members of line management" frequently were required by the policy to be in the direct chain-of-command of the employee making the complaint.

The second variation, in 15 of 25 firms, gave the employee the right to state his complaint to the personnel department usually directly to the personnel manager, as an alternative to line management.

B. Policy and Procedure Programs

Even though 52 companies reported this kind of appeal activity just one basic type program was found. It is the step-by-step procedure. This basic form did, however, have four distinct variations. These variations are (1) line executives only, (2) line and staff executives, (3) a grievance or complaint committee, and (4) a board of review. A breakdown of the use of these four variations by company size is given below:

FIGURE 3

Variations	Firm Size Small	Medium	Large	Total
Line Executives Only	3	4	7	14
Line and Staff Executives	3	7	13	23
Grievance Committee	0	3	1	4
Board of Review	1	1	9	11
Totals	7	15	30	52

Of the four variations in the "policy and procedure" category, the line and staff system was the most prevalent. This method was overwhelmingly selected by medium and large size firms. The staff executives involved were representatives of the personnel or industrial relations departments.

Generally the personnel department entered the appeal activity as a hearing and decision-making stage in the appeal process. This way it gave the employee an opportunity to receive a hearing on his complaint outside the chain-of-command. A characteristic example of this appeal network is shown in Figure 4. It is the Personnel Staff By-Pass.

Another alternative using the staff is shown in Figure 5. According to this procedure, the employee has a choice of either the line route or a staff by-pass.

In considering the participation of staff in the appeal process, it is important to look at the degree of its authority in the settlement of disputes. There are three types of authority in this instance: (1) investigation of grievance only to provide top management with background material for the final hearing; (2) actual settlement authority at some step in the appeal system; and (3) final authority in the settlement of the dispute. A breakdown of twenty respondents shows that staff authority was limited to the first type in two firms, 13 to the second type, and five to the third.

FIGURE 4

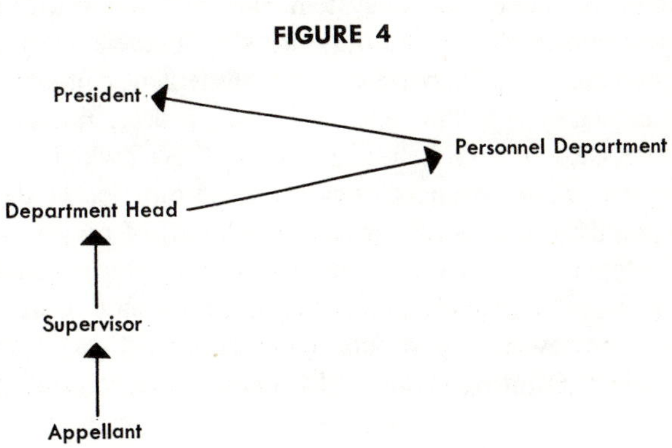

FIGURE 5

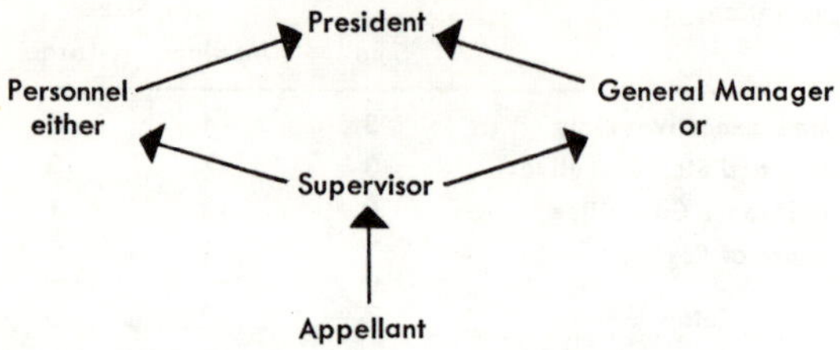

President
Personnel either
General Manager or
Supervisor
Appellant

The second most popular appeal system among the respondents was the "line executive only" method. This procedure involved at least two steps, but more often had three, four, or four-plus. Examples of such systems are as follows in Figure 6.

FIGURE 6

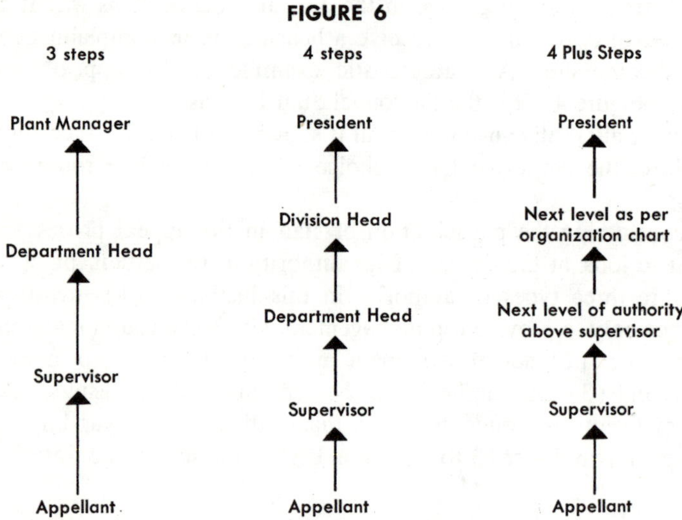

According to the line executive system, the employee must move directly up the chain of command and he may *not* skip a level. He must begin by taking his complaint to his supervisor. If a settlement cannot be reached at this level, he may take it to the next level. This process must continue until he receives a decision or until he reaches the last level, which is generally the president of the firm, whereupon a final decision must be rendered.

Eleven of the 52 respondents employed a board of reviews at a stage in their step-by-step procedure. The membership of the board consisted of company executives. Normally this membership was not permanently established, for after reviewing a particular case, the board was disbanded. The next employee complaint was handled by a new board composed of different executives.

In some firms the board consisted of a line executive appointed by management, a line executive selected by the employee registering the complaint, and the personnel manager. In other companies the board was appointed entirely by management, and included the department head under whom the aggrieved employee's immediate supervisor served. In still other cases the board consisted of five members: two selected by management, two by the employee, and the personnel manager.

Generally the board entered the appeal system at the third step. In five of the eleven companies, board of review decisions were binding on both the company and the employee. In the other six cases, the chief executive had the right to make the final decision.

The fourth variation of the "policy and procedure" appeal systems is the grievance committee. This committee does not constitute an actual step in the appeal network. Its only function is to advise the aggrieved employee and represent him before the staff and line executives reviewing complaints.

The membership of the grievance committee is quite different from that of the board of review. It consists of employees elected to the position. These elected members have the responsibility of processing employee complaints for hearing before the management officers handling the appeal.

6. Conclusions

Based upon analysis of 91 formal appeal programs, I draw the following inferences and conclusions. Some of these points were not developed in this report. They are based upon the findings of the more extensive study which is to be found in my forthcoming book, *Organizational Appeal Systems.*

1. A large number of companies recognize the principle of an employee's right to appeal through the use of an upward channel of communication as *an alternative to the chain of command.*
2. To insure that the rights recognized by the company are understood by employees a policy is developed. This policy, whether formal or informal, puts management on record that it considers legitimate the by-passing of the chain of command for expressing a complaint.
3. In cases where appeal procedures are associated with appeal policies, line executives abdicate some of their authority to veto the decisions of subordinates. Higher levels of management could not reverse a settlement reached at lower levels of the appeal system without risking the destruction of the entire program.
4. Very little was said by responding companies about what they recognize as appealable and nonappealable matters. In just three cases was the statement made that only alleged violations of employee rights *as stated in the employee handbook* are appealable. Apparently in all other cases, the many things which constitute work related complaints are appealable.

5. Most evidence points to the fact that the appeal programs examined were generally designed for the non-exempt employee, either operative or clerical. However nothing is usually stated in the manuals to exclude other categories of employees such as professional, scientific, and executive. Apparently the appeal system is available to all, but just the operative and clerical employees are expected to use it. These observations are gathered from the tone, format, and language used in employee handbooks when appeal rights are discussed.

6. Provision is made by the appeal system to settle all complaints internally. There were provisions in just two cases for an outsider to arbitrate complaints as a final step in the appeal procedure.

7. There is an association between the size of company and the likelihood of finding a formal appeal system. The bigger the company, the greater is this probability. Also the bigger the company, the greater is the chance that the personnel department will have an important role in the appeal system.

8. Based on incomplete information, there seems to be an inverse relationship between mobility in an industry and the prevalency of appeal programs among firms in an industry. This may account for the relatively low number of appeal programs in retail as opposed to manufacturing.

PART SEVEN

Organization Development

The organization development "movement" is of fairly recent origin. Its post-1965 impact has been great and continues to grow. This movement is influencing many managers in the direction of rethinking many of their traditional assumptions and practices.

While the phrase "organization development" can refer to a wide variety of change concepts and strategies related to the human side of organizational life, it connotes some quite specific behavioral science meanings.

In particular, organization development activities center on the work team — improvement of its problem-solving capabilities through the management of its culture and its ability to learn — and on total-system implications. By work team culture, we mean group norms and the realm of sentiments (feelings).

The chief methodologies in organization development activities are (1) interpersonal and group skills transposed from the laboratory training setting to the work team and (2) the "action research model." This does not mean that sensitivity training and organization development are the same thing. They are not. But knowledge and skills in the areas of communications, feedback, and group processes are important in effective organization development efforts. Action research refers to the cycle of data gathering from a system or subsystem, feedback to system members, work with the data, and action planning. This model is clearly visible in several of the selections which follow.

Since the thrust of organization development activities is toward more effective problem solving in organizational work teams, secondary outcomes may be one or more of a variety of changes in such areas as leadership style, work design, work flow, organizational structure, and even technology.

Attention to total system ramifications, however, may be a neglected area in organization development programs. We believe that it is vital in organization improvement efforts to pay attention to the congruency (or lack of it) among a wide range of subsystems, including staffing, job design, appraisal, compensation, development, and justice. This, of course, would include an examination of the underlying assumptions and techniques in the administration of various programs, for instance, management by objectives, incentive systems, and systems of appeal.

A. THE NATURE OF ORGANIZATION DEVELOPMENT

"What is OD?," Selection 29, summarizes the need for organization development, the objective it hopes to attain, and the underlying process it utilizes. Since the strategies and techniques of application are quite varied, this selection helps us to understand the underpinnings of the whole movement.

29

What is OD?

NATIONAL TRAINING LABORATORIES

OD has joined the long list of "initialisms" and acronyms with which we try to tag the complex functions of the modern world. It stands for *Organization Development,* itself a short title for a way of looking at the whole human side of organizational life.

Experiments and studies over 50 years have convinced many behavioral scientists that our organizations are inefficient in realizing the potential of their human resources, that they function on the basis of incorrect assumptions about the nature of man, and that they tend to limit the growth of the persons who work in them. The growing tendency among college students to look with suspicion at a career in industry confirms the findings. It might have been expected, in a society where economic survival is no longer a major issue for the educated, that college graduates would become primarily concerned with their development and experience as complete human beings. OD attempts to help institutions meet that challenge — not only industrial organizations, but also school systems, government agencies, religious and volunteer associations, and others.

Using knowledge and techniques from the behavioral sciences, organization development attempts to integrate individual needs for growth and development with organizational goals and objectives in order to make a more effective organization.

A few of the behavioral science findings and hypotheses underlying the theory and method of OD are here listed:

- Work which is organized to meet people's needs as well as to achieve organizational requirements tends to produce the highest productivity and quality of production.
- Individuals whose basic needs are taken care of do not seek a soft and secure environment. They are interested in work, challenge, and responsibility. They expect recognition and satisfying interpersonal relationships.
- People have a drive toward growth and self-realization.
- Persons in groups which go through a managed process of increasing openness about both positive and negative feelings develop a strong identification with the goals of the group and its other members. The group becomes increasingly capable of dealing constructively with potentially disruptive issues.
- Personal growth is facilitated by a relationship which is honest, caring, and nonmanipulative.
- Positive change flows naturally from groups which feel a common identification and an ability to influence their environment.

The Objectives of OD

Building on these findings and assumptions, OD begins with a process of diagnosing the roadblocks which prevent the release of human potential within the organization. Following are a number of objectives of an OD Project:

1. To create an open, problem-solving climate throughout the organization.
2. To supplement the authority associated with role or status with the authority of knowledge and competence.
3. To locate decision-making and problem-solving responsibilities as close to the information sources as possible.
4. To build trust among individuals and groups throughout the organization.
5. To make competition more relevant to work goals and to maximize collaborative efforts.
6. To develop a reward system which recognizes both the achievement of the organization's mission (profits or service) and organization development (growth of people).
7. To increase the sense of "ownership" or organization objectives throughout the work force.

8. To help managers to manage according to relevant objectives rather than according to "past practices" or according to objectives which do not make sense for one's area of responsibility.
9. To increase self-control and self-direction for people within the organization.

OD Technology

An OD approach is applicable to any type of organization or group function and at any phase of organizational or group life. It is equally appropriate to a team or department and to an entire organization, to current problems and to long-range planning, to start-ups and to reorganizations.

A group undertaking an OD program goes through the following process:

1. Identification of problems.
2. Setting problem priorities.
3. Development and sharing of data concerning these problems. (These data may cover any aspect of the organization's life: technology, systems and structure, interpersonal and personal factors.)
4. Joint action planning, emphasizing alternatives.
5. Implementation and testing of selected alternatives.
6. Periodic review and further action. (Action will tend to fan out as clearer diagnoses and additional alternatives become apparent.)

Basic to all specific OD technology is the principle of maximizing the initiative of the organization's resources. Outside consultants may share the responsibility for the process, but they will work toward increasing the organization's internal capacity to understand and manage its organic growth . . .

B. TYPES OF CHANGE EFFORTS

The emerging role of behavioral scientists and their strategies for applying knowledge toward the improvement of human organizations is reviewed by Bennis (Selection 30). He is concerned with the strategies, methodologies, and conceptual issues which have emerged as a consequence of the assumption of action roles by behavioral scientists. His references to laboratory training, the University of Michigan's Institute for Social Research, Blake's "Managerial Grid," and to Richard Beckhard provide a good lead-in for the articles which follow.

Knowledge about the use of laboratory training as a means of enhancing the effectiveness of organizations is reviewed and evaluated by Buchanan (Selection 31). More specifically, Buchanan discusses the following dimensions to the evaluation, design, and application of laboratory training: (1) the problems and progress in evaluating the impact of laboratory training; (2) the development in theory which attempts to explain what happens in a T-Group; (3) the persistence and types of learning from this experience; (4) the factors influencing learning; and (5) the types of individuals most likely to be affected.

The Baumgartel article (Selection 32) is illustrative of the data gathering and feedback techniques developed by the Institute for Social Research. Its conclusions, we believe, go to the heart of why properly conducted organization development activities have such potential for constructive change:

> *. . . it deals with the system of human relationships as a whole . . . and . . . with each manager, supervisor, and employee in the context of his own job, his own problems, and his own work relationships.*

Change in interpersonal behavior becomes only one of the subsystems or components to organization development in the model presented by Blake, et al. *(Selection 33). Their change strategy involves six phases which may require four or more years for total implementation in a large organization. In general, the initial objective is to change an organization in the direction of "team management" (high concern for people and high concern for production or a 9, 9 system).*

A valuable case study of an organization development program, incorporating a number of the strategies discussed in the previous readings is presented by Beckhard (Selection 34). The setting was a medium-sized decentralized organization. The goals of the OD program were:

• improved communication between various units of the organization

• change in management style from management by control to management by objectives

• improved operating efficiency

• increased problem solving skills of all managers

• establishment of a program for growth and development of all executives.

Beckhard presents the program which the organization followed in working toward these objectives and the role of the consultant in this process.

30

Theory and Method in Applying Behavioral Science to Planned Organizational Change[1]

WARREN G. BENNIS
Massachusetts Institute of Technology

What we have witnessed in the past two or three decades has been called the "Rise of the Rational Spirit" — the belief that science can help to better the human condition (Merton & Lerner, 1951). The focus of this paper is on one indication of this trend: the emerging role for the behavioral scientist and, more specifically, the attempts by behavioral scientists to apply knowledge (primarily sociological and psychological) toward the improvement of human organizations.

The Emergence of the Action Role

Many signs and activities point toward an emerging action role for the behavioral scientist. The *manipulative standpoint,* as Lasswell calls it, is

Reproduced by special permission from *The Journal of Applied Behavioral Science,* "Theory and Method in Applying Behavioral Science to Planned Organizational Change," Warren G. Bennis, pp. 337–360. Copyright 1965 NTL Institute Publications.

becoming distinguishable from the *contemplative standpoint* and is increasingly ascendant insofar as knowledge utilization is concerned.[2] Evidence can be found in the growing literature on planned change through the uses of the behavioral sciences (Bennis, Benne, & Chin, 1961; Freeman, 1963; Zetterberg, 1962; Gibb & Lippitt, 1959; Leeds & Smith, 1963; Likert & Hayes, 1957; Glock, Lippitt, Flanagan, Wilson, Shartle, Wilson, Croker, & Page, 1960) and in such additions to the vocabulary of the behavioral scientist as action research, client system, change agent, clinical sociology, knowledge centers, social catalysts. The shift is also reflected in increased emphasis on application in annual meeting time of the professional associations or in the formation of a Center for Research on the Utilization of Scientific Knowledge within The University of Michigan's Institute for Social Research.

It is probably true that in the United States there is a more practical attitude toward knowledge than anywhere else. When Harrison Salisbury (1960) traveled over Europe he was impressed with the seeming disdain of European intellectuals for practical matters. Even in Russia he found little interest in the "merely useful." Salisbury saw only one great agricultural experiment station on the American model. In that case professors were working in the fields. They told him, "People call us Americans."

Not many American professors may be found working in the fields, but they can be found almost everywhere else: in factories, in the government, in underdeveloped countries, in mental hospitals, in educational systems. They are advising, counseling, researching, recruiting, developing, consulting, training. Americans may not have lost their deep ambivalence toward the intellectual, but it is clear that the academic intellectual has become *engagé* with spheres of action in greater numbers, with more diligence, and with higher aspirations than at any other time in history.

It may be useful to speculate about the reasons for the shift in the intellectual climate. Most important, but trickiest to identify, are those causative factors bound up in the warp and woof of "our times and age" that Professor Boring calls the *Zeitgeist*. The apparently growing disenchantment with the moral neutrality of the scientist may be due, in C. P. Snow's phrase, to the fact that "scientists cannot escape their own knowledge." In any event, though "impurity" is still implied, action research as distinguished from pure research does not carry the opprobrium it once did.

Perhaps the crucial reason for the shift in emphasis toward application is simply that we know more.[3] Since World War II we have obtained large bodies of research and diverse reports on application. We are today in a better position to assess results and potentialities of applied social science.

Finally, there is a fourth factor having to do with the fate and viability of human organization, particularly as it has been conceptualized as "bureaucracy." I use the term in its sociological, Weberian sense, not as a metaphor *à la* Kafka's *The Castle* connoting "red tape," impotency, inefficiency, despair. In the past three decades Weber's vision has been increasingly scrutinized and censured. Managers and practitioners, on the one hand, and organizational theorists and researchers on the other, are more and more dissatisfied with current practices of organizational behavior and are searching for new forms and patterns of organizing for work. A good deal of activity is being generated.

The Lack of a Viable Theory of Social Change

Unfortunately, no viable theory of social change has been established. Indeed it is a curious fact about present theories that they are strangely silent on matters of *directing* and *implementing* change. What I particularly object to — and I include the "newer" theories of neo-conflict (Coser, 1956; Dahrendorf, 1961), neo-functionalism (Boskoff, 1964), and neo-revolutionary theories — is that they tend to explain the dynamic interactions of a system without providing one clue to the identification of strategic leverages for alteration. They are suitable for *observers* of social change, not for practitioners. They are theories of *change,* and not of *changing.*

It may be helpful to suggest quickly some of the prerequisites for a theory of changing. I am indebted here to my colleague Robert Chin (1961, 1963):

a. A theory of changing must include manipulable variables — accessible levers for influencing the direction, tempo, and quality of change and improvement.

b. The variables must not violate the client system's values.

c. The cost of usage cannot be prohibitive.

d. There must be provided a reliable basis of diagnosing the strength and weakness of conditions facing the client system.

e. Phases of intervention must be clear so that the change agent can develop estimates for termination of the relationship.

f. The theory must be communicable to the client system.

g. It must be possible to assess appropriateness of the theory for different client systems.

Such a theory does not now exist, and this probably explains why change agents appear to write like "theoretical orphans" and, more important, why so many change programs based on theories of social change have been inadequate. This need should be kept in mind as we look at models of knowledge utilization.

The Notion of Planned Change

Planned change can be viewed as a linkage between theory and practice, between knowledge and action. It plays this role by converting variables from the basic disciplines into strategic instrumentation and programs. Historically, the development of planned change can be seen as the resultant of two forces: complex problems requiring expert help and the growth and viability of the behavioral sciences. The term "behavioral sciences" itself is of post-World War II vintage coined by the more empirically minded to "safeguard" the social disciplines from the nonquantitative humanists and the depersonalized abstractions of the econometricists. The process of planned change involves a *change agent,* a *client system,* and the collaborative attempt to apply *valid knowledge* to the client's problems.[4]

Elsewhere I have attempted a typology of change efforts in which planned change is distinguished from other types of change in that it entails mutual goal setting, an equal power ratio (eventually), and deliberateness on both sides (Bennis et al., 1961, p. 154).

It may further help in defining planned change to compare it with another type of deliberate change effort, Operations Research. I enter this with a humility bordering on fear and a rueful sense of kinship in our mutual incapacity to explain to one another the nature of our work. There are these similarities. Both are World War II products; both are problem-centered (though both have also provided inputs to the concepts and method of their parent disciplines).[5] Both emphasize improvement and to that extent are *normative* in their approach to problems. Both rely heavily on empirical science; both rely on a relationship of confidence and valid communication with clients; both emphasize a *systems* approach to problems — that is, both are aware of interdependence within the system as well as boundary maintenance with its environment; and both appear to be most effective when working with systems which are complex, rapidly changing, and probably science-based.

Perhaps the most crucial difference between OR and planned change has to do with the identification of strategic variables, that is, with those factors which appear to make a difference in the performance of the system. Planned change is concerned with such problems as (1) the identification of mission and values, (2) collaboration and conflict, (3) control and leadership, (4) resistance and adaptation to change, (5) utilization of human resources, (6) communication, (7) management development. OR practitioners tend to select economic or engineering variables which are more quantitative, measurable, and linked to profit and efficiency. Ackoff and Rivett (1963), for example, classify OR problems under (1) inventory, (2) allocation, (3) queuing, (4) sequencing, (5) routing, (6) replacement, (7) competition, (8) search.

A second major difference has to do with the perceived importance of the relationship with the client. In planned change, the quality and nature of the relationship are used as indicators for the measure of progress and as valid sources of data and diagnosis. Undoubtedly, the most successful OR practitioners operate with sensitivity toward their clients; but if one looks at what they *say* about their work, they are clearly less concerned with human interactions.

A third major difference is that the OR practitioner devotes a large portion of his time to research, to problem solving. The change agent tends to spend somewhat more time on implementation through counseling, training, management development schemes, and so forth. Fourth, planned-change agents tend to take less seriously the idea of the *system* in their approaches. Finally, the idea of an interdisciplinary team, central to OR, does not seem to be a part of most planned-change programs.

One thing that emerges from this comparison is a realization of the complexity of modern organization. Look through the kaleidoscope one way, and a configuration of the economic and technological factors appears; tilt it, and what emerges is a pattern of internal human relations problems. It is on these last problems and their effects upon performance of the system that practitioners of planned organizational change tend to work.

A Focus of Convenience

To develop what George Kelley refers to as a "focus of convenience" for planned organizational change, I want to make two key aspects clearer: the notions of "collaborative relationships" and of "valid knowledge." I see the outcome of planned-change efforts as depending to some considerable extent on the relationship between client and agent. To optimize a collaborative relationship, there need to be a "spirit of inquiry," with data publicly shared, and equal freedom to terminate the relationship and to influence the other.

As to valid knowledge, the criteria are based on the requirements for a viable applied behavioral science research — an applied behavioral science that:

a. Takes into consideration the behavior of persons operating within their specific institutional environments;
b. Is capable of accounting for the interrelated levels (person, group, role, organization) within the context of the social change;
c. Includes variables that the policy maker and practitioner can understand, manipulate, and evaluate;
d. Can allow selection of variables appropriate in terms of its own values, ethics, moralities;
e. Accepts the premise that groups and organizations as units are amenable to empirical and analytic treatment;
f. Takes into account external social processes of change as well as interpersonal aspects of the collaborative process;
g. Includes propositions susceptible to empirical test focusing on the dynamics of change.

These criteria must be construed as an arbitrary goal, not as an existing reality. To my knowledge, there is no program which fulfills these requirements fully. In this focus of convenience, I have arbitrarily selected change agents working on organizational dynamics partly because of my greater familiarity with their work but also because they seem to fulfill the criteria outlined to a greater extent than do other change agents. My choice of emphasis is also based on the belief that changes in the sphere of organizations — primarily industrial — in patterns of work and relationship, structure, technology, and administration promise some of the most significant changes in our society. Indeed it is my guess that industrial society, at least in the United States, is more radical, innovative, and adventurous in adapting new ways of organizing than the government, the universities, and the labor unions, who appear rigid and stodgy in the face of rapid change. If space permitted, however, I would refer also to change agents working in a variety of fields — rural sociology, economics, anthropology — and in such settings as communities, hospitals, cultural-change programs.

Let us turn now to some of the "traditional" models of knowledge utilization.

Eight Types of Change Programs[6]

It is possible to identify eight types of change programs if we examine their strategic rationale: exposition and propagation, élite corps, human relations training, staff, scholarly consultations, circulation of ideas to the élite, developmental research, and action research.

I should like to look at each of these programs quickly and then refer to four biases which seem to me to weaken their impact.

Exposition and propagation, perhaps the most popular type of program, assumes that knowledge is power. It follows that the men who possess "Truth" will lead the world.

Elite corps programs grow from the realization that ideas by themselves do not constitute action and that a strategic *role* is a necessity for ideas to be implemented (e.g., through getting scientists into government as C. P. Snow suggests).

Human relations training programs are similar to the élite corps idea in the attempt to translate behavioral science concepts in such ways that they take on personal referents for the men in power positions.

Staff programs provide a source of intelligence within the client system, as in the work of social anthropologists advising military governors after World War II. The strategy of the staff idea is to observe, analyze, and to plan rationally (Myrdal, 1958).

Scholarly consultation, as defined by Zetterberg (1962), includes exploratory inquiry, scholarly understanding, confrontation, discovery of solutions, and scientific advice to client.

Circulation of ideas to the élite builds on the simple idea of influencing change by getting to the people with power or influence.

Developmental research has to do with seeing whether an idea can be brought to an engineering stage. Unlike Zetterberg's scholarly confrontation, it is directed toward a particular problem, not necessarily a client, and is concerned with implementation and program. (I would wager that *little* developmental research is being done today in the behavioral sciences.)

Action research, the term coined by Kurt Lewin, undertakes to solve a problem for a client. It is identical to applied research generally except that in action research the roles of researcher and subject may change and reverse, the subjects becoming researchers and the researchers engaging in action steps.

These eight programs, while differing in objectives, values, means of influence, and program implications, are similar in wanting to use knowledge to gain some socially desirable end. Each seems successful or promising; each has its supporters and its detractors. Intrinsic to them all, I believe, is some bias or flaw which probably weakens their full impact. Four biases are particularly visible.

Rationalistic Bias: No Implementation of Program

Most of the strategies rely almost totally on rationality. But knowledge *about* something does *not* lead automatically to intelligent action. Intelligent action requires commitment and programs as well as truth.

Technocratic Bias: No Spirit of Collaboration

Change typically involves risk and fear. Any significant change in human organization involves rearrangement of patterns of power, association, status, skills, and values. Some may benefit, others may lose. Thus change typically involves risk and fear. Yet change efforts sometimes are conducted as if there were no need to discuss and "work through" these fears and worries (e.g., F. W. Taylor's failure to consider the relationship between the engineer with the stopwatch and the worker, or Freud's early work when he considered it adequate to examine the unconscious of his patients and tell them what he learned — even to the extent of analyzing dreams by mail).

Individualist Bias: No Organization Strategy Is Involved

This refers to strategies which rely on the individual while denying the organizational forces and roles surrounding him. There is, however, simply no guarantee that a wise individual who attains power will act wisely. It may be that *role corrupts* — both the role of power and the role of powerlessness. In any event, there is no guarantee that placing certain types of people in management — or training them or psychoanalyzing them or making scientists of them — leads to more effective action. Scientists act like administrators when they gain power. And graduates of human relations training programs tend to act like non-alumni shortly after their return to their organizational base.

The staff idea, proposed by Myrdal, is limited by the unresolved tensions in the staff-line dilemma noted by students of organizational behavior and by the conflicts derived from the role of the intellectual working in bureaucratic structures. The élite strategy has serious drawbacks, primarily because it focuses on the individual and not the organization.

Insight Bias: No Manipulability

My major quarrel here is not with the formulation: insight leads to change, though this can be challenged, but with the lack of provision of variables accessible to control. It is not obvious that insight leads directly to sophistication in rearranging social systems or making strategic organizational interventions. Insight provides the relevant variables for planned change as far as personal manipulation goes, but the question remains: How can that lead directly to the manipulation of external factors?

The Elements of Planned Organizational Change

In the October 7, 1963, edition of the *New York Times,* a classified ad announced a search for change agents. It read:

> WHAT'S A CHANGE AGENT? A result-oriented individual able to accurately and quickly resolve complex tangible and intangible problems. Energy and ambition necessary for success . . .

The change agents I have in mind need more than "energy and ambition." They are *professionals* who, for the most part, hold doctorates in the behavioral sciences. They are not a very homogeneous group, but they do have some similarities.

They are alike in that they take for granted the *centrality of work* in our culture to men and women in highly organized instrumental settings; in their concern with improvement, development, and measurement of *organizational effectiveness;* in their *preoccupation with people* and the process of human interaction; in their interest in changing the relationships, perceptions, and values of *existing personnel.* They may be members of the client system, arguing that inside knowledge is needed, or external agents, arguing that perspective, detachment, and energy from outside are needed. They intervene at different structural points in the organization and at different times.

Though each change agent has in mind a set of unique goals based on his own theoretical position and competencies as well as the needs of the client system, there are some general aims. In a paradigm developed by Chris Argyris (1962), bureaucratic values tend to stress the rational, task aspects of work and to ignore the basic human factors which, if ignored, tend to reduce task competence. Managers brought up under this system of values are badly cast to play the intricate human roles now required of them. Their ineptitude and anxieties lead to systems of discord and defense which interfere with the problem-solving capacity of the organization.

Generally speaking, the normative goals of change agents derive from this paradigm. They include: improving interpersonal competence of managers; effecting a change in values so that human factors and feelings come to be considered legitimate; developing increased understanding among and within working groups to reduce tensions; developing "team management"; developing better methods of "conflict resolution" than suppression, denial, and the use of unprincipled power; viewing the organization as an organic system of relationships marked by mutual trust, interdependence, multigroup membership, shared responsibility, and conflict resolution through training or problem solving.

Programs for Implementing Planned Organizational Change

Discussion here will focus on three broad types of change programs that seem to be most widely used, frequently in some combination: training, consultation, and research.

Training

Training is an inadequate word in this context, as its dictionary meaning denotes "drill" and "exercise." I refer to what has been called laboratory training, sensitivity or group dynamics training, and most commonly, T-Group training.[7] The idea originated in Bethel, Maine, under the guidance of Leland Bradford, Kenneth Benne, and Ronald Lippitt, with initial influence from the late Kurt Lewin. The T Group has evolved since 1947 into one of the main instruments for organizational change. Bradford has played a central role in this development as director of the National Training Laboratories. Growth has been facilitated through the active participation of a number of university-based behavioral scientists and practitioners. Tavistock Institute has played a similar role in England, and recently a group of European scientists set up a counterpart to the National Training Laboratories.

The main objective at first was *personal change* or *self-insight.* Since the fifties the emphasis has shifted to *organizational development,* a more precise date being 1958, when the Esso Company inaugurated a series of laboratories at refineries over the country under the leadership of Blake and Shepard (Shepard, 1960).

Briefly, laboratory training unfolds in an unstructured group setting where participants examine their interpersonal relationships. By examining data generated by themselves, members attempt to understand the dynamics of group behavior, e.g., decision processes, leadership and influence, norms, roles, communication distortions, effects of authority on behavioral patterns, coping mechanisms. T-Group composition is itself a strategic issue. Thus the organization may send an executive to a "stranger laboratory" which fills a "seeding" function; "cousin laboratories" may be conducted for persons of similar rank and occupational responsibilities within the company but from different functional groups; "diagonal slices" may be composed of persons of different rank but not in the same work group or in direct relationship; and "family laboratories" may be conducted for functional groups. The more the training groups approach a "family," the more the total organization is affected.

Consulting

The change agent *qua* consultant, perhaps best exemplified in the work of the Tavistock Institute, operates in a manner very like the practicing physician or psychoanalyst: that is, he starts from the chief "presenting symptom" of the client, articulates it in such a way that causal and underlying mechanisms of the problem are understood, and then takes remedial action. Heavy emphasis is placed on the strategy of *role model* because the main instrument is the change agent himself. Sofer (1961) reveals this when he suggests that psychotherapy or some form of clinical experience is necessary preparation for the change agent. Argyris, as consultant, confronts the group with their behavior toward him as an analogue of their behavior *vis-à-vis* their own subordinates.

If the role of the consultant sounds ambiguous and vague, this probably reflects reality. Certainly in the consultant approach the processes of change and the change agent's interventions are less systematic and less programmed than in training or applied research programs. A word about the latter.

Applied Research

I refer here to research in which the results are used systematically as an *intervention*. Most methods of research application collect information and report it. Generally, the relationship ends there. In the survey-feedback approach, as developed primarily by Floyd Mann (1957) and his associates at The University of Michigan's Institute for Social Research, this is only the beginning. Data are reported in "feedback" meetings where subjects become clients and have a chance to review the findings, test them against their own experience, and even ask the researchers to test some of their hypotheses. Instead of being submitted "in triplicate" and probably ignored, research results serve to activate involvement and participation in the planning, collection, analysis, and interpretation of more data.

Richard Beckhard, too, utilizes data as the first step in his work as change agent (in press). In his procedure the data are collected through formal, nonstructured interviews which he then codes by themes about the managerial activities of the client for discussion at an off-site meeting with the subjects.

It should be stressed that most planned-change inductions involve all three processes — training, consulting, researching — and that both agent and client play a variety of roles. The final shape of the change agent's role is not as yet clear, and it is hazardous to report exactly what change agents do on the basis of their reports. Many factors, of course, determine the particular intervention the change agent may choose: among these factors are ones pertaining to cost, time, degree of collaboration required, state of target system, and so on.

Strategic Models Employed by Change Agents

More often than not, change agents fail to report their strategy or to make it explicit. It may be useful to look at two quite different models that are available: one developed by Robert Blake in his "Managerial Grid" system, and one with which I was associated at an Esso refinery and which Chris Argyris evaluated some years later.

Blake has developed a change program based on his analytic framework of managerial styles (Blake, Mouton, Barnes, & Greiner, 1964). Figure 1 shows the grid for locating types of managerial strategies. Blake and his colleagues attempt to change the organization in the direction of "team management" (9, 9 or high concern for people and high concern for production). Based on experience with 15 different factories, the Blake strategy specifies six phases: off-site laboratory for "diagonal slice" of personnel; off-site program focused on team training for "family" groups; training in the plant location designed to achieve better integration between functional groups; goal-setting sessions for groups of 10 to 12 managers.

Blake and his colleagues estimate that these four phases may require two years or longer. The next two, implementing plans and stabilizing changes, may require an additional two years.

Figure 2 (Argyris, 1960) presents another strategy: a change program used in a large oil company to improve the functioning of one of its smaller refineries. A new manager was named and sent to a T-Group training session to gain awareness of the human problems in the refinery. The Headquarters Organizational Development staff then conducted a diagnosis through a survey and interview of the managerial staff (70) and a sample of hourly employees (40/350). About that time the author was brought in to help the headquarters staff and the new manager.

It was decided that a laboratory program of T Groups might be effective but premature, with the result that weekly seminars that focused on new developments in human relations were held with top management (about 20). A one-week laboratory training program followed for all supervisors in diagonal slices, and then another re-evaluation of needs was undertaken. Some structural innovations were suggested and implemented. During the last phase of the program (not shown in the figure), the Scanlon Plan was

FIGURE 1
The Managerial Grid

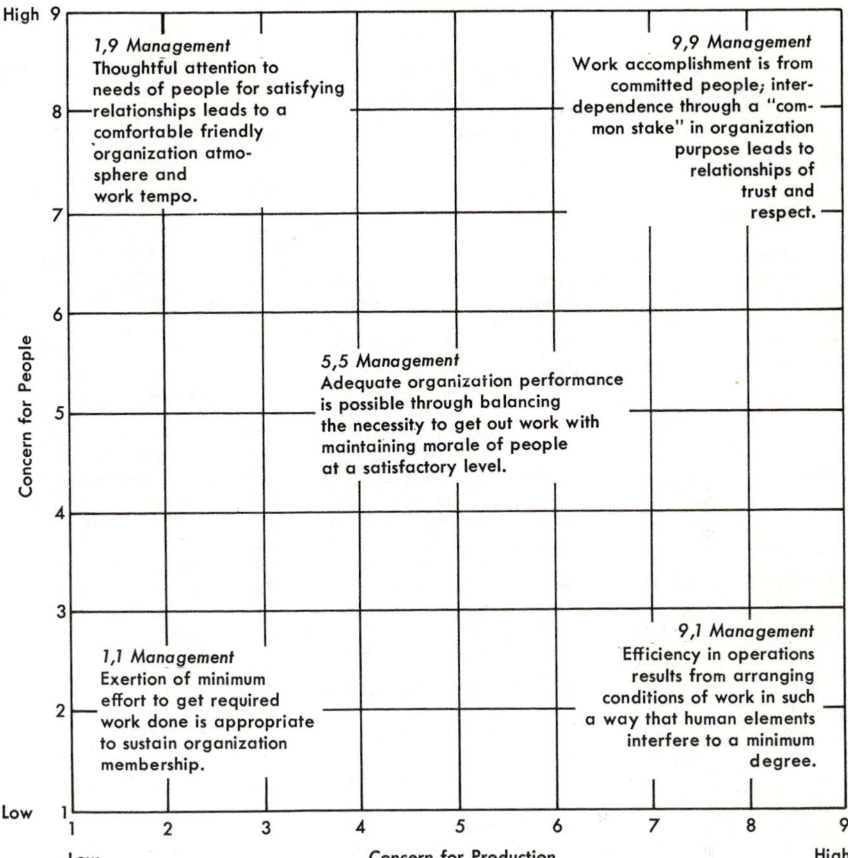

adapted and installed (incidentally, for the first time in a "process" industry and for the first time that a union agreed to the Plan without a bonus automatically guaranteed).

Though it cannot be said with any assurance that these two strategies are typical, it may be helpful to identify certain features: (a) *length of time* (Blake estimates five years; the refinery program took two years up to the Scanlon Plan); (b) *variety of programs* utilized (research, consulting, training, teaching, planning); (c) *necessity of cooperation* with top management and the parent organization; (d) approaching the organization *as a system* rather than as a collection of individuals; (e) *phasing program* from individual to group to intergroup to overall organization; (f) intellectual *and* emotional content.

FIGURE 2

A Change Program

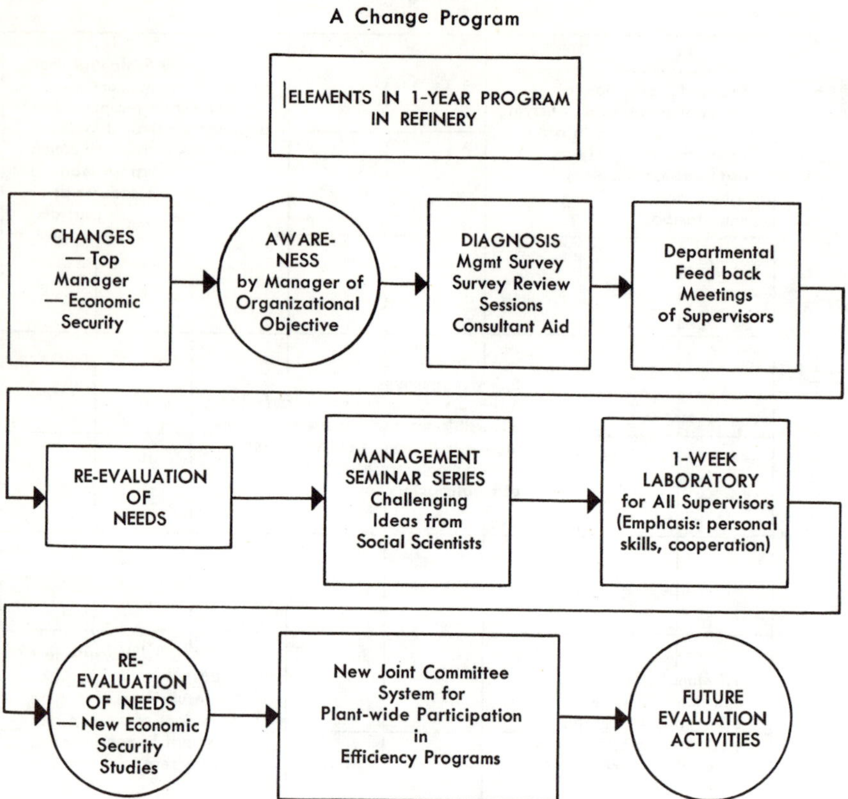

Power and the Role of the Change Agent

How and why do people and organizations change, and what is the nature and source of the power exerted by the change agent? We have to make inferences because change agents themselves tend to be silent on this. It is not *coercive power,* for the change agent generally does not have the ability to reward or punish. Moreover, he would prefer, at least intellectually, not to wield power at variance with his normative goals. Further, there is some evidence that coercive power is less durable than are other kinds of power, except under conditions of vigilant surveillance.

Traditional power? Almost certainly not. The change agent is, in fact, continually working without legitimization. *Expert power?* Possibly some, but it is doubtful whether his knowledge is considered "expert" enough — in the sense that an engineer or doctor or lawyer is seen as expert. *Referent* or *identification power?* Apparently so. Sofer, for example, attributes some influence to the client system's ability and desire to emulate the change agent. Still, this will vary from a considerable degree to not at all.

This leaves us with *value power* as the likeliest candidate of the possible sources of power. Most change agents do emit cues to a consistent value system. These values are based on Western civilization's notion of a scientific humanism: concern for our fellow man, experimentalism, openness and honesty, flexibility, cooperation, democracy. If what I have said about power is correct, it is significant (at least in the United States) that this set of values seems to be potent in influencing top management circles.

Characteristics of Client System

For the most part, the client systems appear to be sub-systems of relatively large-scale international operations who find themselves in increasingly competitive situations, in rapidly changing environments, subjected to what have been called "galloping variables." Often the enterprise was founded through an innovation or monopolistic advantage which is thought to be in jeopardy.

Then there is some tension — some discrepancy between the ideal and the actual — which seems to activate the change program.

Finally, there is some faith in the idea that an intermediate proportion of organizational effectiveness is determined by social and psychological factors and that improvement here, however vague or immeasurable, may improve organizational effectiveness.

The Measurement of Effects

Until very recently, change agents, if they did any evaluation research at all, concentrated almost exclusively on attitudinal and subjective factors. Even so-called "hard" behavioral variables, like absentee rates, sickness and accident rates, and personnel turnover were rarely investigated. Relating change programs to harder criteria, like productivity and economic and cost factors, was rarely attempted and never, to my knowledge, successful.

And again, the research that was conducted — even on the attitudinal measures — was far from conclusive. Roger Harrison attempted an evaluation study of Argyris' work and found that while there was a significant improvement in the individual executive's interpersonal ability compared with a control group, there was no significant "transfer" of this acuity to the real-life organizational setting. In short, there was a fairly rapid "fade-out" of effects obtained in T-Group training upon return to the organization (Harrison, 1962). This study also shows that new tensions were generated between those individuals who attended the training program and those who did not — an example of the lack of a *systems* approach. Shepard's evaluation on the Esso organization shows that the impact of laboratory training was greatest on personal and inter-personal learnings, but "slightly more helpful than useless" in changing the organization.

More recently, though, some studies have been undertaken which measure more meaningful, less subjective variables of organizational effectiveness. Blake, Mouton, Barnes, and Greiner (1964), for example, conducted an evaluation study of their work in a very large (4,000 employees) petrochemical plant. Not only did they find significant changes in the values, morale, and interpersonal behavior of the employees, but significant improvements in productivity, profits, and cost reduction. David (in press), a change agent working on a program that attempts to facilitate a large and complicated merger, attributed the following effects to the programs: increased productivity, reduced turnover and absenteeism, in addition to a significant improvement in the area of attitudes and subjective feelings.

While these new research approaches show genuine promise, much more has to be done. The research effort has somehow to equal all the energy that goes into developing the planned-change programs themselves.

Some Criticisms and Qualifications

The work of the change agents reported here is new and occurs without the benefit of methodological and strategic precedents. The role of the change agent is also new, its final shape not fully emerged. Thus it has both the advantage of freedom from the constraints facing most men of knowledge, and suffers from lack of guidelines and structure. Let us touch quickly on problems and criticisms facing the change agents.

Planned Change and Organizational Effectiveness

I can identify six dimensions of organizational effectiveness: legal, political, economic, technological, social, and personal. There is a good deal of fuzziness as to which of these change agents hope to affect, and the data are inconclusive. Argyris, who is the most explicit about the relationship between performance and interpersonal competence, is still hoping to develop good measures to establish a positive relationship. The connection has to be made, or the field will have to change its normative goal of constructing not only a *better* world but a more *effective* one.

A Question of Values

The values espoused indicate a way of *behaving and feeling;* for example, they emphasize openness rather than secrecy, collaboration rather than dependence or rebellion, cooperation rather than competition, consensus rather than individual rules, rewards based on self-control rather than externally induced rewards, team leadership rather than a one-to-one relationship with the boss, authentic relationships rather than those based on political maneuvering.

Are they natural? Desirable? Functional? What then happens to status or power drives? What about those individuals who have a low need for participation and/or a high need for structure and dependence? And what about those personal needs which seem to be incompatible with these images of man, such as a high need for aggression and a low need for affiliation? In short, what about those needs which can be best realized through bureaucratic systems? Or benevolent autocracies? Are these individuals to be changed or to yield and comply?

The problem of values deserves discussion. One of the obstacles is the emotional and value overtones which interfere with rational dialogue. More often than not, one is plunged into a polarized debate which converts ideas into ideology and inquiry into dogma. So we hear of "Theory X vs. Theory Y," personality vs. organization, democratic vs. autocratic, task vs. maintenance, human relations vs. scientific management, and on and on.

Surely life is more complicated than these dualities suggest, and surely they must imply a continuum — not simply extremes.

Lack of Systems Approach

Up to this point, I have used the term "organizational change" rather loosely. In Argyris' case, for example, organizational change refers to a change in values of 11 top executives, a change which was not necessarily of an enduring kind and apparently brought about some conflict with other interfaces. In most other cases of planned organizational change, the change induction was limited to a small, élite group. Only in the work of Blake and some others can we confidently talk about organizational change — in a systems way; his program includes the training of the entire management organization, and at several locations he has carried this step to include wage earners.

Sometimes the changes brought about simply "fade out" because there are no carefully worked out procedures to ensure coordination with other interacting parts of the system. In other cases, the changes have "backfired" and have had to be terminated because of their conflict with interface units. In any case, a good deal more has to be learned about the interlocking and stabilizing changes so that the total system is affected.

Some Generalizations

It may be useful, as peroration, to state in the most tentative manner some generalizations. They are derived, for the most part, from the foregoing discussion and anchored in experience and, wherever possible, in research and theory.

First, a forecast: I suspect that we will see an increase in the number of planned-change programs along the lines discussed here — toward *less* bureaucratic and *more* participative, "open system" and adaptive structures. Given the present pronounced rate of change, the growing reliance on science for the success of the industrial enterprise, the growing number of professionals joining these enterprises, and the "turbulent contextual environment" facing the firm, we can expect increasing demand for social inventions to revise traditional notions of organized effort.

As far as adopting and acceptance go, we already know a good deal.[8] *Adoption* requires that the *type* of change should be of proven quality, easily demonstrable in its effects, and with information easily available. Its cost and accessibility to control by the client system as well as its value accord have to be carefully considered.

Acceptance also depends on the relationship between the change agent and the client system: the more profound and anxiety-producing the change, the more collaborative and closer relationship required. In addition, we can predict that an anticipated change will be resisted to the degree that the client system possesses little or incorrect knowledge about the change, has relatively little trust in the source of the change, and has comparatively low influence in controlling the nature and direction of the change.

What we know least about is *implementation* — a process which includes the creation of understanding and commitment toward a particular change and devices whereby it can become integral to the client system's operations. I will try to summarize the necessary elements in implementation:

(a) The *client system* should have as much understanding of the change and its consequences, as much influence in developing and controlling the fate of the change, and as much trust in the initiator of the change as is possible.

(b) The *change effort* should be perceived as being as self-motivated and voluntary as possible. This can be effected through the legitimization and reinforcement of the change by the top management group and by the significant reference groups adjacent to the client system. It is also made possible by providing the utmost in true volition.

(c) The *change program* must include emotional and value as well as cognitive (informational) elements for successful implementation. It is doubtful that relying solely on rational persuasion (expert power) is sufficient. Most organizations possess the knowledge to cure their ills; the rub is utilization.

(d) The *change agent* can be crucial in reducing the resistance to change. As long as the change agent acts congruently with the principles of the program and as long as the client has a chance to test competence and motives (his own and the change agent's), the agent should be able to provide the psychological support so necessary during the risky phases of change. As I have stressed again and again, the quality of the client-agent relationship is pivotal to the success of the change program.

Notes and References

1. Drawn from keynote address presented at International Conference on Operational Research and the Social Sciences, Cambridge, England, September 1964.

2. For an excellent discussion of the "value" issues in this development, see Kaplan, A. *The Conduct of Inquiry.* San Francisco: Chandler, 1964, Chapter 10; and Benne, K. D., & Swanson, G. (eds.) "Values and social issues." *J. soc. Issues,* 1960, 6.

3. For a recent inventory of scientific findings of the behavioral sciences, see Berelson, B., & Steiner, G. A. *Human Behavior.* New York: Harcourt, Brace & World, 1964.

4. For a fuller discussion, see Lippitt, R., Watson, J., & Westley, B. *The Dynamics of Planned Change.* New York: Harcourt, Brace & World, 1961; and Bennis et al., 1961.

5. For a brilliant exposition on the contributions of applied research to "pure" theory, see Gouldner, A. "Theoretical requirements of the applied social sciences," in Bennis et al., 1961. Pp. 83–95.

6. For a fuller exposition of these ideas, see my paper, "A new role for the behavioral sciences: Effecting organizational change." *Administrative sci. Quart.,* 1963, 8, 125–165.

7. For a popular account of laboratory training, see Argyris, C. "T-groups for organizational effectiveness." *Harvard bus. Rev.,* 1964, 42, 60–74. For a theoretical background, see Bradford, L. P., Gibb, J. R., & Benne, K. D. (eds.) *T-group Theory and Laboratory Method.* New York: Wiley, 1964; and Schein, E. H., & Bennis, W. G. *Personal and Organizational Change Via Group Methods.* New York: Wiley, 1965.

8. See, in particular, Rogers, E. *The Diffusion of Innovations.* New York: Free Press, 1962; and Miles, M. (ed.) *Innovation in Education.* New York: Bureau of Publications, Teachers College, Columbia Univer., 1964.

Ackoff, R. L., and P. Rivett. *A Manager's Guide to Operations Research.* New York: Wiley, 1963, p. 34.

Argyris, C. *Organization Development: An Inquiry into the Esso Approach.* New Haven: Yale Univer., 1960.

Argyris, C. *Interpersonal Competence and Organizational Effectiveness.* Homewood, Ill.: Dorsey, 1962, p. 43.

Beckhard, R. "An organization improvement program in a decentralized organization." In D. Zand (ed.), *Organization Development: Theory and practice.* In press.

Bennis, W. G., K. D. Benne, and R. Chin (eds.), *The Planning of Change.* New York: Holt, Rinehart & Winston, 1961.

Blake, R. R., Jane S. Mouton, L. B. Barnes, and L. E. Greiner. "Breakthrough in organization development." *Harvard bus. Rev.,* 42 (1964), 133–155.

Boskoff, A. "Functional analysis as a source of a theoretical repertory and research tasks in the study of social change." In G. K. Zollschan and W. Hirsch, *Explorations in Social Change.* Boston: Houghton Mifflin, 1964.

Chin, R. "The utility of system models and developmental models for practitioners." In W. G. Bennis, K. D. Benne and R. Chin (eds.), *The Planning of Change*. New York: Holt, Rinehart & Winston, 1961, pp. 201–214.

Chin, R. "Models and ideas about changing." Paper read at Symposium on Acceptance of New Ideas, Univer. of Nebraska, November 1963.

Coser, L. *The Functions of Social Conflict*. New York: Free Press, 1956.

Dahrendorf, R. "Toward a theory of social conflict." In W. G. Bennis, K. D Benne, and R. Chin (eds.), *The Planning of Change*. New York: Holt, Rinehart & Winston, 1961, pp. 445–451.

David, G. "The Weldon study: An organization change program based upon change in management philosophy." In D. Zand (ed.), *Organization Development: Theory and Practice*. In press.

Freeman, H. E. "The strategy of social policy research." *The soc. welf. Forum,* (1963), 143–160.

Gibb, J. R., and R. Lippitt (eds.). "Consulting with groups and organizations." *J. soc. Issues,* 15 (1959).

Glock, C. Y., R. Lippitt, J. C. Flanagan, E. C. Wilson, C. L. Shartle, M. L. Wilson, G. W. Croker, and H. E. Page. *Case Studies in Bringing Behavioral Science Into Use*. Stanford, Calif.: Inst. Commun. Res., 1960.

Harrison, R. In C. Argyris, *Interpersonal Competence and Organizational Effectiveness.* Homewood, Ill.: Dorsey, 1962, Ch. 11.

Leeds, R., and T. Smith (eds.) *Using Social Science Knowledge in Business and Industry*. Homewood, Ill.: Irwin, 1963.

Likert, R., and S. P. Hayes, Jr. (eds.). *Some Applications of Behavioral Research.* Paris: UNESCO, 1957.

Mann, F. "Studying and creating change: A means to understanding social organization." *Research in Industrial Relations.* Ann Arbor: Industr. Relat. Res. Ass., 1957, Publication No. 17.

Merton, R. K., and D. Lerner. "Social scientists and research policy." In D. Lerner and H. D. Lasswell (eds.), *The Policy Sciences: Recent Developments in Scope and Method*. Stanford, Calif.: Stanford Univer. Press, 1951.

Myrdal, G. *Value in Social Theory*. New York: Harper, 1958, p. 29.

Parsons, R. T. "Evolutionary universals in society." *Amer. sociol. Rev.* 29 (1964), 339–357.

Salisbury, H. E. *To Moscow and Beyond.* New York: Harper, 1960, p. 136.

Shepard, H. Three management programs and the theory behind them." In *An Action Research Program for Organization Improvement.* Ann Arbor: Foundation for Research on Human Behavior, 1960.

Sofer, C. *The Organization from Within.* London: Tavistock, 1961.

Zetterberg, H. L. *Social Theory and Social Practice.* Totowa, N.J.: Bedminster, 1962.

31

Laboratory Training and Organization Development

PAUL C. BUCHANAN
Yeshiva University

A systematic review of the literature on the effectiveness of laboratory training in industry (Buchanan, 1965) resulted in the following conclusions:

1. Laboratory training is effective as a means of facilitating specifiable changes in individuals in the industrial setting
2. It has been used effectively in some programs of organizational development, but not in others
3. Behavioral scientists associated with the National Training Laboratories are actively engaged in subjecting their theories and methods to systematic analysis, and in developing strategies for organization development
4. Some of these strategies, now being studied systematically, are showing exciting results.

The purpose of this paper is to bring the earlier review up to date and to broaden the focus from industry to all types of organizations.

Interest in laboratory training in human relations has expanded significantly. For example, in 1968, National Training Laboratories were conducting 20 per cent more sessions than in the previous year; sensitivity training has become a common activity in workshops and teacher institutes in the field of education; and the number of professionals in the National Training Laboratories has increased from 159 in 1963 to 289 in 1968.

Research on laboratory training has also expanded. There have been 68 technical articles or books which pertain to some aspect of laboratory training published since the earlier review. (Buchanan, 1965). In a bibliography of research prepared by Durham and Gibb (1960), 49 studies were listed for the period 1947–1960, and 76 for the period 1960–1967. Undoubtedly the best single source of background information on the topic up to 1965 is the book by Schien and Bennis (1965).

Studies on laboratory training during the past four years deal with (1)

Taken and adapted from *Administrative Science Quarterly,* Vol. 14, No. 3, Sept. 1969, pp. 466–480. Used by permission.

the methodology of evaluation, (2) theory development, (3) kinds of learning brought about in the laboratories, (4) factors influencing learning in the laboratories, (5) types of individuals who learn from laboratory training, and (6) laboratory training in organization development.

Methodology of Evaluation

The methodology of evaluation continues to be a major problem, yet several recent studies indicate progress.

General Variables in Methodology

House (1967) classified the variables relevant to the problem of evaluation into four categories: objectives of the training, initial states of the learner, initial states of the organization, and methods of inducing change in the learner. Then, considering the methods as input variables, the objectives of the laboratory training as output variables, and the initial states of both the participants and the organization as moderators, he generated a paradigm of relationships that highlighted the issues in planning and assessing organizational development efforts and outlined a specific assessment design to illustrate the paradigm. The result is a clear presentation of relevant types of variables and their interconnectedness, a paradigm that is applicable to the design and assessment of any change in the "person dimension" (Leavitt, 1965) of organization performance. House's study also makes clear that neither the design nor the assessment of any training program is likely to be effective if it does not take into account variables in the *situation* as well as variables in the *person,* a finding highlighted earlier by Fleishman *et al.* (1955), but still often ignored. Equally important, House shows how theory can be used to make it possible for evaluation studies to contribute to a systematic body of knowledge. However, his paradigm is more adequate in providing for moderator than for output variables. As moderators he lists "the nature of the primary work group," "the formal authority system" of the organization, and "exercise of authority by superior"; yet he doesn't list these organization factors as output variables: he lists only changes in knowledge, skill, attitude, and job performance. But it is on the assumption that such changes in the participant will result in changes in the output of the work unit to which the learner belongs that organizations support training. As important as House's work is, therefore, it omits some important variables.

Problems of Design

While House dealt with general problems of design and evaluation, Harrison (1967) has made a thoughtful analysis of some specific issues. First, as he points out it is seldom possible to assign participants randomly to the treatment and a control group. Usually participants are either self-selected, or are assigned for administrative or other organizational reasons. Where control-groups are used for assessment studies, they are usually selected *post hoc* and with little information available about their similarity to the treatment group. For example, in the studies of Bunker (1965) and Bunker and Knowles (1967), control subjects were nominated by participants, and no data are given for the basis of this nomination, about the experiences the controls had during the period covered by the assessment, or the reasons why participants had attended the laboratory and the controls had not. Only two of the studies reviewed in this paper meet requirements for appropriate control groups (Deep, Bass, and Vaughan, 1967; Schmuck, 1968).

But there is an added difficulty in using a control group which Harrison discusses: the fact that being a member of a group influences expectations and thereby introduces bias, if perceptions of behavior are used as criteria. Because of these difficulties, Harrison encourages (and utilizes) assessment designs that examine the relation between (predicted) processes of training and outcomes from training.

A second problem is that of when assessment measures after laboratory training should be taken to obtain a valid evaluation of the impact of training. As Harrison points out, until one knows the pattern of the impact, he doesn't know what kinds of changes to look for and when. For example, the immediate effect on participants may be uncertainty, discomfort, and experimentation, which may then give way to confidence, new behavior patterns, and stabilization. If this were the case, then measures taken only at the end of the training would be very misleading.

Related to the issue of timing of evaluation is that of whether assessment should focus on predicted and/or desired outcomes (what Harrison calls a normative approach), or should be more like a net to catch whatever influences may be apparent. Harrison also discusses difficulties in assessing change on metagoals of laboratory training.

Because of variability in the designs of programs which are called laboratory training it is difficult to specify and apply a design that can be replicated or meaningfully compared with other training methods. As Harrison (1967:6) says, ". . . .we do not yet have adequate enough theory about the effects of different elements of training design even to permit us to classify laboratories according to design."

Miles (1965a, 1965b), for many years an innovator of evaluation designs, met many of the requirements of House's paradigm and Harrison's emphasis on examining process variables. More recently he and his associates have used theory in increasing the rigor of assessment designs (Miles *et al.,* 1965 and 1966; Benedict *et al.,* 1967). This method, which they called a "clinical-experimental approach," has five components: (1) It calls for a clear division of labor between the researcher responsible for assessment, and the change agents responsible for participants. (2) Data are collected both clinically (running account of events before, during, and following the interventions) and experimentally (by pre-planned and periodic measurements of the treatment and a control group. (3) The investigators make theory-based general predictions about the impact that the training is likely to have on specific variables of the organization. (4) The change agent obtains information from the participants, and on this basis formulates specific training activities; then he makes short-range predictions about the variables which the intervention would affect. (5) Careful attention is given to the tactical assessment design. (Miles uses a design involving treatment and control groups and several post-training measurements.) In the study reporting their attempt to use this design (Benedict, *et al.,* 1967) the investigators were not completely successful in meeting their methodological prescriptions; problems arose around keeping the research members and change agents from influencing each other (especially through the exchange of data); and there was questionable similarity between the treatment and the control groups. Even so, the approach of Miles and associates represents a significant improvement in evaluating change efforts.

The study by Marrow *et al.* (1967) is of special significance, partly because it exploited the availability of two large organizations with known similarity and with known "states of health." As in Miles' design, the change agents and the researchers constituted two separate teams. Measurements of human factors and management practices were repeated for both the treatment and the control organization. In addition, economic data were also obtained and systematically analyzed in relation to both short-range and longer-range impact on a number of variables. Further elaboration of the measure used is provided by Likert (1967).

Greiner's study of a grid-based organizational-development project was another methodological advance, in that in addition to the researchers' not being part of the change-agent team, information was obtained about conditions that preceded and in fact apparently led to, the intervention (Greiner, 1965; Blake, *et al.,* 1964).

Many of the studies reviewed have attempted, as Harrison and House suggest, to examine hypothesized relations among independent, intervening, and dependent variables (Rubin, 1967 a, b; Harrison, 1966; Kolb *et al.,* 1968; French *et al.,* 1966; Deep *et al.,* 1967; and Friedlander, 1967). Yet in many the basis of the predicted connection between the training and the measured outcome is not specified (Bunker and Knowles, 1967; Byrd, 1967). Equally important, many do not provide theoretical links between the expected change and improvement in performance on the job.

The practice of assessing the extent of change attributed to a training program by asking participants and their associates to describe any changes they have noted during a specified time after the training (Bunker, 1965; Bunker and Knowles, 1967) has obvious weaknesses such as the demands it makes on memory. But comparisons of responses to questionnaires obtained before and after training also present difficulties. One problem is that the standard of reference used by the respondent may itself be influenced significantly by the training. For example, Blake and Mouton (1968) required participants to rank themselves as to grid styles before and at the end of the seminar, and one of the expected outcomes from the seminar was to increase the use of the "9,9," style by participants. The data (Blake and Mouton, 1968:52) from measures before and after the seminar show a *decrease* of around 32 in the percentage of participants who saw themselves having 9,9 as their most characteristic style. And it is a common experience in groups where questionnaires are used to help the group diagnose and assess its progress on, say, openness, to find no increase or actually a decrease on ratings of openness at the same time that members state (and demonstrate) that they are becoming more open with each other.

There is also the problem of test sensitization, which can influence the responses of a control group. Friedlander (1967:305), in interpreting his data which revealed a decrease in effectiveness of the control group, noted:

> The first administration of the [Group Behavior Inventory] queried comparison group members with blunt questions on sensitive issues which they were unprepared to confront at that time. But after six months of observing those inadequacies that did occur, expectations and standards of the leadership role became clearer. Since current leadership practice did not conform to these expectations, comparison group members now perceived significantly greater inadequacies in the rapport and approachability of their chairman.

To the extent that a decrease occurs in the responses of the comparison group after the laboratory training, statistically significant differences between the treatment and the control group will lead to inaccurate conclusions about the impact of the training upon the treatment group. (They will look better due to an apparent decrease in the control group.) It appears that any measurement scheme involving perceptions are subject to error; therefore greater effort to devise other kinds are much needed.

Some additional shortcomings in the design of the assessment studies reviewed are:

1. In several evaluation procedures, changes noted were given equal weight, even though they appeared to vary greatly in importance (i.e., "listens more" was equivalent in the scoring system to "conducts more effective staff meetings").
2. Results from one study could not be compared with results from other studies, since the training programs evaluated varied in length, in the specific design, in the occupational mix of participants, and in the age and sex of participants. Also, the studies varied in the variables examined, the instrument used to assess change in a given variable, and the time at which measures were gathered after the training period. Thus a body of self consistent knowledge is slow to develop.

3. Where laboratory training was part of an organization development program (Blake and Mouton, 1968; Marrow *et al.,* 1967; Miles *et al.,* 1966), it was difficult to know how much any change effected was due to the laboratory training and how much to other circumstances (Greiner, 1965, 1967).

One must conclude, then, that even though much work has been done to devise more effective evaluation designs, the major shortcomings have not been overcome. This means that the findings summarized below are based on inadequate design and can only be tentative.

Theory Development

In 1964 eight fellows of the National Training Laboratories presented their views on what happens in a T-group. Several important theoretical papers dealing with this issue have appeared since that time.

Theories

Hampden-Turner (1966) developed "an existential learning theory" which he used to integrate findings from three empirical studies of T-group effectiveness. His theory involved a "developmental spiral," wherein he hypothesized that the participant's initial quality of cognition, clarity of identity, and extent of self-esteem would result in his ordering his experience. This ordering in the context of a T-group, leads the participant to risk his competence in interacting with another person; the reaction of the other person stimulates the participant to a new integration of his experiences. This in turn leads to changes in the quality of the participant's cognition, clarity of identity, and extent of self-esteem, and to a repetition of the cycle.

Harrison (1965) formulated a "cognitive model for interpersonal and group behavior" which was intended as a framework for research, and which he later used as a basis for forming training groups (Harrison and Lubin, 1965) and for designing laboratories (Harrison and Oshry, 1965). Harrison sees learning resulting when a participant's way of construing events is "up-ended" by confrontation with other participants who construe the same event differently, and when the participant also feels sufficiently supported by others that he is able to work through the consequences of the disturbing confrontation. This theory clearly has value as a basis for designing training experiences, and there is considerable support for the belief that the type of learning (change) it emphasizes is important. For example, Harvey (1966) has detected several differences in behavior of people who are high on abstract (versus concrete) thinking, a difference which appears to be compatible with Harrison's emphasis on cognitive structure.

Argyris (1965) stated a theory of individual learning from which he derived implications for designing laboratories. Criticism from several fellows of the National Training Laboratories (Argyris, 1967) should dispel any belief that the National Training Laboratories have become complaisant as a result of their present rapid growth and popularity. Argyris also utilized his theory to identify variables in terms of which change could be assessed, devised measures of these variables, and tested his theory (Argyris, 1965).

Clark and Culbert hypothesized that self-awareness develops as a function of mutually congruent therapeutic relations between participants and trainers (Clark and Culbert, 1965).

Schein and Bennis (1965) set forth a theory of learning through laboratory training which consists of a cyclical interplay of a dilemma or disconfirming experience, attitude change, new behavior, new information and awareness, leading to additional change, new behavior, etc.

Smith (1966) formulated and tested a complex theory of learning based on Kelman's model of influence. Bass (1967) made a critique of T-group theory and concluded that the kinds of learning emphasized can be dysfunctional to job performance. As partial evidence for this view, he cites a study (Deep *et al.* 1967) in which it was found that intact T-groups performed less effectively on a business game than groups composed of members from different T-groups. (In the study by Deep *et al.* (1967), the T-group met without trainers and were conducted in what is called "instrumented" laboratory training.)

Laboratory Training and the Improvement of Organizational Performance

Several people have formulated systematic theories about the use of laboratory training in improving the functioning of organizations. Perhaps the most important are those of Blake and Mouton (1964, 1968) in regard to industrial organizations, and Miles and associates (1966) in regard to schools. Blake and Mouton (1968) deal wholly with their plan for organizational development and with guidelines for implementing the plan. Although the basic concepts of planned change which they present are similar to those conceptualized by Lippitt, Watson, and Westley (1958) the value of the study lies in its technology: Blake and Mouton have devised and tested concrete and theoretically sound methods for implementing the concepts.

Miles and his associates (1966) built upon the survey-feedback strategy of planned change, and made a special effort to determine empirically the way in which intervention (or input), intervening, and output variables were interrelated, especially in school systems.

Several other writers have formulated theories about organizations, which are congruent with the values of laboratory training and which emphasize laboratory training as a means of improving the functioning of organizations

(Shepard, 1965; McGregor, 1967; Bennis, 1966; Davis, 1967; Schein and Bennis, 1965).

Greiner (1967) speculates systematically about "antecedents to planned change," asking why the Blake-Mouton interventions had the impact they did. He was able to identify "how the consultants made use of roots put down in the unplanned stages many years before [the beginning of the consultant-planned change] to build top management support for Managerial Grid training," and he relates specific events that occurred during the organization development program to these historic roots. His study thus integrates imaginative observation, survey findings, and theory derived from a variety of related fields into a coherent and nonpolemic theory of organization change. He emphasizes the importance of the historical development of an organization in attempts to change it, a conclusion also reached by Sarason (1966) in his statement that the outcome of a *current* change effort is highly influenced by the outcome of *earlier* change efforts. Failure to cope effectively with the organization's earlier experiences with change also appeared to be one of the reasons for the limited impact of a change project in a recent study (Buchanan, 1968).

From this brief overview of recent theoretical developments, it appears that the primary focus has been on how an individual learns in T-groups, and on processes of planned organizational development. Much less attention has been given to the processes of *group* development. Only two studies (Lakin and Carson, 1964; Psathas and Hardert, 1966) attempted to explore patterns of group development.

Kinds of Learning

Persistence of Learning

In summarizing findings from studies of laboratory training it seems appropriate, first, to consider whether the learning from laboratory training persists. Two studies bear on this question. Schutz and Allen (1966) gathered information on the FIRO-B (Fundamental Interpersonal Relations Orientation—Behavioral) questionnaire from participants (and a control group) at the beginning, the end, and six months after a two-week laboratory. They found that participants changed during the training, and that the changes continued after the training. Harrison (1966) collected information from 76 participants at the beginning, a few weeks after, and a few months after they took part in a laboratory. He concluded that there was a change in the predicted direction at both follow-up periods, but that the difference became significant only between the end of the training and the second follow-up measure; thus the training appeared to be progressive. These findings are consistent with those of Bunker and Knowles (1967), who found significant changes in participants (as compared with a control group) 10–12 months following training. Also, Morton and Bass (1964), in a study of 97 participants, found a marked increase in motivation to improve their performance at the end of the laboratory and substantial changes in job performance in a follow-up 12 weeks later. French *et al.* (1966) also found further changes in participants' self-concepts following the laboratory.

Types of Learning

The next question to be explored concerns what is learned. Here it is difficult to categorize the findings, since researchers rarely look for the same results; and when they do, they typically use different measures, except for the retrospective "behavior change description questionnaire" developed by Miles (1965a) and Bunker (1965) and used in at least three studies.

Reduction of Extreme Behavior

Two studies produce findings, similar in this respect to an earlier study by Boyd and Ellis, which suggest that laboratory training changes people selectively, depending upon their personality. Schutz and Allen (1966) found that (as measured by FIRO-B) very dominant participants become less dominant, while very submissive participants become more assertive. Using the same instrument, Smith (1964) found that his experimental subjects (108 students in 11 training groups) changed significantly more in the direction of a better match between what they *expected* and what they *wanted* on both the control and the affection scales of FIRO-B. Some of the findings of Bunker can also be interpreted as an indication that reduction of abrasive or otherwise undesirable behaviors occurred. Such studies raise the possibility that laboratory training produces other-directed behavior; but Kassajian (1965) found no change in laboratory participants on an instrument which purported to measure other-directedness.

Openness, Receptivity, Awareness, Tolerance of Differences. Changes such as these are most consistently found following laboratory training (and are, of course, among the most commonly stated objectives). Such changes apparently result even from short laboratories. Bunker and Knowles (1967), Morton and Wight (1964), Rubin (1967), Morton and Bass (1964), Schutz and Allen (1966), Smith (1966), and Kolb *et al.* (1968) all report this kind of learning. Such changes probably occurred in the other studies also, but the measures used did not relate to this kind of change.

Operational Skills. This category includes behavior like listening, encouraging the participation of others, use of new techniques, solicitation of feedback, etc. Outcomes of this sort were reported by Bunker and Knowles (1967), Schutz and Allen (1966), Morton and Wight (1964), Sikes (1964), De Michele (1966), and Schmuck (1968).

Because of its design, the study by Schmuck is worth further comment. He studied a four-week laboratory for 20 classroom teachers, where the design included T-groups, problem-solving exercises, and practice in using instruments and procedures for diagnosing classroom problems. Then before the laboratory ended, each teacher formulated specific plans for the following year, applying what she had learned. Follow-up meetings were held bimonthly from September through December. He also met weekly with another set of teachers from the same large school system (and apparently with random assignment of teachers to the two groups), from September to December, covering the same material as in the laboratory except for the T-group work (and of course with much less total time). He found marked differences in the two groups as to the number of practices the participants tried out in their classrooms (5 to 17 by laboratory participants compared with 1 to 2 by the seminar participants), and in the *esprit de corps* among the teachers as indicated by the contacts they made with each other during the fall. What is more significant, he found improvement in the classrooms of the laboratory participants (as compared to both the seminar participants and a small control group), in that the students perceived themselves as having more influence in the class, as being better liked and an integral part of a friendship group in the class, and as being helpful to each other.

Cognitive style. Examples of this type of outcome are findings by Blake *et al.* (1965) that union and managerial participants reflected predicted differential shifts on a managerial grid questionnaire. Harrison (1966) found shifts on the Role Repertory Test from the use of concrete-instrumental toward inferential-expressive modes of thought. Oshry and Harrison (1966) found that many laboratory participants viewed their work environment more humanly and less impersonally, saw themselves more as a significant part of their work problems, and saw more connection between the meeting of interpersonal needs and the effectiveness of their work.

In some studies, however, changes that were expected were not found. Bowers and Soar (1961) found no differences between a group of 25 teachers who took part in half-day training sessions over a three week period and a control group, with respect to their use of group processes in their classrooms during the following academic year. This contrasts with Schmuck's finding significant carry-over into the classrooms (but his intervention consisted of four weeks full time, with systematic follow-up during the fall). Bunker (1965) found no differences between his laboratory participants and controls in initiative and assertiveness. Sikes (1964) failed to find predicted differences between laboratory graduates and a control group in their accuracy in predicting the responses of other members in a discussion group. And Oshry and Harrison (1966) predicted, but did not find, significant changes in sensitivity to the interpersonal needs of others or in the importance attributed to the interpersonal needs of others, when participants returned to their jobs.

Where does laboratory training effect change? There is clear evidence that personal growth results for more participants — they feel better about themselves, have new insights, and consider the training one of the important experiences in their life. Furthermore, participants continually report improvement in their family relations as a result of the experience (Winn, 1966). The value of the laboratory experience for job performance, however, is less convincing: fewer extreme behaviors, greater openness and self-awareness, increased oprational skills, and new alternatives for viewing situations. These seem small advances compared to the powerful forces that maintain a status quo in organizations. But what such change does represent is an increased readiness for "next steps."

Factors Influencing Learning

Several recent studies deal with factors that increase learning by participants in laboratory training; those dealing with the value of laboratory training for organizational development are discussed later.

Group Composition

Perhaps the most clear-cut results have emerged regarding the effects of group composition which have been examined in terms of personality and organizational membership of participants. Harrison (1965:418–9) theorizes about personality factors as follows:

> The process of learning is best facilitated when the individual is placed in a learning situation where either the structure produces dissonance or a significant number of others will act, feel, and perceive in ways which create sharp, clear dissonance for the learner or are contrary to his values. The dissonance must, however, be meaningful to the learner in that the alternatives presented by the others have some anchoring points within his current cognitive systems regarding himself and his interpersonal relationships. . . . we propose that a degree of polarization be created on important issues within the group. This polarization provides the battlefield on which learning by the explorations of opposites can take place. "However, if the individual is exposed only to confrontation and dissonance, he is apt to react in extreme ways. . . . For our learning model to operate, the individual should find in the group some relationships which serve as a refuge and support. Persons with similar cognitive systems, values, and perceptions can provide this support and protection against the destructive efforts of a purely confronting experience. This supportive climate is the castle in our analogy.

After reviewing relevant literature, Harrison concluded that personality variables relevant to obtaining his conditions in the formation of groups were of three types: activity-passivity, high-low affect, and negative-positive affect. He found empirical confirmation of his theory, in that groups homogeneous or mixed on one or more of these variables differed predictably in the way the groups functioned and in the kind of learning. More specifically he concluded (1965:431):

1. Learning is facilitated by a group climate which provides support for one's cognitive, emotional, and behavioral orientation and at the same time confronts one with meaningful alternatives to those orientations.
2. Group climate can be manipulated by relatively crude selection procedures.
3. The models and the research findings reviewed here can be applied to the diagnosis of wide ranges of interpersonal learning difficulties and to the design of learning groups which will provide favorable conditions of support and confrontation. A study by Smith (1966) seems to support Harrison's findings about the importance of personality mix of participants.

Morton and Wight (1964) studied differences in organizational membership. They conducted three instrumented laboratories within a company with groups composed so that participants in six of the D-groups (the designation for T-groups in instrumented laboratories) were all from one department, and all members had direct superior-subordinate relations with others in the group; whereas participants in the other six D-groups did not have direct superior-subordinate relationships, and were from separate units of the plant. The three laboratories were conducted according to the same design. On the basis of critical events (critical event was defined as "anything that has happened since the laboratory which would not have occurred had there been no training") obtained from 90 per cent of the participants three months after the laboratories, they (1964: 35–36) concluded that

> Participants from the more homogeneous groups reported a significantly greater proportion of critical events. In areas of personal responsibility such as supervisor responsibility for his subordinates, his responsibility for individual problem solving, for . . . listening . . . and sensitivity for what was taking place, there was no significant difference in the frequencies with which incidents were reported. When the problems exceeded the limits of the customary personal responsibility and involved the kind of responsibility that results in highly effective team working relations, the homogeneous . . . groups far exceeded the heterogeneous trained groups in the frequencies with which these critical incidents were reported. The post-training activities of the participants have led them into some difficulties. The nature of the difficulties has varied with the homogeneity of the groups. Those who trained in the less homogeneous groups are reporting less accomplished and more resistance of a personal nature. The mem-

> bers of the homogeneous groups, . . . are reporting the greatest number of organizational barriers to applying what they have learned. Whereas the heterogeneous trained groups found their greatest barriers within their primary work group, among those who have not been in the training, the homogeneous trained group report their greatest difficulty in problem solving with those outside their department who have not received training.

These findings must be considered tentative, however, since variables other than the D-group composition could account for the differences between the two types of groups. For example, the report does not make clear the circumstances under which so many members from one department participated in the laboratories; it may have been the supervisor's enthusiasm rather than the D-group composition which accounted for the change. It is also possible that the differences in outcome occurred because many people from the same department had a similar training experience (i.e., participating in a laboratory) rather than that they were in the same D-groups.

Duration of Laboratory

A third variable apparently making a difference in learning outcome is the duration of the laboratory training. Bunker and Knowles (1967) compared the outcomes from two three-week and two two-week summer sessions conducted by National Training Laboratories. They found that the three-week laboratories "fostered more behavioral changes" than the two-week ones; that is, more participants in the three-week ones made changes "toward more pro-active and interactive behavior," while changes made by the two-week participants were in the area of increased receptiveness (i.e., listening, sensitivity, etc.) However, they noted that the laboratories were similar in the amount of time spent in T-groups, but differed greatly in the time devoted to problems relating to their work; thus the differential impact could be due to the design, or interaction between the design and duration, rather than to duration alone. The question of duration merits more study since costs are closely related to duration and almost every study indicates that the trained group shows change.

Trainer Behavior

Interaction effects between trainer and participant orientation on the FIRO-F questionnaire were found to have differential impact upon the "laboratory learning climate" (Powers, 1965) and upon kinds of learning (Smith, 1966). Bolman (1968) also studied the relation of trainer behavior-openness, congruence, and consistency (as judged by participants) to learning by participants. Although the results were inclusive, he succeeded in isolating dimensions of trainer behavior and a way of measuring them. Culbert examined the differential impact of "more" and "less" self-disclosing trainer behavior in two T-groups, and found that although trainer behavior differed as planned, the groups attained the same level of self-awareness (Culbert, 1968).

Goal-setting and Feedback

Several studies have been conducted to examine the effects of goal-setting and feedback. Kolb *et al.* (1968) introduced a procedure in T-groups, by which each participant set a specific change goal for himself and was encouraged to work to meet his goal: then they varied the amount of feedback received during the training, and they attempted to heighten each participant's commitment to the goals he set. They found that differences in both the extent of commitment and in the amount of feedback influenced learning. French, *et al.* (1966) also found that the greater the amount of feedback, the greater the extent of change on self-selected change goals. And Harrison (1966) found that the amount of change in cognitive orientation was significantly related to ratings by participants of how other participants reacted to and utilized feedback during T-group sessions. Those who made it easy for others to give feedback, and who tested the validity of feedback by seeking more, showed the most change. Thus it appears that provision for participants to obtain and utilize feedback is an important factor in laboratory design.

In summary, then, it appears that the climate which develops in the training group, and the kind and/or extent of learning which occurs, are influenced by the personality mix of the participants, the organizational relationships of the participants, and the way the design utilizes feedback. Studies regarding the effect of duration of the laboratory and of trainer behavior are inconclusive.

Type of Laboratory Training and Job Improvement

The question of whether the greatest improvement on the job results from laboratories which focus almost wholly on personal growth or from those which include personal growth, organizational problems, and planning for changes on the job has not been studied with sufficient rigor for meaningful conclusions to be drawn. Bunker and Knowles related their data to the issue; but since the laboratories that they studied varied in duration as well as in the proportion of time spent in T-groups, the differences they found cannot be attributed to the design alone.

Wilson *et al.* (1968) reported results from a follow-up on two 6-day "off-site" laboratories, one of which utilized "the traditional sensitivity approach described by Weschler" and the other Morton's version of an instrumented laboratory. Six months after the instrumented laboratory and 18 months after the "sensitivity" laboratory, a very high and similar proportion of participants of the two laboratories reported that the experience was of value to them as individuals; participants of the instrumented laboratory showed significantly greater improvement as managers, as members of a team, in building team effort in their organizations, and in communicating with others in the work setting. Although the study design was a weak one, as the authors note, the findings were consistent with their predictions.

There are not studies comparing laboratory training with rational training (Ellis and Blum, 1967), "motive acquisition" training (McClelland, 1965), or other forms of training; yet there is certainly a need for such studies.

Types of Individual Influenced

Personality and Organization Variable

In one of the more thorough analyses of learning processes and outcomes, Miles (1965) explored 595 relations among criterion, home organization, treatment, and personal variables. He found significant relations between on-the-job change and sex (males change more), job security (as measured by years as a school principal, the more secure participant changed more), and power (as measured by number of teachers supervised, the more powerful changed more). He did not find significant differences between on-the-job change and age, ego strength (as measured by Barron's scale), flexibility (as measured by Barron's scale), need affiliation (as measured by French's test of insight), a combination of these personality variables, autonomy on the job (as measured by frequency of meetings with superior), perceived power in his work situation, perceived flexibility of his organization, and a combination of these three organizational variables. On the other hand, he found that several of these variables were significantly related to the participant's behavior during the training (specifically to the extent to which he became more communicative, and to the trainer's rating of the extent to which participants changed), and such behavior was in turn related to on-the-job changes.

Unfortunately, there are few replications of Miles' studies. No other study examines age or sex as a factor in learning from laboratories. With respect to personality, Rubin (1967) found that anomy (which as predicted was itself unaffected by laboratory training) significantly influenced the extent of change in self-awareness, which was a factor in the extent of change in acceptance of others. Harrison (1966) found no significant relation between prelaboratory scores on an instrument measuring concrete-instrumental versus inferential-expressive orientation and extent of change as indicated by comparing pre-training with post-training scores on this instrument. He also found no relation between the prelaboratory scores on this instrument and the participants' reactions to feedback during the laboratory — a finding which seems surprising if Harrison's theory about the importance of cognitive orientation is accurate.

In a study of classroom teachers, Bower and Soar (1961) found that an increase in the teachers' use of group processes in the classroom following training was greatest for teachers (a) who were well adjusted and (b) who used group methods before receiving the training. Harrison and Oshry (1965) found that people who were seen as changing most in a T-group were those who were described by colleagues as open to the ideas of others were accepting of others, and listened well. These two studies suggest that laboratory training develops the participant's interpersonal style further rather than reversing it.

There is rather strong evidence that participants who become involved in the T-group learn more than those who are ranked low on involvement (Bunker, 1965; Harrison and Oshry, 1966). Although Miles did not find the relation between involvement and on-the-job change to be significant, he did find involvement significantly related to trainer ratings of the participants' effectiveness in the group, which was in turn significantly related to on-the-job change. Perhaps involvement in the training group is a function of the amount of dissonance produced — or of having "a castle and a battlefield," as Harrison suggests.

The direction that research should take, in the tradition of Miles' study, is exemplified by Smith (1966). Using a complex model of training based on Kelman's model of influence, and four separate measures of learning, Smith explored the relations among group climates (as indicated by the mix of participant orientation, trainer styles, and types of influence underlying the trainer-participant interaction process) and types of learning. He found support for his predictions that (a) the compliant learning pattern, found among groups with authority-oriented participants and trainers, showed highest learning in diagnostic ability, and (b) the internalizing learning pattern, found in groups with data-oriented participants and people-oriented trainers, showed the greatest favorable changes on FIRO scores and on interpersonal awareness. (This study was based on 31 T-groups, but since the laboratories varied in duration, and the participants in age and occupational background, it is difficult to know the extent to which extraneous factors clouded the findings.)

Influence of Background

Bunker and Knowles (1967) found that human relations laboratory participants from religious and governmental organizations showed significant change after a three-week laboratory but not after a two-week one; whereas participants from industry, education, and social service changed significantly after a two-week session, but the differences between the two-week and the three-week session were not significant. However, in this study the data on participants' background did not permit more than rough groupings, so little confidence can be placed in the findings.

In summary, these studies provide some support for the prediction that sex, job security, organizational power, anomy of the participant, trainer-participant interaction patterns, the openness of the participant, and the participant's involvement in the T-group make a difference in how much the participant learns; but clearly this is a topic which merits much more systematic exploration.

Laboratory Training in Organization Development

The evidence rather clearly indicates that laboratory training has a predictable and significant impact on most participants; yet it is also clear that from the standpoint of organizational improvement, laboratory training by itself is not enough. Several researchers have addressed themselves to facilitating "transfer of learning" (Winn, 1966, Bass, 1967, Oshry and Harrison, 1966). Bass has identified eight different approaches currently being tried as a means of increasing transfer. In varying degrees, these methods involve including in the training people and/or activities associated with participants on the job, while still retaining a focus on behavior in the laboratory. Laboratory training systematically undertaken throughout the company, using combinations of stranger, work, and interface groups, was a major intervention in the program at the Space Technology Laboratories (Davis, 1967), in Non-Linear Systems (Kuriloff and Atkins, 1966), and in a division of Alcan (Winn, 1966). And the indications are that in all three companies the development efforts were effective.

Laboratory Training as Part of a Development Program

In several strategies, however, laboratory training is one component of a multiphased program, as in Harwood Manufacturing Company's revitalization of Weldon (Marrow, *et al.,* 1967), in Beckhard's work (1966) with a large hotel company, in Blake's and Mouton's work (1968), and in several projects in school systems (Buchanan, 1968; Miles *et al.,* 1966). In all of these cases of organization development, it is difficult to assess how important the laboratory training was in the impact of the total program (and of course it is equally difficult to assess the effectiveness of the total program itself). In an attempt to learn (Buchanan, 1967) what characterized effective programs of organization development eight successful programs and three unsuccessful ones were examined in the hope of finding some crucial variable. The use of laboratory training (or any other formal training) was not a crucial variable. Neither of the two cases (Guest, 1962; Jaques, 1951) where there was the clearest evidence of success involved formal training. One of the variables that did emerge as crucial was the introduction of new and more fruitful concepts for diagnosing current problems of the organization and for setting improvement goals. Having new concepts for diagnosing current practices seemed to provide members of the organization with a means of getting from symptoms to variables which provided leverage for change; having new concepts for setting targets was important in working out clear ideas of potentiality and in developing dissonance and thus motivation for change. Information which has become available since that study was made is consistent with the conclusion about the development of new concepts as a crucial issue in organization development. In a project of organization development, analysis of the case reports on work done with two schools indicated that in the more effective of the two projects much more time was given to developing new concepts and the skills of key participants before diagnosis and planning for system change was undertaken (Buchanan, 1968). In the school system where there was more change, the superintendent had participated in a laboratory conducted by National Training Laboratories, and he and the key members of the system took part in a one-week laboratory of their own. In the other system, the superintendent did not have prior laboratory experience, and he and his key staff had a two-day laboratory of their own. In two other cases of organizational development where there was little evidence of effectiveness (Benedict *et al.,* 1967; Miles *et al.,* 1966), diagnosis of current conditions in the system was undertaken before any effort was made to develop new concepts. In contrast, Blake and Mouton (1968) continually stress the understanding of grid theory and the development of skills required in its application as an essential first step in each phase of their strategy. They begin by exposing the key person in the treatment organization to the managerial grid concept and to alternative styles of management and their implications. This is followed by familiarizing a representative sample of participants with the same concepts. Then all members of management are exposed to the same concepts, and only then are needs diagnosed and improvement goals set by individuals and teams for themselves and for the total organization. A case study recently reported by Bartlett (1967), in which the development effort appeared to be successful, also involved development of new concepts and skills as the first step in the program.

Cognitive Changes

Quite clearly formal training is one effective means for developing cognitive changes as an opening step in organizational development. At the same time, it is also clear that there are other means of creating cognitive changes. The question, then, is whether laboratory training and, in fact, what *kind* of laboratory training provides the most useful concepts and skills for organizational development. Answers to this question can be sought from two sources: from theories about effective organization functioning, and from outcomes of organizational development programs that utilize different methods for introducing new concepts and skills. Although the latter method would be more convincing, at this time there is little such information available. One must therefore look to theory for support of the utility of laboratory training as a means of providing relevant cognitive changes in participants in programs of organizational development. Blake and Mouton have made a case for laboratory training based on grid theory; Shepard, Likert, Argyris, Bennis, and McGregor have provided relevant theory in the case of non-grid laboratory training; and Miles has systematically sought empirical data relevant to the question as it pertains to school systems.

One can summarize this review of the literature as to the value of laboratory training as follows:

1. It facilitates personal growth and development, and thus can be of value to the individual who participates.
2. It accomplishes changes in individuals which according to several theories are important in effecting change in organizations and in effectively managing organizations.
3. One study, in which an instrumented laboratory was compared with sensitivity training, provides some indication that more organizational change resulted from the instrumented approach.
4. The findings from this literature search are compatible with the conclusions reached in a similar review made four years ago (Buchanan 1965).

References

Argyris, Chris. "Explorations in interpersonal competence — I and II." *Journal of Applied Behavioral Science,* I (1965), 58–83; 255–269. ———. "On the future of laboratory education." *Journal of Applied Science,* 3 (1967), 153–183.

Bartlett, Alton C. "Changing behavior as a means to increase efficiency." *Journal of Applied Behavioral Science,* 3 (1967), 381–403.

Bass, Bernard M. "The anarchist movement and the T-group." *Journal of Applied Behavioral Science,* 3 (1967), 211–226.

Benedict, Barbara, Paula Calder, Daniel Callahan, Harvey Hornstein, and Matthew B. Miles. "The clinical-experimental approach to assessing organizational change efforts." *Journal of Applied Behavioral Science,* 3 (1967), 347–380.

Bennis, Warren G. *Changing Organizations.* New York: McGraw-Hill, 1966.

Beckhard, Richard. "An organization improvement program in a decentralized organization." *Journal of Applied Behavioral Science,* 2 (1966), 3–26. ———. "The confrontation meeting." *Harvard Business Review,* 45 (1967), 149–155.

Blake, Robert R., and Jane S. Mouton. *The Managerial Grid.* Houston: Gulf, 1964. ———. "Some effects of managerial grid seminar training on union and management attitudes toward supervision." *Journal of Applied Behavioral Science,* 2 (1966), 387–400. ———. *Corporate Excellence through Grid Organization Development.* Houston: Gulf, 1968.

Blake, Robert R., Jane S. Mouton, Lewis B. Barnes, and Larry E. Greiner. "Breakthrough in organization development." *Harvard Business Review*, 42 (1964), 133–155.

Blake, Robert R., Jane S. Mouton, and Richard L. Sloma. "The union management intergroup laboratory: strategy for resolving intergroup conflict." *Journal of Applied Behavioral Science,* 1 (1965), 25–57.

Bolman, Lee. "The Effects of Variations in Educator Behavior on the Learning Process in Laboratory Human Relations Education." Doctoral dissertation, Yale University, 1968.

Bowers, N. D., and R. S. Soar. "Evaluation of laboratory human relations training for classroom teachers. Studies of human relations in the teaching-learning process: V. final report." Columbia: University of South Carolina, 1961.

Buchanan, Paul C. "Evaluating the effectiveness of laboratory training in industry." In Explorations in Human Relations Training and Research, Report No. 1. Washington: National Training Laboratories, 1965. ———. "Crucial issues in organizational development." In Goodwin Watson (ed.), *Change in School Systems.* Washington: National Training Laboratories, 1967. ———. Reflections on a Project in Self-renewal in Two School Systems. Washington: National Training Laboratories, 1968.

Bugental, James, and Robert Tannenbaum. "Sensitivity training and being motivation." *Journal of Humanistic Psychology,* III (1963), 76–85.

Bunker, Douglas R. "Individual applications of laboratory training." *Journal of Applied Behavioral Sciences,* 1 (1965), 131–148.

Bunker, Douglas R., and Eric S. Knowles. "Comparison of behavioral changes resulting from human relations training laboratories of different lengths." *Journal of Applied Behavioral Science,* 3 (1967), 505–524.

Byrd, Richard E. "Training in a non-group." *Journal of Humanistic Psychology,* VII (1967), 18–27.

Clark, James, and Samuel A. Culbert. "Mutually therapeutic perception and self-awareness in a T-group." *Journal of Applied Behavioral Science,* 1 (1965), 180–194.

Culbert, Samuel A. "Trainer self-disclosure and member growth in two T-groups." *Journal of Applied Behavioral Science,* 4 (1968), 47–73.

Davis, Sheldon A. "An organic problem-solving method of organizational change." *Journal of Applied Behavioral Science,* 3 (1967), 3–21.

Deep, S., Bernard Bass, and James Vaughan. "Some effects on business gaming of previous quasi-T-Group affiliations." *Journal of Applied Psychology,* 51 (1967), 426–431.

De Michele, John H. "The Measurement of Rated Training Changes Resulting from a Sensitivity Training Laboratory of an Overall Program in Organization Development." Doctoral dissertation. New York University, 1966.

Ellis, Albert, and Milton Blum. "Rational training: a new method of facilitating management and labor relations." *Psychological Reports,* 20 (1967), 1267–1284.

Fleishman, Edwin A., E. F. Harris, and H. E. Burtt. *Leadership and Supervision in Industry.* Columbus: Bureau of Educational Research, Ohio State University, 1955.

French, J. R. P., J. J. Sherwood, and D. L. Bradford. "Change in self-identity in a management training conference." *Journal of Applied Behavioral Science,* 2 (1966), 210–218.

Friedlander, Frank. "The impact of organizational training laboratories upon the effectiveness and interaction of ongoing groups." *Personal Psychology,* 20 (1967), 289–308.

Greiner, Larry E. "Organization Change and Development: A Study of Changing Values, Behavior, and Performance in a Large Industrial Plant. Doctoral dissertation. *Harvard Business School,* 1965. ———. "Antecedents of planned organization change." *Journal of Applied Behavioral Science,* 3 (1967), 51–86.

Guest, Robert. *Organizational Change.* Homewood, Ill.: Dorsey, 1962.

Hampden-Turner, C. M. "An existential 'learning theory' and the integration of T-group research." *Journal of Applied Behavioral Science,* 2 (1966), 367–386.

Harrison, Roger. "Group composition models for laboratory design." *Journal of Applied Behavioral Science,* 1 (1965), 409–432. ———. "Cognitive change and participation in a sensitivity training laboratory." *Journal of Consulting Psychology,* 30 (1966), 517–520. ———. "Problems in the design and interpretation of research on human relations training." In *Explorations in Human Relations Training and Research,* Report No. 1. Washington: National Training Laboratories, 1967.

Harrison, Roger, and B. Lubin. "Personal style, group composition, and learning." *Journal of Applied Behavioral Science,* 1 (1965), 286–301.

Harrison, Roger, and Barry Oshry. "The design of one-week laboratories." In E. H. Schein and W. G. Bennis (eds.), *Personal and Organizational Growth through Group Methods.* New York: Wiley, 1965, pp. 98–106. ———. "The Impact of Laboratory Training on Organizational Behavior: Methodology and Results." Working paper, National Training Laboratories, 1966.

Harvey, O. J. *Experience, Structure, and Adaptability.* New York: Springer, 1966.

House, Robert J. " 'T-group' training: some important considerations for the practicing manager." *New York Personnel Management Association Bulletin,* 21 (1965), 4–10. ———. "Manager development: a conceptual model, some propositions, and a research strategy for testing the model." In *Management Development: Design, Evaluation & Implementation.* Ann Arbor: University of Michigan, 1967.

Jaques, E. *The Changing Culture of a Factory.* London: Tavistock, 1951.

Kassarjian, H. "Social character and sensitivity training." *Journal of Applied Behavioral Science,* 1 (1965), 433–440.

Knowles, Eric S. "A bibliography of research — since 1960." In *Explorations in Human Relations Training and Research,* Report No. 2. Washington: National Training Laboratories, 1967.

Kolb, D. A., S. K. Winter, and D. E. Berlew. "Self-directed change: two studies." *Journal of Applied Behavioral Science,* 4 (1968), 453–471.

Kuriloff, A., and S. Atkins. "T-group for a work team." *Journal of Applied Behavioral Science,* 2 (1966), 63–93.

Lakin, M., and R. Carlson. "Participant perception of group process in group sensitivity training." *International Journal of Group Psychotherapy,* 14 (1964), 116–122.

Leavitt, H. "Applied organizational change in industry: structural, technological, and humanities approaches." In James G. March (ed.), *Handbook of Organizations.* Chicago: Rand McNally, 1965, pp. 1144–1170.

Likert, Rensis. *The Human Organization.* New York: McGraw-Hill, 1967.

Lippitt, Ronald, Jeanne Watson, and Bruce Westley. *The Dynamics of Planned Change.* New York: Harcourt, Brace and World, 1958.

McClelland, David C. "Toward a theory of motive acquisition." *American Psychologist,* 20 (1965), 321–333.

McGregor, Douglas. *The Professional Manager.* New York: McGraw-Hill, 1967.

Marrow, A., D. Bowers, and S. Seashore. *Participative Management.* New York: Harper and Row, 1967.

Medow, Herman. "Sensible non-sense." *Journal of Applied Behavioral Science,* 3 (1967), 202–203.

Miles, M. B. "Learning processes and outcomes in human relations training: a clinical-experimental study." In E. H. Schein and W. G. Bennis (eds.), *Personal and Organizational Growth through Group Methods.* New York: Wiley, 1965(a), pp. 244–254. ———. "Methodological Problems in Evaluating Organizational Change: Two Illustrations." Working paper, Columbia University, 1965(b).

Miles, M. B., J. R. Milavsky, D. Lake, and R. Beckhard. "Organizational Improvement: Effects of Management Team Training in Bankers Trust." Unpublished monograph, Bankers Trust Company, New York, 1965.

Miles, M. B., P. Calder, H. Hornstein, D. Callahan, and S. Schiavo. "Data Feedback and Organizational Change in a School System." Working paper, Columbia University, 1966.

Morton, R. B., and B. M. Bass. "The organizational training laboratory." *Training Directors Journal,* 18 (1964), 2–18.

Morton, R. B., and A. Wight. "A Critical Incidents Evaluation of an Organizational Training Laboratory." Working paper, Aerojet General Corporation, 1964.

Oshry, B., and R. Harrison. "Transfer from 'here-and-now' to 'there-and-then': changes in organizational problem diagnosis stemming from T-group training." *Journal of Applied Behavioral Science,* 2 (1966), 185–198.

Powers, J. R. "Trainer orientation and group composition in laboratory training." Doctoral dissertation, Case Institute of Technology, 1965.

Psathas, G., and R. Hardert. "Trainer interventions and normative patterns in the T-group." *Journal of Applied Behavioral Science,* 2 (1966), 149–169.

Rubin, I. "Increased self-acceptance: a means of reducing prejudice." *Journal of Abnormal and Social Psychology,* 5 (1967) (a), 233–238. ———. "The reduction of prejudice through laboratory training." *Journal of Applied Behavioral Science,* 3 (1967) (b), 29–50.

Sarason, Seymour B. *The School Culture and Processes of Change.* College Park: College of Agriculture, University of Maryland, 1966.

Schein, E. H., and W. G. Bennis. *Personal and Organizational Growth through Group Methods.* New York: Wiley, 1965.

Schmuck, R. A. "Helping teachers improve classroom group processes." *Journal of Applied Behavioral Science,* 4 (1968), 401–435.

Schutz, W. C. "An Approach to the Development of Human Potential." Washington: National Training Laboratories, Subscription Service Report No. 6, 1964. ———. *Joy.* New York: Grove, 1967.

Schutz, W. C., and V. Allen. "The effects of a T-group laboratory on interpersonal behavior." *Journal of Applied Science,* 2 (1966), 265–286.

Shepard, H. A. "Changing relationships in organizations." In James G. March (ed.), *Handbook of Organizations.* Chicago: Rand McNally, 1965, pp. 1115–1143.

Sikes, W. "A Study of Some Effects of a Human Relations Training Laboratory." Doctoral dissertation, Purdue University, 1964.

Smith, P. B. "Attitude changes associated with training in human relations." *British Journal of Social and Clinical Psychology,* 3 (1964), 104–112. ———. "T-group Climate, Trainer Style, and Some Tests of Learning." Working paper, University of Sussex, England, 1966.

Tannenbaum, R., and James Bugental. "Dyads, clans, and tribe: a new design for sensitivity training." *NTL Training News,* 7 (1963), 1–3.

Wilson, J. E., D. P. Mullen, and R. B. Morton. "Sensitivity training for individual growth — team training for organization development." *Training and Development Journal,* 22 (1968), 1–7.

Winn, A. "Social change in industry: from insight to implementation." *Journal of Applied Behavioral Science,* 2 (1966), 170–185.

32

Using Employee Questionnaire Results for Improving Organizations: The Survey "Feedback" Experiment

HOWARD BAUMGARTEL
The University of Kansas

During the thirty years since the pioneering human-factors research in the Western Electric Company, literally hundreds of interview, observation, and questionnaire studies have been carried out in business, governmental, and military organizations. Often, in the course of these studies, researchers and management personnel have been faced with the problem of how to make productive use of the research findings for benefiting organizations in which the research was carried out.

The use of systematic data on operations — measures of cost, production, sales and nowadays, measures of "human factors" — is one of the key problems in rational administration. How can managers make effective use of information about the functioning of their own organizations?

Ordinarily, internal information on the organization's behavior is used in making routine business decisions. However, we know, for example, that data showing increasing costs do not automatically set in motion the necessary forces to reduce costs. The data must be interpreted and the corrective action must be planned as a consequence.

This article presents the findings of an experiment in which the results of a questionnaire survey of employee perceptions and attitudes were used not only as an aid in decision-making but, essentially, as a planned program of management development and organizational change. The results of this study as well as evidence from other research in applied Social Psychology indicate that a series of intensive, overlapping group conferences on the problems identified in an employee survey can have markedly beneficial effects on the subject organization. This discovery is one of the exciting new developments in the field of executive management.

Taken and adapted from *Kansas Business Review,* Vol. 12, No. 12, Dec. 1959, pp. 2–6. Used by permission.

The process of reporting research findings back into a business organization (or to any other group) has come to be called "feedback" because of the obvious analogy with the feedback principle in the household thermostat and other automatic systems-control devices. By conceptualizing this feedback process it can be better understood as a management tool and perhaps used by businessmen to greater advantage.

Our interest in testing the effectiveness of this survey feedback program as a method of improving organizational functioning stemmed from several sources. First, the frequent failure of the usual industrial supervisory training programs to produce measurable improvement had led to a review of the whole problem of organizational change.[1,2] However, the trial and error experience of human-relations researchers in implementing the results of research in client companies had resulted in the promising but experimentally untested conclusion that an intensive "working through" of survey findings could dramatically improve organizational effectiveness.[3,4] Second, "information theory" and "general system theory," as developed by electronics engineers, automation theorists, and the like, had emphasized the importance and significance of "feedback" and "servo-mechanism" processes in the effective functioning of any system.[5,6] Third, Social Psychologists had been perennially interested in how more accurate information about the perceptions and attitudes of others influence one's own feelings and motives.[7,8] Finally, Group Dynamics researchers had been interested in the effects of the feedback process on group effectiveness[9] and community change[10] in a variety of social settings.

These various theoretical as well as practical interests led to the design and execution of this experimental study of a survey feedback program. Experimental designs, while often requiring planning and control beyond the tolerance of many administrators, can provide a conceptual model for thinking about organizational change.

How the Study was Conducted

The electric light and power company in which this study was carried out had for a number of years been supporting an extensive program of research on human relations, absenteeism, morale and so forth. A collaborative relationship between the Company and the Survey Research Center had been established to provide for a mixture of basic and applied research and for consultation. This experimental study was originated and carried out in the course of this company-researcher relationship. The research work was done in the Accounting Division of the Company.

Careful plans were worked out with officials in the Personnel Planning Department and with the top officials in the Company's Accounting Division to carry out the proposed experiment in the use of survey data to improve organizational functioning. Six accounting departments were included; these departments employed about 60 supervisors and about 640 nonsupervisory personnel. Four of the departments received the "feedback program"— conferences on results of a questionnaire survey — during the year 1951–52 and were called the experimental departments. The other two "control" departments received no special attention from the management or research group other than the regular and routine administrative and management activities characteristic of the normal practices throughout the company. In 1950 before the experiment, and again in 1952 after the program, all supervisors and nonsupervisory personnel filled out lengthy fixed-response questionnaires[11] which covered a wide variety of attitudes and feelings concerning the major aspects of the work situation. Many of the questions specifically referred to certain theoretically important human relations variables and concepts. A comparison of the changes in questionnaire responses in the experimental group with changes in the control group would, in this research design, demonstrate the effects of the feedback program in the four departments.

The material for the feedback program was developed out of the "before" or 1950 questionnaire data as well as from an earlier survey carried out in 1948. A booklet was prepared for all supervisors and nonsupervisory employees in each department. The results of the responses to the questionnaire surveys were presented in the four sections of the booklet. The first section presented a comparison of employee responses to a set of morale-type questions asked in both the 1948 and 1950 surveys, thus indicating change over time. The departmental employee and the division employee responses to another set of questions were compared in the second section. The third section of the report referred to the dramatic differences in the way nonsupervisory employees and supervisors responded to an identical set of questions about supervisor-worker relationships. The final section reported extensive quotations from employee comments written on the last page of the questionnaire. The booklet gave managers and employees very complete and detailed information about each department and its comparison with the division as a whole as well as how attitudes had changed since 1948.

The most important part of the study was, of course, the actual program of meetings and conferences at which time the survey findings were discussed with Company personnel. After a short series of meetings with the top officials in the Accounting Division and the four department heads, the researcher worked individually with the department heads to plan and execute a conference program. The basic device was the establishment of a relatively undirected series of group discussions of the meaning, implications, and action possibilities of the survey data. Individual conferences with department heads led to lengthy meetings between the department head and his supervisors. In most cases, the researcher had one or more conferences with individual supervisors in addition to his participation in the group meetings. The entire program lasted eight months.

The goal of the researcher was not to tell or interpret the meaning and action implications of the data but rather to facilitate the process of personal and group discovery of important human problems and their solutions.[12] Although the researcher's objective was to conclude the survey feedback program with a discussion meeting of each supervisor with his employees, this did not happen in all cases. Those supervisors who had the most "problems," as in other training efforts, also had the greatest difficulty in benefiting from this program. However, consistent with the voluntary principle, each person was free to choose how far he wanted to go in the program — the researcher acted merely as a staff helper.

The Experimental Results

Change was measured by a 120-item questionnaire asked in the feedback and nonfeedback departments on the 1950 and 1952 surveys. Of these 120 questions, 61 were asked in identical form on both surveys. Seventeen new questions were asked on the 1952 survey about how various aspects of supervision and the job environment had changed since the previous survey. These 17 questions were called the "perceived change" items.[13] Appropriate tests of statistical significance[14] were used throughout the analysis of comparative changes in order to ascertain the meaningfulness of such changes. (See asterisk Figure 1 and Figure 2.) Item changes were classified according to the level of statistical significance. Those at the one per cent level of confidence represented the most marked changes (the least likely to have occurred by chance). No significance was attached to those changes which did not attain the 10 per cent level of confidence.

The prediction of over-all positive change in the experimental group was supported by the findings. In the experimental departments, 34 per cent of the 61 identical items showed statistically significant "improvement" as measured by the question phrasing. Fifteen of the 17 "perceived change" items showed significant positive change in the feedback departments as compared with the two control departments. In other words, the questionnaire results showed marked improvements in the departments which had experienced the change program.

Figure 1 shows the questionnaire items asked both before and after the program which changed significantly in the experimental groups as compared with the control groups. The particular changes are noteworthy. To mention only the most important differences, one notes that after the program relatively more nonsupervisory employees expressed more interest in their work, felt their work was more important, felt their supervisors were better at "handling" people, felt supervisors made more specific efforts to give recognition by training and reports, and felt their supervisors were better "leaders" and more "likeable." In addition, employees felt more satisfied with their progress in the company.

FIGURE 1

Items Which Indicate High Favorable Change in Experimental Departments Compared with Control Departments*

A. Relative differences significant at 1 per cent level:

Q 2. What do you think of the job you are on (interest)?

Q 6. How important do you feel your work is?

Q 8. How good is your supervisor at handling people?

Q21. How does your supervisor give recognition for good work done by the employees in your work group?

(5) Trains for better jobs.

(6) Makes note of it in his reports.

Q25. From your dealings with your supervisor, how well would you say the following comments fit him?

(4) Is a "leader" of men.

(8) Likeable.

Q38. How do you feel about the progress you have made in the company up to now (satisfaction)?

B. Relative difference significant between 1 and 5 per cent level:

Q 1. How do you feel about the amount of responsibility you have in your job (satisfaction)?

Q12. How does your supervisor usually treat employees with complaints?

Q21. How does your supervisor give recognition for good work done by employees in your work group?

(10) Gives privileges.

Q24. How can you tell what your supervisor thinks of the work you do?

(1) He tells me what he thinks.

Q25. From your dealings with your supervisor, how well would you say the following comments fit him?

(1) Considerate.

(3) Reasonable in what he expects.

(5) Bossy (inverted).

Q46. How do you feel your group compares with other groups doing similar work in getting the job done?

C. Relative difference significant between 5 and 10 per cent level:

Q 7. Considering your job as a whole, how well do you like it?

Q21. How does your supervisor give recognition for good work done by the emlyoyees in your work group?

(4) Tells his supervisors.

Q25. From your dealings with your supervisor, how well would you say the following comments fit him?

(7) Is a "driver" (inverted).

Q26. How often are there group meetings in which employees in your work group can discuss things with the supervisor?

Q33. Taking all things into consideration, how satisfied are you with your supervisor?

* Significance of differences in Mean differences (uncorrelated).

FIGURE 2

"Perceived Change" Questionnaire Items Which Indicate High Favorable Change in Experimental Departments Compared with Control Departments*

Question 57. What changes, if any, took place in the following areas since the last survey in May 1950?

A. Differences significant at 1 per cent level:

(2) How your work group compares with other groups in getting the job done.
(9) How free you feel to talk to your supervisor about job problems.
(10) How much your supervisor understands the way employees look at and feel about things.
(13) How well the supervisors in your department get along together.
(17) How much you understand the way your supervisor sees things.

B. Differences significant at 1–5 per cent level:

(3) How often your supervisor holds meetings with the work group as a whole.
(5) How often your supervisor praises you or gives you credit for good work.
(6) How sure you are how you stand with your supervisor.
(11) How well you feel you know your supervisor.
(12) How much emphasis your supervisor places on getting out the work.
(14) How you feel about the amount of information you get on what is going on in the company.
(15) How your supervisor usually handles complaints.
(16) How willing your supervisor is to try new ideas.

C. Differences significant at 5–10 per cent level:

(4) How good these meetings are.
(7) How your supervisor handles suggestions made by the employees.

* Significance of differences in Means (uncorrelated).

Figure 2 shows the "perceived change" items which varied most favorably in the experimental departments in comparison with the nonfeedback departments. Here the results showed, among other things, that more employees in the experimental departments felt:

that their group was better at getting the job done,
that they were freer to take job problems to their supervisors,
that their supervisors better understood their point of view,
that their supervisors got along better with each other,
that they understood better how their supervisor sees things.

Many of these same questionnaire items and the variables they measure have been found to be related to individual and group productivity, absenteeism, and turnover in other research settings.[15,16]

Conclusions

The results of this experimental study lend support to the idea that an intensive, group discussion procedure for utilizing the results of an employee questionnaire survey can be an effective tool for introducing positive change in a business organization. It may be that the effectiveness of this method, in comparison to traditional training courses, is that *it deals with the system of human relationships as a whole* (superior and subordinate can change together) and that *it deals with each manager, supervisor, and employee in the context of his own job, his own problems, and his own work relationships.*

We have speculated that the following conditions are essential for such a feedback program to be effective in any organization. There is reason to believe that the same principles apply in the use of sales and production information as well as with data concerning human factors:

- The information must be about the organization itself — often research findings from other companies do not convince the present management.
- The information must be quantitative and objective — personal opinions and impressions are often distorted; there must be some external point of reference.

The information must have some stimulating quality by being: new information — a good cost accounting system provides new data on departmental costs; information contrary to common belief — several studies, for example, have shown that older workers produce more than younger workers; information about things not ordinarily discussed — how many times do personal feelings about the boss ever get talked out in staff meetings?

- The information must provide directions for or alternative ways of achieving positive change — just knowing that there is high turnover and low "morale" in department X isn't enough; one needs to know what factors create the problem.

The results of this study suggest that the creative use of new information for conferences and meetings at all levels of departmental organization may be one of the best and most dynamic avenues to management development and organizational growth.

Notes

1. F. Mann, "Studying and Creating Change: A Means to Understanding Social Organization," in Industrial Relations Research Association's *Research in Industrial Human Relations* (New York: Harper & Bros., 1957).
2. A. Zaleznek, *Foreman Training in a Growing Enterprise* (Boston: Division of Research, Harvard Graduate School of Business Administration, 1951).
3. E. Jacobson, R. Kahn, F. Mann, and N. Morse (eds.), "Human Relations Research in Large Organizations." *The Journal of Social Issues,* Vol. VII, No. 3 (1951).
4. E. Jaques, *Changing Culture of a Factory* (New York: Dryden, 1952).
5. R. W. Deutsch, "On Communication Models in the Social Sciences," *The Public Opinion Quarterly* (Fall, 1952).
6. *Scientific Monthly* (September, 1952).

7. T. M. Newcomb, *Social Psychology* (New York: Dryden, 1950).

8. M. Sturm, *Attitude Change as Related to Perception of Group Consensus* (unpublished Ph.D. dissertation, University of Michigan, 1953).

9. D. H. Jenkins, "Feedback and Group Self-Evaluation," *Journal of Social Issues,* Vol. IV, No. 2 (1948).

10. C. Selltiz and M. H. Wormser, "Community Self-Surveys: An Approach to Social Change," *Journal of Social Issues,* Vol. V, No. 2 (1949).

11. Respondents indicated by checking which of several alternative answers to questions most suited them. On many attitudinal items, the five-step, Likert-type responses were used, i.e. from "very much" to "very little."

12. H. Baumgartel, "Escape from Facts," *Adult Leadership,* Vol. III, No. 8 (February, 1955). This article describes in more detail the kinds of experiences in a program of this type.

13. H. Baumgartel, "An Analysis of the Validity of 'Perceived Change' Measures" (Ann Arbor: Survey Research Center, University of Michigan, 1954). (Mimeographed.)

14. Tests of statistical significance are for the purpose of reducing the possibility of attributing meaning to quantitative differences which could have occurred by chance alone.

15. D. Katz and R. L. Kahn, "Some Recent Findings in Human Relations Research in Industry," *Readings in Social Psychology,* eds. G. Swanson, T. Newcomb, and E. Hartley (New York: Holt, 1952).

16. R. L. Kahn and D. Katz, "Leadership Practices in Relation to Productivity and Morale," *Group Dynamics,* eds. D. Cartwright and A. Zander (Evanston: Row, Peterson, 1953).

Breakthrough in Organization Development

ROBERT R. BLAKE
Scientific Methods, Inc.

JANE S. MOUTON
Scientific Methods, Inc.

LOUIS B. BARNES
Harvard University

LARRY E. GREINER
Harvard University

This article describes how behavioral science concepts of team learning from a link between individual learning and total organization development. The link is important because it suggests some answers to a long-standing problem in industry: how to test and demonstrate the large-scale usefulness of human relations research and teaching. In the process, the article also describes a rather new approach to management development and, more broadly, to organization development.

Barriers to Success

Strangely enough, large-scale organization development is rare, and the measurement of results is even rarer. Even though management has sought for years to grasp and implement the important findings of behavioral science research, the task has proved more difficult than it first seemed. Many findings are subtle and complex. Other findings relate to individual insights or knowledge which is hard to build into the organization's life stream. In addition, most behavioral scientists do a better job of communicating technical findings to each other than they do of communicating the relevance of their research to practicing managers.

Robert R. Blake, Jane S. Mouton, Louis B. Barnes, and Larry E. Greiner, "Breakthrough in Organization Development," *Harvard Business Review*, Vol. 42, Nov.–Dec. 1964, pp. 133–138.

There have been many earnest attempts to make the behavioral sciences useful to business, government, and service institutions. But, because of the complexities, success has been elusive. Consider:

• Within many organizations, pockets of human relations enthusiasts form. They typically find themselves bucking a complacent or skeptical management. The enthusiasts retaliate by overselling their beliefs (which simply generates more skepticism) or by withdrawing from accusations of being "soft" on workers, profits, and tough-minded traditions of management.

• Selected executives are sent to management development programs which feature human relations concepts. Quite often, companies send "those who need it most." Particularly in "sensitivity training"-type programs, these men are placed under considerable strain. Though psychiatric problems rarely occur, they are a source of concern for staffs and faculties of such programs. Companies sometimes inadvertently send men with histories of previous mental illness. Under these conditions, psychiatric problems can occur and program effectiveness decrease for all concerned.[1]

• Other executives return from human relations programs highly enthusiastic. In at least some of these cases, there does seem to be real evidence of increased insight and individual learning. The problem for these men is one of implementation. Unless they have considerable organizational influence and/or a new, supportive climate, they will probably be forced back into old behavioral patterns and relationships.

• Occasionally, a total working group or department will be given human relations training within a company. At best, these efforts generate high morale and productivity within the group. At worst, the "chosen" group becomes the target or scapegoat of others in the organization, and the intergroup difficulties increase.[2]

• Most typically, in-company human relations training programs are established for foremen or other lower level managers. The almost universal response of participants in these programs is, "I wish my boss could learn what I've been learning." Then, as in the famous study of the International Harvester training program, most trainees go back to the job and apparently conform to their bosses' expectations, often at the expense of human relations concepts set forth in the program.[3]

In short, the over-all results of human relations and behavioral science training are questionable, at best, for on-the-job practitioners. Individual benefits are thought to be great, and personal testimonials are abundantly favorable.[4] However, the question of mobilizing these insights into collective organizational efforts has remained a serious issue.

Step Forward

The large-scale program in organization development described in this article may be a major step forward. It was regarded as highly successful both by the businessmen involved and by outside observers; the results *were* measured.

New to most executives in concept and design, the program makes use of a "Managerial Grid" approach to more effective work relationships. The Grid helps to give businessmen a language system for describing their current managerial preferences. It also involves classroom materials and an educational program for designing more productive problem-solving relationships. Even more important, the program is meant to be taught and applied by line managers over a time span involving six overlapping phases. These phases will be described briefly in Part I of this article; here you can see how a Managerial Grid program *should* work.

Then, in Part II you can see how such a program *did* work. The evaluation took place in a large plant (about 4,000 employees), which was part of a very large multiplant company. The parent company will be called "Piedmont" and the relevant plant unit "Sigma," for purposes of disguise. The Sigma plant had a reputation within Piedmont of being technically competent and had consistently been able to meet production goals over past years. Among Sigma's 4,000 employees were some 800 managers and technical staff personnel. These managers and staff personnel were all exposed to a Managerial Grid training program beginning late in 1962. At the request of the research manager in Piedmont's employee relations department, an evaluation study was designed shortly thereafter to follow up the effects of that program. The study included questionnaires, interviews, observations, and a combing of company records in order to separate program effects from nonprogram effects. The findings suggest that, even allowing for the nonprogram effects, the results of the Grid program were impressive. In brief:

- There is some evidence that Sigma's organization development program was responsible for at least several million dollars of controllable cost savings and profit increase. In addition, the program seems to have been responsible for a sizable increase in employee productivity during its first year.
- Sigma's managers began follow-up projects having total organization implications to a degree never experienced prior to the organization development program.
- The relationships between Sigma and Piedmont were considerably improved, partly as a result of the program. In addition, both union and community relationships were better than they had been in the past.
- There is some evidence that major shifts occurred in the behavioral patterns, dominant values, and attitudes found among managers at Sigma. These shifts were in line with the goals of the Managerial Grid program. Improved boss-subordinate, group, and intergroup relations were reported by Sigma managers.

• Colleague support seemed to be more important than boss support as a factor in managerial improvement, according to subordinate managers.

HOW THE GRID PROGRAM SHOULD WORK*

The Managerial Grid identifies five theories of managerial behavior, based on two key variables found in organizations. One variable reflects concern for production or output; the other variable, concern for people. In this instance the term "concern for" refers to the degree of concern, not the actual results. That is, it does *not* represent real production or the extent to which human relationship needs are actually met. It *does* indicate managerial concern for production and/or people and for how these influence each other.

Managerial Grid

These two variables and some of their possible combinations are shown in Figure 1. The horizontal axis indicates concern for production, and the vertical axis indicates concern for people. Each is expressed on a scale ranging from 1, which represents minimal concern, to 9, which represents maximal concern.

Briefly, the lower left corner of the Grid diagram in Figure 1 shows a 1,1 style. This represents minimal concern for production and minimal concern for people. The 1,9 style in the upper left corner depicts maximal concern for people but minimal concern for production. The 9,1 style in the lower right corner portrays maximal concern for production and minimal concern for human relationships. The 9,9 style in the upper right-hand corner represents maximal concern for both human relationships and production. The 5,5 style in the center of the diagram is "middle of the road" in both areas of concern.

Once managers have studied the classroom material accompanying the Grid, it is possible for them to revise practices and procedures so as to work toward a 9,9 organizational climate. These efforts use an educational program as the core, in contrast to more conventional ways of getting better organizational results, (e.g., changing organizational structure, leadership replacement, tightened accounting controls, or simple pressuring for more output).

Educational Steps

The educational steps are simple in concept, though complex in execution. They include the following:

• An investigation by each man of his own managerial style, using certain

* Editor's note: The authors of this section are Robert R. Blake and Jane S. Mouton.

FIGURE 1

The Managerial Grid

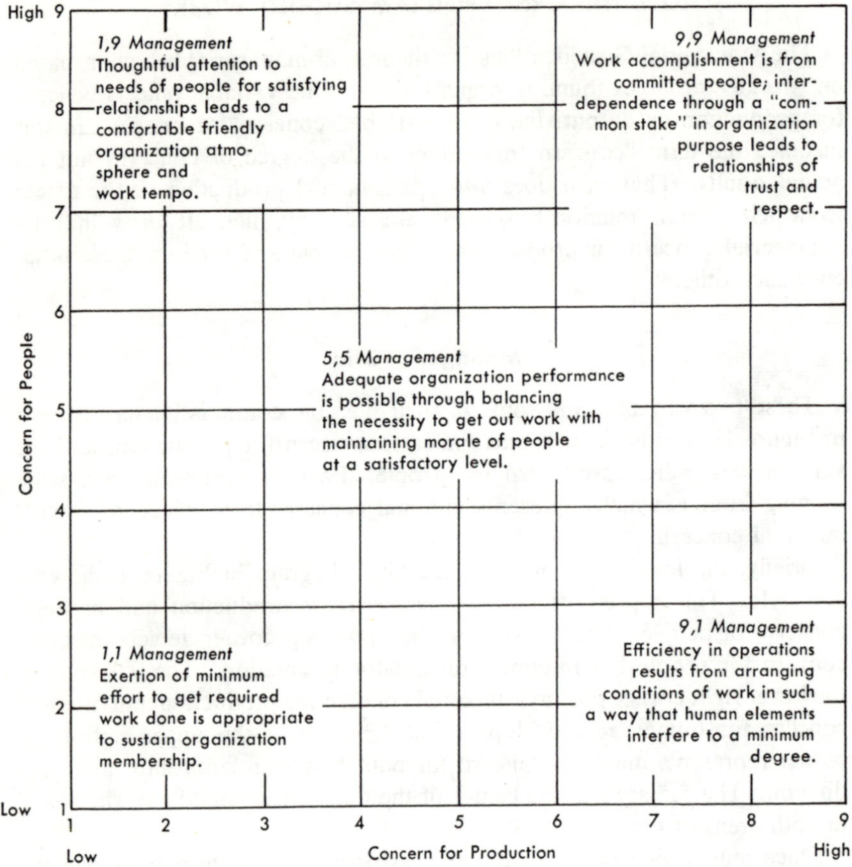

Managerial Grid forms of analysis. These include self-evaluation instruments, self-administered learning quizzes, in-basket procedures, and organizational simulations.

• A detailed and repeated evaluation of team effectiveness by groups which work with each other.

• Diagnosis of major organization problem areas; e.g., long-range planning, profitability of operation, union-management relations, promotion policies, incentive awards, new-product development, absenteeism, utilities conservation, and safety.

We should emphasize that this entire approach to organization development is self-administered by management except for occasional consultation regarding major issues. As of now, the Managerial Grid approach has been used in both industry and government. Changes in the near future will be in degree rather than in basic approach.

Six-Phase Program

At the present time, we describe these organization development programs in terms of six overlapping phases. Taken sequentially, these phases can cover from three to five years, but they can also be compressed into a shorter period of time within a company.

Manager Development

The six phases can be divided realistically into two major parts. The first two phases involve *management* development so that the other four phases can help managers work toward the 9,9 goals of *organization* development. Here are two management development phases:

1. *Laboratory-Seminar Training.* This is a one-week conference designed to introduce the manager to Grid concepts and material. From 12 to 48 individuals are assigned as members of problem-solving teams during each Laboratory-Seminar. These Seminars are conducted by line managers who already have been through the Seminar and thus know its material and schedules.

The Seminar begins with the study and review of one's own Managerial Grid style of behavior as outlined in a series of questionnaire booklets completed by each manager. It continues with 50 hours of intensive problem solving, evaluation of individual and team results, and critiques of team performance. The problems typically simulate organizational situations in which interpersonal behavior affects task performance. Each team regularly evaluates its own behavior and problem-solving capabilities. A team which performs poorly on one problem exercise is able to assess and adjust its problem-solving style in time for the next exercise. In addition, one exercise involves an attempted 9,9 "feedback" from team members to each individual concerning *team* impressions of his managerial styles.

Though Grid Seminars are sometimes compared with "T-Group" or "Sensitivity" training, the two training experiences are quite different. The strongest similarity comes in the face-to-face feedback experience of Phase #1. Even here, however, the Managerial Grid Seminars take a more structured approach by focusing on managerial styles rather than on personal behavior characteristics which may or may not be related to management.

Phase #1 is not intended to produce immediate organization improvement. It serves more as the trigger which creates a readiness to really work on human problems of production. Participation in a Grid Seminar is set up so as to include a "diagonal slice" of the organization chart. No man is in the same group as his boss or immediate work colleagues. At the same time, this diagonal slice arrangement permits many organizational levels and departments to be represented in each session.

2. *Team Development.* This represents an on-the-job extension of Phase #1. The general 9,9 concepts and personal learning of the Grid Seminars are transferred to the job situation after each work group or department decides on its own 9,9 ground rules and relationships. Team development usually starts with the boss and his immediate subordinates exploring their managerial styles and operating practices as a work team. The ground rules of openness and candor which were established in Phase #1 can now become the daily operating style of Phase #2.[5]

Taken together, Phases #1 and #2 provide management development conditions which are designed to:

> . . . enable managers to learn Managerial Grid concepts as an organizing framework for thinking about management practices;
>
> . . . increase the self-examination of personal performance characteristics;
>
> . . . increase a manager's willingness to listen, to face and appreciate work-related conflict, to reduce and work out interpersonal frictions, and to reject compromise as a basis for organizational decision making;
>
> . . . build improved relationships between groups, among colleagues at the same level, and between superiors and subordinates;
>
> . . . make managers more critical of outworn practices and precedents while extending their problem-solving capacities in interdependent situations. Words like "involvement" and "commitment" become real in terms of day-to-day tasks.

Organization Development

The last four phases build on this management development and help managers work toward the more complex goals of organization development.

3. *Intergroup Development.* This involves group-to-group working relationships and focuses on building 9,9 ground rules and norms beyond the single work group. Situations are established whereby operating tensions that happen to exist between groups are identified and explored by group members and/or their representatives.

The goal is to move from the appallingly common "win-lose" pattern to a joint problem-solving activity. This seems to be possible when competing groups work their problems through to resolution using intergroup procedures developed in behavioral science studies.

A second type of intergroup development helps to link managers who are at the same level but belong to different work units (e.g., foremen, district sales managers, department managers, and so forth). Their competitiveness may increase organizational productiveness, but it may also result in departmental goals being placed ahead of more important organizational goals. Here, the problem is again met using joint problem-solving efforts which confront interpersonal issues according to 9,9 ground rules and norms.

4. *Organizational Goal Setting.* This involves issues of major importance to all managers. Organization development moves beyond team areas into problems that require commitment at all levels. Such broad problems include: cost control, union-management relations, safety, promotion policies, and over-all profit improvement. These problems are identified by special task groups which may again come from a "diagonal slice" of the organization chart. Departmental groups may also help to define goals and assign roles. The goals prove to be "practical" when managers who must implement them also establish responsibilities for implementation. Commitment gained from the goal-setting procedures of this phase also avoids those negative responses now groupsd under "resistance to change."

5. *Goal Attainment.* This uses some of the same educational procedures used in Phase #1, but here the issues are major organizational concerns and the stakes are real.

For example, when problem areas are defined by the special task groups, other teams are set up throughout the organization. These teams are given a written "task paragraph" which describes the problem and the goal. Team members are also given packets of information on the issue under discussion. This information is usually studied overnight, after which individual managers check themselves on a true-false test designed by the special task group. Once individuals have studied the information and the test, the teams begin discussion on the same items, checking their agreed-on answers against an answer key. This way, agreement is reached on the nature of the problem and its key dimensions. From this point on, the team members work toward a better statement of the problem and toward corrective steps. They also begin to assign responsibility for these corrective action steps.

Phase #5 also relies on a manager serving as a coordinator during Phases #4 and #5. His primary goal is to help achieve the goals set during Phase #4. His secondary aim is to help identify previously unrecognized problems. He should have neither line nor staff responsibility in the conventional sense, but should hold a position similar to an industrial medical officer. He would be a specialist in organization development and intervene at those times when proposed steps seem inconsistent with 9,9 theory. He would seek action based on understanding and agreement, not because of any formal authority he holds. This approach, though more difficult than access through authority, reduces resistance. It also improves the quality of joint effort.

6. *Stabilization.* This final phase is designed to support the changes brought about in the earlier phases. These changes are assessed and re-

inforced so as to withstand pressures toward "slip-back" and regression. This also gives management an opportunity to evaluate its gains and mistakes under the organization development program.

Summary

In this section we have briefly outlined the concepts and phases that go into an organization development program using Managerial Grid material. In some respects, the program sounds simple, and yet any manager recognizes the difficulties involved in influencing a large organizational unit toward changes in values and performance. . .

Notes

1. See Chris Argyris, "T-Groups for Organizational Effectiveness," HBR March–April 1964, p. 60.

2. See Alex Bavelas and George Strauss, "Group Dynamics and Intergroup Relations," in W. F. Whyte, Melville Dalton, et al., *Money and Motivation* (New York, Harper & Brothers, 1955), pp. 90–96.

3. E. A. Fleishman, E. F. Harris, and E. H. Burtt, *Leadership and Supervision in Industry* (Columbus, Personnel Research Board, Ohio State University, 1955).

4. Instances of individual learning are documented in a series of HBR articles by Kenneth R. Andrews: see "Is Management Training Effective? I. Evaluation by Managers and Instructors," January–February 1957, p. 85; "Is Management Training Effective? II. Measurement, Objectives, and Policy," March–April 1957, p. 63; and "Reaction to University Development Programs," May–June 1961, p. 116.

5. See R. R. Blake, J. S. Mouton, and M. G. Blansfield, "How Executive Team Training Can Help You and Your Organization," *Journal of the American Society of Training Directors* (now called *Training Directors Journal*), January 1962, p. 3.

34

An Organization Improvement Program in a Decentralized Organization

RICHARD BECKHARD
Richard Beckhard Associates

In the past few years, some "giant steps" have been taken in the application of behavioral science knowledge to the problems of organization improvement and growth. It is becoming increasingly possible for organization managers to scientifically diagnose the conditions in their organization both in terms of practices, procedures, and ways of producing integrated effort and in terms of motivation, attitudes, and values of the people who make up the organization. It is also possible, from such diagnosis, to make a realistic assessment of the state of an organization's health and from this assessment to plan systematic steps for improving its health and effectiveness.

Some Assumptions About Organization Change

Organization Diagnosis

In introducing change into a system, it is assumed that the following phases of initial diagnosis would apply:

Defining the change problem;
Determining the appropriate client systems within the total organization system;
Determining each system's readiness and capacity to change;
Determining appropriate change objectives;
Assessing the change agent's own resources.

It is also assumed that for change to take place, the current status or set of conditions must be unfrozen, new inputs made available, and the system refrozen in a new set of conditions. For this to occur effectively in an organization, the education or change program needs to be organic; that is, it should grow out of itself and out of the needs identified as relevant to the organization's purposes. Specifically:

The program must be *goal-related,* that is, clearly related to organization purposes;

The program must be seen as *relevant* to *individual purposes* as well as to organization purposes by the people participating in it;

The program should have maximum *spread potential* throughout the organization.

Induction of Change

The change strategy should ensure that the organization can continue to learn from its own experience. This implies activities and tactics that provide for operating units to look at their own operations, test them against alternatives, and plan future improvement. It also implies a process of systematic information collecting, feedback, and action planning based on the information. For such purposes the organization should be divided into learning groups such as work families, peer groups, or project groups.

Change goals need to be clearly defined in terms of the *types* of changes desired. One type is change in *organizational climate* (as evidenced in the organization's practices, its communications, its ways of handling conflict). A second type is change in *attitudes* and *values* of the people in the organization (for example, treating conflict as an appropriate and necessary condition of organization life or recognizing that frank and open communication is a desirable value). A third type is a change in *skills* (e.g., in problem solving or interpersonal relationships).

Although all of these types of change goals are existent in any organization change effort, it is important that relatively explicit priorities be established.

In the management of change it is necessary to find appropriate educational methods to achieve any of these change goals. The function of the educational consultant is to help the organization provide conditions in which it can introduce appropriate educational methods, collect more systematic data on its own organizational functioning, increase its ability to use such data in improvement planning, and build a training and educational orientation into its line management so that organization improvement becomes a way of life.

The Organization

Let us look at this particular organization, its purposes, and general structure.

The company is a medium-sized concern which operates 26 hotel properties in the United States, Canada, the Caribbean, and Great Britain. At the time the improvement program started, the company managed five hotels with about 2,000 employees. Today, its activities include hotels, motor hotels, and motor lodges, with about 7,000 employees. The period covered by this report, 1958 to 1963, was one of rapid growth resulting from the building and establishment of new hotels. The requirements for staffing, financing, and operating each new property made extreme demands on management personnel as well as on the finances of the company. Also, during this period conditions in the hotel industry changed. A rapid increase in the number of hotel and motor hotel units led to increased competition in rates and special services. These outside influences, plus rapid expansion and major investment in new properties, made the company's profit position precarious. At the time of this writing, however, a major upturn is being reported.

The organization improvement program with which we are concerned begins in the spring of 1958 and deals with the hotel division of the company. The president of the hotel division had reporting to him at central headquarters a staff consisting of the directors of five departments: operations, sales and advertising, purchasing and food, personnel employment, and controller. The general managers of each of the hotels also reported directly to the president. (See Figure 1.) The company had moved to an administratively decentralized operating policy. Each general manager was quite autonomous in terms of decision making, with the exception of a central accounting and control system and certain corporate policies relative to centralized purchasing. Large capital expenditures were approved centrally. General managers did not have actual profit targets, but profit estimates were a standard procedure. Each of the hotel properties was a unique unit with a very few of the characteristics of a "chain" operation.

During the period of the change effort with which this paper is concerned, the company moved into the motor hotel field, developed a motor hotel division, and later, a motor lodge division.

Identification of the Need for Improvement

The president initiated the change program. In the spring of 1958 he attended a workshop at which the consultant was a trainer. In discussing his organization, the president identified as a serious managerial problem the communication difficulties between corporate or central staff and line top managers. He felt that, although he had brought these two elements of the organization together regularly at quarterly management meetings, there still existed a lack of trust, openness, and clarity in terms of decision-making authority. The causes for these difficulties were perceived to be both organizational and interpersonal. The president also felt that the communication from the top group to second-level line managers in the hotels was not so effective as it should be. He was looking for help.

FIGURE 1

1958 Organization Chart

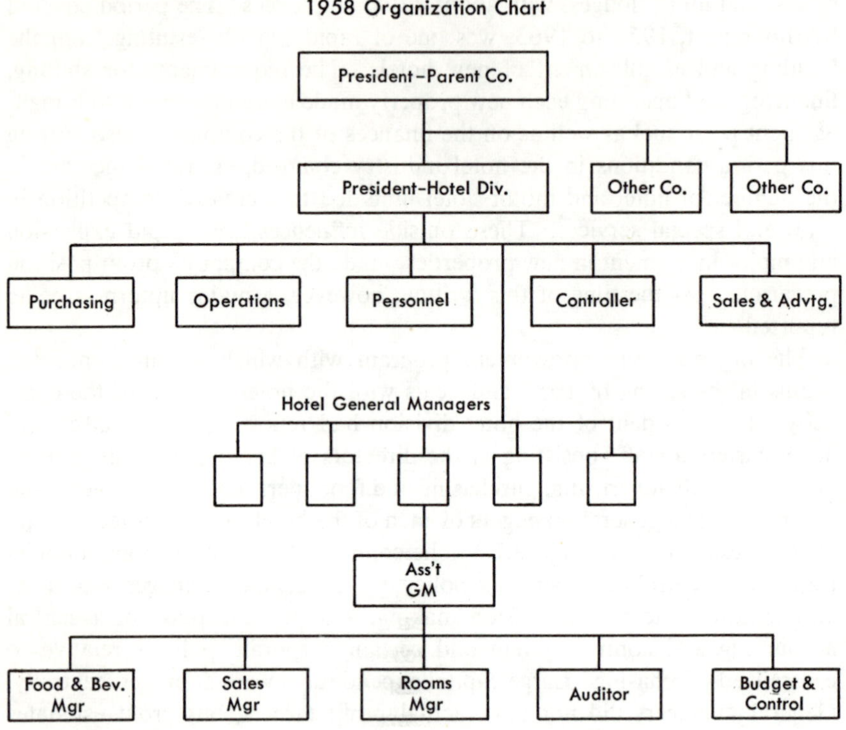

In describing his concern, the president pointed to various evidences of the problem:

Central staff reported considerable difficulty in trying to initiate new ideas or improvement efforts into the hotels. They felt there were too many debates with general managers as to what could or could not be done in an improvement effort. In some cases staff were required to communicate *only* through general managers rather than through counterpart department heads.

On the other hand, general managers complained to the president about the confusion caused by the central staff's coming into hotels and making recommendations and suggestions. Some general managers saw this as an intrusion by people who lacked the experience and know-how of the hotel business. In a few cases general managers had barred central staff from their hotels, unless specifically requested by the general manager.

Although attempts had been made during the quarterly meetings to work through these problems, there seemed to be a lack of willingness to deal openly with them.

Because of the background of the hotel industry, essentially entrepreneurial, and because of the managerial styles of the general managers, relatively little direct communication existed between several of the general managers and their operating subordinates except on necessary operational matters. Furthermore, social distance was reinforced by the economics of the situation, as illustrated by the fact that the general manager's compensation is approximately 100 per cent more than that of the next nearest subordinate staff member.

First Phases of the Program

Proceeding on the assumption that information collecting, feedback, and action planning are three essential steps in initiating change, the consultants suggested that a program be developed with the top group with the purposes of further defining the problem, broadening its base of information, and setting some conditions for joint planning to deal with it.

Information Collection Through Interviews

As a first step, an interview was held with each of the general managers, each of the central staff department heads, with a sample of the subordinates of the general managers, and a sample of the subordinates of the central staff heads. In each of these interviews, the respondents were told why the interview was being held, what use would be made of the data, that there would be a meeting of the general managers and central staff heads to work on improving communications and operations, and that they as individual respondents could contribute to the effectiveness of this meeting by sharing their information about the causes of difficulties and by giving their suggestions as to ways for improving communications.

In each case these interviews lasted from one to two hours, were nondirected, and ranged over a wide variety of topics. The interviewer recorded information, and at the close of the interview reported back to the respondent what he had heard. He also cleared with the respondent the information to be reported out, with the assurance that the identity of the respondent would be held confidential.

The material from all these interviews was organized into a series of management process headings such as —

1. Communications between president and line (or staff)
2. Line-staff communications
3. Location of decision making
4. Role clarification or confusion
5. Communications procedures.

The interview results were then listed under these categories and color-coded to identify the category of respondent (i.e., general manager, staff head, staff assistant, and so on).

Feedback of Information from Interviews and Initiation of Planning

A three-day meeting was convened at an off-site area. This meeting was attended by the president, the general managers, the central staff heads, and two consultants. On the first half-day of the meeting the findings from the interviews were presented. During this presentation, the members of the group could check for clarification, but no discussion of the information was allowed.

In the second phase of the meeting the group as a whole went through the list and determined the priority items. As the group analyzed the findings and the sources of information, it became clear that solutions to most of the problems listed could be achieved only through the joint efforts of those present. The type of information could not be dealt with by legislation from the top but required problem solving by all those affected. Sample items were —

From staff heads: The president expects us to introduce changes and maintain and upgrade quality but the general managers won't let us into the hotels to do it.

From general managers: The advertising policy of the corporation is ridiculous. We talk decentralization and yet we have no voice in setting our own advertising policy.

From subordinates of general managers: Where are we going in this organization? We have no feeling of belonging to a corporation but only to a hotel.

There were over 90 individual items representing issues on which the group would need to work. The process of selecting priority issues for discussion took the better part of the first day. On reconvening the first night, as a change of pace, and with the purpose of giving a framework for looking at the difficulties the group would be facing as it worked on the issues in subsequent days, the consultants introduced some theory about communications in organizations.

The second and third days were spent in digging into some of the central issues, bringing up the conflicts that existed among the various groups, and looking for areas of agreement and ways of working through the problems. This process involved identification of the causes of an issue in terms of past backgrounds of the staff and the managers, the behavior of the president, the problems of structure, and the nature of the business. The group explored possible changes in practices, procedures, and attitudes that would be required for correcting some of the problems that had been identified.

During the discussions, the consultants' contributions pinpointed how the group was functioning, guidelines for working on a problem, bringing conflict to the surface where it could be worked on, and systematic diagnosis of the causes of some of the problems that were identified.

The three days were active, volatile, and tiring. But by the end of this period, the group felt that it had made only a start and that it needed to continue. A meeting was therefore scheduled for one month later.

The second meeting was held in a hotel and was less exciting than the first. The members of the group came with the expectation of picking up where they had been, that is, with the climate of openness and problem solving that had existed at the end of the first session. They were surprised to discover that in the intervening time there had been considerable regression. In order for discussions to continue profitably, it was necessary to spend a few hours in re-establishing the earlier climate of trust.

A significant outcome of this second meeting was the top management's recognition of, and attention to, concerns of subordinates about the state of affairs. Some of the concerns that had been reported were that subordinate managers did not feel they could influence the corporate management in any significant way; that they considered their primary rewards and punishments as coming from the general manager of their hotel, that therefore their primary and almost exclusive loyalty lay there; and that they thought no one at corporate headquarters was much concerned with their needs, career plans, or current performance. Related to this, they felt little identification with the corporation's future objectives and plans, but saw their career planning in terms either of their own unit or of the total industry.

Most felt a lack of communication with counterparts in other of the organization's hotels. For example, sales managers had never had a meeting together, nor had other functional counterparts. In a number of cases, due to the entrepreneurial management style, subordinates did not see themselves as part of a management team but rather as individuals reporting to "the boss."

The management group decided that it would be desirable to set up a series of meetings, modeled after the ones they themselves were having, for the subordinate manager group. They set up two sets of meetings: one with sales, food, and rooms managers (customer-contact departments) and another with assistant general managers, auditors, and budget and control directors (administrative departments). Second-level central staff counterparts were assigned to meet with the relevant groups.

It was agreed that for these meetings there would again be a need for collecting information from those attending and for providing a method to feed this information back and make it available for group work. In creating these sets of conferences, the management group recognized that it would be necessary to ensure some follow-up from the output of the conferences if any real organization improvement were to occur. During discussion on this point, the consultants suggested that, to deal with the feelings of lack of connection with the corporation that were repeatedly expressed by their subordinates, it might be desirable to include some face-to-face contact with the president of the division during these meetings. This was programmed into the meetings. It was also suggested that the meetings should try to deal simultaneously with a variety of stated needs, including: need for communication between counterparts, need for improved problem solving between staff and line at the same level, need for strengthening of hotel teams, and need for establishing communication between the hotel teams and the system.

The hotel managers agreed that they would report and present the plan to their teams and that they would build in follow-up meetings in the hotels so that the outputs of the conferences could be built back into the hotel organizations. To establish some identifying label, the series of meetings were called "Key Executive Conferences."

Key Executive Conferences

The methodology of these conferences was similar to that of the top management conference. Consultants interviewed the participants, organized the material by categories, and scheduled problem-solving meetings.

The first phase of each of these meetings was concerned with the feedback of information. The second phase differed slightly from the top management meetings in that the groups were asked by the consultant to go through the agenda and rate each item as —

1. An item we want to recommend to top management
2. An item we want to discuss and work through
3. An item that no longer seems relevant.

The items that were seen as ready for immediate recommendation were accumulated throughout the conference on a separate list. The items identified as needing discussion by the group became the group's major agenda during the three-day period. As each of these items was discussed, it was either attached to the list of recommendations or identified as completed and therefore eliminated from the agenda.

The cumulative list of recommendations to the corporation was presented to the president in a confrontation meeting held on the last half-day of the conference. He discussed each item and noted some action. That is, he made a decision, yes or no, or referred a question to a task force or to some other part of the organization. A specific issue will serve to illustrate this process.

One question of central concern to a number of people was: "How can we reorganize advertising policy to allow hotels to have more voice in planning their own advertising programs?"

After discussion of this issue, the group sent a delegation to the president to discuss it with him in detail. At this confrontation he announced that with the information he now had from the field (previously screened from him) he was hereby appointing a field-oriented man (a member of the group attending) as sales and advertising director to provide the needed liaison between the field and central office. This was a major policy change from highly centralized advertising direction by a corporate vice-president with little or no field consultation. It also demonstrated dramatically a successful and useful influence effort on the part of second-level management on top management.

These key executive conferences were scheduled twice a year. On the third round the groups reviewed the status of the conferences, their original purposes, and their current relevance. It was felt that the need for across-the-board problem-solving meetings had diminished as intrahotel communications improved and channels to the top were clearly opened. However, the need for technical counterpart meetings was stronger than ever.

It was decided, and agreed to by top management, that the key executive conferences would be terminated and that technical meetings on a periodically scheduled basis would be instituted.

Problem-Solving Conferences in Hotels

Emerging from these conferences was a general improvement in the communications and working effectiveness of the top team in each hotel. Some of the managers suggested that similar conferences within hotels would be profitable, and such programs were set up.

The format of these hotel "self-survey, action-planning meetings" was essentially similar to that of the meetings already described. After interviews with all middle- and first-line supervision, the information was categorized and fed back to the respondents who met in working groups composed of representatives of all departments. These groups worked through the agenda and made recommendations to top (hotel) management. The recommendations were then fed back to the top team and a confrontation meeting similar to those described above was held, but with the general manager conducting the meeting and setting the action plans.

These meetings have proved to be continuously effective and are held today on a semiannual or annual basis in all of the hotels. They have become a "way of life" for identifying current concerns, organizing work to deal with them, and planning action. The consultants' role has become that of "sponge" (collecting their data), "water faucet" (giving the information back to them), and "catalyst" (bringing all elements of management together).

A Redefinition of the Change Goals

This initial improvement effort was designed to deal with the effects of decentralization, the needs for improvement of interunit and interpersonal communications skills, and with techniques for better problem solving. The same set of goals guided the activities with the key executives and the initial efforts within the hotels.

Concurrently with the development of this program, the nature of the mission of the organization changed as the coporation went into the motor hotel business. This expansion necessitated a structural reorganization. From it emerged an organization in which two group vice-presidents reported to the president, one for motor hotels and one for hotels. (Later a motor lodge group was added.) Reporting to the group vice-president for hotels were the general managers of all the hotels and a small staff of specialists. Reporting to the group vice-president for motor hotels were the general managers of the motor hotels. Reporting to the president at a staff level were directors of corporate service: planning (for new hotels), purchasing, personnel, and sales and advertising.

During the period previously described, the president had attended a National Training Laboratories human relations laboratory and had subsequently encouraged his key executives to attend. The two group vice-presidents, several of the hotel general managers, and two or three of the staff directors had done so. As a result of these and other activities, the president became quite explicit in his desire to move the entire organization toward a management-by-objectives or Theory-Y orientation.

The president convened a two-day planning conference with the central staff directors and group vice-presidents to explore how far the organization had progressed in this direction and what would be needed to move the total culture toward a Theory-Y or management-by-objectives orientation. (See Figure 2.) At this conference the group reviewed the relationships between the president and staff and line management. These were seen to be quite improved although there were still difficulties between line management and some central office departments, and between the president and his staff. It was agreed that a periodic series of organization improvement meetings should be held with this group, with the minimum of one annual off-site conference and a series of on-site, shorter meetings.

The group recognized that a systematic target-setting[1] or goal-setting program was a necessary tool of any management-by-objectives operation. It was agreed that a unit-by-unit goal-setting process would be instituted during the coming year and that an individual performance-improvement target-setting process would be developed within the top management and corporate staff group.

A need was also felt for a program with the motor hotel management group working toward the development of a concept of team management. Another area identified was building a team for a new hotel; another was building inter-group relationships between the planning division (the corporate representatives in building and preparing a new hotel) and the general manager and his team (who take over its operation when it opens).

FIGURE 2

1964 Organization Chart

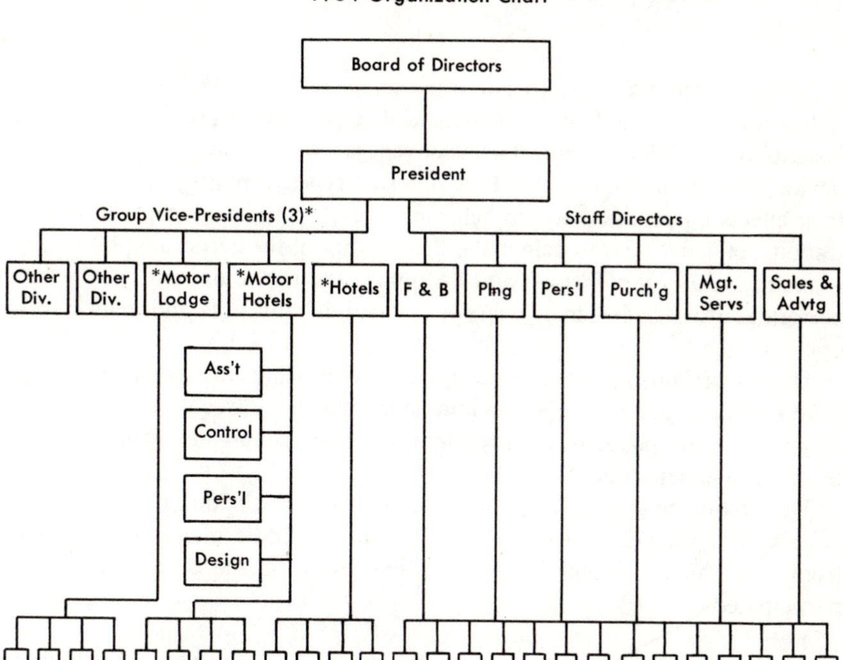

In looking ahead, it was obvious to all that a speed-up in the development of potential general management talent was a major organization requirement. The rapid expansion of the industry, the policy of rotation within the organization, and the proposed additional expansion for the late sixties, all combined to require acceleration in the preparation of management talent.

Management Development Training

Several factors combined to influence the next major effort:

1. The expansion program and organization policy discussed above
2. The experience of the president and most of the corporate staff heads with laboratory training
3. The need for additional technical development and training for new management trainees
4. The needs of existing middle managers who had come up through one phase of the business but had little training in either management or other technical phases of the business.

Organization Improvement Activities

It was therefore proposed that there should be three types of educational efforts.

Management School. A one-week management workshop using laboratory training methods was scheduled. The purposes were to increase the insights of participants into the effectiveness of their own managerial behavior; to help them understand the different types of managerial styles and their effects on productivity; to help them develop some concepts of organizational effectiveness; to help make them aware of the corporate philosophy of *management by objectives* and its application to the units in which they performed; to broaden their concept of team effectiveness and team development.

These workshops were staffed by a faculty of behavioral scientists. They were scheduled for a group of 24 middle management executives selected by a task force composed of the president, the two group vice-presidents, and the personnel department head.

The first of these workshops was held in 1962 and additional workshops have since been held twice a year. The entire middle management group from the hotel and motor hotel operations and from the central staff have participated.

Technical Seminars. To deal with the broadening of technical skills, a series of technical meetings on food and beverage, budget and control, and auditing have been established. Participants from a variety of settings within the organization have attended these sessions.

Counterpart Meetings. The regularly scheduled technical counterpart meetings mentioned earlier have broadened their agenda to include some training and development work on problem solving, communications, and management. A series of special workshops on interviewing and consulting have been given to large numbers of managers.

In addition to the above specific educational efforts, the personnel office provides a central clearing house for off-site educational activities both in hotel operations and management.

Target and Goal Setting

As reported earlier, one of the major areas identified at the planning conference as needing attention was the process of goal setting in hotel units, in the field, and in individual performance improvement.

A program was established by which, on a semiannual basis, the top management of each hotel meet with the group vice-president of their division, the president of the corporation, and the key central staff, to review unit goals and jointly determine what is necessary to implement the goals for the coming year or months. This process requires the active participation of the management team within the unit. This has had the effect of building in much more involvement throughout the organization and a feeling of "ownership" in the unit and organization goals.

Personal performance improvement via systematic goal setting was established initially by the president and the group vice-presidents. This included the preparation of position descriptions by subordinates; the setting of improvement targets; the sharing of perceptions between the president and his subordinates about the reality and achievability of these various targets; their priority; and the periodic, joint review of progress toward targets. By constant evaluation of the process as well as by the refinement of the techniques employed, this has become a useful method of continuous information collecting and planning for the top group. Several of the general managers felt the method would be a helpful management tool in their hotels, and two of them introduced it within their organizations. In one case, the program included a series of training meetings for the entire management group in which they were given lectures on the process, opportunities to develop position descriptions, practice in interviews, and so forth. The process received substantial favorable lip service. However, because of pressure from the general manager to "do" the program, it met with considerable resistance in practice. As soon as the pressure abated, the program fell apart. This was one of the more dramatic failure incidents in this total effort and serves to reinforce the fact that an externally imposed program, without real involvement and participation on the part of those responsible for its implementation, is probably doomed from the start.

On the other hand, the unit goal setting which is organic to the corporate requirements has been seen as relevant by all concerned and has become an increasingly effective instrument for planning and communication among the several field units and the central office.

Team Training — Intergroup Staff and Line in New Hotels

One of the innovations in the organization improvement program has been the training of new management teams. The hotel industry is constantly developing new management teams as new properties open. It also sets up temporary systems which are established for a limited time only, such as the team that comes into existence to design and supervise the building and furnishing of a new hotel. This team goes out of existence when the hotel opens.

There were two specific sets of groups that were identified by the staff and the group vice-presidents as needing help in improving their communications and teamwork. One was the technical team responsible for the planning and construction supervision of a new hotel. The other was the general manager and his top team who would operate the hotel. A specific area of concern was the interface between these two groups (the planning team and the operating team) during the period of the final phases of construction and the preopening activities.

A series of conferences was held with the technical staff to analyze the problems of multiple authority, change-over from staff to line operation, problems of the preopening period, selection of personnel for the new hotel (previously handled by central staff), and training of staff (by central specialists or line heads). A result of these joint meetings was a series of revised procedures whereby the general manager was brought into the picture at a much earlier date, had a more active role in the selection of his own staff, and had more influence on the final design of the facility.

Training Operating Teams

The training of new hotel management operating teams was established as a high priority need. In order to understand the significance of this training, one needs a picture of previous practice.

The selection of people to serve as department heads in new hotels had been based on their proved technical competence in their own fields, such as housekeeping, engineering, food preparation, and so on. Each of the members making up a new management team came from a background of experience in which he had learned to operate *with* a particular managerial style and *under* a particular managerial style. The general manager, in each case an experienced man, had his own managerial style and ways of work which he intended to employ in his future operations. When the team came together on the job, the demands of the work required their fullest effort in the technical area. No time was spent on discussion of ways of work, relationships, communications procedures. For the first few months after the hotel opened, all the problems of a new property created similar demands and pressures. Matters of relationship, communication, and so forth usually did not get much attention by the team until well along in the first year. Consequently, considerable inefficiency might well have been avoided had better communication been established earlier among the several key members of the management team.

It was hypothesized that the effective building of a new team could be accomplished more efficiently if, as a part of their earliest experiences as a team, they could spend some time concentrating on the building of a culture. This would include explicit discussion of norms and procedures to be followed in terms of communication, decision making, and job responsibilities.

Experiments were set up with three hotels which were due to open within a year or two. In each case, the first activity of the top management team (general manager and key department heads) was to attend a two- or three-day off-site conference with the purpose clearly to begin building the management team.

The format of these conferences was as follows: After an opening statement by the head of the team (general manager), the group built an agenda of relevant concerns and problems to be tackled in the area of team effectiveness, work relationships, communications, training, and the like. Explicit attention was paid to the establishment of an open communications climate through such devices as asking each member to share with the group his reasons for taking the job, what his career aspirations were, and so on. Another mechanism was for each member to describe for the group how he saw his responsibilities and authority in the new unit. The general manager then reacted to this statement, as did the colleagues, and a consensus was arrived at relative to each job.

Other agenda items included plans for communication (staff meetings, among others); training programs for staff coordination and use of resources; clarification of practices — for example, what things needed approval; relationships to the technical planning staff; and special problems of the "opening week."

In each of these three experiments, follow-up meetings were held approximately six to eight months after the opening to check on results and to review the various commitments made at the earlier meeting. Respondents reported considerable progress toward more openness and improved communication; but, in each case, there were some regressions which were reviewed and worked through again.

As reported by the president, the corporate staff, the board of directors, the general managers involved, and the teams themselves, the openings of these three hotels were the smoothest in the corporation's history. Teams were able to deal with a much larger number of complex problems; turnover was reduced dramatically as compared with experience at previous openings in similar hotels; and, contrary to the trend for new hotels, there was virtually no turnover in the middle management groups within the first year. These activities were seen by the participants and the corporate leadership as highly useful in terms of developing the health of the organization.

Operations Improvement Committees

With the continually increased need to improve its competitive position, an operations improvement program was introduced into the organization. Profit improvement or operations improvement committees were developed in most units with rank-and-file and management participation. The mission of these committees was to develop innovations, service improvements, and more efficiency in the quality and handling of food, lodging, and service.

These activities have produced a high degree of involvement on a fairly broad base and have resulted in a considerable number of improvements in performance, in increased service and reduced costs. Management reports much more concern for profit and costs on the part of rank-and-file employees. This shows up in such ways as reduced breakage in the kitchens, less waste in handling laundry, and so on.

Overhead Cost Reduction Program

With the tightening economic conditions, due to overexpansion in the industry, there was the need for an appreciable cut in overhead costs at the central staff level.

The president brought together the heads of staff departments and told them of the amounts of cuts that would probably be required, using two figures: a minimum and a maximum. He asked each staff head, in consultation with two or three of his colleagues from other departments, to form task forces to think through what he and his department would do if the minimum cut or the maximum cut were required and also to think through what the consequences would be to the corporation this year, and for several years ahead. Staff heads were asked to include some colleagues with points of view different from their own.

A historian for this project was selected early in the program to keep a record of the processes operating throughout the program. Some bases for selection of task forces were recorded as follows:

Knowledge of the activity of the other department
Use of the services of the other department
Involvement in effects of reduction
Range of ideas and viewpoints
Challenge to certain items
Individual bias in favor of the particular department's services
Need to be involved in the decision making
Special skills
Decision-making power and importance of approval.

Following the series of task force meetings, a general meeting was held during which each staff head explained his present budget, his recommendations for reducing his budget, and the consequences on both a long- and short-term basis of these reductions.

The final results as indicated in the report were as follows:

Individual department reductions range from zero to $50,000. The total effect of this program, provided all recommendations are put into effect, results in reducing the central office budget by approximately $225,000 and in reducing the number of persons employed in central office by 12.

Significant aspects of this effect, in addition to the obvious savings in dollars, are the high degree of shared commitment to the solution of the problem and the ability to cope with layoffs and belt-tightening without any loss to the viability of the organization.

Program Effects

Dramatic profit improvement was recorded in 1964, with highest earnings in the company's ten-year history. This profit was against an industry trend of stabilized profits. It is impossible to correlate this profit improvement fully with the educational effort; but it is clear that the program has made a significant contribution through developing attitudes of commitment to company objectives, a shared value of concern for costs, and a measurable increase in operating efficiency of almost all units.

Specific evidence of changes in organization climate include very low turnover in a highly mobile industry, an increase in rotation of management personnel, the promotion into higher positions of more than a hundred management people, an increase of performance effectiveness in most units in terms of costs as related to sales, more efficient staffing, and reduction of costs with no appreciable decrease of service.

There are clear indications that the organization is able to handle crises in much more effective ways. The organization has recently withstood a reorganization at the corporate level, major modifications in proposed expansion plans, major relocations of numbers of management personnel into new assignments, yet has shown an increase in performance return.

Increasingly, the units of the organization are learning from their own experience, are able to function more effectively with less dependence on outside help, and, at the same time, are making more creative use of a variety of resources within the organization.

Summary

The change effort started with the president's recognition of the need for improving problem-solving skills, interpersonal communication skills, and intergroup communication as a function of the decentralization policy. The key line management and the corporate staff management, together with the president, were seen as an initial learning group; first efforts were with them, to help identify and work through the problems of the organization as they perceived them.

The next major effort was with the subordinates of the above-mentioned key line and staff executives. Here the primary concerns (in addition to improving skills and individual effectiveness) were to change the influence pattern between middle management and the top management of the organization, to build the effectiveness of the team within each operating unit, and to establish communication links between counterparts in various segments of the system.

Building team effectiveness, improving communications, and problem solving in the several individual units made up the next major phase, with emphasis on improved linkage between the corporate headquarters and the middle line management through top management of each unit, intergroup and interpersonal communication within a unit, and vertical communication between the general manager and the rest of his team. Increased operating effectiveness in terms of better procedures and more generally shared concern for costs, controls, and efficiency were the organization goals of this phase.

The major goal shifted to moving the entire organization toward a management-by-objectives or "Theory-Y" orientation.[2] Changing external conditions and increasing requirements for management talent also meant speeding up the preparation of existing management personnel to enable them to handle greater responsibilities.

To meet these goals, new learning groups were created. Groups of peers from across the system were brought together in one-week management laboratories for intensive exploration of their own managerial styles and of organization behavior. Technical sessions dealing with food and beverage preparation, budget and controls, auditing procedures, and so on, were held for specialists in these fields and for others in management who wished to broaden their repertoire of skills.

Goal-setting programs were introduced for all operating units on a systematic basis; and performance-improvement, target-setting sessions were instituted at the central staff level and in some of the operating units. The training of new hotel teams received major emphasis.

When economic conditions required tightening of the belt, improved efficiency throughout the organization, and reduction in overhead costs, the *total resources* of the organization were mobilized. Operations improvement committees consisting of rank-and-file management personnel in all units were set up in each hotel, and a series of task forces was developed to achieve a rather drastic cut in central staff overhead costs.

Notes

1. Target setting, a management practice, reverses the traditional method of performance appraisal in which the supervisor writes the job description and evaluates the subordinate's performance against his, or the organization's, criteria for effective performance. In target setting, the subordinate develops his own position description and discusses this with his supervisor, with joint agreement on the position description. The incumbent then sets performance-improvement targets for a short period, such as six months. These improvement targets are discussed with the supervisor and become the joint goals of the supervisor and subordinate for the subordinate's performance improvement. At the end of the period, the incumbent analyzes his results in terms of goals achieved or not achieved, and this analysis provides a basis for joint discussion with the supervisor and for the joint replanning and setting of new goals for the next period. The process requires that the supervisor function as a consultant and at

the same time represent organization requirements. It may produce some strain on the subordinate who must now commit himself to improvement targets rather than work toward targets set for him by either the supervisor or the organization.

2. Management by objectives, or Theory Y, was developed by Douglas McGregor in *The Human Side of Enterprise* (New York: McGraw-Hill, 1960). McGregor describes the traditional management assumptions and calls them Theory X. He postulates a new set of assumptions which he calls Theory Y. These latter basically include the concept of self-control throughout the organization.

C. MEASUREMENT IN ORGANIZATION DEVELOPMENT

Measurement of results is very difficult and is conspicuously absent in many organization development efforts. The conceptual models and techniques developed by Rensis Likert, Floyd Mann, and others at the Institute for Social Research, show great promise, not only for diagnosis, but for measuring changes and for studying the interrelationships of variables.

In the selection which follows, Likert et al. *(Selection 35), while somewhat overlapping with the earlier selection by Likert and Bowers, presents such a model for analyzing variables which influence organizational behavior over time. Preliminary results from the testing of the model indicate that it is useful for increasing the lead time in dealing with human problems which are beginning to develop.*

35

How to Increase a Firm's Lead Time in Recognizing and Dealing with Problems of Managing its Human Organization

RENSIS LIKERT
University of Michigan

DAVID G. BOWERS
University of Michigan

ROBERT M. NORMAN
University of Michigan

Social scientists engaged in research on management and organizational performance initially expected to find a marked and consistent relationship between the management style of the leader, the attitudes and loyalties of his subordinates, and the productivity of his organization. A number of studies done in the decade following World War II, however, revealed a variety of relationships between managerial style, employee attitudes, and the productivity of the organization. Many studies found a positive relationship between employee attitudes and productivity; i.e., more favorable attitudes were accompanied by higher productivity. Other research projects, however, found a negative relationship: poorer attitudes associated with greater productivity. Several reviews summarizing studies of the relationships between leadership styles, attitudes of subordinates and their productivity have concluded that all of the studies taken together show that there is no consistent, dependable relationship among the three major kinds of variables.

What accounts for the failure to find consistently the expected relationship among these variables? Several factors appear to be responsible and have been discussed elsewhere.[1] The variable which appears to be particularly important, however, is *time*.

Taken and adapted from *Michigan Business Review,* Vol. 11, No. 1, Jan. 1969, pp. 12–17. Used by permission.

As so often happens in research, it was the failure to obtain expected results in an experiment which called to the attention of the investigators the importance of this neglected variable. In two separate large-scale field experiments, the Institute for Social Research obtained findings contrary to the predictions which had been made when the research projects were designed. In both instances, evidence emerged in the analyses, or in subsequent developments, to show that the time intervals between changes in the causal variables[2] and the related changes in the intervening and finally in the end-result variables took much longer than investigators expected.

Evidence from other sources also points to the importance of time as a major factor which influences the observed relationships among the causal, intervening, and end-result variables. When measurements of these three kinds of variables are obtained at a particular point in time, the relationships among them often show a pattern which suggests that time is an important dimension affecting these relationships. For example, when the correlations among all the different causal, intervening, and end-result variables are computed using data collected at one point in time, they often will show a pattern which suggests that the closer any two variables are in the causal — intervening — end-result sequence — i.e., they occur at about the same point in time — the more marked the observed relationship tends to be. The farther apart the variables are in the sequence and the greater the probable time interval between changes in one and changes in the other, the lower the correlations tend to be.

Yuchtman has provided additional evidence concerning the importance of time as a key factor influencing the relationships among the causal, intervening, and end-result variables.[3] He found, for example, that for even the short time lag of a single year, the size of the correlations between causal and end-result variables increased over the correlations obtained when all measurements were made at a single point in time.

Further evidence demonstrating the importance of time as a variable and revealing the sequence of changes among the variables over time is reported in a recent book by Marrow, Bowers, and Seashore.[4]

All of these findings indicate that to obtain valid conclusions concerning the interrelationships among the causal, intervening, and end-result variables, it is necessary to analyze the data over an appreciable period of time. The Institute for Social Research, consequently, has started a major research project, the inter-company longitudinal studies, which will provide for the first time the extensive data required for these analyses.

The Research Plan for Analyzing Relationships Over Time

Collection of measurements from the same company locations over about a five-year period will be required to obtain sufficient data for testing the relationships among the causal, intervening, and end-result variables. To make participation in the project worth the expenditure of this amount of time to companies, an organizational development program will be undertaken in each firm. This program will apply fully all available research findings along with the specific measurements obtained in each firm. The latter will be used for organizational diagnoses as well as for feedback to each manager or supervisor of data for his own unit.

FIGURE 1

Schematic Relationships among Causal, Intervening, and End-result Variables

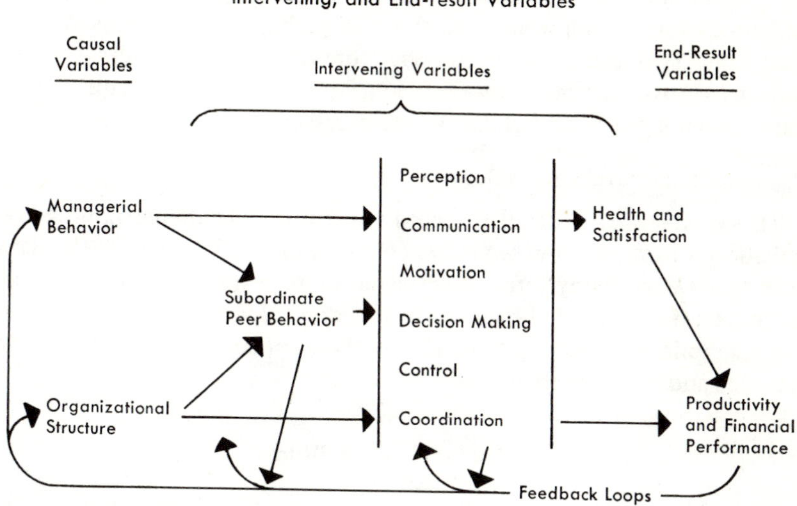

Pilot studies for this project were started two years ago. Activities to date have involved twenty organizational sites, including over 11,000 persons in eight different companies. Since February, 1966, a core questionnaire has been developed and computer programs have been created which are adequate to process the data in the form required for the major venture. In addition, pilot efforts have been conducted in the participating firms in applying existing knowledge and current data to help each firm improve its organizational capabilities and performance.

The following describes briefly the kinds of data being collected in each participating division of firm:

Questionnaire Data

Questionnaires will be administered at least once a year, initially by ISR personnel. In addition, questionnaires will be administered in most firms on a sample basis more often than once a year in order to obtain evidence concerning changes in relationships among the variables not adequately reflected in the annual measurements.

The instrument to be employed is based upon the accumulated experience of the Institute for Social Research in conducting studies of organization during the past 20 years. This standard instrument contains a core of organizational measures covering both causal and intervening variables. This core consists of 18 indices based on 48 multiple-choice items and reflects a theory of organizational structure and functioning.[5]

Performance Data

A major problem in this project is that of establishing comparable criteria of production and financial performance from one organizational unit to another. Within any one firm, or perhaps among firms from the same industry, these measures may be more or less comparable. For comparisons across all firms, however, some transformation to equivalent or standard units will be undertaken where necessary.

Organizational Development Data

These data will be detailed records of the organizational improvement activities undertaken by both the company and ISR personnel. These records will take many forms, such as accurate reports and copies of content covered and data fed back, tape recordings, kinescopes, photos, narrative descriptions of training content, and diaries of coaching and intervention activities and response elicited.

Analyses of the Data

Since this project requires extensive analyses of large quantities of data, a preprogrammed system of data processing and analysis has been developed. Relationships will be computed after each questionnaire administration among the causal, intervening, and end-result variables (in the form of a correlation matrix). The computations will include all current questionnaire indices, all questionnaire indices from preceding measurements, and all performance criteria for an appropriate number of months. At the outset, this will be six months preceding and six months following the measurement point; later analyses will include a much greater number of months subsequent to each questionnaire administration. By inspection, peaks in the correlations can be located and the time periods and levels of maximum relationships discovered.

Research on Principles and Processes of Organizational Change and Improvement

The necessity of assisting companies to apply the findings and measurements obtained in this study provides an extraordinary opportunity to explore and test various approaches and strategies for organizational improvement and management development. As the efforts to bring about organizational improvement proceed, opportunities will occur to conduct rigorous quantitative studies designed to learn more about which principles and methods are most effective for training managers and building highly effective human organizations.

The organizational development techniques to be tested experimentally will vary among and within the companies as the situations permit. The number of units and the time interval over which this study will be conducted will permit several different strategies and methods of organizational development to be tried along with adequate experimental controls.

The initial efforts to bring about organizational and managerial improvement will employ the best principles and procedures currently available. As the work proceeds, studies will be done to discover better ways of applying new knowledge. As more effective principles and methods of management development and organization building are discovered, they will be incorporated in the application efforts of the project.

Some Potential Benefits from this Project

At present, organizations in every field of administration are expending substantial funds on organizational development and managerial training. All of the training given managers in organizational development programs assumes that certain leadership styles and managerial behavior are more likely than are other styles to yield high productivity and better overall performance. This assumes that there are consistent and dependable relationships over time among the causal, intervening, and end-result variables. The findings from this project, consequently, will make a major contribution to all efforts devoted to educating managers and to improving organizational effectiveness. It will increase appreciably the return achieved from funds spent on organizational development.

The second contribution from this project concerns management's need in all fields of administration for better operating information. A two-year study by a major committee of the American Accounting Association has stated this need in a monograph issued in August, 1966. This report, entitled *A Statement of Basic Accounting Theory,* states:

> Accounting for internal management use . . . while based broadly upon economic concepts, must also include the concepts arising from the growing body of knowledge about management. This is particularly true of the parts of this knowledge and technology which are now sufficiently objective, well documented, and extensive to be regarded as essentially a theory of management. (p. 2)
>
> Recognizing and defining the problem requires an information system that brings problems to the attention of management and then permits the particular conditions involved to be isolated and understood . . . For de-

> fining the problem, information is required in sufficient detail to permit not only an awareness of its existence but an understanding of cause and effect. Thus, signals sent out by the control system must be capable of amplification and extension upon management's request. (p. 46)
>
> The control function is tied in planning through the feedback it provides on how well the plans have been conceived and implemented and in bringing to light problems that require managerial attention. To be effective, the information must be structured to reflect the activity or organizational unit under examination. Further, the information should reveal cause and effect relationships that exist so that the proper problems are highlighted while something can still be done about them. (p. 49)

The progress which can be made on these and other recommendations in this report of the American Accounting Association will be influenced appreciably by whether there are dependable and sizable relationships among the causal, intervening, and end-result variables. The preliminary findings from this project are providing evidence that dependable and sizable relationships actually do exist.

Some Preliminary Results from the Longitudinal Research

From the pilot studies started a couple of years ago we are now beginning to obtain our second year of measurements. The early data are confirming our expectations that measurements over at least a few years' time are necessary to obtain correct estimates of the relationships which actually exist among the causal, intervening, and end-result variables. Some initial results can be presented to show the findings beginning to emerge.

In one continuous process plant employing more than 500 persons, measurements of the causal and intervening variables obtained in 1966 were related by work groups (N = 40 groups) to performance data for the same period of time. Three indices of managerial behavior were used. The first index reflects the extent to which the manager is seen as being supportive and applying the principle of supportive relationships. This index is called "managerial support." The second refers to his efforts to use group problem solving in dealing with work problems and to build his work group into a cohesive, effective team, and is called "managerial interaction facilitation." The third reflects the manager's attempts to aid his subordinates on job problems and to provide the knowledge and technical resources they need for their work and is labeled "managerial work facilitation."

These three measures of managerial behavior were related to monthly performance measurements for these forty work groups for the four successive months just prior to and subsequent to the period when the causal variables were measured. The performance measurements were actual costs incurred expressed as a per cent of the standard; the lower this ratio of costs, the better the performance. None of the twelve possible cofficients of correlation (three managerial variables related to performance for four separate months, or 3 x 4) were large enough to be statistically significant.

When these measurements of managerial behavior, obtained in 1966, were related to monthly performance measured *one year later,* all twelve of the correlation coefficients were statistically significant and varied from −.48 to −.58. These statistical relationships revealed that managerial behavior in early 1966 was the cause of approximately one-third of the variation among departments in cost performance one year later. Preliminary findings indicate that predictions over a two-year span are likely to be even more accurate.

Similar results were obtained when the analysis was based on peer leadership within the work group. The same three leadership variables were used, but dealt with the extent to which work group members saw their own colleagues providing peer leadership in the form of support, interaction facilitation, and work facilitation.

Comparable findings were obtained also for five different indices measuring intervening variables. These variations reflect the level of (1) work motivation; (2) communication, upward, downward, and lateral; (3) control, including managements' capacity to control work group behavior; (4) inter-departmental coordination; and (5) decision-making. When the 1966 measurements of these five intervening variables were related to 1967 performance data, i.e., one year later, all of the correlation coefficients were statistically significant (varied from −.37 to −.68). For the communication index, the correlations with the four months performance indices were −.57, −.58, −.67, and −.68.

Although measurements of the intervening variables may not provide management with as much increase in lead time in recognizing problems as do measurements of the causal variables, nevertheless the increase is appreciable. It can be helpful also in confirming or modifying conclusions based on the causal measurements.

These results indicate that measurements of the causal and intervening variables will give every level of management a substantial increase in lead time in dealing with the problems of managing the human organization of the firm. Each manager will have data available showing him the problems which are beginning to develop, the causes producing them, and the kinds of remedial action most likely to yield a constructive solution. These data will reveal, moreover, the efficacy of remedial steps at an early phase. By catching and correcting problems in their incipient stage, managers will avoid costly breakdowns and achieve more successful performance. These pilot findings indicate that these measurements will give managers from one to three years greater lead time than they now have.

Notes

1. Likert, Rensis, *The Human Organization: Its Management and Value.* New York: McGraw-Hill, 1967.

2. In this paper, reference will be made to three broad classes of variables, labeled, respectively, causal, intervening, and end-result. They can be defined briefly as follows:

a. The *causal* variables are independent variables which determine the course of developments within an organization and the results achieved by it. Causal variables include only those independent variables which can be altered or changed by the organization and its management. The variable, "general business conditions," for example, although an independent variable, is not viewed as causal since the management of a particular enterprise can do little about it. Causal variables include the structure of the organization and management's policies, decisions, business and leadership strategies, skills, and behavior.

b. The *intervening* variables reflect the internal state and health of the organization, e.g., the loyalties, attitudes, motivations, performance goals, and perceptions of all members and their collective capacity for effective interaction, communication, and decision making.

c. The *end-result* variables are the dependent variables which reflect the achievements of the organization, such as its productivity, costs, scrap loss, and earnings.

3. Yuchtman, E., A Study of Organizational Effectiveness. Unpublished doctoral dissertation, University of Michigan, 1966.

4. Marrow, A. J., Bowers, D. G., and Seashore, S. E. *Management by Participation: Creating a Climate For Personal and Organizational Development.* New York: Harper & Row, 1967.

5. The theory is presented in Likert, Rensis, *New Patterns of Management,* New York: McGraw-Hill, 1961 and *The Human Organization: Its Management and Value,* New York: McGraw-Hill, 1967. A much-simplified version of the concepts is shown in Figure 1.

D. PROBLEMS IN ORGANIZATION DEVELOPMENT

Finally, Bennis (Selection 36) outlines for us the "practical, tough problems" which must be confronted if organization development is to reach its potential. He does not assert that OD has made no contributions. Rather, he claims OD has not made the contributions it should make and is potentially capable of making. For, he concludes:

> *. . . Organizational Development is one of the few educational programs I know of that has the potential to create an institution vital enough to cope with the unparalleled changes ahead.*

36

Unsolved Problems Facing Organizational Development

WARREN G. BENNIS
State University of New York at Buffalo

> Out of all this has come the first clear recognition of an inescapable fact; we cannot successfully *force* people to work for management's objectives. The ancient conception that people will do the work of the world only if they are forced to do so by threats or intimidation, or by the camouflaged authoritarian methods of paternalism, has been suffering from a lingering fatal illness for a quarter of a century. I venture the guess that it will be dead in another decade. — Douglas McGregor, 1950

McGregor may have been overly-optimistic about the death of authoritarianism, but he was unerring, as usual, in putting his finger on the right

Taken and adapted from *The Business Quarterly,* Vol. 34, No. 4, Winter 1969, pp. 80–84. Used by permission.

issue. Given the retroactive insight of almost twenty years, we can say that Organizational Development is essentially an evolutionary hypothesis. It asserts that every age develops an organizational form and life style most appropriate to the genius of that age. Most organizations reflect the uneasiness of transition for they were built upon certain assumptions about man and his environment. The environment was thought to be placid, predictable, and uncomplicated. Man was thought to be placid, predictable and uncomplicated. "All you have to do," said Henry Ford in one of his speeches to the Ford executives, "is to set the work before the men, and they will do it." Organizations based on these assumptions will fail; if not today, then tomorrow. They will fail for the very same reasons that dinosaurs failed: the environment changes suddenly at the peak of their success.*

The environment now is busy, clogged and dense with opportunities and threats; it is turbulent, uncertain, and dynamic. The people who work for organizations are more complicated than ever before. They have needs, motives, anxieties, and to make matters even more complicated, they bring higher expectations than ever before to our institutions. The institutions themselves are changing, through the press of environmental challenges and the internal demands of its people. Organizational Development is a response to these complex challenges, an educational strategy which aims to bring about a better fit between the human beings who work in and expect things from organizations and the busy, unrelenting environment with its insistence on adapting to changing times.

This is a tremendous task. One should not expect sudden success from such a new practice, I suppose, but it might be useful to examine some of the unsolved problems facing Organizational Development. In doing so, the hope exists that Organizational Development's potential can be realized, rather than forfeiting future achievement through a complacency about current accomplishments. In my view, Organizational Development will be unable to reach its true strength unless it confronts a series of practical, tough problems.

The Politics of Change

Organizational Development practitioners rely exclusively on two sources of influence, truth and love. Somehow the hope prevails that man is reasonable and caring, and that valid data, coupled with an environment of trust

* A recent editorial in the *Boston Globe* quoted Benson Snyder, M.I.T. psychiatrist, apropos dinosaurs and change. Musing about a recent trip to some California universities, he wrote: "There is another consequence of this response to rapid change. The climate of society becomes suffused and distrait, positions ossified, and one hears expressions of helplessness increase, like dinosaurs on the plains of mud. Each in his own way frantically puts on more weight and thinks this form of strength will serve him. He doesn't know he has lost touch until the mud reaches the level of his eyes . . ."

(and love), will bring about the desired change. "All's fair in love and war"; it really is, but you really must know which you're playing. Organizational Development seems most appropriate under conditions of trust, truth, love, and collaboration. But what about conditions of war, conflict, dissent, and violence? Putting it differently, there seems to be a fundamental deficiency in models of change associated with Organizational Development. It systematically avoids the problem of power, or the politics of change.

This deficiency is serious enough from a theoretical point of view, but it is more deadly in practice. For, fundamentally, the Organizational Development consultant tends to use the truth-love model when it may be inappropriate and has no alternate model to guide his practice under conditions of distrust, violence, and conflict. Essentially, this means that in pluralistic power situations, in situations which are not easily controlled, Organizational Development practice may not reach its desired goals. This may explain why Organizational Development has been reasonably successful in industry and other closed, hierarchical structures where power is relatively centralized and there is a basic (if uneven) consensus about organizational goals. At the same time Organizational Development, to my knowledge, has not met with success in diffuse power structures such as cities, large-scale national organizations, or the urban ghetto.

Another concern that stems from this almost total reliance on the truth-love strategy of social change is that only the wealthy organizations and those with firm control over its constituents can be reached through present Organizational Development programs leading to what Blake and Mouton have referred to as "Corporate Darwinism," or more simply, the rich get richer. So IBM, Esso, Union Carbide, ALCAN, AT&T, etc. reap more advantages while impoverished and disadvantaged groups, such as local government, civil rights movements, universities, hospitals, communities are untended.

Still another equally serious problem has to do with the T-Group coloration that almost all Organizational Development programs take on. It should be emphasized that Organizational Development should not be confused with sensitivity training or T-Groups. Yet the need to state this testifies to the confusion, which is not unrelated to the fact that most Organizational Development cases that finally reach print focus almost exclusively on the T-Group as the basic strategy of intervention. In the *Journal of Behavioral Sciences,* I wrote an editorial in 1968 which underlined this point.

"I have yet to see an Organizational Development program that uses an interventional strategy other than an interpersonal one, and this is serious when one considers that the most pivotal strategies of change in our society are political, legal, and technological. We call ourselves 'change agents', but the real changes in our society have been wrought by the pill, the bomb, the automobile, industrialization, communication media, and other forces of modernization. The change agents in our society are the lawyers, the architects, the engineers, the politicians, and the assassins. (I should add students to this list, for even as I write this they are rioting and shooting and clamoring for 'real power,' institutional leverage which they have never before sought.)"

I have no easy answer to this dilemma that faces every Organizational Development consultant and change agent: How can he operate in situations of dissension and conflict to help people in those situations to discover and affirm the values of collaboration and commit themselves to its achievement?

Recently, I set forth some general principles that may lead toward a wiser handling of the dilemma:

1. Collaboration is an achievement, not a given condition. The ways of effective collaboration must be learned.
2. Conflict is not to be avoided by a change agent. Rather, he faces conflict in himself and in others and seeks ways to channel the aggressive energies of conflict and power toward the achievement of personal and social gain for all concerned.
3. Power is not a bad thing, though much behavioral science literature treats it as such through indifference or ignorance.
4. Social action depends on power just as physical movement depends on energy. Nothing changes in human affairs until new power is generated or until old power is redistributed.
5. The Organizational Development consultant strives to utilize power that is based on and guided by rationality, valid knowledge, and collaboration and to discount power based on and channeled by fear, irrationality, and coercion. The latter kind of power leads to augmented resistance to change, unstable changes, and dehumanized and irrational conflicts. Still and all, one had better understand these irrational and powerful forces.

Unless models can be developed that include the dimensions of power-conflict in addition to truth-love, Organizational Development will find fewer and narrower institutional avenues open to its influence. And in so doing, it will slowly and successfully decay.

Structure Versus Climate

Organizational Development pays lip-service only to structural (or technological) changes while relying only on a change in organizational "climate." I mean by "climate" a set of values or attitudes which affect the way people relate to each other, such as "openness," authority patterns and social relations, etc. This is no mean feat, of course, but again — related to the preceding point — it is seriously restrictive. The Organizational

Development literature is filled with vague promises about "restructuring" or "organizational design" but with some exceptions . . . few outcomes are actually demonstrated. Program budgeting, computerization, new communication systems, structural imagination, "open posting" of new positions (e.g. Polaroid plan), a job enlargement, for example, may have far more impact than a dramatic shift of "organizational climate." It is difficult to understand the effects of climate, as a matter of fact, unless the attitudinal-value complex is reflected in concrete organizational designs. Far more has to be done in bridging an engineering design approach with Organizational Development change strategies before it will be possible for the goal of "socio-technical" approaches to be anything more than respectable jargon.

The Profession of Organizational Development

Typically, a "profession" is considered to be a "calling" based on foundation of knowledge directed toward a "clientele" and with an ethical posture towards its clientele and members of the profession. To some extent, the practice of Organizational Development is a profession with a growing number of competent practitioners. In other ways, its falls short when compared with other more mature professional callings.

Several areas of concern come to mind. For one thing, there is no integrated theory of organizational change with a set of interrelated hypotheses and variables. This goal is not met, incidentally, in many other professions, such as medicine, law, engineering. However, and far more serious, in my view, is that there is, as yet, no tradition of *adding knowledge cumulatively* to the general theory of practice. The law is established case by case and in engineering, medicine, and even teaching, there is a steady accumulation upon an accepted framework for practice. I am not aware that Organizational Development is at this stage of development.

Related to this point is the overall disinterest in long-term research projects. Again, with some striking exceptions, the Organizational Development consultant rarely does research on his client system, except for infrequent "evaluation" studies. Now these evaluative studies are terribly important and I do not, in any way, mean to disparage them. But it seems to me that the most significant research to be done on Organizational Development must be related to what Organizational Development is all about, the *development* of an organization over time. Thus, Organizational Development research should deal with long term processes, induced by certain interventions, and leading to certain predictable outcomes. We know a good deal about the interventions — e.g., a confrontation meeting, data-feedback, sensitivity training, etc. — and have a moderately good idea of what these interventions do by way of outcomes. We have very little to say about the processes and mechanisms of organizational change. This seems especially paradoxical when the processes of change are exactly what the Organizational Development consultant has to concern himself with.

Most professionals also have on hand a set of instruments which rather quickly assess the client's present health or illness. Organizational Development practice certainly has a need for a variety of thermometers that can be inserted into the client system in order to identify the status of the client along a whole host of dimensions. For example, an Organizational Development consultant would surely want to examine the value system of the client and the extent to which there was consensus or dissension regarding the core values. An Organizational Development consultant would surely want to understand the nature of the goal structure, communication patterns, decision structure, authority relations, and so on. Over the years, researchers, using a variety of methods from survey methods to group discussion, have been able to develop instrumentation for diagnosis. Yet there is no agreed upon set of instruments to "work up" the diagnosis. This also is paradoxical because Organizational Development practitioners have likely acquired more knowledge about the diagnosis of an organizational system than organizational theorists could tell them.

About the training of competent Organizational Development practitioners, much more needs to be said. The first generation of any new profession is always the most gifted and the most erratic. This is certainly true of Organizational Development practitioners from my vantage point. Some extremely gifted practitioners like Richard Beckhard, Herb Shepard, Shel Davis, are making history through their creative practice. Others, I am afraid, can possibly jeopardize the growth of Organizational Development in the usual ways that new professions become vulnerable: through routine hackwork, malpractice, and ethical blunders. My main concern here is that we educate and then develop the next generation of Organizational Development practitioners. The universities are not doing it; in fact, my impression is that organizations have "rolled their own," that is, set up their own training program, independent of the university. There is a lot to be said for that, of course, but homemade programs require nourishment from other sources of knowledge and theory not necessarily contained within the organization. In a sense, I am challenging universities to open their doors to new departments of Organizational Development, applied social sciences, policy sciences, etc. The name is not important. What is important is the need for well-trained, full-time practitioners of Organizational Development. For without these new men, who will design the future and help create the organizations that can release our human potential and master the environment?

Expressing these qualms, I hope, will not discourage the reader. Rather, I hope to inspire him, for basically Organizational Development is one of the few educational programs I know of that has the potential to create an institution vital enough to cope with the unparalleled changes ahead.